Communications
in Computer and Information Science   1896

Rationale

The CCIS series is devoted to the publication of proceedings of computer science conferences. Its aim is to efficiently disseminate original research results in informatics in printed and electronic form. While the focus is on publication of peer-reviewed full papers presenting mature work, inclusion of reviewed short papers reporting on work in progress is welcome, too. Besides globally relevant meetings with internationally representative program committees guaranteeing a strict peer-reviewing and paper selection process, conferences run by societies or of high regional or national relevance are also considered for publication.

Topics

The topical scope of CCIS spans the entire spectrum of informatics ranging from foundational topics in the theory of computing to information and communications science and technology and a broad variety of interdisciplinary application fields.

Information for Volume Editors and Authors

Publication in CCIS is free of charge. No royalties are paid, however, we offer registered conference participants temporary free access to the online version of the conference proceedings on SpringerLink (http://link.springer.com) by means of an http referrer from the conference website and/or a number of complimentary printed copies, as specified in the official acceptance email of the event.

CCIS proceedings can be published in time for distribution at conferences or as post-proceedings, and delivered in the form of printed books and/or electronically as USBs and/or e-content licenses for accessing proceedings at SpringerLink. Furthermore, CCIS proceedings are included in the CCIS electronic book series hosted in the SpringerLink digital library at http://link.springer.com/bookseries/7899. Conferences publishing in CCIS are allowed to use Online Conference Service (OCS) for managing the whole proceedings lifecycle (from submission and reviewing to preparing for publication) free of charge.

Publication process

The language of publication is exclusively English. Authors publishing in CCIS have to sign the Springer CCIS copyright transfer form, however, they are free to use their material published in CCIS for substantially changed, more elaborate subsequent publications elsewhere. For the preparation of the camera-ready papers/files, authors have to strictly adhere to the Springer CCIS Authors' Instructions and are strongly encouraged to use the CCIS LaTeX style files or templates.

Abstracting/Indexing

CCIS is abstracted/indexed in DBLP, Google Scholar, EI-Compendex, Mathematical Reviews, SCImago, Scopus. CCIS volumes are also submitted for the inclusion in ISI Proceedings.

How to start

To start the evaluation of your proposal for inclusion in the CCIS series, please send an e-mail to ccis@springer.com.

Jiachi Chen · Bin Wen · Ting Chen
Editors

Blockchain and Trustworthy Systems

5th International Conference, BlockSys 2023
Haikou, China, August 8–10, 2023
Proceedings, Part I

Springer

Editors
Jiachi Chen 🆔
Sun Yat-Sen University
Zhuhai, China

Bin Wen 🆔
Hainan Normal University
Haikou, China

Ting Chen 🆔
University of Electronic Science
and Technology of China
Chengdu, China

ISSN 1865-0929   ISSN 1865-0937 (electronic)
Communications in Computer and Information Science
ISBN 978-981-99-8100-7   ISBN 978-981-99-8101-4 (eBook)
https://doi.org/10.1007/978-981-99-8101-4

This Springer imprint is published by the registered company Springer Nature Singapore Pte Ltd.
The registered company address is: 152 Beach Road, #21-01/04 Gateway East, Singapore 189721, Singapore

Paper in this product is recyclable.

Preface

Blockchain has become a hot research area in academia and industry. The blockchain technology is transforming industries by enabling anonymous and trustful transactions in decentralized and trustless environments. As a result, blockchain technology and other technologies for developing trustworthy systems can be used to reduce system risks, mitigate financial fraud, and cut down operational cost. Blockchain and trustworthy systems can be applied to many fields, such as financial services, social management, and supply chain management.

This proceedings volume contains the papers from the 2023 International Conference on Blockchain and Trustworthy Systems (BlockSys 2023). This conference was held as the fifth in its series with an emphasis on state-of-the-art advances in blockchain and trustworthy systems. The main conference received 93 paper submissions, out of which 45 papers were accepted as regular papers. All papers underwent a rigorous peer review process – each paper was reviewed by 2-4 experts. The accepted papers together with our outstanding keynote and invited speeches led to a vibrant technical program. We are looking forward to future events in this conference series.

The conference would not have been successful without help from so many people. We would like to thank the Organizing Committee for their hard work in putting together the conference. First, we would like to express our sincere thanks to the guidance from the Honorary Chair: Dusit (Tao) Niyato. We would like to express our deep gratitude to the General Chairs: David Lo, Weizhe Zhang, and Xiuzhen Cheng for their support and promotion of this event. We would also like to thank the program chairs: Bin Wen, Jiachi Chen, and Ting Chen supervised the review process of the technical papers and compiled a high-quality technical program. We also extend our deep gratitude to the program committee members, whose diligent work in reviewing the papers led to the high quality of the accepted papers. We greatly appreciate the excellent support and hard work of the Publicity Chairs: Changlin Yang, Taotao Li, and Tao Zhang; Publication Chairs: Jiangshan Yu, Jieren Cheng, and Peilin Zheng; Organizing Chairs: Chun Shan, Rao Zeng, Yuxin Su, and Ziqiang Luo; Industrial Chairs: Jiashui Wang and Huizhong Li; Special Track Chairs: Lulu Wang, Pengcheng Zhang, Shunhui Ji, Xiaobin Sun, xiaoxue, Zhangbing Zhou, Huaiguang Wu, Siqi Lu, Xueming Si, and Yongjuan Wang; Advisory Board: Huaimin Wang, Jiannong Cao, Kuan-Ching Li, and Michael R. Lyu; and Steering Committee: Hong-Ning Dai, Xiapu Luo, Yan Zhang, and Zibin Zheng. Most importantly, we would like to thank the authors for submitting their papers to BlockSys 2023.

We believe that the BlockSys conference provides a good forum for both academic researchers and industrial practitioners to discuss all technical advances in blockchain and trustworthy systems. We also expect that future BlockSys conferences will be as successful, as indicated by the contributions presented in this volume.

August 2023

David Lo
Weizhe Zhang
Xiuzhen Cheng
Bin Wen
Jiachi Chen
Ting Chen

Organization

Honorary Chair

Dusit (Tao) Niyato   Nanyang Technological University, Singapore

General Chairs

David Lo   Singapore Management University, Singapore
Weizhe Zhang   Harbin Institute of Technology, China
Xiuzhen Cheng   Shandong University, China

Program Chairs

Bin Wen   Hainan Normal University, China
Jiachi Chen   Sun Yat-sen University, China
Ting Chen   University of Electronic Science and Technology
  of China, China

Organizing Chairs

Chun Shan   Guangdong Polytechnic Normal University, China
Rao Zeng   Hainan Normal University, China
Yuxin Su   Sun Yat-sen University, China
Ziqiang Luo   Hainan Normal University, China

Publicity Chairs

Changlin Yang   Sun Yat-sen University, China
Taotao Li   Sun Yat-sen University, China
Tao Zhang   Macau University of Science and Technology,
  China

Publication Chairs

Jiangshan Yu	Monash University, Australia
Jieren Cheng	Hainan University, China
Peilin Zheng	Sun Yat-sen University, China

Industrial Chairs

Jiashui Wang	Ant Group, China
Huizhong Li	WeBank, China

Special Track Chairs: Anomaly detection on blockchain

Lulu Wang	Southeast University, China
Pengcheng Zhang	Hohai University, China
Shunhui Ji	Hohai University, China
Xiaobin Sun	Yangzhou University, China

Special Track Chairs: Edge Intelligence and Metaverse Services

xiaoxue	Tianjin University, China
Zhangbing Zhou	China University of Geosciences, China

Special Track Chairs: Blockchain System Security

Huaiguang Wu	Zhengzhou University of Light Industry, China
Siqi Lu	Henan Key Laboratory of Information Security, China
Xueming Si	Fudan University, China
Yongjuan Wang	Henan Key Laboratory of Information Security, China

Advisory Board

Huaimin Wang	National University of Defense Technology, China
Jiannong Cao	Hong Kong Polytechnic University, China

Kuan-Ching Li   Providence University, China
Michael R. Lyu   Chinese University of Hong Kong, China

Steering Committee

Hong-Ning Dai   Hong Kong Baptist University, China
Xiapu Luo   Hong Kong Polytechnic University, China
Yan Zhang   University of Oslo, Norway
Zibin Zheng   Sun Yat-sen University, China

Web Chair

Renke Huang   Sun Yat-sen University, China

Program Committee

Alexander Chepurnoy   IOHK Research, China
Ali Vatankhah   Kennesaw State University, USA
Andreas Veneris   University of Toronto, Canada
Ao Zhou   Beijing University of Posts and
                                   Telecommunications, China
Bahman Javadi   Western Sydney University, Australia
Bo Jiang   Beihang University, China
Bu-Qing Cao   Hunan University of Science and Technology,
                                   China
Bijun Li   Hainan Normal University, China
Bin Wen   Hainan Normal University, China
Bing Lin   Fujian Normal University, China
Chang-Ai Sun   University of Science and Technology Beijing,
                                   China
ChangLin Yang   Sun Yat-sen University, China
Claudio Schifanella   University of Turin, Italy
Chunhua Su   Osaka University, Japan
Chunpeng Ge   Nanjing University of Aeronautics and
                                   Astronautics, China
Chuan Chen   Sun Yat-sen University, China
Daojing He   Harbin Institute of Technology (Shenzhen), China
Debiao He   Wuhan University, China
Fangguo Zhang   Sun Yat-sen University, China

Fenfang Xie	Sun Yat-sen University, China
Gerhard Hancke	City University of Hong Kong, China
Guobing Zou	Shanghai University, China
Haibo Tian	Sun Yat-sen Univeristy, China
Han Liu	Tsinghua University, China
Huawei Huang	Sun Yat-sen Univeristy, China
Jan Henrik Ziegeldorf	RWTH Aachen University, Germany
Jiakun Liu	Singapore Management University, Singapore
Jieren Cheng	Hainan University, China
Jiwei Huang	China University of Petroleum, China
Jiang Xiao	Huazhong University of Science and Technology, China
Jiajing Wu	Sun Yat-sen University, China
Kai Lei	Peking University, China
Kenneth Fletcher	University of Massachusetts Boston, USA
Kouichi Sakurai	Kyushu University, Japan
Laizhong Cui	Shenzhen University, China
Liehuang Zhu	Beijing Institute of Technology, China
Linfeng Bao	Zhejiang University, China
Liang Chen	Sun Yat-sen University, China
Lingjun Zhao	University of Aizu, Japan
Mario Larangeira	IOHK/Tokyo Institute of Technology, Japan
Meng Yan	Chongqing University, China
Muhammad Imran	King Saud University, China
Mingdong Tang	Guangdong University of Foreign Studies, China
Nan Jia	Hebei GEO University, China
Omer Rana	Cardiff University, UK
Pengcheng Zhang	Hohai University, China
Pengfei Chen	Sun Yat-sen University, China
Qianhong Wu	Beihang University, China
Qinghua Lu	CSIRO, Australia
Qian He	Guilin University of Electronic Technology, China
Raja Jurdak	Commonwealth Scientific Industrial and Research Organization, Australia
Shangguang Wang	Beijing University of Posts and Telecommunications, China
Shijun Liu	Shandong University, China
Shiping Chen	CSIRO, Australia
Shizhan Chen	Tianjin University, China
Shuiguang Deng	Zhejiang University, China
Sude Qing	China Academy of Information and Communications Technology, China

Tao Xiang	Chongqing University, China
Taotao Li	Sun Yat-sen University, China
Ting Chen	University of Electronic Science and Technology of China, China
Tingting Bi	CSIRO, Australia
Tsuyoshi Ide	IBM, China
Tianhui Meng	Shenzhen Institute of Advanced Technology, Chinese Academy of Sciences, China
Walter Li	Beijing University of Technology, China
Wei Luo	Zhejiang University, China
Wei Song	Nanjing University of Science and Technology, China
Weifeng Pan	Zhejiang Gongshang University, China
Wuhui Chen	Sun Yat-sen University, China
Weibin Wu	Sun Yat-sen University, China
Weili Chen	Sun Yat-sen University, China
Xiaodong Fu	Kunming University of Science and Technology, China
Xiaoliang Fan	Xiamen University, China
Xiangping Chen	Sun Yat-sen University, China
Xiaohong Shi	Guangzhou University, China
Xiapu Luo	Hong Kong Polytechnic University, China
Yu Jiang	Tsinghua University, China
Yuan Huang	Sun Yat-sen University, China
Yucong Duan	Hainan University, China
Yutao Ma	Wuhan University, China
Yuhong Nan	Sun Yat-sen University, China
Yiming Zhang	National University of Defense Technology, China
Yu Li	Hangzhou Dianzi University, China
Zekeriya Erkin	Delft University of Technology, The Netherlands
Zhe Liu	Nanjing University of Aeronautics and Astronautics, China
Zhihui Lu	Fudan University, China
Zhiying Tu	Harbin Institute of Technology, China
Zhiyuan Wan	Zhejiang University, China
Zihao Chen	Meta, China
Zihao Li	Hongkong Polytechnic University, China
Zoe L. Jiang	Harbin Institute of Technology, Shenzhen, China
Zibin Zheng	Sun Yat-sen University, China

Contents – Part I

Empirical Study and Surveys

Federated Learning for Blockchain

Contents – Part II

Blockchain Architecture and Optimization

Protocols and Consensus

Anomaly Detection on Blockchain

Blockchain Scam Detection: State-of-the-Art, Challenges, and Future Directions

Shunhui Ji[1], Congxiong Huang[1], Hanting Chu[1], Xiao Wang[1], Hai Dong[2], and Pengcheng Zhang[1(✉)]

[1] College of Computer and Information, Hohai University, Nanjing, China
pchzhang@hhu.edu.cn
[2] School of Computing Technologies, RMIT University, Melbourne, Australia

Abstract. With the rapid development of blockchain platforms, such as Ethereum and Hyperledger Fabric, blockchain technology has been widely applied in various domains. However, various scams exist in the cryptocurrency transactions on the blockchain platforms, which has seriously obstructed the development of blockchain. Therefore, many researchers have studied the detection methods for blockchain scams. On the basis of introducing the mainstream types of scams, including Ponzi scheme, Phishing scam, Honeypot, and Pump and dump, this paper provides a thorough survey on the detection methods for these scams, in which 48 studies are investigated. The detection methods are categorized into the analysis-based methods and the machine learning-based methods in terms of the adopted techniques, and are summarized from multiple aspects, including the type of dataset, the extracted feature, the constructed model, etc. Finally, this paper discusses the challenges and potential future research directions in blockchain scam detection.

Keywords: Blockchain · Smart contract · Ponzi scheme · Phishing scam · Honeypot · Pump and dump · Scam detection

1 Introduction

Blockchain [1], as a distributed ledger technology, demonstrates the advantages of data immutability, security, transparency, and anonymity, which has facilitated the development of various applications. Blockchain-based trading platforms allow users to trade cryptocurrencies without being supervised by a third party. Smart contracts have extended the functionality of blockchain. Users deploy customised smart contracts on the blockchain platform and the smart contracts will be executed automatically according to their embedded programs.

However, various financial scams were launched on blockchain platforms to defraud users, which may compromise users' account passwords and transfer their assets for illicit profits. According to the survey [2], cryptocurrency crime with illicit addresses on the blockchain platform earned $7.8 billion in 2020,

J. Chen et al. (Eds.): BlockSys 2023, CCIS 1896, pp. 3–18, 2024.
https://doi.org/10.1007/978-981-99-8101-4_1

while the value reached \$14 billion in 2021. The increasing scams on blockchain platforms have caused huge financial losses and a crisis of trust in the blockchain environment, which has seriously obstructed the development of blockchain. Therefore, many researchers have conducted research on scams on the blockchain and proposed corresponding detection methods. Some detection methods aim at specific types of scams, such as Ponzi scheme [3] and Honeypot [4]. And some detection methods do not target at specific types, detecting abnormal transactions between blockchain addresses and consequently identifying malicious and illegal entities [5] that may be involved in scams, gambling, etc.

Specifically, Li et al. [6] surveyed works about the blockchain anomaly detection using data mining technology. Blockchain anomaly detection methods were analyzed and sorted from two aspects: general detection methods and specific detection methods. And some of the detection methods for Ponzi schemes and Pump and dumps were summarised in specific detection methods. Bartoletti et al. [7] reviewed studies on cryptocurrency scams, in which cryptocurrency scams were classified and summarized. Aida et al. [8] surveyed studies on anomaly and fraud detection using data mining techniques with blockchain big data, in which the key elements of these methods were summarized and analyzed. Wu et al. [9] reviewed studies on network-based anomaly detection methods for cryptocurrency transaction networks, in which the works were summarized from four perspectives: entity identification, transaction pattern identification, illegal activity identification, and transaction tracking.

The aforementioned works mainly summarized the works from the perspective of *anomaly detection*, with less focus on specific *scam detection*. The scope of anomalies is broad and its boundary is not clearly defined. In contrast, scam has a clear definition and limited scope, which can be considered as a type of anomaly. In this regard, this paper provides a systematic review and analysis for the studies on the detection of specific blockchain scams, including Ponzi scheme, Phishing scam, Honeypot, and Pump and dump.

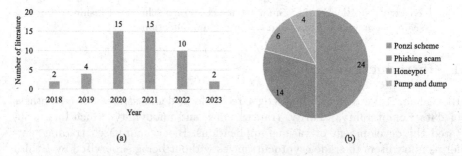

(a)   (b)

Fig. 1. Distribution of papers in terms of publication time and scam type

To systematically investigate the related studies, firstly, the keywords "Ponzi scheme", "Blockchain scam detection", "Phishing scam", "Honeypot", "Pump and dump", etc. were set to search for relevant papers on major academic search engines (e.g. Google Scholar, DBLP, Web of science). Secondly, we screened these papers and retained papers that were highly relevant to the research question and of good quality. Thirdly, the related works and references in these papers were reviewed to search for additional relevant papers. Finally, 48 papers were selected, including Ponzi scheme detection (24 papers), phishing scam detection (14 papers), Honeypot detection (6 papers), and Pump and dump detection (4 papers). The distribution of papers in terms of publication time and scam type are respectively shown in Fig. 1(a) and (b).

The rest of this paper is organized as follows. Section 2 introduces the mainstream types of scams on the blockchain. Sections 3 and 4 provide detailed overviews of the analysis-based detection methods and the machine learning-based detection methods, respectively. Section 5 discusses the inadequacy of existing scam detection methods and the further research directions. Finally, Sect. 6 concludes the paper.

2 The Mainstream Types of Scams

2.1 Ponzi Scheme

Ponzi scheme is a fraudulent investment trap, also known as a high yield investment project. Ponzi scheme usually promises investors a return on investment that is much higher than that of ordinary projects, thus attracting a large number of investors to participate in the project. However, the profit return mechanism of the scheme is using the investment funds of later investors as the return for previous investors, with which the creator of the scheme and previous investors usually make a huge profit. For the other investors, it needs more investors to participate for obtaining the promised benefits, which becomes increasingly difficult to achieve. When the number of investors reaches the bottleneck, the scam will collapse and the later participants will lose their investment [3].

2.2 Phishing Scam

Phishing scam occurs a lot in the transactions on the Internet. Scammers use various means, such as creating fake websites that look legitimate, sending emails from trusted sources, to induce users to open URLs or attachments that contain malicious software. Then malicious software will be installed to monitor user behaviour for stealing private information, such as bank card number and password, with which the money will be withdrawn from the user's account. Scammers also may disguise themselves as trustworthy organizations, enticing users to transfer money to their accounts. The widespread popularity of cryptocurrencies and the convenience of trading on blockchain platforms have made blockchain a new target for phishing scams. Phishing scams on blockchain spread through fake emails, websites, and decentralised applications, stealing users' private keys and transferring assets to the designated address [10].

2.3   Honeypot

Honeypot is a new type of scam on Ethereum, which utilizes the difficulties of smart contract programming technology to create a series of traps to confuse users who are not familiar with the mechanism of Solidity and the EVM (Ethereum Virtual Machine). Honeypot makes the users mistakenly believe that they understand the logic of the smart contract code and can benefit from sending cryptocurrency to the smart contract, but ultimately they will lose all their investment.

The scammer designs a smart contract with obvious vulnerabilities or intuitive conditions for obtaining benefits. It seems that exploiting existing vulnerabilities or conditions will definitely result in benefits. Then the source code of the smart contract is published on the blockchain platform and advertised widely to attract users who have a certain understanding and programming ability in smart contracts and try to profit from them. These users are attracted by the apparent vulnerability and the profit conditions, but do not notice the deeper trap hidden behind the code. Once the user invests cryptocurrency into the smart contract, the contract will not work as expected and the invested cryptocurrency cannot be withdrawn. Eventually, the creator of the smart contract extracts all cryptocurrencies through a designed backdoor [4].

2.4   Pump and Dump

Pump and dump is a price manipulation scam. In the cryptocurrency trading market, scammers purchase the cryptocurrencies at a lower or average price for a period of time. And then they artificially raise the price of the cryptocurrency and entice other investors to buy at a higher price by spreading false information on social media. After the scammers sell their holdings of cryptocurrency, the price usually falls, causing significant losses for buyers. This kind of scam typically targets micro and small cryptocurrencies because they are more easily manipulated [11].

3   Analysis-Based Detection Methods

For the smart contracts which are successfully deployed on the Ethereum platform, the bytecodes, ABI (Application Binary Interface), transaction records, and other information are available on the Etherscan website[1], and the verified Solidity source codes of some smart contracts are released[2]. With the source code of smart contract, program analysis techniques can be used to detect scams. With the transaction records, transaction analysis can be performed. The existing analysis-based detection methods mainly aim at two types of scams: Ponzi scheme and Honeypot.

---

[1] https://etherscan.io/.
[2] https://docs.soliditylang.org/en/v0.8.19/.

3.1 Ponzi Scheme Detection

Chen et al. [12] proposed a semantic-aware detection method SADPonzi based on a heuristic guided symbolic execution technique. The execution paths and symbolic contexts for the investment and return behaviours in a contract were generated and combined with internal call relations to obtain overall semantic information. The semantic information was then combined with the control flow graph of the opcode to analyze whether Ponzi scheme exists through the mode of fund allocation.

Bartoletti et al. [3] proposed a Ponzi scheme detection method based on string similarity analysis. NLD (Normalised Levenshtein Distance) algorithm was used to calculate the similarity of the bytecodes between the target smart contract and Ponzi scheme contract. Contracts whose NLD value is less than 3.5 were considered as potential Ponzi schemes, which filtered out the simple and repetitive scam contracts.

Sun et al. [13] proposed a detection method PonziDetector based on similarity analysis for contract behaviour forest. Software testing technique was used to uncover the contract behaviour during the interactions between the test cases and the smart contract, which was then described as the behavioural forest. Then the similarity between the behavioural forests was calculated by the AP-TED (All Path Tree Edit Distance) algorithm to detect Ponzi scheme by setting the similarity threshold.

Song et al. [14] detected Ponzi scheme by analyzing the amount of funds transferred between various accounts. A virtual transaction network was created to simulate trading behaviour among accounts. They divided the accounts in the transaction network into different types of accounts, such as master account, investing account, partner account, etc. Then a series of rules were set to compare the amount of Ether transferred between different accounts to determine whether a contract is Ponzi scheme.

3.2 Honeypot Detection

HoneyBadger [4, 15] is a tool that employs symbolic execution and heuristics to detect Honeypots. With bytecode as input, it constructs the control flow graph and symbolically executes its different paths to perform symbolic analysis. With the results of the symbolic analysis, cash flow is analyzed to detect whether the contract is capable to receive as well as transfer funds. Finally, different honeypots are identified via heuristics.

Ji et al. [16] proposed a Honeypot detection method based on anisotropic features. They refined the attack model of honeypots and summarized the complete attack process. Then they conducted feature mining on ten honeypot families to extract the anisotropic features and constructed the honeypot genealogy. With the guidance of honeypot genealogy, the anisotropic feature matching was performed to detect Honeypots.

4   Machine Learning-Based Detection Methods

The key of machine learning-based detection methods is feature extraction from the smart contracts or the transaction records in the dataset. For the smart contract codes, feature extraction is usually carried out using language processing techniques. Some studies treat the scam detection problem as image classification problem by transforming bytecodes into images. For the transaction records, transaction features are mainly extracted by analyzing the trading behaviour among accounts, such as fund allocation, account balance changing, etc. Transaction network model construction can also be used to extract feature information of nodes and edges in the network model.

4.1   Ponzi Scheme Detection

Table 1 shows the existing machine learning-based detection methods for Ponzi scheme, which lists the types of extracted features and the classification models used for detection. According to the type of the dataset, machine learning-based detection methods for Ponzi scheme are classified into five categories: opcode, bytecode, source code, transaction record, and combined data oriented detection.

Table 1. Summary of machine learning-based detection methods for Ponzi scheme

Data	Ref.	Feature	Model
Opcode	[17]	n-gram TF	PonziTect
	[18]	n-gram TF	OB
	[19]	n-gram TF, TF-IDF, TF-OUR	LR, DT, SVM, ET, etc.
Bytecode	[20]	image	CNN
	[21]	matrice	OC-SVM, IF
Source code	[22]	AST	DT, SVM
	[23]	token sequence	Transformer
Transaction record	[24]	Tran-Feature	PIPPER, BN, RF
	[25]	Tran-Feature	GCN
Combined data	[26]	TF, Tran-Feature	XGBoost
	[27]	TF, Tran-Feature	DT
	[28]	TF, Tran-Feature	J48, RF
	[29]	TF, Tran-Feature	LSTM
	[30]	TF, Tran-Feature, bytecode similarity	LightGBM
	[31]	TF, Tran-Feature, sequence	CTRF
	[32]	TF, sequence, ABI call	SE-CapsNet
	[33]	2-gram TF-IDF, bytecode similarity	CatBoost
	[34]	TF, n-gram TF-IDF, sequence, counting vector	BT, XGBoost, etc.
	[35]	Tran-Feature, node feature	GCN
	[36]	numerical feature	XGBoost

Opcode Oriented Detection. Opcode, which is obtained by disassembling bytecode, is the most common type of data used in Ponzi scheme detection. In the existing works, the features extracted from opcode include n-gram TF, TF-IDF (Term Frequency - Inverse Document Frequency), and TF-OUR.

The n-gram TF feature is the frequency of the term which is combined by n consecutive opcodes. Fan et al. [17,18] extracted n-gram TF features ($1 \leq n \leq 4$) after eliminating stop words and splitting opcodes. With the extracted features, the PonziTect algorithm [17] and the OB (Ordered Boosting) algorithm [18] were used to detect Ponzi scheme contracts.

TF-IDF measures the importance of each opcode for a document within a set of documents. The more frequently an opcode appears in a document, but the less frequently it appears in other documents, the more representative it is for that document. Peng et al. [19] proposed TF-OUR feature, which was calculated by dividing the frequency of the term by the frequency of the maximum prefix term for the term. Eight classification models, such as DT (Decision Tree), RF (Random Forest), LR (Logistic Regression), etc., were combined with n-gram TF, TF- IDF, and TF-OUR features ($1 \leq n \leq 5$) to explore the best solution for Ponzi scheme detection.

Bytecode Oriented Detection. The bytecode of smart contract is compiled from the source code which is programmed with the high-level language, such as Solidity. It consists of a series of hexadecimal numbers that are highly sequential and abstract.

Lou et al. [20] used code visualisation technique to convert bytecodes into images, which were then employed to construct CNN (Convolutional Neural Network) model for Ponzi scheme detection, in which spatial pyramidal pooling approach was used to make the CNN adapt to different sizes of images.

Shen et al. [21] transformed the bytecodes into high-dimensional matrices by taking two bytes as one feature value. The PCA (Principal Component Analysis) algorithm was then used to reduce the dimensionality of the matrices and eliminate the noise in the matrices. Finally, the OC-SVM (One-class-Support Vector Machine) and IF (Isolation Forest) models were constructed to detect Ponzi schemes.

Source Code Oriented Detection. Compared with opcodes and bytecodes, the source codes of smart contracts have more intuitive semantic information, which can be transformed into AST (Abstract Syntax Trees) for further processing.

Ibba et al. [22] parsed the structure of the AST and replaced all mathematical operators with corresponding semantic meaning. With the AST transformed into semantic document, the DT and SVM (Support Vector Machine) models were constructed to perform classification.

Chen et al. [23] converted the AST to specially formatted code token sequences. The Transformer model was employed to learn the structure features, semantic features, and long-range dependencies in the code token sequences for classification.

Transaction Record Oriented Detection. Transaction records of blockchain addresses also can offer related features to distinguish between Ponzi and non-Ponzi schemes.

Bartoletti et al. [24] extracted Tran-Features (Transaction features), including the Gini coefficient of the values transferred to the address, the lifetime of the address, etc., to detect Ponzi schemes on Bitcoin with three classification models: RIPPER, BN (Bayes Network) and RF.

Yu et al. [25] collected the transaction records to establish TN (Transaction Network), from which Tran-Features were extracted. And the GCN (Graph Convolutional Network) model was constructed for Ponzi scheme detection.

Combined Data Oriented Detection. In the existing studies about Ponzi scheme detection, many researchers extracted multiple features from various data to construct detection models.

Chen et al. [26–29] extracted opcode TF and Tran-Feature features to construct the Ponzi scheme detection models. Except for the TF and Tran-Feature features, the similarity of the bytecodes between the target smart contract and Ponzi scheme contract was incorporated to construct the LightGBM model [30], and the sequence of bytecode was incorporated to construct the CTRF (Code and Transaction Random Forest) model [31].

In addition, in the detection model construction, the TF, sequence of bytecode, and ABI call features were extracted [32]; the 2-gram TF-IDF and bytecode similarity features were extracted [33]; the features, including TF, n-gram TF-IDF ($2 \leq n \leq 3$), sequence and count vector which represents the occurrence of each word in the bytecode, were extracted [34]; the Tran-Feature features from the transaction records and the node features from auxiliary heterogeneous interaction graph, which contains the information of externally owned account and contract account, were extracted [35].

Fan et al. [36] extracted numerical features associated with DApp (Decentralized Application) submitter's information, such as transaction time and investor's address, to construct the detection model. To protect the user's sensitive information, the clients of different DApps jointly trained the XGBoost model by federal learning without sharing the original data.

4.2   Phishing Scam Detection

The machine learning-based detection methods for Phishing scam usually extract features from the transaction records to construct the detection model. Table 2 provides a summary of the machine learning-based detection methods for phishing scam, listing the representation network of transactions, the feature extraction methods, the types of extracted features, and the classification models.

Table 2. Summary of machine learning-based detection methods for Phishing scam.

Ref.	Network	Extraction method	Feature	Model
[37]	TN	node2vec	latent	OC-SVM
[38]	TN	Line_graph2vec	latent	SVM
[39]	TN	trans2vec	node	SVM
[40]	TN	INSS	node	GCN
[41]	TN	MP	node	GCN
[42]	TN	LTFE	network, time series	LR
[43]	TN	manual-designed	account, network	SVM, KNN, AdaBoost
[10]	TN	GCF	cascade	DElightGBM
[44]	TN	GCN	structural	LightGBM
[45]	TN/TSGN/ Directed-TSGN	Graph2Vec, Diffpool	node/handcrafted	RF
[46]	Ego-Graph	node relabeling	structural, attributed	DT
[47]	TTAGN	edge2node	structural	LightGBM
[48]	SRG	GCN	edge	LR, SVM, XGBoost
[49]	TPG	GNN	transaction pattern	MCGC

Many researchers convert transaction records into TN (Transaction Network) or TG (Transaction Graph), which are referred as TN in this paper, to extract features using graph embedding or self-defined algorithms. Yuan et al. [37,38] respectively used the node2vec algorithm and the Line_graph2vec algorithm to extract the latent features to construct the OC-SVM and SVM models. The trans2vec algorithm [39] which takes the transaction amount and timestamp into consideration, the INSS (important neighbors subgraph sampling) method [40] which extracts features from the neighbor information of node, and the MP (Message Passing) algorithm [41] which computes the passed information between the nodes, were used to extract the node features. Wan et al. [42] used LTFE (Local network structures and Time series of transactions feature extraction) method to extract network features and time series features. Wen et al. [43] extracted the account features (such as the number of large transactions) and network features (such as the number of in-degree neighbors) to construct the SVM, KNN (K-Nearest Neighbor) and AdaBoost models. Chen et al. [10] used the GCF (Graph-based Cascade Feature extraction) method to extract cascade features, including node features and n-order features which contain the node features of the n-order friends, to construct DElightGBM (lightGBM-based Dual-sampling Ensemble algorithm) model. Chen et al. [44] used GCN (Graph Convolutional Network) to extract the structural features for constructing the LightGBM model.

Wang et al. [45] extracted TSGN (Transaction SubGraph Network) from TN, and expanded TSGN to Directed-TSGN which introduces the direction attributes. Then they respectively used graph2vec and Diffpool algorithm to extract node features from TN, TSGN, and Directed-TSGN. They also extracted handcrafted features from the three networks. The RF models constructed with the nine sets of features were compared. Xia et al. [46] constructed k-hop directed Ego-Graph for each address. Then they used a graph embedding method based on node relabeling strategy to extract both structural and attributed features. Li et al. [47] proposed TTAGN (Transaction Aggregation Graph Network), in which the edge representations around the node to fuse topological interactive relationships were aggregated into the representation of the node. Then they used edge2node algorithm to extract structural features. Fu et al. [48] transformed the TG into SRG (Sender and Receiver Graph), and used GCN to learn edge features in the graph. Zhang et al. [49] extracted transaction pattern features with GNN (Graph Neural Network) from TPG (Transaction Pattern Graph), which reduced the computational complexity through graph classification, to construct the MCGC (Multi-Channel Graph Classification) model.

4.3   Detection of Other Scams

Table 3 shows a summary of machine learning-based detection methods for other scams, including Honeypot and Pump and dump, listing the types of extracted features and the classification models.

Honeypot. The existing honeypot detection methods are all based on code features or transaction features to construct the detection model. Chen et al. [50] extracted n-gram TF features ($1 \leq n \leq 3$) from the opcode to construct the LightGBM model. Hara et al. [51] employed to extracted the distributed representation features from bytecode with the word2vec method and the TF-IDF features from opcode to construct the XGBoost model. Camino et al. [52] extracted the source code features (such as the number of lines in the source code) and the transaction features to construct the XGBoost model.

Table 3. Summary of machine learning-based detection methods for other scams.

Scams	Reference	Feature	Model
Honeypot	[50]	n-gram TF	LightGBM
	[51]	TF-IDF, distributed representation	XGBoost
	[52]	source code, Tran-Feature	XGBoost
Pump and dump	[11]	coin feature	RF, GLM
	[53]	moving window	RF, LR
	[54]	moving window	RF, AdaBoost
	[55]	social	CNN, LSTM

Pump and Dump. Xu et al. [11] extracted coin features before Pump and dump in the dataset based on the analysis of the market movements of coins. Then the coin features were employed to construct the RF, GLM (Generalized Linear Model) models for Pump and dump detection. Morgia et al. [53,54] split the historical trading data in chunks of seconds and defined a moving window. The moving window related features, such as the moving standard deviation of the number of trades, were extracted to construct the detection models. Nghiem et al. [55] extracted social features (such as the total number of forum comments on the coin) from the historical social data to construct the CNN and LSTM models for detecting the Pump and dump.

5 Discussion

5.1 Challenges

Existing methods for scam detection are mainly divided into two areas: analysis-based detection and machine learning-based detection. We will discuss the challenges in the two areas respectively.

(1) Challenges in analysis-based detection
Existing analysis-based detection methods mainly use code analysis techniques, such as symbolic execution, to analyze the execution paths and behaviour of the smart contract. The detection depends on the patterns of scams, which are defined manually by collecting and analyzing the existing blockchain scams. These detection methods perform well in detecting known scams. However, when facing unknown scams, or when scammers deliberately disguise scams, the performance will be greatly affected. With the increasing number of smart contracts, it is challenging in terms of the expandability and efficiency of such methods since it requires to define new patterns for new scams in the detection.
(2) Challenges in machine learning-based detection
Machine learning-based detection methods do not require defining patterns manually and are more expandable than the analysis-based detection methods. In addition, these methods can maintain good efficiency and certain effectiveness in the face of the increasingly large amount of data on the blockchain.

For the code features based detection methods, the obvious shortcoming is that the extracted features are simple and incomplete. For example, the frequency of opcodes is commonly employed to construct the detect model in most of the works. On the one hand, the opcode frequency cannot represent the complete semantic information of the smart contract. On the other hand, scammers can manually insert redundant codes into the smart contract to obfuscate the feature difference between scams and non-scams.

For the transaction features based detection methods, the detection performance depends on the existing transaction records. And the detection for the target address also requires its transaction records. If there is no enough transaction information for the target address, the detection can not be performed. Especially for the Pump and dump, of which the research is still in the early stage, the related data is insufficient. Since the detection for Pump and dump depends on the changes in cryptocurrency prices, it is challenging to detect the Pump and dump in real time. In addition, for transaction network based detection methods, various network structures are defined and various features are extracted. However, there is no comparison with the same dataset among these methods. It is difficult to evaluate the effectiveness of these methods.

The effectiveness of machine learning-based detection methods is related to the dataset. On the blockchain platforms, a lot of scam addresses are not identified and labelled. The number of scams is small, which cause the imbalance between positive and negative samples in the dataset. In addition, with the rapid development of blockchain over the years, a significant portion of data becomes meaningless historical data, which may be still used in existing research. This will affect the efficiency in detecting future scams.

5.2   Future Directions

Based on the above discussion about the shortcomings of existing blockchain scam detection methods, this paper summarizes the following future research directions.

Constructing Standard Datasets for Various Scams. The datasets for each scam used in the existing works are different. It is necessary to construct the standard datasets for various scams, which are of large scale and contain enough scam samples, so that researchers can employ them to construct detection models and perform experimental evaluation. Existing datasets can be integrated and supplemented with the latest data on the blockchain platforms. For the data imbalance problem, on the one hand, the existing addresses on the blockchian platform can be analyzed with the existing effective scam detection methods to identify the scams; on the other hand, new scams can be created based on the defined scam patterns. With these scams integrated into the dataset, the data imbalance can be solved.

Improving the Code Oriented Feature Extraction. The existing code oriented feature extraction methods mainly focus on the frequency-related features, which are simple and incomplete. To make the machine learning based model perform better in scam detection, the training data should contain as many scam related features as possible, such as the control flow information and data flow information in the smart contract. The pattern of each scam should be analyzed to determine which elements are the scam related features. And corresponding feature extraction methods need to be studied to extract these features.

Studying a Method to Detect Multiple Scams. All the existing scam detection methods are designed to detect one type of scam. There is no detection method that can detect multiple types of scams. However, the data and features used in some detection methods for different scams may be of the same type. For example, Refs. [18] and [50] both extracted frequency features from the opcodes of smart contracts to detect Ponzi scheme and Honeypot. It is possible to design a method to detect multiple scams. With such a method, it can easily judge whether there is a scam at the target address and what type of scam it is.

6 Conclusion

This paper surveyed the existing detection methods for blockchain scams, including Ponzi scheme, Honeypot, Phishing scam, and Pump and dump. The detection methods were categorized into analysis-based methods and machine learning-based methods. More specifically, the detection methods for each scam type were summarized from various aspects, such as the type of dataset, the extracted feature, the constructed model, etc. Finally, the challenges in analysis-based detection and machine learning-based detection were analyzed respectively. And the future research directions were discussed.

Acknowledgments. The work is supported by the National Natural Science Foundation of China (No. 62272145 and No. U21B2016), the Fundamental Research Funds for the Central Universities of China (B220202072, B210202075), the Natural Science Foundation of Jiangsu Province (BK20191297, BK20170893), the CloudTech RMIT Green Bitcoin Joint Research Program/Laboratory, and the Cooperative Research Centres Projects (CRC-P) funding scheme "Fast and Secure Crypto Payments for E-Commerce Merchants" (CRCPXIII000145).

References

1. Yli-Huumo, J., Ko, D., Choi, S., et al.: Where is current research on blockchain technology?-a systematic review. PLoS ONE **11**(10), e0163477 (2016)
2. CHAINALYSIS: The 2022 crypto crime report (2022). https://go.chainalysis.com/2022-crypto-crime-report.html
3. Bartoletti, M., Carta, S., Cimoli, T., Saia, R.: Dissecting Ponzi schemes on ethereum: identification, analysis, and impact. FGCS **102**, 259–277 (2020)
4. Torres, C.F., Steichen, M., State, R.: The art of the scam: demystifying honeypots in ethereum smart contracts. In: USENIX Security 2019, pp. 1591–1607 (2019)
5. Kumar, N., Singh, A., Handa, A., Shukla, S.K.: Detecting malicious accounts on the ethereum blockchain with supervised learning. In: Dolev, S., Kolesnikov, V., Lodha, S., Weiss, G. (eds.) CSCML 2020. LNCS, vol. 12161, pp. 94–109. Springer, Cham (2020). https://doi.org/10.1007/978-3-030-49785-9_7
6. Li, J., Gu, C., Wei, F., Chen, X.: A survey on blockchain anomaly detection using data mining techniques. In: Zheng, Z., Dai, H.-N., Tang, M., Chen, X. (eds.) BlockSys 2019. CCIS, vol. 1156, pp. 491–504. Springer, Singapore (2020). https://doi.org/10.1007/978-981-15-2777-7_40
7. Bartoletti, M., Lande, S., Loddo, A., et al.: Cryptocurrency scams: analysis and perspectives. IEEE Access **9**, 148353–148373 (2021)
8. Kamišalić, A., Kramberger, R., Fister Jr., I.: Synergy of blockchain technology and data mining techniques for anomaly detection. Appl. Sci. **11**(17), 7987 (2021)

9. Wu, J., Liu, J., Zhao, Y., et al.: Analysis of cryptocurrency transactions from a network perspective: an overview. J. Netw. Comput. Appl. **190**, 103139 (2021)
10. Chen, W., Guo, X., Chen, Z., et al.: Phishing scam detection on ethereum: towards financial security for blockchain ecosystem. In: IJCAI, vol. 7, pp. 4456–4462 (2020)
11. Xu, J., Livshits, B.: The anatomy of a cryptocurrency pump-and-dump scheme. In: USENIX Security Symposium, pp. 1609–1625 (2019)
12. Chen, W., Li, X., Sui, Y., et al.: SADPonzi: detecting and characterizing Ponzi schemes in ethereum smart contracts. POMACS **5**(2), 1–30 (2021)
13. Sun, W., Xu, G., Yang, Z., et al.: Early detection of smart Ponzi scheme contracts based on behavior forest similarity. In: QRS, pp. 297–309 (2020)
14. Song, L., Kong, X.: A study on characteristics and identification of smart Ponzi schemes. IEEE Access **10**, 57299–57308 (2022)
15. Torres, C.F., Baden, M., State, R.: Towards usable protection against honeypots. In: ICBC, pp. 1–2 (2020)
16. Ji, T., Fang, B., Cui, X., et al.: CADetector: cross-family anisotropic contract honeypot detection method. Chin. J. Comput. **45**(4), 877–895 (2022)
17. Fan, S., Fu, S., Xu, H., et al.: Expose your mask: smart Ponzi schemes detection on blockchain. In: IJCNN, pp. 1–7 (2020)
18. Fan, S., Fu, S., Xu, H., et al.: Al-SPSD: anti-leakage smart Ponzi schemes detection in blockchain. Inform. Process. Manag. **58**(4), 102587 (2021)
19. Peng, J., Xiao, G.: Detection of smart Ponzi schemes using opcode. In: Zheng, Z., Dai, H.-N., Fu, X., Chen, B. (eds.) BlockSys 2020. CCIS, vol. 1267, pp. 192–204. Springer, Singapore (2020). https://doi.org/10.1007/978-981-15-9213-3_15
20. Lou, Y., Zhang, Y., Chen, S.: Ponzi contracts detection based on improved convolutional neural network. In: SCC, pp. 353–360 (2020)
21. Shen, X., Jiang, S., Zhang, L.: Mining bytecode features of smart contracts to detect Ponzi scheme on blockchain. CMES **127**(3), 1069–1085 (2021)
22. Ibba, G., Pierro, G.A., Di Francesco, M.: Evaluating machine-learning techniques for detecting smart Ponzi schemes. In: WETSEB, pp. 34–40 (2021)
23. Chen, Y., Dai, H., Yu, X., et al.: Improving Ponzi scheme contract detection using multi-channel TextCNN and transformer. Sensors **21**(19), 6417 (2021)
24. Bartoletti, M., Pes, B., Serusi, S.: Data mining for detecting bitcoin Ponzi schemes. In: CVCBT, pp. 75–84 (2018)
25. Yu, S., Jin, J., Xie, Y., Shen, J., Xuan, Q.: Ponzi scheme detection in ethereum transaction network. In: Dai, H.-N., Liu, X., Luo, D.X., Xiao, J., Chen, X. (eds.) BlockSys 2021. CCIS, vol. 1490, pp. 175–186. Springer, Singapore (2021). https://doi.org/10.1007/978-981-16-7993-3_14
26. Chen, W., Zheng, Z., Cui, J.: Detecting Ponzi schemes on ethereum: towards healthier blockchain technology. In: WWW 2018, pp. 1409–1418 (2018)
27. Chen, W., Zheng, Z., Ngai, E.C.H., et al.: Exploiting blockchain data to detect smart Ponzi schemes on ethereum. IEEE Access **7**, 37575–37586 (2019)
28. Jung, E., Le Tilly, M., Gehani, A., et al.: Data mining-based ethereum fraud detection. In: Blockchain, pp. 266–273 (2019)
29. Wang, L., Cheng, H., Zheng, Z., et al.: Ponzi scheme detection via oversampling-based long short-term memory for smart contracts. Knowl.-Based Syst. **228**, 107312 (2021)
30. Zhang, Y., Yu, W., Li, Z., et al.: Detecting ethereum Ponzi schemes based on improved LightGBM algorithm. IEEE TCSS **9**(2), 624–637 (2021)
31. He, X., Yang, T., Chen, L.: CTRF: ethereum-based Ponzi contract identification. Secur. Commun. Netw. **2022**, 10 (2022)

32. Bian, L., Zhang, L., Zhao, K., et al.: Image-based scam detection method using an attention capsule network. IEEE Access **9**, 33654–33665 (2021)
33. Zhang, Y., Kang, S., Dai, W., et al.: Code will speak: early detection of Ponzi smart contracts on ethereum. In: SCC, pp. 301–308 (2021)
34. Aljofey, A., Jiang, Q., Qu, Q.: A supervised learning model for detecting Ponzi contracts in ethereum blockchain. In: Tian, Y., Ma, T., Khan, M.K., Sheng, V.S., Pan, Z. (eds.) ICBDS 2021. CCIS, vol. 1563, pp. 657–672. Springer, Singapore (2021). https://doi.org/10.1007/978-981-19-0852-1_52
35. Jin, C., Jin, J., Zhou, J., et al.: Heterogeneous feature augmentation for Ponzi detection in ethereum. IEEE Trans. Circuits-II **69**(9), 3919–3923 (2022)
36. Fan, S., Xu, H., Fu, S., et al.: Smart Ponzi scheme detection using federated learning. In: HPCC/SmartCity/DSS, pp. 881–888 (2020)
37. Yuan, Q., Huang, B., Zhang, J., et al.: Detecting phishing scams on ethereum based on transaction records, In: ISCAS. pp. 1–5 (2020)
38. Yuan, Z., Yuan, Q., Wu, J.: Phishing detection on ethereum via learning representation of transaction subgraphs. In: Zheng, Z., Dai, H.-N., Fu, X., Chen, B. (eds.) BlockSys 2020. CCIS, vol. 1267, pp. 178–191. Springer, Singapore (2020). https://doi.org/10.1007/978-981-15-9213-3_14
39. Wu, J., Yuan, Q., Lin, D., et al.: Who are the phishers? Phishing scam detection on ethereum via network embedding. IEEE Trans. Syst Man Cybern.-Syst. **52**(2), 1156–1166 (2020)
40. Tang, J., Zhao, G., Zou, B.: Semi-supervised graph convolutional network for ethereum phishing scam recognition. In: ECNCT, vol. 12167, pp. 369–375 (2022)
41. Yu, T., Chen, X., Xu, Z., et al.: MP-GCN: a phishing nodes detection approach via graph convolution network for ethereum. Appl. Sci. **12**(14), 7294 (2022)
42. Wan, Y., Xiao, F., Zhang, D.: Early-stage phishing detection on the ethereum transaction network. Soft. Comput. **27**(7), 3707–3719 (2023)
43. Wen, H., Fang, J., Wu, J., et al.: Transaction-based hidden strategies against general phishing detection framework on ethereum. In: ISCAS, pp. 1–5 (2021)
44. Chen, L., Peng, J., Liu, Y., et al.: Phishing scams detection in ethereum transaction network. TOIT **21**(1), 1–16 (2020)
45. Wang, J., Chen, P., Yu, S., Xuan, Q.: TSGN: transaction subgraph networks for identifying ethereum phishing accounts. In: Dai, H.-N., Liu, X., Luo, D.X., Xiao, J., Chen, X. (eds.) BlockSys 2021. CCIS, vol. 1490, pp. 187–200. Springer, Singapore (2021). https://doi.org/10.1007/978-981-16-7993-3_15
46. Xia, Y., Liu, J., Wu, J.: Phishing detection on ethereum via attributed ego-graph embedding. IEEE Trans. Circuits-II **69**(5), 2538–2542 (2022)
47. Li, S., Gou, G., Liu, C., et al.: TTAGN: temporal transaction aggregation graph network for ethereum phishing scams detection. In: WWW, pp. 661–669 (2022)
48. Fu, B., Yu, X., Feng, T.: CT-GCN: a phishing identification model for blockchain cryptocurrency transactions. Int. J. Inf. Secur. **21**(6), 1–10 (2022)
49. Zhang, D., Chen, J., Lu, X.: Blockchain phishing scam detection via multi-channel graph classification. In: Dai, H.-N., Liu, X., Luo, D.X., Xiao, J., Chen, X. (eds.) BlockSys 2021. CCIS, vol. 1490, pp. 241–256. Springer, Singapore (2021). https://doi.org/10.1007/978-981-16-7993-3_19
50. Chen, W., Guo, X., Chen, Z.: Honeypot contract risk warning on ethereum smart contracts. In: JCC, pp. 1–8 (2020)
51. Hara, K., Takahashi, T., Ishimaki, M., et al.: Machine-learning approach using solidity bytecode for smart-contract honeypot detection in the ethereum. In: QRS-C, pp. 652–659 (2021)

52. Camino, R., Torres, C.F., Baden, M., et al.: A data science approach for detecting honeypots in ethereum. In: ICBC, pp. 1–9 (2020)
53. La Morgia, M., Mei, A., Sassi, F., et al.: Pump and dumps in the bitcoin era: real time detection of cryptocurrency market manipulations. In: ICCCN, pp. 1–9 (2020)
54. Morgia, M.L., Mei, A., Sassi, F., et al.: The doge of wall street: analysis and detection of pump and dump cryptocurrency manipulations. ACM Trans. Internet Tech. **23**(1), 1–28 (2023)
55. Nghiem, H., Muric, G., Morstatter, F., et al.: Detecting cryptocurrency pump-and-dump frauds using market and social signals. Expert Syst. Appl. **182**, 115284 (2021)

ScamRadar: Identifying Blockchain Scams When They are Promoting

Xinzhe Zheng[1,2], Pengcheng Xia[1], Kailong Wang[3], and Haoyu Wang[3(✉)]

[1] Beijing University of Posts and Telecommunications, Beijing 100000, China
[2] The University of Hong Kong, Hong Kong, China
[3] Huazhong University of Science and Technology, Wuhan 430000, China
haoyuwang@hust.edu.cn

Abstract. The vigorous growth of cryptocurrencies has infiltrated into social media, manifested by extensive advertisement campaigns popping up on platforms such as Telegram and Twitter. This new way of promotion also introduces an additional attack surface on the blockchain community, with a number of recently-identified scam projects distributed via this channel. Despite prior efforts on detecting scams, no existing works systematically study such promotion channels for detecting on-going scam projects. In this paper, we take the first step to propose a novel approach that leverages promotion messages to detect on-going blockchain-themed scam projects. We extract features spanning four dimensions: word frequency, sentiment analysis, potential profit margin and URL information. For automated detection, we first construct two datasets, and then train a classifier on them that achieves a high accuracy (over 90%). Through our large-scale study, we have identified $69,148$ highly suspicious scam messages, relating to $8,247$ blockchain addresses. By tracing the confirmed scam addresses, we further identify a cumulative illicit income of around 900 ETH. Our findings should help the blockchain community understand and promptly detect scam projects when they are promoting.

Keywords: Cryptocurrency · Blockchain scams · Promotional messages · Scam detection · Semantic analysis

1 Introduction

Since Satoshi Nakamoto introduced the first digital cryptocurrency based on blockchain in 2008, many cryptocurrencies have emerged in the following years due to the evolving technology. According to CoinMarketCap [1], the global cryptocurrency market capitalization has reached $1.76 trillion in 2022. The prosperous market has also generated tremendous financial opportunities and profits for investors. *Where there is sunshine, there is shadow*—cryptocurrencies are also intensively targeted by scammers. According to Federal Trade Commission [2], scams have incurred more than $80 million loss on cryptocurrency investments,

J. Chen et al. (Eds.): BlockSys 2023, CCIS 1896, pp. 19–36, 2024.
https://doi.org/10.1007/978-981-99-8101-4_2

with an increase of over ten-fold year-over-year in 2021. In particular, there have been numerous high-profile frauds in the past years at staggering scales. For example, the PlusToken Wallet Ponzi scheme impacted 2.4 million users, involving $2.9 billion total losses [3]. In 2017, two ICOs issued by the same company, Pincoin and iFan, attracted approximately 32,000 investors [4] with $660 million incurred losses from them.

The tricks exploited by scammers are continuously evolving. In the past, scammers typically sent phishing messages to investors via email or forums. With the rise of social media in recent years, scammers are taking advantage of them (e.g., Telegram) to reach out to investors with lucrative offers (e.g., promising them high returns for a huge upfront payment and subsequent fees [5]). The reason behind such shift is the low cost of posting fraudulent information on social media platforms such as BitcoinTalk [6], Twitter [7] and Telegram [8]. The overwhelming influx of information from various sources thus confuses investors, which renders it feasible to trick them with various types of frauds such as airdrop scam [9], Ponzi scheme [10], ICO scam [11,12], counterfeit token scam [13], etc. Researchers in the cryptocurrency community have already combated with scams [13–18]. However, most of the existing scam detection techniques rely on the transaction histories of scam addresses. Consequently, they can only be used to identify scams after victims falling into the traps.

This raises the research question: *Can we identify blockchain scams, even before they succeed in tricking victims?* (**First question**) Our preliminary exploration suggests that answer is yes. Based on our observation, scammers usually post "attractive" promotional information to maximally lure unsuspecting victims, which is significantly different from the advertising information of benign blockchain projects. This pattern can be utilized as a good indicator to flag blockchain scams when they are promoting, and raise warnings to investors before they are fallen into the scams. However, it is not straightforward to the research community how to effectively leverage this newly found pattern. In other words, *how to determine whether a message is a scam promotional message?* (**Second question**)

Our Work. In this paper, we seek to promptly identify blockchain scams based on their promotional messages. To answer the first question, we begin with harvesting two ground truth datasets, one is manually collected from various social media sources and the other is automatically collected based on the target blockchain addresses (to be detailed in Sect. 3.1). The former dataset contains 658 messages and the latter contains 18,692 messages. Through feature visualization, we have observed distinct characteristics between scam and benign messages against the features including word vectors, sentimental analysis, profit margin and embedded URLs.

The observed distinctions also motivate the scam message detection process. As an answer to the second question, we have implemented SCAMRADAR, a machine learning based classifier to pinpoint scams using features extracted from the four feature dimensions. Evaluation results suggest that SCAMRADAR can achieve excellent performance, with an accuracy of over 90%. Thus the second remaining question is solved. We further apply SCAMRADAR to 103,057 blockchain promotional messages collected from Telegram, and identify 69,148 suspected scam messages connecting with 8,247 suspicious scam addresses, which have not been previously revealed by our community.

Contributions. In summary, this paper makes the following main research contributions:

- **Detecting scams at promoting stage.** To the best of our knowledge, this is the first attempt from our community to identify blockchain scams at their promoting stage. This method is complementary to existing techniques, which can act as a whistle blower to identify blockchain scams at their early stage before they create a huge impact.
- **An effective tool.** We develop SCAMRADAR, a practical tool to identify scam promotional messages and their related scam addresses based on various kinds of features. Evaluation on our curated large-scale benchmark shows that SCAMRADAR can achieve great performance, i.e., with an accuracy of over 90%.
- **A large-scale study.** We apply SCAMRADAR to a large-scale dataset of promotional messages collected from Telegram, and identify 69,148 suspected scam messages connecting with 8,247 suspicious scam addresses, which were not previously aware by our community. We further revealed the characteristics of these scams.

To facilitate further research, we released SCAMRADAR with all the data to the research community.

2   A Motivating Example

According to our preliminary investigation, Telegram has been actively involved with blockchain scams. A specific example is an airdrop scam advertising the fake MCO token, circulated in a Telegram group, as depicted in Fig. 1(a). The enticing investment opportunity (i.e., very high profit margins) generates a substantial reward at a minimal input. For example, one of the listed purchase options offers 20 MCO tokens (worth up to 1 ETH) at 0.1 ETH. The irrationality and abnormality behind such promotion information indicate its malicious nature. Under this airdrop message, the users who transfer ETHs to the address will never receive the promised MCO tokens back. By checking the transactions into the scam address, we found that 5 victims lost a total of 0.17 ETH to this scam. Even though the loss incurred in this scam is not exceptionally high, tens of thousands of such scams would cost a lot to honest investors.

3   Approach

We propose a systematic approach leveraging structural and semantic characteristics from texts: word vectors, sentimental analysis, URL analysis, and profit margin, as shown in Fig. 1(b).

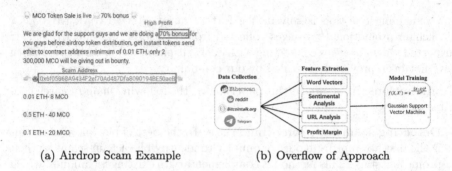

(a) Airdrop Scam Example   (b) Overflow of Approach

Fig. 1. Sample Scam and Overview of Approach

3.1   Data Collection

We assemble two ground-truth datasets, both consisting of six types of scam and benign messages. The first dataset (referred to as **MS** hereafter) contains scam messages from a wide range of social media sources (e.g., Telegram groups including airdropscams [19], Bitcoins SCAM Warner [20] and SCAM Detector [21]) and online open-source databases (e.g., the anti-cryptocurrency scam project CryptoScamDB [22]). It also contains benign messages from official accounts and groups. In total, **MS** includes 658 messages (359 scam and 299 benign messages), as listed in Table 1. The second dataset (referred to as **AS** hereafter) is automatically crawled using keys that are comprised of target Ethereum addresses (i.e., tagged as phishing, scam and benign) from etherscan.io [23]. More specifically, we call the Telegram API to crawl the neighboring sentences surrounding a key (three sentences before and after) to form a sample. After further screening and excluding irrelevant samples, **AS** contains 18, 692 messages including 3741 scam and 14951 benign messages. In addition to the ground-truth datasets, we further assemble a dataset of sentences with unknown labels for analysis in this work. They are collected using similar channels as the two datasets, counting to a total of 230, 188 messages.

Table 1. Manually Tagged Set

	Type	Number
Benign	–	299
Scam	Airdrop Scam	78
	Ponzi Scam	62
	Counterfeit Token	45
	Unknown Scam	53
	Mining Scam	64
	Pump Down	57

3.2   Feature Extraction

Word Vectors. We aim to first identify characteristic words belonging to each category, and then construct the word vector based on their occurrence frequencies. In particular, we adopt TF-IDF [24] to get feature words for the six types of scam messages and the benign messages, after preprocessing to remove the meaningless tokens. The word vector w_i can be further derived as:

$$\mathbf{w_i} = \{c_{i1}, c_{i2}, ..., c_{i15}\} \tag{1}$$

where c_{ij} represents the frequency of the j_{th} feature word of message type i.

Then, the data in vector $\mathbf{w_i}$ is normalized, given by:

$$\mathbf{w_i} = \text{Norm}[\mathbf{w_i}] = \{\frac{c_{i1}}{\sum\limits_{k=1}^{15} c_{ik}}, \frac{c_{i2}}{\sum\limits_{k=1}^{15} c_{ik}}, ..., \frac{c_{i15}}{\sum\limits_{k=1}^{15} c_{ik}}\} \tag{2}$$

For each message, we calculate its six types of scam vectors and the benign vector. To enable effective scam detection, the final word vector is constructed by combining the seven word vectors into one, given by Eq. 3. The first part is the result of adding six scam word vectors, and the second part is the word vector of the benign type. To balance the vector modulus size of scam and benign types for better differentiation, we multiply benign type word vector by 5.

$$v = \{v_{scam}, 5 \times v_{normal}\} = \{\sum_{i=1}^{6} \mathbf{w_i}, 5 \times \mathbf{w_7}\} \tag{3}$$

where v denotes the word vector of a specific message.

Sentimental Analysis. The text sentimental information could serve as another key indicator for detecting scam messages. This is based on our observation that scam messages typically include overly attractive offers to trap investors. As a comparison, benign messages tend to describe their investment campaigns neutrally, without exaggeration. In this work, we use vaderSentiment [25, 26] for sentiment analysis. It outputs four indicators of a message: positive probability, neutral probability, negative probability and compound score. The compound score is computed by summing the valence scores of each word in the lexicon, adjusted according to the rules and then normalized to be between -1 (most extreme negative) and $+1$ (most extreme positive). The difference between the scam and benign messages can be distinguished through these four indicators.

Profit Margin. Scam messages commonly advertise unrealistically high investment returns (e.g., over 100% profit in 30 min), which is one of the defining features. In comparison, the profit margin is much lower in those benign ones, if not null. Considering that there are various standards for advertising the profit margin (i.e., calculated over days, months, or even minutes), we set or convert the unit with reference to a daily rate to facilitate direct comparison. If a single message contains several levels of profit margins, the average result is calculated to represent its daily profit rate. For a message that does not contain profit information, its profit margin is zero.

URL Analysis. For messages embedded with URLs instead of blockchain addresses, we seek to investigate the relevance between the URLs and scams to utilize them as one of the differentiating features. We use search engines from VirusTotal [27] to scan for malicious URLs in the messages. For each URL, VirusTotal will return a list of numbers on the detection results, representing analysis tags including "harmless", "malicious", "suspicious", "timeout" and "undetected". Here we use numbers of "malicious" and "suspicious" as the final features of a URL. For a message, all the features of its related URLs are accumulated to represent its final feature to be used for our analysis. For the identified URLs of scam messages, Besides, we use an IP-geolocation mapping database [28] to obtain where the IP addresses of URLs belong.

3.3 Gaussian Kernel Support Vector Machine

We use support vector machine (SVM) to train a classification model. Based on the four analyses, the input data size of a specific message is 36 (30 on word vector + 4 on sentiment analysis + 1 on profit margin analysis + 1 on URL analysis). The task of the SVM is to find out the hyperplane that can separate these two types of messages in the 36-dimensional space. We adopt the Gaussian kernel function, which can map finite-dimensional data to a higher-dimensional space. The SVM model is set as medium fineness to avoid over-fitting.

4   Evaluation

In this section we aim to study the effectiveness of proposed features in distinguishing the scam and benign messages. We focus on multi-dimensional aspects including feature visualization, model performance, and realistic scam detection.

4.1   Feature Visualization

We visualize the four features separately to show their capability for distinguishing scam and benign messages.

Visualization of Word Vectors. We utilize the 359 scam messages and 299 benign messages from **MS** for comparison. Investigating the feature words derived from TF-IDF model, we have observed characteristic patterns for difference scam types.

For feature words related to *airdrop scam messages*, the TF-IDF value of the word "bot" is very high. This is because such scams are generally related to the chat bots on Telegram. They trick the participants to complete the registration process, and collect their blockchain addresses and private keys. For feature words related to *Ponzi scams*, most focus on time and profit, such as "daily", "hour", "profit", "withdrawal", advertising extremely high profit margin in a short period. In comparison, the feature words related to *benign messages* are relatively neutral: "distribute", "join", "follow", "reward". Official airdrop projects typically promise a token reward after completing fixed tasks, without participants' further actions (e.g., sending token to a specific addresses) or other complex rewards schemes.

To confirm that the word vectors can distinguish the scam from benign messages, we calculate those for all messages in **MS** and adopt t-SNE method [29] for dimension reduction. After processing, we are able to plot them as two-dimensional vectors, as shown in Fig. 2(c). The read dot represents scam type, and the blue cross represents benign type.

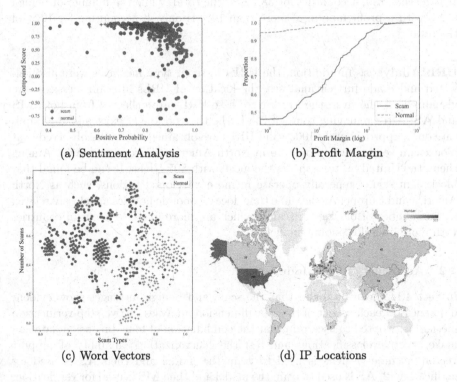

(a) Sentiment Analysis

(b) Profit Margin

(c) Word Vectors

(d) IP Locations

Fig. 2. Visualization Results

Visualization of Sentiment Analysis. Then the results of sentiment analysis are analyzed. In order to facilitate visualization, only the positive probability and compound score are considered. Again, the data in **MS** is shown in Fig. 2(a). It can be seen that the distribution of different sentimental levels in scam messages is more extensive than that in the benign messages. When the positive probability is within the range of 0.8–1.0, the proportion of scam messages is much higher, consistent with the previous conjecture that the participants are more willing to invest after reading the scam messages. On the compound score, some scam messages get a compound score of 1.0, while almost no benign type ones get 1.0. Although the visualized results show a large overlap between scam and benign type of messages, the potential disparate characteristics can still be found between them.

Visualization of Profit Margin. The statistical result of profit margin is shown in Fig. 2(b), the cumulative distribution functions of scam type and benign type demonstrate that the average profit margin of scam type is grater than that of benign type. The number of fraud types with a profit margin of more than 10% reaches 139, accounting for 38.7% of the total, while the number of benign types with a profit margin of more than 10% is only 4, accounting for 1.3% of the total.

URL Analyses. In addition, the URLs in scam type messages were also collected and made further analyses. the location of URLs in scam messages are visualized, as shown in the Fig. 2(d). These URLs are collected from both **MS** and **AS**. After removing some of the URLs that no longer exist and the duplicate ones, approximately 1000 valid URLs are obtained. It can be observed that blockchain scams mainly operate in North America, Europe and Asia. Among them, the United States appears the most, with 505 URLs. It can be found that blockchain scams generally operate in more developed regions, such as North America and Europe. At the same time, local economic policies are closely related to the number of blockchain scams, which are more likely to occur in countries with more liberal economic models.

4.2   Accuracy of the Model

In Sect. 4.1, it can be found that the scam and benign messages show evident differences in each aspect of the four-dimension analyses. A two-step verification method is adopted to ascertain that the combination of four-dimension data can make effective classifications and test the generalization capability of support vector machine: 1. **MS** is used to train the model and then **AS** is used for verification. 2. **AS** is used to train the model and then **MS** is used for verification. The results of the two-step verification method based on support vector machines are presented in Table 2.

Firstly, **MS** is used as the training set, and **AS** is used as the verification set. Using **MS** as the training set, a considerable result is obtained. The accuracy of the classification results is about 90%. Although the precision item in the result is not that high, the recall rate of scam messages is approximately 100%, which

Table 2. Two-step Verification Result

Training Set	Validation Set	Accuracy (%)	Precision (%)	Recall (%)	F1 (%)
Ms	As	90.79	68.62	99.44	81.21
As	Ms	96.5	99.7	93.87	96.7

means the model can perfectly find scam messages, and this is more important for the investors. Then, the two data sets are swapped and the steps above are repeated. As the results demonstrate, the results of the validation set reach a certain high degree.

Through two-step verification of the model, it can be learned that the classification model has strong generalization ability, especially for scam detection, and the data of four-dimensional analysis can be used to effectively distinguish the scam and benign type messages.

4.3   Detecting Suspected Scam Projects

The purpose of training the classification model is to find more suspected scam messages. In this section, the **MS** and **AS** are combined into one data set, and some suspicious scam messages in the unknown type data set are marked with the trained classification model. Further analysis of the suspected scam messages is then carried out.

First, the messages of unknown type are preprocessed. The length of the shortest message in the combination data set is calculated as a minimum length, and the messages of unknown type which are less than the minimum length are excluded. In this way, a preliminary 103,057 messages are obtained out of 230,188 messages, and the number of blockchain addresses extracted from these messages is 9,029. The pre-trained classification model is used to mark the messages corresponding to these addresses, and finally 69,148 messages and 8,247 suspected scam addresses are finally obtained.

The number of messages for the suspected scam addresses is first calculated and sorted, and then the API on etherscan.io is used to collect the transaction information for these addresses. In Table 3, the ten addresses with the largest number of corresponding messages and their associated information are shown.

Number of messages indicates the number of messages corresponding to the address, and the "Value In" indicates the amount of Ethers transferred to the address.

According to the statistical results, the number of messages corresponding to suspected scam addresses is relatively large, with the largest number reaching 5,291, and most of the addresses will have hundreds of corresponding messages. That is to say, in the collection of about 100,000 effective messages, a large proportion of the messages is similar. They are quickly copied and spread among Telegram groups.

The ten addresses suspected of scam type are then studied manually, and it is confirmed that they are all scam addresses. Addresses No. 1, 3, 4, 7, 9 and

Table 3. Suspected Scam Addresses: Top 10

Address	Number of Messages	Scam Token	Value In	Number of Out Transactions	Number of In Transactions
0x281a0b47d9fb15592a21e2a7c1b8cc3453860a1b	5291	Basic Attention Token	5.106	11	18
0x273622b6481bf50eb9d1a897ec31aa6248af985b	3597	True USD	7.170	9	10
0x301d811c4a87f9cc0cabc4b85fc3b2d51ca5dd15	3252	Basic Attention Token	2.997	5	6
0x769bbb7f4ca5264e83458e3c20f298cbfc21d9cc	3186	Basic Attention Token	12.762	17	26
0x51ed115b7ecaf1c27a66a0a3f34bd51bf5da9d36	2433	Paxos Standard	4.341	7	4
0xb5cb84924eedba7995756aa823c82fcf942ade56	2045	Ether Diamond	17.461	1696	509
0x6251a79f79f68631b12fa64940d004e09ddfd16d	2032	Basic Attention Token	3.085	8	7
0x859963c26df5bac19a1baa2938186988d57448b1	1924	Litecoin Token	3.824	20	21
0x6bae242e72a82f8be420a95121b65fc0b2459419	1293	Basic Attention Token	0.110	130	11
0xc70d49ab06128f0fe8028ad8d489cb5e97b8ee7e	1078	Basic Attention Token	3.900	11	9

10 correspond to the Basic Attention Token (BAT) sale. Basic Attention Token is a legit project, however, the fraudsters exploited its authority to cheat the investors. The corresponding report can be found on Bitcointalk forum. The sixth address corresponds to an scam project called Ether Diamond, which has been flagged as a fake token by users on the Bitcointalk forum [30]. This address has many out transactions, which can make it harder for people to track these scammed funds, and we have a deeper analysis on it in Sect. 4.4.

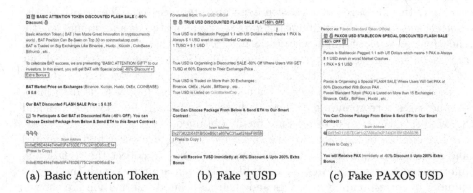

(a) Basic Attention Token   (b) Fake TUSD   (c) Fake PAXOS USD

Fig. 3. Scam Messages

After reviewing the messages of these addresses, it is found that although some of the scam messages fall under different projects, they have highly similar patterns. As shown in Fig. 3, it is not difficult to find that the messages of Basic Attention Token, fake TUSD and fake PAXOS USD are highly similar. In other words, fraudsters often do not need to modify too much content to re-launch a blockchain scam, and by setting up a robot in Telegram, these scam type of messages can be spread widely and quickly, which is almost zero cost for fraudsters.

The claimed investment strategy for scam addresses are also similar, with the money being transferred as soon as the victim transfers a certain amount of ETH to these addresses, rarely more than a day in between. And it is found that most Ethers obtained by BAT scam project were withdrawn from FTX Exchange [31] after several rounds of transactions.

4.4   Identifying More Scam Messages

With the ten confirmed scam addresses and the transaction records of all these 8,247 suspected addresses, more scam messages can be found out through some address expansion heuristics.

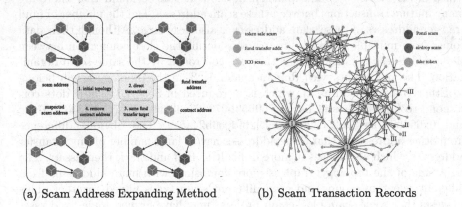

(a) Scam Address Expanding Method   (b) Scam Transaction Records

Fig. 4. Expand Method and Result

As shown in Fig. 4(a), after building the initial topology through the transaction records of all addresses, the solution of expanding more scam addresses consists of three main steps. The first step is to find out the addresses which have direct transaction records with the ten scam addresses among suspected scam addresses. If an address has a direct transaction record with the ten scam addresses, it is considered as a scam address. And the second step is to find the address that has the same fund transfer address as the scam address. Although not directly linked to a confirmed scam address, this transaction behaviour greatly increases the likelihood that the address is of the scam type. There are two kinds of addresses, one is account address, the other is contract address. It is noticed that if the fund transfer address is a contract address, it is hard to confirm whether the suspected scam address is actually a scam address. Buying tokens or invoking smart contracts is totally legitimate. So, in the last step, by calling the Ethereum browser API to determine whether the fund transfer address is a benign account address or a contract address, we remove the addresses found in the second step whose fund transfer address is a contract address. After everything is done, these scam addresses and their corresponding text messages are manually confirmed to ensure that they are truly scam addresses. And finally, a total of 71 scam addresses are expanded, with 392 transaction records involved. Along with the 10 scam addresses mentioned in Sect. 4.3, although only 71 scam addresses are obtained finally, these addresses correspond to 29, 739 scam messages, which account for almost half of the total 69, 148 suspected scam messages.

Based on the obtained results, a topology graph of scam address transaction records is presented in Fig. 4(b).

According to the topology, we can find some patterns of scam address transactions and its operation mode. The green dots, which are the token sale scam type of addresses. For example, the aforementioned address 0x281a0b47d9fb15592a21-e2a7c1b8cc3453860a1b, and 0x76f531a15563f684af1e5f292caa6aea79b99806, which is discovered by our expansion method. It can be found that there are many mutual transactions between these scam addresses, and the number of fund transfer addresses of these scam addresses is also very large. Although their data comes from multiple telegram groups, considering the close connection between these addresses, it indicates that they are controlled by the same scam organization. The yellow dots with Roman numeral "I" in the topology graph belong to Ether Diamond addresses, which is introduced in Sect. 4.3. These dots correspond to ETH addresses like 0x750b53b273463cd3aa9c37867cad2f3433b9730c and 0x666b547aa15a6256a254e63c392bfd0e6b24a5c9. The obvious difference from other addresses is that these addresses have a large number of fund transfer addresses, which also makes it more difficult to find and track their assets. The right side of the topology graph is more confusing, with many addresses from different telegram groups and even different scam types mixed together. This suggests that some scam blockchain projects may have formed some fixed asset transfer paths and their workflows are very mature.

Table 4. Scam Organizations We Identified.

Scam Organization	Scam Type	# of Scam Address	Active Year	High-frequency Trading Period (day)	Value In	Transaction Interval (hour)	# of Fund Transfer Address
Char Token	Fake token	6	2020	75.4	503.7	35.7	747
Ether Diamond	ICO scam	6	2020	269.2	146.9	19.7	416
Unknown	Token sale scam	28	2020	74.9	137.8	16.3	114
Unknown	Ponzi scam	6	2020	150.4	75.8	18.3	40
Minereum Token	Airdrop scam	8	2021	249.5	11	189.7	10
Futurax	ICO scam	3	2019	115.4	5.1	192.2	51

Further, as shown in Table 4, we perform analysis on several relatively large scam organizations related to these scam addresses, including the scam types, active years, high-frequency trading periods of the address and etc. It is simple to obtain the active year of each organization as we can get when these messages were sent out on Telegram. As for the high-frequency trading periods of the address, the timestamps of transactions are first obtained. Then, these timestamps are clustered according to the adaptive DBSCAN clustering algorithm [32]. If a set of timestamps are very close, the clustering algorithm will classify them into one category. If the distribution of timestamps occurs in significantly different time periods, the clustering algorithm will classify them into 2 or even more. After the clustering step, the category containing the largest number of timestamps is picked and its time span is calculated as the high-frequency trading period of the address. The high-frequency trading period of addresses can show the active time of scam addresses to a certain extent, that is, the main time of fraud. The following analysis is based on these aforementioned indicators.

For example, Char Token, whose addresses are shown in Fig. 4 as orange dots with Roman numeral "II", is the most profitable scam organization in our dataset, with more than 500 Ethers being transferred to its scam address. One of the scam addresses in the picture is 0x22f7bbffd86cfea6cd7ad97fc8089343a1f52852. The group is described on the Bitcointalk forum as a faken token scam that the organizer team is fake. The profile pictures on the project's website were computer-generated, with fake LinkedIn profiles attached. In addition, the scam addresses of the first unknown organization which belong to token sale scam and Ether Diamond group also involve a large number of Ethers. They earned 137.8 and 146.9 Ethers respectively. The smallest scam organization in our dataset was Futurax, where 5.1 Ethers were transferred. And its scam addresses, like 0xf52a310fb1f7bcb9b29a8bbfe606d36365ee6649, are shown in the topology graph as yellow dots with Roman numeral "III". Although only a few scam organizations are listed, a considerable number of assets are involved. Blockchain scam projects have caused considerable damage to both investors and the market.

According to statistical data, we also found that most of these scam projects appeared around 2020. At that time, the cryptocurrency market had just experienced the black swan event on March 12, 2020 and the average decline in cryptocurrencies reached 38% on that day [33]. The unstable market gave these scammers some opportunity to exploit the situation. It is also found that these scam projects may persist for a considerable period of time, such as the Ether Diamond group, whose scam addresses have a high-frequency trading period of up to 269 days. On this metric, other organizations also exceeded 70 days, which means that there have been investment victims for a long period of time, and these scam projects have not been blocked in a short period of time.

In addition, we further study time interval between the victims' time of being scammed and the attackers' time of fund transfer. In specific, We analyzed a group of in and out transactions at similar timestamps. If the amount of ETH in the out transactions is equal to the total amount of incoming ETH, then this group of transaction records is regarded as one fund transfer behavior. And the time interval is calculated by subtracting the latest in transaction timestamp from the earliest out transaction timestamp. The data shown in the table is the result of averaging. We find these scam projects usually transfer the funds within a short period of time after receiving the funds. The fact that most organizations transfer funds out within a day shows that fraudsters are desperate to withdraw these tokens, or distribute them, to keep the funds safe. The number of fund transfer addresses is also quite large, and in common, organizations with larger funds tend to have more corresponding fund transfer addresses. These scam organizations are obviously of a certain size and are well-organized.

To sum up, many scam messages are successfully found through the pre-trained classification model. An in-depth analysis of these scam messages and their corresponding blockchain addresses is then conducted. Some of these scam messages have very similar context and transaction patterns. These scam messages often use very similar words to attract investors with more positive emotions, which can be easily distinguished from type of messages. Some even share the same token purchase options. All kinds of analysis can find that scam organizations are not scattered, but organized and efficient, and they are constantly planning frauds one after another in the dark side.

5   Related Work

With the development of cryptocurrency market, cryptocurrency scams have emerged across the world. Not only the total amount of money lost in cryptocurrency scams are increasing, but the categories of the scams are becoming more diverse. such as airdrop scam [9], Giveaway scam, Ponzi scam [10], ICO scam [11], counterfeit token scam [13], pump-and-dump scam [34] and so on.

In response to the growing number of blockchain scams, extensive research has been conducted. Among them, Ponzi scams and ICO scams are studied more. For example, Vasek et al. [35] studied the Ponzi scam ecosystem in Bitcoin. Through survival analysis, they identified some factors that affect the persistence of a scam: the frequency of interaction with the victim and the time when the fraudsters register the scam account. Chen et al. [36] built an automatic classification model to detect smart Ponzi schemes through the transaction information of scam addresses and the code in Ethereum smart contracts. There are also studies on pump-and-dump schemes that focus on the performance of trades in certain groups [37]. The most related work to us is Bian et al. [11]. For ICO scams, they analyzed four characteristics: ICO white paper, webpage information, GitHub repositories at the time of ICO, and founding teams, using a neural network model to detect scam ICO. Their work relies on rich messages on ICO projects' whitepapers and webpages, and thus their method does not deal with relatively short promoting messages well enough to detect other scams.

In addition, we also find that most of the scams occur on Ethereum, which is related to the mature DeFi (Decentralized Finance) ecology of Ethereum. Researchers have used a number of different methodologies to detect scams in

Ethereum, such as data mining [38], machine learning [39], analyzing transactions on Ethereum to detect phishing [40], and sentiment analysis [41]. In addition, some researchers have identified and analyzed the fraudulent behaviors from the source: social media [42].

Few efforts focused on detecting scams when they are promoted. Via the above studies, we analyzed the scams they mentioned and further found some underlying patterns in blockchain scams, which constitutes some indicators to implement the classification model of this work.

6 Discussion

6.1 Implication

The research results of this work can help the blockchain community to a certain extent, including blockchain project investors and developers. First of all, this paper designs a classification model with generalization ability, which can judge whether a blockchain project is a scam according to the text messages when they are promoting. It can help investors understand the existence of many scam blockchain projects and learn the pattern of scam messages to improve awareness. Second, considering the prevalence of scam messages we find on social media, the governance of the ecosystem needs to be improved. Third, we can find more scam addresses based on some heuristics through confirmed scam addresses. And there may be many mutual transactions between the scam addresses. This finding could help developers or researchers find more scam addresses or scam blockchain projects and alert blockchain investors in a timely manner.

6.2 Limitation

This study also has some limitations. First, although the classification model in this paper can effectively classify blockchain projects by relying on the messages, most of the messages are collected from Telegram, and their lengths are usually relatively short. It may be hard to detect ICO scams through their whitepapers. It is hoped that the work in this area can be carried out in the future to improve the model's performance. Second, if fraudsters modify the text pattern of scam type messages according to our work, the classification model in this paper may not be effective in scam detection. Therefore, the characteristics of scam type messages may be studied from other perspectives in the future to enrich the dimensions of the detection model. Third, the method proposed in this paper to find more scam addresses based on confirmed scam addresses can only find a small part of the results. It is also worth thinking about combining text information with blockchain address transactions and detecting scam blockchain projects from multiple perspectives.

7   Conclusion

This paper systematically studied the scam blockchain projects from their texts and addresses. The proposed classification model proved that scam-type messages often have a significantly different text pattern than benign blockchain ads. The scam blockchain address analysis shows that these scam blockchain projects are well organized, and their attacks may have certain concealment and long periodicity. Shockingly, only a small group of attackers can control a wide range of scam blockchain projects. The meager crime cost of scammers and a large amount of defrauded assets indicate that the blockchain community should invest more research to fight against these scams in order to maintain the good ecosystem of the blockchain. Though the work done in this paper proposed some effective methods to track these scam projects, these methods can only uncover the tip of the iceberg of scam blockchain projects. A lot more research should be done in the future to learn more about these scams and prevent them to a certain extent.

References

1. https://coinmarketcap.com/. Accessed 5 Oct 2022
2. FTC data shows huge spike in cryptocurrency investment scams (2021). https://www.ftc.gov/news-events/press-releases/2021/05/ftc-data-shows-huge-spike-cryptocurrency-investment-scams?utm_source=govdelivery
3. Cryptocurrency anti-money laundering report, 2019 Q2 (2019)
4. Gareth Jenkinson. Unpacking the 5 biggest cryptocurrency scams (2018). https://cointelegraph.com/news/unpacking-the-5-biggest-cryptocurrency-scams
5. Caporal, J.: Study: crypto and investment scams skyrocket in 2020 and 2021 (2021)
6. Bitcoin talk (2021). https://bitcointalk.org/
7. Twitter. it's what's happening/twitter (2021). https://twitter.com/
8. Telegram messenger (2021). https://telegram.org/
9. Mina Down on. How to profit from crypto airdrops and avoid scams along the way | hacker noon (2018). https://hackernoon.com/a-guide-to-navigating-the-world-of-cryptocurrency-airdrops-cef2777427db
10. Fan, S., Fu, S., Xu, H., Zhu, C.: Expose your mask: smart Ponzi schemes detection on blockchain. In: 2020 International Joint Conference on Neural Networks (IJCNN), pp. 1–7 (2020)
11. Bian, S., et al.: IcoRating: a deep-learning system for scam ICO identification. arXiv preprint arXiv:1803.03670 (2018)
12. Liebau, D., Schueffel, P.: Crypto-currencies and ICOs: are they scams? An empirical study. An Empirical Study (2019)
13. Gao, B., et al.: Tracking counterfeit cryptocurrency end-to-end. Proc. ACM Meas. Anal. Comput. Syst. 4(3), 1–28 (2020)
14. Xia, P., et al.: Trade or trick? Detecting and characterizing scam tokens on uniswap decentralized exchange. Proc. ACM Meas. Anal. Comput. Syst. 5(3), 1–26 (2021)
15. Huang, Y., et al.: Understanding (mis) behavior on the EOSIO blockchain. Proc. ACM Meas. Anal. Comput. Syst. 4(2), 1–28 (2020)
16. Xia, P., et al.: Don't fish in troubled waters! Characterizing coronavirus-themed cryptocurrency scams. In: 2020 APWG Symposium on Electronic Crime Research (eCrime), pp. 1–14 (2020)

17. Wu, J., et al.: Who are the phishers? Phishing scam detection on ethereum via network embedding. IEEE Trans. Syst. Man Cybern.: Syst. **52**(2), 1156–1166 (2022)
18. Wang, K., et al.: Characterizing cryptocurrency-themed malicious browser extensions. In: SIGMETRICS (2023)
19. Telegram group: airdropscams. https://t.me/airdropscams. Accessed 5 Oct 2022
20. Telegram group: CryptoScamWarner. https://t.me/CryptoScamWarner. Accessed 5 Oct 2022
21. Telegram group: ScamDetector11. https://t.me/ScamDetector11. Accessed 5 Oct 2022
22. CryptoScamWarner. https://cryptoscamdb.org/. Accessed 5 Oct 2022
23. etherscan. https://etherscan.io/. Accessed 5 Oct 2022
24. Chowdhury, G.G.: Introduction to Modern Information Retrieval. Facet publishing (2010)
25. Hutto, E.G.C.J.: vadersentiment (2014). https://github.com/cjhutto/vaderSentiment
26. Hutto, C., Gilbert, E.: VADER: a parsimonious rule-based model for sentiment analysis of social media text. In: Proceedings of the International AAAI Conference on Web and Social Media, vol. 8, no. 1, pp. 216–225 (2014)
27. virustotal. https://www.virustotal.com. Accessed 5 Oct 2022
28. https://api.chinaz.com/ApiDetails/IP . Accessed 5 Oct 2022
29. Van Der Maaten, L., Hinton, G.: Visualizing data using t-SNE. J. Mach. Learn. Res. **9**(2605), 2579–2605 (2008)
30. Telegram group navigation for major altcoins and exchanges (2020). https://bitcointalk.org/index.php?topic=5241151.0. Accessed 15 June 2023
31. FTX Exchange. https://ftx.com/. Accessed 23 Oct 2022
32. Li, W., Yan, S., Jiang, Y., Zhang, S., Wang, C.: Research on method of self-adaptive determination of DBSCAN algorithm parameters. Comput. Eng. Appl. **55**(5), 1–7 (2019)
33. Yarovaya, L., Matkovskyy, R., Jalan, A.: The effects of a "black swan" event (COVID-19) on herding behavior in cryptocurrency markets. J. Int. Finan. Mark. Inst. Money **75**, 101321 (2021)
34. Pump and dump cryptocurrency: how does it happen (2018). https://www.icoholder.com/blog/pump-and-dump-cryptocurrency/
35. Vasek, M., Moore, T.: Analyzing the bitcoin Ponzi scheme ecosystem. In: Zohar, A., et al. (eds.) FC 2018. LNCS, vol. 10958, pp. 101–112. Springer, Heidelberg (2019). https://doi.org/10.1007/978-3-662-58820-8_8
36. Chen, W., Zheng, Z., Ngai, E.C.-H., Zheng, P., Zhou, Y.: Exploiting blockchain data to detect smart Ponzi schemes on ethereum. IEEE Access **7**, 37575–37586 (2019)
37. Nghiem, H., Muric, G., Morstatter, F., Ferrara, E.: Detecting cryptocurrency pump-and-dump frauds using market and social signals. Expert Syst. Appl. **182**, 115284 (2021)
38. Jung, E., Le Tilly, M., Gehani, A., Ge, Y.: Data mining-based ethereum fraud detection. In: 2019 IEEE International Conference on Blockchain (Blockchain), pp. 266–273. IEEE (2019)
39. Poursafaei, F., Hamad, G.B., Zilic, Z.: Detecting malicious ethereum entities via application of machine learning classification. In: 2020 2nd Conference on Blockchain Research & Applications for Innovative Networks and Services (BRAINS), pp. 120–127. IEEE (2020)

40. Yuan, Q., Huang, B., Zhang, J., Wu, J., Zhang, H., Zhang, X.: Detecting phishing scams on ethereum based on transaction records. In: 2020 IEEE International Symposium on Circuits and Systems (ISCAS), pp. 1–5. IEEE (2020)
41. Sureshbhai, P.N., Bhattacharya, P., Tanwar, S.: KaRuNa: a blockchain-based sentiment analysis framework for fraud cryptocurrency schemes. In: 2020 IEEE International Conference on Communications Workshops (ICC Workshops), pp. 1–6. IEEE (2020)
42. Mirtaheri, M., Abu-El-Haija, S., Morstatter, F., Ver Steeg, G., Galstyan, A.: Identifying and analyzing cryptocurrency manipulations in social media. IEEE Trans. Comput. Soc. Syst. 8(3), 607–617 (2021)

Based on Financial Characteristics to Capture the Source of Funds of the Ponzi Scheme on Ethereum with Graph Traversal Technology

Yuxi Zhang[1], Haifeng Guo[1]([✉]), Biliang Wang[2], Yunlong Wang[2], and Jianfu Luo[2]

[1] Department of Finance, School of Management, Harbin Institute of Technology, Harbin 150001, China
haifengguo@hit.edu.cn

[2] School of Finance, Southwestern University of Finance and Economics, Chengdu 610000, China

Abstract. Detecting Ponzi schemes in blockchain is an urgent task due to the various illegal transactions generated on the blockchain, among which Ponzi schemes are difficult to identify. The high returns promised by Ponzi schemes lure more and more people into the fraud. To prevent further economic losses, this paper proposes a detection method based on the financial features of Ponzi schemes and graph theory. By constructing a transaction subgraph of the fund sources of Ponzi schemes and traversing the subgraph, the proposed method can locate the fund source nodes of Ponzi schemes according to the matched subgraph structure. This paper is the first to combine the financial features of Ponzi schemes with graph algorithm techniques to study the simultaneous de-anonymization of multiple nodes in Ponzi schemes.

Keywords: Ethereum · Ponzi Scheme · Transaction Subgraph · Graph Traversal

1 Introduction

Ponzi schemes have been a major problem for the financial industry for decades, and with the rise of blockchain technology and cryptocurrencies, new forms of Ponzi schemes have emerged. One of the main challenges in combating these schemes is the difficulty in detecting and monitoring fraudulent transactions on blockchain networks. In recent years, there has been a growing interest in research on blockchain-based transaction monitoring and fraud detection, with a focus on identifying Ponzi schemes.

The anonymization of the blockchain is one of the primary difficulties in the identification of Ponzi schemes. There is no authentication mechanism, which makes it difficult to trace the transaction to its real initiator and recipient, thus increasing the difficulty of identifying Ponzi schemes. Secondly, according to the transaction characteristics of Ethereum account nodes and contracts, a unique product of Ethereum, the transaction types of Ponzi schemes are more diverse. Different Ponzi schemes may use different means and methods to carry out fraud, so in Ethereum Identifying Ponzi schemes online

J. Chen et al. (Eds.): BlockSys 2023, CCIS 1896, pp. 37–44, 2024.
https://doi.org/10.1007/978-981-99-8101-4_3

requires a high degree of flexibility and adaptability. Third, there are millions of transactions in the Ethereum network every day, which makes it easy for Ponzi scheme transactions to be drowned in the huge transaction volume, thus increasing the difficulty of identifying Ponzi schemes. In addition, Ponzi schemes usually involve transactions between multiple accounts, and the transaction links may be very complicated, which increases the difficulty of identifying Ponzi schemes.

In this paper, we propose a method capable of identifying nodes in Ponzi schemes that make transfers to scammers or Ponzi contracts. This method is based on the principle of graph theory to construct the subgraph structure of the non-Euclidean space with the identified node as the core to finally identify the node.

The rest of the paper is organized as follows. The second section presents the related research background and work, which mainly includes the types of Ponzi schemes on Ethereum and the detection of illegal behavior on blockchain by other scholars using graph algorithms. The third section introduces the Ponzi scheme case studied in this paper, as well as its financial characteristics. The fourth section explains the main principles of the model. The fifth section discusses and validates the experimental results through visualization. The final section provides a summary of the entire paper.

2   Background and Related Work

2.1   Ponzi Scheme on Ethereum

In the Ethereum network, Ponzi schemes can be divided into the following types:

(1) **Transaction-profit Ponzi schemes.** This type of Ponzi scheme usually promises participants high returns through trading cryptocurrencies, etc. In reality, the profits mainly come from new investors rather than actual trading gains. The typical characteristics of these schemes are to attract new investors with high returns, and many victims are often novice investors or people who lack knowledge of the cryptocurrency industry. For example, *Bitconnect* is a transaction-profit Ponzi scheme on the *Ethereum* network that promised participants monthly returns of 1% to 10%. However, the project was actually a Ponzi scheme that ultimately defrauded more than $2 billion in digital assets.

(2) **Token issuance Ponzi schemes.** This type of Ponzi scheme usually promises participants high returns by buying newly issued tokens. In reality, these tokens have no real use case or value, and investors' returns mainly come from new investors. The typical characteristics of these schemes are to emphasize the future value and market prospects of tokens, attracting a large number of investors to join. For example, *OneCoin* is a token issuance Ponzi scheme on the Ethereum network that promised participants high returns by buying *OneCoin* tokens. However, the project was actually a Ponzi scheme that ultimately defrauded more than $4 billion in digital assets.

(3) **Smart contract Ponzi schemes.** Smart contracts are one of *Ethereum*'s core features that can automatically execute contract conditions and transfer funds to beneficiaries. These Ponzi schemes exploit the features of smart contracts to commit fraud, typically by enticing users to invest funds in a seemingly secure smart contract that is actually manipulated by scammers to defraud users of their funds.

2.2 Anomaly Detection on Blockchain Based on Graph Structure

Mark Weber et al. [1], used Graph Convolutional Networks (GCN) to predict illegal transactions in elliptic data sets. Tam et al. [2] used the mechanism of sampling transaction neighbors which is similar to the subgraph extraction. They characterized edges by embedding the temporal features from the time-series of transactions and incorporating them into the graph convolution network. Jiajing Wu et al. [3] proposes an approach to detect phishing scams on Ethereum by mining its transaction records. Specifically, they first crawl the labeled phishing addresses from two authorized websites and reconstruct the transaction network according to the collected transaction records. Then, by taking the transaction amount and timestamp into consideration, they propose a novel network embedding algorithm called trans2vec to extract the features of the addresses for subsequent phishing identification.

3 Case Description and Financial Characteristics of Funding Source Nodes

3.1 The Illegal Fund-Raising Case Description About *"PlusToken"*

This paper discusses the analysis of the *Plustoken* case, the first cryptocurrency pyramid scheme that was cracked down by the Chinese Ministry of Public Security in 2020. The suspects set up the *"PlusToken* platform" and developed related applications to engage in Internet pyramid schemes. The platform uses blockchain technology as a gimmick and uses digital currencies such as Ethereum as a transaction medium, claiming to provide digital currency value-added services and promising high rebates to attract a large number of people to participate. The platform is divided into technology, marketing, customer service, and withdrawal groups, responsible for technical operation and maintenance, promotion, consultation and reply, and review of withdrawals. Participants can become members by recommending and paying more than $500 worth of digital currency as a "threshold fee," and receive the platform's self-created *"Plus"* coins according to the value of the digital currency paid, forming a hierarchical relationship based on the order of joining. The platform divides members into five levels, including members, big clients, big shots, masters, and creators, and distributes a corresponding amount of *"Plus"* coins as rewards and rebates according to the number of downlines and the amount of investment. In order to attract more people to participate, the criminal gang used the Internet to promote the platform's joining method, operation mode, bonus system, and profit prospects, and even hired foreign personnel to impersonate the founder of the platform and package the so-called "international platform" and "foreign projects." They also organized periodic meetings, concerts, tours, and other offline activities to promote the platform, and even spent a lot of money to hold large-scale promotion conferences overseas several times. It is estimated that the platform developed more than 2 million members and had more than 3,000 hierarchical relationships during its existence, collecting several million digital currencies such as Ethereum from members, with a total amount involved of over 40 billion yuan (calculated based on the market situation at the time of the case).

3.2 Financial Characteristics of Funding Source Nodes

From the view of financial, if the Ponzi scheme is split according to the label category, it can be mainly divided into three types of labels. As shown in Fig. 1, the most important label is "Ponzi node", which is the main node for absorbing illegal funds from the public. The second type of node is the funding source node of the Ponzi scheme, that is, the node that injects funds into the "Ponzi node". The third type of node is the transfer node of the funds absorbed by the Ponzi scheme, which is the next-level node of the "Ponzi node" fund transfer.

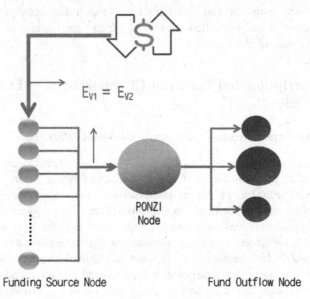

Fig. 1. Ponzi scheme main node structure

The research in this paper is based on the subgraph construction of the Ponzi scheme funding source nodes. Through the analysis of the case and data, it is found that this case is an online and offline joint publicity, and the victim group is not very familiar with the concept of "*Blockchain*" and "*Ethereum*" and the actual operation. Most of the actual users projected by the source of funding nodes do not belong to the group of people who have been conducting transactions on Ethereum for a long time. The virtual currency used by these people when investing in Ponzi nodes does not come from their own long-term accumulation or transaction income in the *Ethereum* network, and even most users have never had account nodes in the *Ethereum* network. Therefore, the historical transactions of these "funding source nodes" are simple and pure, and the transaction logic is as follows: investors or victims purchase a certain amount of E_{v1} virtual currency offline through fiat currencies and exchanges or other trading node accounts with virtual currency, and then Transfer the purchased virtual currency to the Ponzi node at one time or in batches, and the total amount is E_{v2}. $E_{v1} = E_{v2}$, and the funding source node has no other transaction nodes except these two types of account nodes.

4 Model Framework

4.1 Generate Target Node Vector

This article extracts 1073 transaction records from the *"PLUSTOKEN"* case, which are used for subgraph extraction in this article. When dealing with graph data, each node needs to be represented as a vector (or called feature vector) so that we can use these nodes in the neural network for learning and matching.

In this paper, the node feature matrix is generated for the Ponzi scheme node A, the deposit node B of the Ponzi scheme, and other adjacent first-order nodes C of node B. For each node, we generated two random features. These features can be regarded as the attributes of the node, which can be the attributes of the node's degree, degree centrality, proximity centrality, betweenness centrality, etc., or external features obtained from other data sources.

Specifically, it can be expressed as:

Displayed equations are centered and set on a separate line.

$$A = \{(a_i, feature1_i, feature2_i)|i = 1, 2, \ldots, n_A\} \qquad (1)$$

$$B = \{(b_i, feature1_i, feature2_i)|i = 1, 2, \ldots, n_B\} \qquad (2)$$

$$C = \{(c_i, feature1_i, feature2_i)|i = 1, 2, \ldots, n_C\} \qquad (3)$$

4.2 Generate Directed Edge Vectors

Based on the concept of edge list in graph theory, it represents the edge of the graph. Each line contains the identifiers of two nodes, indicating that there is an edge between these two nodes. Specifically, this paper generates directed edges for two nodes with a transaction relationship. The origin of the edge is the initiator of the transaction, and the end of the edge is the recipient of the transaction.

4.3 Create Non-Euclidean Space Subgraphs

This paper establishes the non-Euclidean space graph of nodes through the topological relationship between nodes. This directed graph object can be represented as a mathematical first-order adjacency matrix, where the rows and columns of the matrix represent nodes respectively. If there is an edge from a row node to a column node, the corresponding element in the matrix is 1, otherwise it is 0. Since our graph is directed, the adjacency matrix is an asymmetric matrix. For example, if there is an element (2, 3) in the edge list, the second row and third column of the adjacency matrix are 1, indicating that there is an edge from node 2 to node 3. We'll use this directed graph object to build our target subgraph. Specifically, we extract the transaction subgraph of Funding Source Node B: $G = (A, B, C, E_v, y_i)$, where V represents the set of accounts in this subgraph, E_v represent the directed edge set that contain information about transaction volume, y_i is the label of subgraph G.

4.4 Illegal Fund-Raising Link Subgraph Traversal and Funding Source Node Retrieval

In order to confirm how many qualified deposit nodes around this Ponzi node transfer money to it, this paper use the form of graph traversal to conduct a structured traversal search on the historical transaction records of illegal fund-raising nodes based on the established subgraph. To locate deposit nodes that meet the characteristics.

This paper needs to find a specific type of path in the original graph, i.e. from a start node to an intermediate node, and then to a termination node, with edges having equal weights between the start and termination nodes. To find such paths, we can use breadth-first search or depth-first search algorithms to traverse the original graph. When we traverse the graph, we record information such as labels and weights of nodes, so that when we find a qualified path, we can directly add this information to the target subgraph object. This paper uses a simple nested loop to implement this algorithm, which has high time complexity, but it is feasible for small graph applications.

5 Graph Visualization

5.1 Sub-graph

This paper firstly visualizes the non-Euclidean graph for each eligible deposit node, and the graph structure formed is shown in Fig. 2:

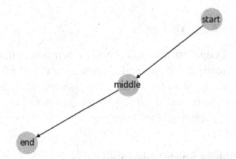

Fig. 2. Fund source node transaction subgraph

Among them, middle is the deposit node, end is the illegal fundraising node, and start is the exchange account that provides the original Ethereum for the deposit node or other anonymous active nodes on Ethereum. The 1,078 pieces of transaction data selected in this article capture a total of 285 sub-pictures of the complete illegal fund-raising link of the Ponzi scheme.

5.2 Graph

Because there is not only one transaction between nodes among many nodes, this paper merges the recurring nodes in the visualization link. As shown in Fig. 3, the number of capital source nodes captured is still 285, but the number of nodes of exchanges or other accounts that provide the capital source nodes with the Ethereum used for investment is greatly reduced.

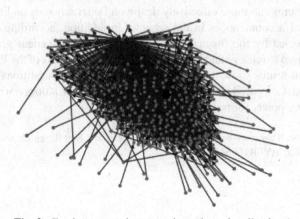

Fig. 3. Fund source node transaction subgraph collection 1

In order to verify the wider feasibility of this model, this paper also randomly selected 3199 transaction data in this case, of which a total of 1638 transaction subgraphs were constructed, the structure of which is the same as that in Fig. 2. After merging the subgraphs, there are a total of 1560 fund source nodes. The merged subgraph is shown in Fig. 4. It can be seen that the fund source nodes are still far more than the account nodes that provide the original Ethereum.

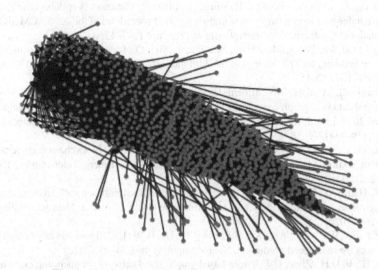

Fig. 4. Fund source node transaction subgraph collection 2

6 Conclusion

Traditional deanonymization on Ethereum is often a pure algorithmic technology, but for specific types of financial crimes like Ponzi schemes, fully combining financial features with graph structures can more effectively deal with Ponzi schemes on Ethereum. Deanonymization of account nodes in the scheme. In addition, according to the graph structure constructed by the financial characteristics, the subsequent graph traversal search mode is used to retrieve and locate the funding source nodes of the Ponzi scheme. The experimental results show that it is more efficient than the traditional single node exclusion method. Compared with other more complex models, it does not need to spend a lot of computing power for training.

Acknowledgments. This work was supported by The National Key Research and Development Program of China(2020YFB1006104).

References

1. Weber, M., et al.: Anti-money laundering in bitcoin: Experimenting with graph convolutional networks for financial forensics. *arXiv preprint* arXiv:1908.02591, (2019)
2. Tam, D.S.H., Lau, W.C., Hu, B., Ying, Q.F., Chiu, D. M., Liu, H.: Identifying illicit accounts in large scale e-payment networks–a graph representation learning approach. *arXiv preprint* arXiv:1906.05546 (2019)
3. Wu, J., et al.: Who are the phishers? phishing scam detection on ethereum via network embedding. IEEE Trans Syst. Man, Cybern. Syst. **52**(2), 1156–1166 (2020)
4. Zhao, C., Guan, Y.: A graph-based investigation of bitcoin transactions. In: Peterson, G., Shenoi, S. (eds.) DigitalForensics 2015. IAICT, vol. 462, pp. 79–95. Springer, Cham (2015). https://doi.org/10.1007/978-3-319-24123-4_5
5. Bollacker, K., Evans, C., Paritosh, P., Sturge, T., Taylor, J.: Freebase: A collaboratively created graph database for structuring human knowledge. In: Proceedings of the 2008 ACM SIGMOD International Conference on Management of Data, pp. 1247–1250 (2008)
6. Tang, J., Qu, M., Wang, M., Zhang, M., Yan, J., Mei, Q.: Line: largescale information network embedding. In: Proceedings of the 24th International Conference on World Wide Web, pp. 1067–1077 (2015)
7. Schlichtkrull, M., Kipf, T.N., Bloem, P., van den Berg, R., Titov, I., Welling, M.: Modeling relational data with graph convolutional networks. In: Gangemi, A., et al. The Semantic Web. ESWC 2018. LNCS, vol 10843, pp. 593–607. Springer, Cham (2018).https://doi.org/10.1007/978-3-319-93417-4_38
8. Djenouri, Y., Srivastava, G., Belhadi, A., Lin, J.C.W.: Intelligent blockchain management for distributed knowledge graphs in IoT 5G environments. Trans. Emerg. Telecommun. Technol. e4332 (2021)
9. Gu, P., Han, Y.Q., Gao, W., Xu, G.D., Wu, J.: Enhancing session-based social recommendation through item graph embedding and contextual friendship modeling. Neurocomputing **419**, 190–202 (2020)
10. Lu, Z.L., Lv, W.F., Cao, Y.B., Xie, Z.P., Peng, H., Du, B.W.: LSTM variants meet graph neural networks for road speed prediction. Neurocomputing **400**, 34–45 (2020)
11. Tang, H., Ji, D.H., Zhou, Q.J.: Triple-based graph neural network for encoding event units in graph reasoning problems. Inf. Sci. **544**, 168–182 (2021)
12. Zhao, J., Liu, X.D., Yan, Q.B., Li, B., Shao, M.L., Peng, H.: Multi-attributed heterogeneous graph convolutional network for bot detection. Inf. Sci. **537**, 380–393 (2020)

IntelliCon: Confidence-Based Approach for Fine-Grained Vulnerability Analysis in Smart Contracts

Yiming Shen[1], Kunhua Li[1], Lin Mao[2], Wenkai Li[1], and Xiaoqi Li[1(✉)]

[1] School of Cyberspace Security, Hainan University, Haikou 570208, China
csxqli@gmail.com
[2] School of Computer Science and Technology, Hainan University, Haikou 570208, China

Abstract. Ethereum smart contracts are programs that execute transactions on a distributed ledger platform without intermediaries. However, they are prone to various types of vulnerabilities that can affect their security and functionality. In this paper, we present INTELLICON, a novel framework that leverages a pre-trained identifier-aware encoder-decoder CodeT5 model and confident learning to detect seven types of vulnerabilities in Ethereum smart contracts. Confident learning is a technique that improves dataset quality by identifying and correcting noisy labels, particularly in the presence of multiple annotators with varying levels of accuracy. We fine-tune CodeT5 on a dataset of 27,426 smart contracts annotated by multiple tools and pruned by confident learning to ensure that the model learns genuine vulnerability features rather than tool-specific features. Furthermore, we utilize abstract syntax tree (AST) analysis to extract code gadgets with sliding windows to locate the function that may contain code vulnerabilities. We evaluate the effectiveness of our framework in vulnerability detection with F1-score. Our results indicate that INTELLICON achieves high Micro-F1 (0.9591) and Macro-F1 (0.9293), outperforming existing methods. Moreover, our framework demonstrates its ability to handle imbalanced data, noisy labels, and complex code structures. INTELLICON contributes to improving the security and reliability of smart contracts, providing insights for future research on code generation tasks.

Keywords: Blockchain · Smart Contract · Confident Learning · Vulnerability Detection · Deep Learning

1 Introduction

Recently, blockchain [1] technology has experienced rapid development in various fields (e.g., finance, healthcare, supply chain, and IoT) [2]. However, the vulnerabilities of smart contracts have given significant concerns, resulting in financial losses, system failure, and damage to the platform's reputation. According to the

© The Author(s), under exclusive license to Springer Nature Singapore Pte Ltd. 2024
J. Chen et al. (Eds.): BlockSys 2023, CCIS 1896, pp. 45–59, 2024.
https://doi.org/10.1007/978-981-99-8101-4_4

Blockchain Security and AML Analysis Annual Report of SLOWMIST [3], 30.3% of the 303 blockchain security events recorded in 2022 were due to contract vulnerabilities. Notably, high-profile security incidents in the RONIN NETWORK, and the WORMHOLE NETWORK resulted in losses exceeding \$610 million and \$300 million, respectively [4]. These incidents emphasize the urgent need for enhanced security measures to safeguard users' assets and mitigate potential security risks.

Smart contract vulnerabilities pose a significant risk to the security and integrity of blockchain systems, necessitating the development of effective techniques for their detection and mitigation [5]. Traditional methods for detecting smart contract vulnerability rely on static or dynamic analysis. Static analysis examines the source code or bytecode of smart contracts without executing them, while the dynamic analysis runs smart contracts with test inputs or fuzzing techniques. However, these methods have limitations such as slow processing, high false positives/negatives rates, low coverage, and scalability issues. To address the limitation of traditional methods for detecting smart contract vulnerabilities, machine learning-based methods [6] have been proposed. These methods leverage various algorithms or models to learn patterns or features from code snippets and classify them as vulnerable or non-vulnerable.

Moreover, existing large datasets (e.g., SmartBugs [7]) are often labeled by multiple traditional vulnerability detection tools. While models trained on these datasets can achieve high performance, they are limited by these traditional tools. In essence, as long as the neural network replicates expert-defined rule, it can achieve a high F1 close to 1. Therefore, these training results merely simulate or synthesize the functions of the original tools, rather than truly learning the underlying causes of vulnerabilities.

In this paper, we propose INTELLICON, a CodeT5-based detection framework for smart contracts that address the limitations of traditional methods. The source code of the smart contract is processed as an abstract syntax tree (AST) to collect code gadgets and then fed to the CodeT5 model. Our framework also utilizes confident learning technology during training to improve the labeling consistency of the dataset. To provide a measure of confidence in the accuracy of our model, we construct a set of prediction ranks around its predictions. By leveraging these prediction ranks as a decision criterion, potentially incorrect forecasts can be filtered out, leading to an improvement in the overall accuracy of the model. The experimental results demonstrate that our framework achieves a micro-F1 score of over 95%, and a macro-F1 score of over 92%, outperforming the existing popular pre-training frameworks (e.g., Bert and T5) in terms of detection ability.

The main contributions of this paper are as follows:

- We propose a novel framework that leverages identifier-aware CodeT5 and multi-label learning to identify seven types of vulnerabilities in Ethereum Smart contracts.
- We are the *first* to utilize confident learning to improve the quality of datasets that involve multiple traditional analysis tools with varying levels of accuracy

in smart contracts vulnerability labels. By identifying and correcting noisy labels, we enable the model to acquire genuine vulnerability features during subsequent training.

- We enhance interpretability in machine learning-based vulnerability detection methods by providing fine-grained code gadgets that can potentially expose the sources of these vulnerabilities.

The remainder of this paper is organized as follows. In Sect. 2, the background of our research was reviewed. Section 3 presents our INTELLICON framework. Section 4 evaluates our framework and compares it to other approaches. Section 5 introduces the related work. Finally, we conclude our work and provide directions for future research in Sect. 6.

2 Background

2.1 Ethereum Smart Contract Security Threats

The Ethereum [8] is a blockchain platform that supports smart contracts, which are programs that record transactions and perform logic. However, smart contracts can also pose security risks [9], such as reentrancy, integer overflow, denial of service, unchecked low calls, and improper access control. These risks can lead to malicious attacks or exploits, resulting in loss of funds.

2.2 Pre-trained Language Model

Pre-trained language models in natural language processing (NLP) involve obtaining general language representations from large datasets. It results in a better semantic representation that can be applied to the downstream tasks (e.g., text classification). As the need for semantic representation and static word embeddings to deep semantic word embeddings through word vectors, more pre-training models have gained significant attention (e.g., GPT, BERT, T5).

2.3 Text Classification Task

Text classification is a process of assigning labels to text data. Given $X = \{x_1, x_2, ..., x_n\}$ and $Y = \{y_1, y_2, ..., y_k\}$, where each x_i is a document consisting of a sequence of words $\{w_1, w_2, ..., w_m\}$, each y_i represents a class label. Text classification learns a function $f : X \rightarrow Y$ that maps each x_i to its corresponding label. Once the model is trained, the function can be used to predict the label of a new document X_{new}. X_{new} feed to f, which outputs a predicted label $\hat{y}$ based on the learned mapping from the X to Y.

3 IntelliCon

In this Section, we will give a detailed description of INTELLICON, a confident learning-based approach for fine-grained vulnerability detection in Ethereum smart contracts, leveraging the identifier-aware CodeT5 model.

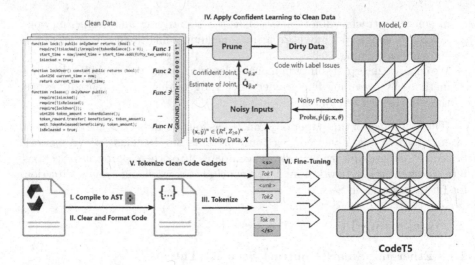

Fig. 1. Training Phase of the INTELLICON Framework

3.1 Overview

The INTELLICON framework consists of two main phases: model training in Fig. 1 and vulnerability detection in Fig. 2. The first phase is to train a code-aware fine-grained encoder-decoder model that can identify seven types of vulnerabilities in Ethereum smart contracts with confident learning. We adopt CodeT5 [10], a state-of-the-art pre-trained model for code understanding based on the T5 architecture. In addition, we apply self-confidence learning to improve the quality of our dataset by removing noisy data, thereby enhancing the learning effectiveness of the vulnerability features.

The second phase is to analyze the input code to interpret the specific code gadgets that caused the vulnerability. We compile to parse the input code and generate an abstract syntax tree (AST) representation to gather code gadgets. Then we tokenize and feed code gadgets into the fine-tuned CodeT5 model, classifying the vulnerabilities. Details about the vulnerability detection phase will be discussed in Sect. 3.4.

3.2 Model Details

In this section, we will introduce our model in the following steps: pre-processing, feature extraction, fine-tuning, confident learning, and vulnerability detection.

Pre-processing. First, the smart contract undergoes an initial conversion to an AST, followed by extracting code fragments from the AST. Specifically, a rule-based approach is employed to extract code gadgets from the AST that pertain to each vulnerability type, guided by their corresponding definitions and characteristics. For example, in the reentrancy vulnerability, code gadgets are

Table 1. Contract Simplification Rules

Level	Remove Rules
Source Layer	i. The code describing the version of source files ii. The code for importing other contracts iii. Comment lines in various formats iv. Spaces and line breaks
Contract Layer	i. Event definition ii. Library definition
Function Layer	Functions of pure and view types

identified that represent external calls made to untrusted contracts or functions. Second, according to Ethereum Yellow Paper [11], we summarize the following Table 1 that needs to be deleted from the source code.

Feature Extraction. To prepare code gadgets for fine-tuning with CodeT5, it is necessary to convert them into numerical features that the model can process. In this study, we utilized RobertaTokenizer, which divides each code gadget into a sequence of subword tokens and truncates or pads the sequence with $<pad>$ tokens to attain a fixed length. Additionally, the tokenizer includes special tokens, $<s>$ and $</s>$, at the start and end of the sequence, respectively. Finally, the sequence is mapped numerically to the appropriate IDs based on the CodeT5 vocabulary.

Fine-Tuning. In this study, we fine-tune the CodeT5 model for our multi-label vulnerability detection task. Given an input code x and its corresponding binary label vector $y = (y_1, ...y_n)$, where y_i indicates the presence and absence of vulnerability types i in x. However, due to severe class imbalance and discrepancies in the learning difficulties among labels, we have adopted the Zero-Level Positive and Negative Relationship (ZLPR) loss function and a class-weighted imbalanced sampler.

In Eq. 1, ZLPR optimizes pairwise comparisons of target class scores with non-target class scores and effectively balances the weight of each item using LogSumExp properties.

$$Loss = log(1 + \sum_{i \in \Omega_{neg}} e^{s_i}) + log(1 + \sum_{j \in \Omega_{pos}} e^{-s_j}) \tag{1}$$

where Ω_{pos}, Ω_{neg} are the positive and negative class sets of the samples, respectively, s_i represents the score of the i-th class, while s_j is the j-th class.

As Eq. 2 shows, the sampler sampling probabilities to each label combination by tallying their occurrences. It helps to determine the optimal ratio of oversampling and undersampling.

$$p(N_i) = \frac{(\frac{1}{count(N_i)})}{\sum\limits_{i=1}^{n \leq 2^k} (\frac{1}{count(N_j)})} \tag{2}$$

3.3   Confident Learning

To solve the issue of inconsistent and noisy labeling caused by the use of multiple tools for dataset annotation, We employ confident learning (CL) [12]. Specifically, CL assumes a class-conditional noise process, where the noisy labels depend only on the latent true labels, not on the data. By utilizing CL probabilistic thresholds and ranking examples to train with confidence, CL can estimate the joint distribution between noisy and true labels.

Using a fine-tuned CodeT5 model, we have calculated the out-of-sample probability of each smart contract instance via cross-validation. The resulting out-of-sample probability, combined with the noisy label, served as the input for CL leveraging rank pruning [12] to compute the problem label. We evaluated the confidence score of the data to correct potential label errors in the dataset.

Rank Pruning. We define the dataset as having n training instances, where each instance x has a true label $y \in \{0, 1\}$ and a corresponding noisy label $s \in \{0, 1\}$. The observed dataset can be expressed as $\{(x_1, y_1), (x_2, y_2), \ldots, (x_n, y_n)\}$. The set of positive instances is defined as $\widetilde{P} = \{x|s = 1\}$ and the set of negative instances is defined as $\widetilde{N} = \{x|s = 0\}$.

To map s to y, we employ a classifier g along with the parameters LB, UB, ρ_0, and ρ_1. For a given instance x, the predicted value of $g(x)$ is transformed into $\hat{s}$, which takes a binary value of 0 or 1. The threshold $LB_{y=1}$ is used to determine the true label for x. If the $g(x)$ of higher than $LB_{y=1}$, indicating that x has a true label of $y = 1$ with high confidence. Similarly, for $UB_{y=0}$, if $g(x)$ is lower than $LB_{y=1}$, x has a true label of $y = 0$ with high confidence.

The noise rates are defined as $\rho_1 = P(s = 0|y = 1)$ and $\rho_0 = P(s = 1|y = 0)$. Let p_{s1} denote the observed positive label $P(s = 1)$, and p_{y1} denote the true positive label $P(y = 1)$. Thus, the reverse noise rates can be calculated as Eq. 3.

$$\pi_0 = P(y = 1 \, s = 0) = \frac{\rho_1 p_{y_1}}{(1 - p_{s_1})}$$

$$\pi_1 = P(y = 0 \, s = 1) = \frac{\rho_0(1 - p_{y_1})}{(1 - p_{s_1})} \tag{3}$$

Therefore, p_{y1} can be derived by combining ρ_1, ρ_0, π_0, and π_1.

To approximate this result under trivial conditions, confident learning uses confidence counts to estimate the original noise rates. The noisy labels are assumed to be uniformly random with the Eq. 4.

$$\hat{\rho}_1 = \frac{\tilde{N}_{y=1}}{\tilde{N}_{y=1} + \tilde{P}_{y=1}}; \qquad \hat{\rho}_0 = \frac{\tilde{P}_{y=0}}{\tilde{N}_{y=0} + \tilde{P}_{y=0}}$$

$$\hat{\pi}_1 = \frac{\hat{\rho}_0}{p_{s1}} \times \frac{1 - p_{s1} - \hat{\rho}_1}{1 - \hat{\rho}_1 - \hat{\rho}_0}; \qquad \hat{\pi}_0 = \frac{\hat{\rho}_1}{1 - p_{s1}} \times \frac{p_{s1} - \hat{\rho}_0}{1 - \hat{\rho}_1 - \hat{\rho}_0} \tag{4}$$

where:

$$LB_{y=1} = P(\hat{s} = 1 | s = 1) = E_{x \in \tilde{P}}(g(x)) = (1 - \rho_1)(1 - \pi_1) + \rho_0 \pi_1$$
$$UB_{y=0} = P(\hat{s} = 1 | s = 0) = E_{x \in \tilde{N}}(g(x)) = (1 - \rho_1)\pi_0 + \rho_0(1 - \pi_0)$$
$$\tilde{P}_{y=1} = \{x \in \tilde{P} | g(x) \geq LB_{y=1}\}; \quad \tilde{N}_{y=1} = \{x \in \tilde{N} | g(x) \geq LB_{y=1}\} \tag{5}$$
$$\tilde{P}_{y=0} = \{x \in \tilde{P} | g(x) \leq UB_{y=0}\}; \quad \tilde{N}_{y=0} = \{x \in \tilde{N} | g(x) \leq UB_{y=0}\}$$

The pruning can be performed as follows steps. First, select the $\hat{\pi}_1|\tilde{P}|$ instances with the smallest $g(x)$ as the set $\tilde{P}_{conf}$, and the $\hat{\pi}_0|\tilde{N}|$ instances with the highest $g(x)$ as $\tilde{N}_{conf}$, $X_{conf} = \tilde{P}_{conf} \cup \tilde{N}_{conf}$. Next, defining yi as the predicted label for sample i, the loss function for Rank Pruning is represented by the class-conditional weighted loss function on X_{conf}:

$$\tilde{l}(\hat{y}_i, s_i) = \frac{1}{1 - \hat{\rho}_1} l(\hat{y}_i, s_i) \cdot \mathbb{I}[[x_i \in \tilde{P}_{conf}]] + \frac{1}{1 - \hat{\rho}_0} l(\hat{y}_i, s_i) \cdot \mathbb{I}[[x_i] \in \tilde{N}_{conf}] \tag{6}$$

We incorporate this method to correct label errors by manually removing low-confidence items. To show the effectiveness, we evaluate the CL on our dataset quality and model performance in Sect. 4.4.

3.4   Vulnerability Detection

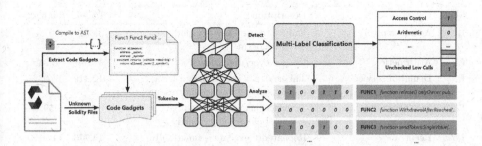

Fig. 2. Detection Phase of the INTELLICON Framework

To detect vulnerabilities in smart contracts, we first fine-tuned a CodeT5 model on a pruned dataset using preprocessing and CL methods. We then compiled the contract to be analyzed and performed AST analysis to traverse its syntax paths and parse all the function fragments into code gadgets. Tokenization was applied to the code gadgets, and the sliding window and fragment integration techniques described in Sect. 4.2 were utilized to split the code gadget tokens that exceeded the maximum input length set by the model. The fine-tuned CodeT5 model was used to encode them into latent representations using a transformer encoder. A linear layer was applied on top of the encoder outputs to generate the multi-label vectors for each code gadget, indicating the presence of each vulnerability type. The detection phase is depicted in Fig. 2.

4   Experiment

In this section, we will introduce the experimental results of the INTELLICON.

4.1   Experimental Settings

Dataset. We use the SmartBugs-Wild dataset [7] as our source of smart contract code gadgets for fine-tuning CodeT5. This dataset contains 47,398 smart contracts extracted from the Ethereum network and analyzed by SmartBugs [13]. However, the labeling of the SmartBugs-Wild is based on nine categories of traditional tools. It may result in variations in detection capabilities and accuracy, thus may introducing potential noise and inconsistency labels. Furthermore, the smart contracts in the dataset comprise the entire source code, as opposed to code snippets that focus on specific vulnerabilities. This may present challenges for the model to learn the relevant features and patterns from the code. Additionally, as shown in Table 2, the class distribution of data points in the dataset is significantly imbalanced, which may have implications for model performance.

Table 2. The Description of Dataset

Mark	Category	Description	Label	Percent
L1	Access control	Failure to use function modifiers or use of tx.orgin	3,801	3.07%
L2	Arithmetic	Integer over/underflows	37,597	30.36%
L3	Denial of service	The contract is overloaded with requests or computational resources	12,419	10.03%
L4	Front running	Transactions are included in a block before being mined	8,161	6.59%
L5	Reentrancy	Repeatedly execute a function by exploiting an external contract's callback function	14,773	11.91%
L6	Time manipulation	Miner can manipulate the timestamp of a block	4,069	3.29%
L7	Unchecked low level calls	call(), delegatecall() or send() fails	14,656	11.84%
–	Others	Contracts with none or unknown vulns	28,355	22.90%
Total Labels			123,805	100%

After Pre-processing mentioned in Sect. 3.2, a new dataset of 27,426 code gadgets was gathered, including seven vulnerability types (i.e., access control, arithmetic, denial of service, front running, reentrancy, time manipulation, and unchecked low-level calls).

Environment. We conducted our experiments on a server with an AMD EPYC 7543 CPU (2.80 GHz, 32 cores), 28 GB of RAM, and an NVIDIA RTX A5000 GPU (24 GB of memory) on Ubuntu 20.04LTS. We used PyTorch 1.12.1 and Transformers 4.16.2 to implement and run the CodeT5 model with a pre-trained checkpoint from HuggingFace's model hub. We used Cleanlab 2.3.1 to apply the confident learning technique to prune the dataset. We performed our experiments in April 2023 using a stable network connection.

4.2 Model Tricks

INTELLICON aims to provide a smart contract vulnerability detection service under real conditions. In this experiment, the maximum sequence length is set to 521 (>512) to demonstrate that CodeT5 can surpass the length limit of traditional transformer structures of 512 and handle long sequence text tasks. It is worth noting that 521 is only an arbitrary value set for batch processing, and considering the size of video memory, INTELLICON can actually handle the text of any sequence length.

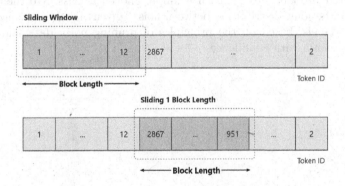

Fig. 3. Diagram of Sliding Window

At the same time, considering the performance of real devices, we provide an alternative prediction method based on fragment integration, which enables INTELLICON to successfully process ultra-long sequence text (sequence length more than 1000000) under low GPU memory. In this method, Our framework split the ultra-long sequence by setting part_length and obtaining multiple blocks with a length of part_length. Finally, INTELLICON predicts each part through a sliding window shown in Fig. 3 and synthesizes the results. We also apply this method to locate vulnerabilities by repeatedly splitting unit blocks until the model cannot recognize them, finding the minimum block where $\sum(label) \neq 1$, thus achieving vulnerability location.

To ensure the model is fast, stable, and accurate, We use AdamW as an optimizer with a learning rate of 5e−5, adam_epsilon of 1e-8, warmup_steps of 100 and a batch size of 8 for 100 epochs. In our approach, training sets, validation sets, and test sets are divided into 6:2:2. We added a dropout layer to the downstream classifier with a dropout probability of 0.5 to further avoid overfitting the model. We also use an early stopping mechanism with a patience value of 5.

INTELLICON uses Cleanlab [12] and manual evaluation methods to denoise data. Cleanlab is an open-source project based on confidence learning that provides corresponding modules to discover, evaluate, and repair datasets.

Moreover, to rectify the issue of class imbalance present in our dataset, we have implemented the ZLPR loss function in conjunction with an imbalanced dataset sampler, which serves to restore balance to the class distribution. In addition, we have incorporated dropout layers and early stopping techniques to mitigate the concern of overfitting.

4.3   Data Pruning with Confident Learning

We first split our dataset into a training set, a validation set, and a test set. We use the training set to train our identifier-aware CodeT5 model and obtain the predicted probabilities for each example and each class. We then use CL to estimate the joint distribution between noisy (given) labels and uncorrupted (unknown) labels, based on the principles of pruning noisy data and ranking examples to train with confidence.

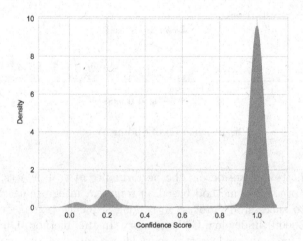

Fig. 4. Data Confidence Distribution Chart

The density plot of the data confidence score distribution for the dataset is shown in Fig. 4, which shows that the vast majority of the data has a confidence score near 1.000, with approximately 10% of the data having a label confidence score of less than 0.207, indicating a higher likelihood of label errors. After manually inspecting this portion of the data, and removing labels that were confirmed to be incorrect, We obtained our Pruned Dataset.

We then retrain our identifier-aware CodeT5 model on the Pruned Dataset and evaluate its performance on the validation set. We compare the results with the baseline model that is trained on the original training set without CL in the next section.

4.4 Evaluation

In this section, we present a comparison between our identifier-aware CodeT5 model with CL (CodeT5+CL) and other models that utilize various architectures and techniques to detect vulnerabilities in Ethereum smart contracts. Our baselines include BERT, T5, and CodeT5 models trained with and without confident learning to prune datasets.

We use the F1-score as the main metric to evaluate the performance of each model on each vulnerability type. The results are shown in Table 3.

From Table 3, we can see that our CodeT5+CL model outperforms all the baselines on all the vulnerability types and achieves the highest Micro-F1 score of 0.9591 and Macro-F1 score of 0.9293. This shows that our model can effectively and precisely detect vulnerabilities in Ethereum smart contracts by using identifier-aware CodeT5 and confident learning (Fig. 5).

Table 3. Performance of models with and without CL

Model	Method	Micro -F1	Macro -F1	F1-Score						
				L1	L2	L3	L4	L5	L6	L7
Bert	–	0.8992	0.8509	0.7493	0.9597	0.9507	0.7988	0.7912	0.8111	0.8957
Bert	CL	0.9320	0.8869	0.7929	0.9764	0.9478	0.8685	0.8599	0.8235	0.9395
T5	–	0.8971	0.8516	0.7443	0.9506	0.9379	0.8216	0.7991	0.7953	0.9126
T5	CL	0.9370	0.9045	0.8254	0.9775	0.9569	0.8961	0.8526	0.8626	0.9486
CodeT5	–	0.9338	0.8855	0.7579	0.9752	0.9739	0.8667	0.8673	0.8086	0.9490
CodeT5	**CL**	**0.9591**	**0.9293**	**0.8290**	**0.9855**	**0.9757**	**0.9222**	**0.9081**	**0.9151**	**0.9696**

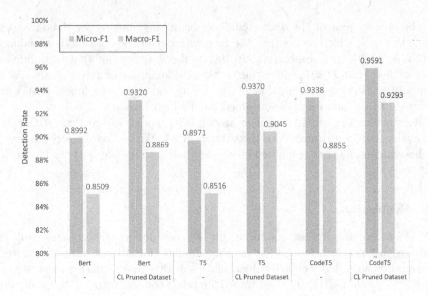

Fig. 5. F1 Score of models

We can also observe that using CL to prune the dataset improves the performance of both BERT and T5 models by about 5.12% on average F1-score, compared to using the original dataset without CL. This evidence illustrates that the utilization of CL can significantly augment the quality of dataset labeling performed by multiple annotators, especially when their individual accuracies vary. Additionally, it effectively mitigates the adverse effects of erroneous or imprecise labels on the subsequent phases of model training and evaluation.

4.5   Discussion

Our work evaluated the effectiveness of confident learning in detecting vulnerabilities in smart contracts. The results show that our proposed model achieves a Micro-F1 score of 0.9591 and a Macro-F1 score of 0.9293, which outperforms Bert, Bert+CL, T5, T5+CL, and CodeT5. This demonstrates the efficacy of our model and confident learning in improving label quality.

INTELLICON has the potential to effectively and efficiently assist in detecting and analyzing seven types of vulnerabilities in smart contracts, thereby enhancing the security of blockchain-based applications and providing valuable insights for developers and auditors in the blockchain industry.

Future research directions include applying our framework to other blockchain platforms(e.g., Fisco Bcos), exploring multitask learning approaches, and investigating other ways of enhancing the interpretability of our framework. These potential directions for future research could further enhance the performance and practicality of our framework and contribute to the advancement of smart contract security.

5   Related Work

In this section, we review the existing methods for vulnerability detection in Ethereum smart contracts.

5.1   Traditional Detection Methods

Traditional detection methods rely on manual or semi-automated techniques and expert-defined rules to identify vulnerabilities in smart contracts. They can be further divided into static analysis and dynamic analysis. Static analysis methods analyze the source code or bytecode of smart contracts without executing them. Tikhomirov et al. [14] presents *SmartCheck*, which works by translating Solidity source code into an XML-based intermediate representation and checking it against XPath patterns. Feist et al. [15] describe *Slither*, a static analysis framework that converts Solidity smart contracts into an intermediate representation called SlithIR, which allows for the application of commonly used program analysis techniques. However, they may suffer from high false positives or negatives due to the complexity and ambiguity of smart contract semantics. Moreover, they may not be able to handle dynamic features such as external calls or state changes.

Dynamic analysis methods execute smart contracts on a simulated or real blockchain environment and monitor their runtime behaviors. They can detect vulnerabilities that depend on specific inputs by generating test cases or observing transactions. Luu et al. [16] firstly performed dynamic symbol execution tools called *Oyente* to analyze vulnerability. Still, these methods may require more time and resources to execute smart contracts and collect data and not cover all possible execution paths and inputs of smart contracts.

Fuzzing methods are a special type of dynamic analysis that generates mutated inputs randomly for smart contracts and observe their exceptions. They can detect vulnerabilities that cause abnormal behaviors such as crashes or reverts by applying coverage-guided heuristics or evolutionary algorithms. Jiang et al. [17] presents *ContractFuzzer* to test Ethereum smart contracts for security vulnerabilities. The fuzzer generates fuzzing inputs, defines test oracles, instruments the EVM to log runtime behaviors, and analyzes these logs to report vulnerabilities. Fuzzing methods may be ineffective and impractical due to the high cost of executing smart contracts on a blockchain network and depend on the availability and accuracy of environments.

5.2   Machine Learning-Based Detection Methods

Machine learning-based detection methods leverage data-driven techniques to identify vulnerabilities in smart contracts. Zhuang et al. [18] propose using graph neural networks (GNNs) to represent the structure of a smart contract function and use a degree-free graph convolutional neural network (DR-GCN) and a temporal message propagation network (TMP) to learn from the normalized graphs for vulnerability detection. Lutz et al. [19] introduce *ESCORT*, a deep neural network-based multi-output method that supports lightweight transfer learning for new security vulnerabilities.

NLP-based methods can leverage pre-trained models on large-scale code corpora to improve the performance and generalization ability of vulnerability detection. For instance, Sun et al. [20] propose a new framework called *ASS-Bert* for smart contract vulnerability detection that leverages active and semi-supervised learning with a bidirectional encoder representation from transformers network.

However, due to most of the large datasets being annotated by multiple traditional vulnerability detection tools with limited accuracy [7], training on them will make the model a simulator for these tools, and the noisy labels and false positives of these tools will also affect the performance of the model. Furthermore, they may not be able to explain their predictions due to the lack of interpretability of neural networks.

6 Conclusion

In this paper, We provide a novel approach, INTELLICON, for detecting smart contract vulnerability by utilizing CodeT5 and confident learning techniques. Our work represents the *first* attempt to utilize confident learning for cleaning noisy labels to enhance detection. Moreover, we interpret specific code gadgets that cause vulnerabilities by traversing functions extracted via the AST analysis method for each vulnerability type. Experimental results demonstrated that over 95.9% micro-F1 score and 92.9% macro-F1 score could be achieved in detecting 7 types of vulnerabilities in smart contracts, outperforming the baseline models. Our work contributes to the advancement of smart contract security and provides valuable insights for developers and auditors in the blockchain industry.

References

1. Nakamoto, S.: Bitcoin: a peer-to-peer electronic cash system. Decentralized business review, pp. 21260–21268 (2008)
2. Zhang, S., Li, W., Li, X., Liu, B.: AuthROS: secure data sharing among robot operating systems based on Ethereum. In: Proceedings of the QRS (2022)
3. Slowmist: Blockchain security and aml analysis annual report (2023). https://www.slowmist.com/report/2022-Blockchain-Security-and-AML-Analysis-Annual-Report(EN).pdf
4. Li, W., Jiuyang, B., Li, X., Peng, H., Niu, Y., Zhang, Y.: A survey of DeFi security: challenges and opportunities. J. King Saud Univ. Comput. Inf. Sci **34**(10), 10378–10404 (2022)
5. Li, X., Chen, T., Luo, X., Yu, J.: Characterizing erasable accounts in Ethereum. In: Susilo, W., Deng, R.H., Guo, F., Li, Y., Intan, R. (eds.) ISC 2020. LNCS, vol. 12472, pp. 352–371. Springer, Cham (2020). https://doi.org/10.1007/978-3-030-62974-8_20
6. Sürücü, O., et al.: A survey on ethereum smart contract vulnerability detection using machine learning. Disrupt. Technol. Inf. Sci. VI **12117**, 110–121 (2022)

7. Durieux, T., Ferreira, J.F.: Empirical review of automated analysis tools on 47,587 Ethereum smart contracts. In: Proceedings of the ICSE, pp. 530–541 (2020)
8. Li, W., Bu, J., Li, X., Chen, X.: Security analysis of DeFi: vulnerabilities, attacks and advances. In: Proceedings of the Blockchain, pp. 488–493 (2022)
9. Li, X., Chen, T., Luo, X., Wang, C.: CLUE: towards discovering locked cryptocurrencies in Ethereum. In: Proceedings of the SAC, pp. 1584–1587 (2021)
10. Wang, Y., Wang, W., Joty, S., Hoi, S.C.: Codet 5: identifier-aware unified pretrained encoder-decoder models for code understanding and generation. In: Proceedings of the EMNLP, pp. 8696–8708 (2021)
11. Wood, G., et al.: Ethereum: a secure decentralised generalised transaction ledger. Ethereum Proj. Yellow Pap. **151**(14), 1–32 (2014)
12. Northcutt, C., Jiang, L., Chuang, I.: Confident learning: estimating uncertainty in dataset labels. J. Artif. Intell. Res. **70**, 1373–1411 (2021)
13. Ferreira, J.F., Cruz, P., Durieux, T.: Smartbugs: a framework to analyze solidity smart contracts. In: Proceedings of the ASE, pp. 1349–1352 (2021)
14. Tikhomirov, S., Voskresenskaya, E.: Smartcheck: static analysis of ethereum smart contracts. In: Proceedings of the ICSE, pp. 9–16 (2018)
15. Feist, J., Grieco, G., Groce, A.: Slither: a static analysis framework for smart contracts. In: Proceedings of the WETSEB, pp. 8–15 (2019)
16. Luu, L., Chu, D.H., Olickel, H.: Making smart contracts smarter. In: Proceedings of the CCS, pp. 254–269 (2016)
17. Jiang, B., Liu, Y., Chan, W.K.: Contractfuzzer: fuzzing smart contracts for vulnerability detection. In: Proceedings of the ASE, pp. 259–269 (2018)
18. Zhuang, Y., Liu, Z., Qian, P.: Smart contract vulnerability detection using graph neural network. In: Proceedings of the IJCAI, pp. 3283–3290 (2020)
19. Sendner, C., Chen, H., Fereidooni, H.: Smarter contracts: detecting vulnerabilities in smart contracts with deep transfer learning. In: Proceedings of the NDSS, pp. 1–18 (2023)
20. Sun, X., Liangqiong, T., Zhang, J., Cai, J., Li, B., Wang, Yu.: ASSBert: active and semi-supervised bert for smart contract vulnerability detection. J. Inf. Secur. Appl. **73**, 103423 (2023)

Edge Intelligence and Metaverse Services

Dynamic Computation Offloading Leveraging Horizontal Task Offloading and Service Migration in Edge Networks

Yang Bai[1], Zhangbing Zhou[1,2(✉)], and Xiaocui Li[1]

[1] School of Information Engineering, China University of Geosciences (Beijing), Beijing 100083, China
zhangbing.zhou@gmail.com
[2] Computer Science Department, TELECOM SudParis, 75006 Paris, France

Abstract. Amidst the progressive proliferation of user petitions in the realm of *Internet of Things* (*IoT*), the concept of *Edge Computing* (*EC*) is being hailed as a beacon of promise, epitomizing multifaceted dexterity and sound service delivery methodologies. Given the finite resource allocation of *IoT* devices, it is plausible to assert that those *IoT* devices that are burdened with arduous workloads might fail to adequately address latency-sensitive requests from users in a prompt manner. In order to surmount the obstacle at hand, we posit a dynamic methodology of computation offloading, whereby a multiplicity of elements are taken into account. These elements include, but are not limited to: (I) The proposition of the intermediate node concept serves to curtail the latency experienced by user requests, via the dynamic consolidation of task offloading and service migration tactics. (II) The intricacies of the intermediate node selection issue are expounded as a multi-faceted *Markov Decision Process* (*MDP*) realm, the boundaries of which are contingent on the burden placed upon the incumbent network. As a means of diminishing the expansiveness of the aforementioned *MDP* sphere and facilitating prompt judgments, a profound reinforcement learning methodology has been custom-tailored. According to the experimental results, this particular modus operandi exemplifies a more pronouncedly impactful curtailment of turn-around time requisite to abide by user requests.

Keywords: Computation Offloading · Service Migration · Deep Reinforcement Learning · Dynamic Resource Configuration · Edge Networks

1 Introduction

There has been a concentrated effort in numerous academic investigations to mitigate the issue of service response latency via computational offloading. The endeavors of these investigations have had a singular focus on the optimization of both resource allocation and offloading determinations [1]. Most studies in

J. Chen et al. (Eds.): BlockSys 2023, CCIS 1896, pp. 63–76, 2024.
https://doi.org/10.1007/978-981-99-8101-4_5

this realm place emphasis solely on task offloading as a means of resolving service response delay. Yet, the highly dynamic nature of user service requests in practical scenarios often remains neglected. Frequent service transfer from cloud to edge servers may lead to longer wait times for users and increased power consumption in IoT devices. One solution that could address this issue is transferring services across edge servers [2], which would bring the services closer to user devices. To strike the perfect balance between service excellence and migration expenses, and to offer convenience to end-users, it becomes pivotal to identify the appropriate time and location for service migration [3]. The adept selection of the service migration pathway necessitates the adoption of a decision theory-based algorithm by the authors [4]. Prior research mainly concentrates on searching for the most suitable algorithm to diminish the latency of task offloading or service migration. However, the algorithm's decision-making duration is commonly overlooked. Circumstances that pose time sensitivity and operate in unstable network surroundings necessitate a decision algorithm with robustness and intricacy to support prompt decision-making [5]. In essence, the utilization of a $Markov$ $Decision$ $Process$ (MDP) has the potential to offer solutions to job offloading and service relocation conundrums [6]. Employing a reinforcement learning algorithm to ascertain the most effective MDP strategy manifests prudence [7]. The Q-learning algorithm is unparalleled in its ability to make swift decisions compared to competing reinforcement learning algorithms [8]. To that end, we were spurred to investigate a hybridized $Deep$ Q-leaning $Network$ (DQN) model for reinforcement learning, which amalgamated Q-learning with cutting-edge deep learning techniques [9].

Collaboration across edge servers, including job offloading and service migration, is the core of the EC paradigm aimed at boosting service quality. Despite this, prior works have treated both cooperation strategies as unrelated. In order to address this issue, this paper proposes a potent approach for computing offloading that effectively minimizes processing expenditures through the dynamic integration of task offloading and service migration techniques. The central premise of our work can be succinctly summarized as follows:

- A novel approach to dynamic computation offloading has been proposed, which integrates both computation offloading and service migration to identify intermediary nodes possessing adequate resources. This strategy effectively curtails the expenses associated with catering to user requests.
- Formulating the problem of selecting optimal intermediate nodes as a MDP and employing a reinforcement learning technique in conjunction with deep learning to compress the MDP space and expedite decision-making.

The forthcoming sections of this essay have been organized as such: Sect. 2 features a comprehensive analysis and debate of similar literature. Section 3 outlines the three-layer system model, delay model, and problem characterization. In Sect. 4, we expound at length on our dynamic computing method and technique. This method employs a deep reinforcement learning approach, which we thoroughly describe in this section. Section 5 contains elaborate simulation experiments aimed at proving the effectiveness of our algorithm. Finally, Sect. 6 serves as a summary of our work.

2   Related Work

The migration of computational operations and service displacement have gained significant traction in the field of *EC* due to the proliferation of tasks that require high computational intensity and the diverse range of service requisitions. Numerous scientists have dedicated their efforts towards the enhancement of *Quality of Service* (*QoS*) and cost minimization by designing effective algorithms. Below is a discussion of related algorithms and models.

2.1   Offloading of Tasks in Edge Computing (EC)

The determinants that impact task deviation judgments hold paramount importance in the edge network. Certain studies center on employing partial unloading methodologies to curtail task processing delays [1]. The predicament of task arrival offloading has been rectified through the creation of an ingenious online primal-dual algorithm coupled with a dynamic edge computation model [10]. The literature [11] elucidates a pioneering optimization model that employs the game theory paradigm to maximize the anticipated speed of an agent's unloading process. Additionally, a technique rooted in meta-reinforcement learning was introduced to advance the offloading algorithm's ability to generalize, as a means to improve the approach for task offloading [12]. The *Fog Resource* aware *Adaptive Task Offloading* (FRATO) framework has been proposed for enabling the flexible selection of an optimal offloading approach, leveraging uncertain resources [13]. This is backed by a computational offloading technique called *Deep Deterministic Policy Gradient* (*DDPG*), that is grounded in the deep reinforcement espoused in relevant literature [22].

2.2   Migration of Services in Edge Computing (EC)

Researchers have presented a user mobility-driven technique for service migration across edge services, which aims to achieve flawless computing with minimal latency [14]. As the transfer of user devices takes place, services are concurrently shifted to the alternate edge servers. The available literature [15] suggests a highly effective optimization method to diminish the cost of migration, utilizing a repeated relaxation and rounding approach. Given the fleet of agile vehicles, the challenge of service migration is transformed into an ambiguous conundrum of decision optimization. Consequently, a novel approach to service migration, the *Latency-aware Service Migration* method based on *Decision* theory (LSMD), has been developed. The endeavor to swiftly transform something is arduous due to the significant time complexity of conventional heuristic approaches. In order to emulate the decision-making processes for service migration, a one-dimensional *MDP* is employed [16]. Reinforcement learning appears to be a suitable approach for decision-making pertaining to the relocation of services. Within the realm of literature [17], the question of service migration is presented as a complex optimization issue, with the ultimate goal being to develop a strategy that is optimal in nature. To achieve this, deep reinforcement learning is utilized.

In our research, we have incorporated the notion of deep reinforcement learning to facilitate prompt decision-making. Furthermore, we have efficiently merged job offloading and service relocation to enhance the overall performance. Our strategy of dynamic computing offload has a direct impact on the selection of appropriate time and location to shift the corresponding services of a task.

3   Formulation of Problems and Modeling

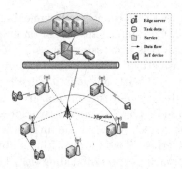

Fig. 1. Organizational structure

3.1   Model for the System

Figure 1 demonstrates the composition of the organizational structure of the system, which consists of three layers, namely the user layer, edge server layer, and cloud layer [18]. The IoT devices effectively accumulate relevant data for diverse services, transmit it wirelessly to the nearest edge server, and consequently begin the operation, whereas both IoT devices and edge servers are geographically distant from the cloud layer.

Based on the model system mentioned above, we suggest several notations for the purpose of this article. The collection of edge servers can be represented by $E = \{E_1, E_2, \ldots, E_n\}$, which is described by the following characteristics: the $E_i.id$, a distinctive identifier assigned to each server, the geographical location $E_i.loc = (L_x, L_y)$, the ability of the edge server to manage $E_i.cap$, the present roster of services being hosted by $E_i.hostLst$, and the current list of tasks that $E_i.pt$ can handle. The main goal of this article is not to delve into the heterogeneity of edge servers, but rather to discover a more effective method of minimizing task handling latency. Thus, the assumption is made that all edge servers share a common set of physical resources such as CPU processing power, memory, bandwidth, and storage. In an actual setting, there is an array of services that are highly varied. For the sake of clarity, yet without compromising its all-encompassing nature, we posit that the layer of edge servers comprises m services denoted by $F = \{F_1, F_2, \ldots, F_m\}$. These services are typified by two defining properties: $F_i.id$ as a distinct identifier for each service, and $F_i.bytes$ as its corresponding capacity. Divide the given time period T into equal time slots, denoted by $T = \{T_1, T_2, \ldots, T_t\}$, and assume that during each time slot, the IoT devices from the user layer will request k tasks, labeled as $CC = \{C_1, C_2, \ldots, C_k\}$. These tasks are characterized by various attributes, such as a unique identifier ($C_i.id$), geographic location ($C_i.loc = (L_x, L_y)$), required service type ($C_i.F_j$), amount of data to be processed ($C_i.bytes$), and the number of CPU cycles needed for task processing ($C_i.cir$).

3.2   Delay Model

In the interest of this paper, the latency modes encompass task offloading, task queuing, task processing, and service migration. The comprehensive elaborations and formulations of these latency models are as follows.

Task Offloading Delay. The concept of task offloading latency refers to the duration necessary for the transmission of data between the local edge server and the intended destination edge server. The amount of time needed to offload tasks is contingent on both the amount of data to be transferred and the transfer rate. Consequently, the duration of data transfer latency at a specific time slot T_t, originating from user C_i and directed towards edge server E_j, can be expressed in the following manner.

$$d_{to}^{i,j,t} = \frac{C_i.bytes}{V_{tr}^{i,j,t}} \tag{1}$$

If we denote the volume of the task data as $C_i.bytes$, we can define the data transfer rate $V_{tr}^{i,j,t}$.

$$V_{tr}^{i,j,t} = Blog_2(1 + \frac{P_{tx}^i G^{i,j,t}}{N_{noise}}) \tag{2}$$

In the given scenario, where B represents the channel bandwidth, P_{tx}^i denotes the transmitted power of the user's device C_i, $G^{i,j,t}$ signifies the channel gain between the user's device C_i and the edge server E_j, and N_{noise} represents the bandwidth of the background noise.

Task Processing Delay. The primary contributor to processing latency is attributed to the computational speeds of the edge servers. The expression of task requirements delay can be characterized as such

$$d_{pr}^{i,j,t} = \frac{C_i.cir}{E_j.cap} \tag{3}$$

The variable $C_i.cir$ represents the quantity of CPU cycles required to execute a given task, while $E_j.cap$ stands for the computational ability of the edge server as determined by its CPU frequencies.

Task Queuing Delay. Once all tasks have been queued and processed, the edge server initiates the proper service to handle the present task. Assuming that the K task precedes the current task, as deduced from the Eq. (3).

$$d_{tq}^{i,j,t} = \sum_{k=1}^{K} \frac{C_k.cir}{E_j.cap} \tag{4}$$

Service Migration Delay. The primary factor that directly impacts this latency is the volume of the service and its transfer rate. Decision time for migration may not have a significant impact when compared to the transfer latency [19]. The representation of migration latency can be done in the following manner:

$$d_{cm}^{i,t} = \frac{F_i.bytes}{V_{tr}^{j,j',t}} + d_r \tag{5}$$

Assuming that $S_i.bytes$ signifies the extent of service capacity, $V_{tr}^{j,j',t}$ denotes the velocity of transmission from source edge server j to destination edge server j', and d_r denotes the time required for service reconfiguration.

3.3 Problem Formulation

Our algorithm aims to reduce the latency of the edge network. By commencing from user i's time slot t, we can provide the equation for the total time delay.

$$d_{total}^{i,t} = d_{to}^{i,t} + d_{pr}^{i,t} + d_{tq}^{i,t} + d_{cm}^{i,t} \tag{6}$$

The time lag of the network can be unmistakably construed as a weighted accumulation of the summation of delays of all tasks. Therefore, the overall expense denoted by the letter C can be expressed as:

$$C = \omega_1 \sum_{i=1}^{n} d_{total}^{i,t} \tag{7}$$

The weights of d_{total} and e_{total} in the objective function are denoted by ω_1 and ω_2, respectively. By tweaking the values of ω_1 and ω_2, one can alter the impact of delay on the overall cost.

4 Algorithm

In order to minimize the total cost C as given in Eq. (7), we present a new *Dynamic Computation Offloading Strategy DCOSS* based on deep reinforcement learning. In Sect. 4.1, we describe the strategy in detail.

4.1   Dynamic Computation Offloading Strategy

As per the service migration policy, it is imperative to transfer services from either the cloud or any other edge server configurations to the corresponding local edge server for efficient task management, in case the latter is not equipped with the aforementioned service. Dividing the execution of a task into three stages, namely the transfer, queuing, and computation stages, as illustrated by Fig. 2, is a widely accepted approach. While offloading and migration procedures govern the transfer process in the aforementioned policies, they impose limitations on the location where tasks are processed, which is constrained to certain servers in the network, thereby failing to fully leverage the capabilities of cooperative edge servers.

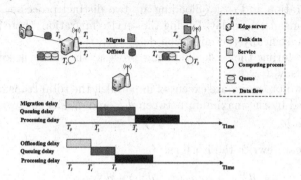

Fig. 2. Task processing for migration and offloading strategies

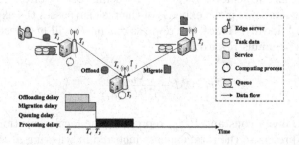

Fig. 3. Task processing for dynamic computation offloading strategy

At T_3, as illustrated by Fig. 3, E_1 was inundated with a hefty workload that resulted in a prolonged queue duration for a task requested by a user. Owing to the absence of any associated amenities at E_1, the task was consequently divested to the go-between node E_2, which boasted significant computing capabilities.

Furthermore, the task's corresponding service was transferred from E_3 to E_2 to align with the relocated task.

It is apparent that the queuing duration is eradicated by implementing tasks on E_2, courtesy of its free state. Additionally, given that E_2 is stationed between E_1 and E_3, the transfer distances for both the offloading and the migration are shortened, in contrast to the same processes between E_1 and E_3 that Fig. 2 illustrates. As a result, the delay encountered during transmission is correspondingly curtailed. Furthermore, as the two transmission processes are carried out simultaneously, there is a degree of **overlap** between the offloading and migration intervals.

From the aforementioned description, it can be inferred that the process of transmitting our policy can be categorized into three distinct scenarios.

- Service migration and task offloading are two distinct processes that impact the total transmission delay. During the service migration, there is a delay in migration, specifically the migration delay d_{cm}.
- Meanwhile, during the task offloading process, the delay is known as the offloading delay d_{to}.
- When the two processes are executed in parallel, the total transmission delay is determined by the maximum between d_{cm} and d_{to}, as encapsulated in the $max(d_{cm}, d_{to})$.

Therefore, we can rewrite the Eq. 6 as:

$$d_{total}^{i,t} = max(d_{to}^{i,t}, d_{cm}^{i,t}) + d_{pr}^{i,t} + d_{tq}^{i,t} \tag{8}$$

Q-Network Update. The primary objective of our algorithm is to curtail the total expenses denoted by $\mathcal{C}$. The system, therefore, will be eligible for a positive benefit once it achieves its goal of reducing costs. Conversely, there will be negative repercussions if the expense of the task surpasses the expenditure of executing the job locally. Hence, the rewards during T_i will manifest in the form of either a plus or minus reward.

$$r_i = M - \frac{\mathcal{C}_{local}^{T_i}}{\mathcal{C}^{T_i}(s_i, a_i)} \tag{9}$$

whereas M remains a constant, $\mathcal{C}_{local}^{T_i}$ represents the local execution cost at T_i, while $\mathcal{C}^{T_i}(s_i, a_i)$ refers to the total expense incurred in selecting a_i when in state s_i.

As for Q-learning, $Q(s, a)$ signifies the Q-value of a particular state-action pair (s, a). This Q-value denotes the targeted reward for executing a task at state s, i.e., determining an edge server as the appropriate execution spot for the job at hand. Therefore, the optimal policy for a given state s can be expressed as such:

$$\pi^*(s) = \arg\max_{a \in \mathbb{A}} Q^*(s, a) \tag{10}$$

Algorithm 1. Q-Network Update

Input: $s_\tau, a_\tau, r_\tau, s_{\tau+1}, \mathbb{M}$
Output: θ
1: Store $(s_\tau, a_\tau, r_\tau, s_{\tau+1})$ in $\mathbb{M}[i \bmod |\mathbb{M}|]$
2: Sample $\mathbb{M}_\tau \subset \mathbb{M}$
3: **for** $(s_{\tau-1}^{(j)}, a_{\tau-1}^{(j)}, r_{\tau-1}^{(j)}, s_\tau^{(j)})$ in $\mathbb{M}_\tau$ **do**
4:    Calculate $Q(s_\tau^{(j)}, a_\tau^{(j)}; \theta')$
5:    Calculate target network's Q-value Q_{target}
6:    Compute the error between $Q(s_\tau^{(j)}, a_\tau^{(j)}; \theta')$ and Q_{target}
7: **end for**
8: $\theta = argmin_\theta L(\theta)$
9: From time to time reset $\theta' = \theta$
10: Return θ

The attainment of the optimal Q-value for the state-action pair (s, a) is represented by $Q^*(s, a)$. As a result, determining the Q-value of all available actions $a \in \mathbb{A}$ is essential to derive the optimal policy for the current state s. In the Q-learning algorithm, every $Q(s, a)$ can be revised through the use of the learning principle:

$$Q(s,a) = Q(s,a) + \alpha\big(R(s,a) + \gamma \max_{a' \in \mathbb{A}} Q(s',a') - Q(s,a)\big) \qquad (11)$$

where $\alpha \in (0, 1]$ is the learning rate and γ is the discount parameter.

A crucial component of the deep Q-learning algorithm involves training the *DNN* using historical data stored in the experience replay memory $\mathbb{M}$ [21]. During the *t-th* time slot, a batch of training data samples is randomly chosen from $\mathbb{M}$. The Adam algorithm [20] is applied to update the *DNN*'s weights θ, effectively reducing the averaged cross-entropy loss.

$$L(\theta_t) = -\frac{1}{|\mathbb{M}|} \sum_\tau^M \Big((\mathbf{a}_\tau^*)^\mathsf{T} \log f_{\theta_t}(\mathbf{s}_\tau) + (1 - \mathbf{a}_\tau^*)^\mathsf{T} \log\big(1 - f_{\theta_t}(\mathbf{s}_\tau)\big)\Big) \qquad (12)$$

Algorithm 1 demonstrates the detailed steps for updating the Q-network. The size of the memory space $\mathbb{M}$ is fixed, and it is updated during each iteration. Historical data can be utilized to decrease the variance of θ_t, while random sampling reduces the correlation among the training data, leading to a faster convergence of $L(\theta)$. Additionally, because the recent strategies consistently improve the algorithm's decision, the *DNN* learns from the most recent data samples. We omit the update procedure of the Adam algorithm for the sake of simplicity.

DCOS. Algorithm 2 introduces the *DCOS*, a dynamic computation offloading algorithm based on *DQN*. The algorithm comprises two segments- the reinforcement settings and the Q-network update. The reinforcement settings and Q-network update are comprehensively explained in Algorithm 1.

Considering the intricate computational nature of Algorithm 2, the fundamental constituents of the network blueprint are stated in Sect. 3.1. It includes

---

Algorithm 2. DCOS

Input: $\theta, \mathbb{M}$
Output: a_i
 1: **for** episode $= 1$, N **do**
 2:    Observe s_0
 3:    $\mathbb{M} = \emptyset$
 4:    Initialize $\mathbb{M}$
 5:    **for** i $= 1$, t **do**
 6:       /*Action Selection*/
 7:       Select a_i according pre-defined policy
 8:       Observe s_{i+1}
 9:       Calculate r_i by Eq. (9)
10:      /*Call Algorithm 1*/
11:      $\theta = QNetworkUpdate\,(s_i, a_i, r_i, s_{i+1}, \mathbb{M})$
12:      Output a_i
13:    **end for**
14: **end for**

---

n edge servers, m service categories, and k task petitions issued in every time slot. The time complexity of Algorithm 2 principally centers on the Q-network update and the settings of reinforcement learning. In order to procure the system, the time complexity is correlated with the magnitude of the state having the $O(2n + 3m)$ significance. The computation of rewards incurs a time complexity of $O(n + m + k)$. As far as the selection of actions is concerned, two possibilities arise depending on the value of ϕ. Contemplating both circumstances simultaneously, the time complexity remains $O(n)$. When it comes to updating the Q-network, the time complexity is contingent on the scale of the experience replay memory $\mathbb{M}$, which varies in proportion to the magnitude of the state space $\mathbb{S}$ and the action space $\mathbb{A}$. Thus, the time complexity for this phase approaches $O(n^2)$. The execution of Algorithm 2 takes place in a sequence, thereby resulting in a polynomial time complexity.

5 Experiments

To elaborate on the experimental settings, Sect. 5.1 provides an insight into the key aspects. Furthermore, in Sect. 5.2, we endeavor to perform simulation experiments for the proposed dynamic computation offloading algorithm.

5.1 Experimental Settings

In the simulation settings of the system model, we define a region of 500 by 500 m^2, which encompasses 50 edge servers that have been deployed randomly. The time-slot duration ranges from 20 to 30 ms, and during each time-slot, k task requests are generated by the *IoT* device. The relevant parameters have been explicitly mentioned in Table 1.

Table 1. Simulation parameters

Parameters	Simulation value	Description
$E.cap$	2 GFz	The processing capability of edge server
T_i	random in [20, 30] ms	The i-th time slot
n	50	The number of edge servers
k	30	The max number of task requests at each time slot
m	50	The number of service classes
$F.bytes$	random in [0.2, 5] MB	The capacity of service
$C.cir$	uniform in [2, 12] cycles/bit	The number of CPU circles required by the task
$C.bytes$	random in [0.5, 5] MB	The capacity of task
B	500 MFz	The channel bandwidth
N_{noise}	−100 dBm	The background noise
ω_1	0.8	Weight of delay in total cost $\mathcal{C}$

The efficacy of the DQN algorithm is significantly influenced by the deep neural network design. Our research demonstrates that a modest four-layer network framework containing one input layer, two hidden layers, and one output layer yields better convergence results. The two hidden layers comprise 100 and 60 hidden neurons respectively and employ the $Relu$ activation function. In the output layer, the sigmoid activation function is utilized to generate the ultimate action. We have configured the DQN parameters as follows: the learning rate is α is 0.01, the discount parameter γ has been set to 0.9, the training batch size is 100, and the experience replay memory size is 200.

In order to demonstrate the superiority of the $DCOS$ algorithm with respect to delay, we have conducted a comparative analysis against two basic models: the $Deep$ $Deterministic$ $Policy$ $Gradient$ ($DDPG$) [22] and the $Extensive$ $Service$ $Migration$ Model (ESM) [17].

– In the $DDPG$ model, task scheduling is based solely on the task offloading strategy, and the optimal offloading target node is determined by the DQN network.
– As for the ESM model, the task is processed on the local node and if that node lacks the necessary service configuration, the system model will migrate the service in accordance with the optimal policy relating to the migration costs.

5.2 Performance Evaluation

The analysis of delay in user requests' performance is conducted in response to a shift in task density.

To assess how varying task densities impact different algorithms, we carried out experiments on densities of 10, 25, 40, and 55 tasks per second. This range of task densities represents a gradient from low to high workload states for the network. In Fig. 4, a comparison of delays for different task densities is plotted.

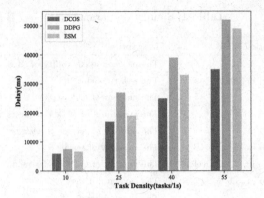

Fig. 4. Delay comparison on different task densities

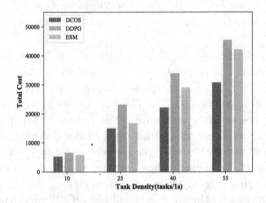

Fig. 5. Total cost comparison on different task densities

Figure 5 depicts the comparison of total costs. As evinced by Fig. 4, in case the density of tasks amounts to 15, the computing resources attributed to an individual edge server are capable of fulfilling the majority of task solicitations, thereby mitigating the need for coordination. Consequently, the interval of latency amid the aforementioned triad of collaborative techniques is trifling. Should the task density escalate to 25, the proficiency levels of *DCOS* and *ESM* tend to converge, since the *ESM* proposition restricts the task execution location to local. In the long run, the task burden is uniformly distributed among all the edge servers, consequently, the variance in performance between the two algorithms is trifling in low-workload scenarios. In direct correlation with the marked augmentation of both task density and overall workload, evident is the progressively expanding divide between the temporal resource consumption of the *DDPG* and *ESM* algorithms in comparison to that of the *DCOS*. Further, as the network becomes saturated, the *DCOS* algorithm seamlessly diverts assigned tasks to peripheral intermediary nodes, adequately equipped with computational resources, thereby ultimately mitigating any existing task queuing delay.

As evinced by the observations articulated in Fig. 5, our presented *DCOS* algorithm demonstrates notable constancy in the face of augmented task densities. The results reveal that the *DCOS* algorithm executes the calculation-disburdening function in a financially expedient manner across all scenarios. Notably, the data trends portrayed in both Fig. 4 and Fig. 5 remain nearly identical, largely owing to the intense delay that characterizes end-user requests. Indeed, the amplified task densities correlate proportionately with superior *DCOS* algorithmic performance.

6   Conclusion and Future Works

In an effort to unleash the complete capacity of a collective periphery server, a dynamic computational offloading game plan that draws qualitative inspiration from deep learning, reinforced by a complementary framework, has been proffered. Through the utilization of simulation experiments, it has been demonstrated that the methodology in question possesses the potential to efficiently harness the available computing resources of an edge server and subsequently enable superior decision-making capabilities of said server, while simultaneously reducing the delay experienced by users requesting services, all within the confines of the experimental environment. Furthermore, the stability and flexibility of the presented algorithm have been aptly demonstrated upon comparison with two existing baseline algorithms. Of particular importance is the fact that our algorithm fails to substantially ameliorate the latency associated with user requests when anomalous network activity occurs. Further efforts will be directed towards the effective initialization of network service settings, which in turn will serve to enhance the algorithm's efficiency to overcome this challenge.

References

1. Yuan, X., Xie, Z., Tan, X.: Computation offloading in UAV-enabled edge computing: a Stackelberg game approach. Sensors **22**(10), 3854 (2022)
2. Chen, X., et al.: Dynamic service migration and request routing for microservice in multi-cell mobile edge computing. Internet Things J. **9**(15), 13126–13143 (2022)
3. Xu, M., Zhou, Q., Wu, H., Lin, W., Ye, K., Xu, C.: PDMA: probabilistic service migration approach for delay-aware and mobility-aware mobile edge computing. Softw.: Pract. Exp. **52**(2), 394–414 (2022)
4. Liu, Z., Xu, X.: Latency-aware service migration with decision theory for internet of vehicles in mobile edge computing. Wirel. Netw. 1–13 (2022)
5. Chen, S., Tang, B., Wang, K.: Twin delayed deep deterministic policy gradient-based intelligent computation offloading for IoT. Digit. Commun. Netw. **9**, 836–845 (2022)
6. Wang, S., Urgaonkar, R., Zafer, M., He, T., Chan, K., Leung, K.K.: Dynamic service migration in mobile edge computing based on Markov decision process. IEEE/ACM Trans. Netw. **27**(3), 1272–1288 (2019)
7. Liu, J., Ji, W.: Evolution of agents in the case of a balanced diet. Int. J. Crowd Sci. **6**(1), 1–6 (2022)

8. Watkins, C.J., Dayan, P.: Q-learning. Mach. Learn. **8**(3), 279–292 (1992)
9. Mnih, V., et al.: Human-level control through deep reinforcement learning. Nature **518**(7540), 529–533 (2015)
10. Wang, H., Xu, H., Huang, H., Chen, M., Chen, S.: Robust task offloading in dynamic edge computing. Trans. Mob. Comput. **22**(1), 500–514 (2021)
11. Zhou, J., Tian, D., Sheng, Z., Duan, X., Shen, X.: Distributed task offloading optimization with queueing dynamics in multi-agent mobile-edge computing networks. Internet Things J. **8**(15), 12311–12328 (2021)
12. Wang, J., Hu, J., Min, G., Zomaya, A.Y., Georgalas, N.: Fast adaptive task offloading in edge computing based on meta reinforcement learning. Trans. Parallel Distrib. Syst. **32**(1), 242–253 (2020)
13. Tran-Dang, H., Kim, D.S.: FRATO: fog resource based adaptive task offloading for delay-minimizing IoT service provisioning. Trans. Parallel Distrib. Syst. **32**(10), 2491–2508 (2021)
14. Kim, T., et al.: MoDEMS: optimizing edge computing migrations for user mobility. J. Sel. Areas Commun. (2022). https://doi.org/10.1109/JSAC.2022.3229425
15. Liang, Z., Liu, Y., Lok, T.M., Huang, K.: Multi-cell mobile edge computing: joint service migration and resource allocation. Trans. Wirel. Commun. **20**(9), 5898–5912 (2021)
16. Li, C., Zhang, Y., Gao, X., Luo, Y.: Energy-latency tradeoffs for edge caching and dynamic service migration based on DQN in mobile edge computing. J. Parallel Distrib. Comput. **166**, 15–31 (2022)
17. Park, S.W., Boukerche, A., Guan, S.: A novel deep reinforcement learning based service migration model for mobile edge computing. In: 2020 IEEE/ACM 24th International Symposium on Distributed Simulation and Real Time Applications (DS-RT), pp. 1–8 (2020)
18. Jiao, Y., Wang, C.: A blockchain-based trusted upload scheme for the internet of things nodes. Int. J. Crowd Sci. **6**(2), 92–97 (2022)
19. Wang, S., Urgaonkar, R., Zafer, M., He, T., Chan, K., Leung, K.K.: Dynamic service migration in mobile edge-clouds. In: 2015 IFIP Networking Conference (IFIP Networking), pp. 1–9 (2015)
20. Kingma, D.P., Ba, J.: Adam: a method for stochastic optimization. arXiv preprint arXiv:1412.6980 (2014)
21. Rouzbahani, H.M., Karimipour, H., Lei, L.: Optimizing scheduling policy in smart grids using probabilistic delayed double deep Q-learning (P3DQL) algorithm. Sustain. Energy Technol. Assess. **53**(102712), 2213-1388 (2022)
22. Qinghua, Z., Ying, C., Jingya, Z., Yong, L.: Computation offloading optimization in edge computing based on deep reinforcement learning. In: 2020 5th International Conference on Mechanical, Control and Computer Engineering (ICMCCE), pp. 1552–1558 (2020)

Blockchain-Assisted Authentication and Key Agreement Protocol for Cloud-Edge Collaboration

Peng Liu[1,2], Qian He[1,2(✉)], Bingcheng Jiang[1,2], and Ming Jiang[2]

[1] State and Local Joint Engineering Research Center for Satellite Navigation and Location Service, Guilin University of Electronic Technology, Guilin 541004, China
heqian@guet.edu.cn
[2] Guangxi Key Laboratory of Cryptography and Information Security, Guilin University of Electronic Technology, Guilin 541004, China

Abstract. In response to the urgent need for scalable, lightweight, low-latency, anonymous, and highly secure identity authentication and key agreement protocol schemes in cloud-edge collaborative environments, we propose a blockchain-assisted lightweight authentication and key agreement protocol. In this protocol, a distributed environment based on a consortium blockchain is created with the assistance of cloud servers and edge nodes, reducing reliance on a single trusted authority. Anonymous real identity authentication and blockchain storage mechanisms ensure the credibility of identity information and the security of privacy information. In addition, most of the computational overhead of the authentication and key agreement process is transferred to the edge nodes and cloud services, reducing latency and reducing the computational burden on IoT devices. Security analysis shows that the protocol is secure against common attacks, and performance comparison analysis with similar protocols shows that our protocol is more secure and efficient, making it more suitable for resource-limited IoT devices.

Keywords: Blockchain · Mutual Authentication · Key Agreement · Cloud-Edge Collaborative · IoT Devices

1 Introduction

With the development of mobile communication technology and wireless sensing technology, the widespread application of the Internet of Things (IoT) has ushered humanity into an era of intelligent interconnection of all things, accompanied by a massive amount of data closely related to human production and life [1,2]. However, the limited computing and storage capabilities of IoT devices are key factors constraining their development [3]. Cloud computing technology has been introduced into the IoT field as a new service paradigm, which can efficiently and conveniently realize information and resource sharing. In the cloud computing environment, IoT intelligent devices (such as sensors, smart meters,

J. Chen et al. (Eds.): BlockSys 2023, CCIS 1896, pp. 77–90, 2024.
https://doi.org/10.1007/978-981-99-8101-4_6

wearable devices, etc.) upload data collected to remote cloud servers, and the cloud server stores and analyzes the data. Users can access the data by accessing the cloud server, which inevitably brings additional communication overhead and transmission delays [4]. By leveraging edge computing technology, gateways and access points located at the edge of the network can be used as edge nodes to assist cloud servers in completing local data storage and analysis, which can effectively alleviate this problem [5]. In the edge computing environment, edge nodes are deployed in unmanned environments, and the communication environment is vulnerable to various attacks. Authentication and key agreement protocols are crucial for ensuring secure access and transmission of IoT data and protecting user privacy. Wu et al. [6] presented a lightweight authentication and key agreement protocol for social vehicular networks using fog nodes, which only utilizes hash functions for identity authentication and key agreement, but this scheme is susceptible to internal and session attacks.

There have been some schemes for mutual authentication and key agreement among the IoT devices, edge nodes, and cloud services in cloud-edge collaborative environments. A lightweight authentication protocol for IoT devices in distributed cloud computing environments was proposed by Amin et al. [7], in which a shared session key is used between smart terminals and cloud services. However, the computational and communication overheads of the agreement process are high, making this scheme unsuitable for resource-constrained smart terminals. Wazid et al. [8] proposed a key management scheme for authentication in vehicular networks based on cloud-edge architecture, but the protocol is vulnerable to man-in-the-middle attacks and lacks forward security. Ma et al. [9] introduced edge computing into bidirectional session key agreement between smart terminals and cloud services, involving the cloud, edge, and terminal entities. However, Eftekhari et al. [10] pointed out the risks of internal attacks and session key attacks in the protocol [9]. Jia et al. [11] proposed a tripartite authentication key exchange protocol based on bilinear pairs, which enables mutual authentication between smart terminals and edge nodes through a cloud server, generating a shared public session key among the three communication entities. This protocol completes mutual authentication and key agreement with only one round of communication. Wu et al. [12] proposed a secure authentication and key agreement scheme that addresses the shortcomings of scheme [11], and have conducted a informe security analysis and BAN logic analysis of the proposed scheme. Xu et al. [13] proposed a three-factor anonymous authentication scheme for industrial Internet, which has high efficiency based on hash and elliptic curve encryption, but is less scalable. However, in the aforementioned authentication schemes, all user identity information is managed by a centralized authentication center. This approach is vulnerable to security issues such as identity data tampering, malicious denial of authentication services, and exploitation of user privacy data for profit. Furthermore, if the centralized authentication server is attacked, the entire authentication system may be paralyzed. In the cloud-edge collaborative environment, it is challenging to meet the needs for IoT device authentication and communication security.

The consortium blockchain is a permissioned blockchain [14], which boasts advantages such as decentralization, tamper-resistance, and ease of auditing. It consists of multiple nodes that maintain a distributed ledger, but each node must be verified before joining the alliance blockchain. The consortium blockchain retains many characteristics of public blockchains, such as establishing trust between nodes and making data tampering difficult. In addition, compared to public blockchains, the consortium blockchain features faster transaction speeds and better protection of data privacy [15]. Guo et al. [16] proposed a blockchain-based distributed authentication system for edge computing. In their approach, device identities are generated through a smart contract and then downloaded and stored on the device side. However, the blockchain stores detailed information that can prove the authenticity of device identities, and the openness and transparency of the blockchain may lead to the leakage of device information. Cheng et al. [17] presented a certificateless mutual authentication scheme between edge servers and IoT devices based on blockchain in the edge computing collaboration. The protocol protects users' identity information anonymously, but during the legitimate identity acquisition phase, users do not undergo true identity verification, which enables adversaries to easily obtain legitimate identities. Wang et al. [18] proposed a key management scheme for anonymous authentication and edge computing infrastructure of smart grid based on blockchain. The scheme achieves low-cost user revocation and key update, but the size of the blockchain increases as the number of devices increases, which leads to edge nodes being unable to perform blockchain operations.

The current blockchain-based authentication and key agreement schemes can solve some security issues that traditional centralized authentication methods cannot, such as malicious identity tampering and denial of authentication service. However, they still lack a secure real identity verification mechanism during the legal identity and key agreement stages, as well as the privacy information leakage caused by non-anonymized information storage in the blockchain. Moreover, the computing and storage capabilities of IoT devices in the cloud-edge collaboration environment are limited. Therefore, there is an urgent need for a scalable, lightweight, low-latency, anonymized, and highly secure authentication and key agreement scheme. In this paper, we propose a blockchain-assisted authentication and key agreement protocol for cloud-edge collaboration, and the main contributions of our scheme can be summarized as follows:

(1) We have constructed a three-layer architecture by integrating blockchain into the cloud-edge collaborative environment. The channel isolation strategy of the Hyperledger Fabric blockchain network was used to enable multiple cloud servers and edge nodes to coexist in a single blockchain network.

(2) We propose a blockchain-assisted lightweight authentication and key agreement protocol, where anonymous real identity verification and blockchain storage mechanism ensure the reliability of identity verification and privacy information security, achieving secure three-party data transmission between IoT terminals, edge nodes, and cloud servers.

(3) Security analysis demonstrates that the proposed scheme can achieve privacy-preserving mutual authentication and session key agreement, and is secure against known attacks. Comparison with similar schemes shows that our proposal provides better security protection for the cloud-edge collaboration scenario.

The remainder of our paper is organized as follows. Section 2 introduces the system model. Section 3 presents the formal construction of the our protocol. Then, We presented security analysis and performance analysis separately in Sect. 4 and Sect. 5, respectively. Finally, we conclude this paper in Sect. 6.

2   System Model

2.1   System Model

The system model for our proposed scheme is shown in Fig. 1, which consists of three layers: the Internet of Things (IoT) device layer, edge layer, and cloud layer. The system model includes the following components: trusted authority (TA), cloud server (CS), edge nodes (EN), smart terminal (ST), and blockchain (BC).

(1) TA. The trusted authority is primarily used for system initialization and entity registration. It is a registered entity responsible for registering ST and EN and providing identity authentication parameters to registered entities. TA serves as the administrator of the blockchain network and is responsible for installing chaincodes on the blockchain peers. Data in the cloud ledger can be added or updated through APIs using TA.

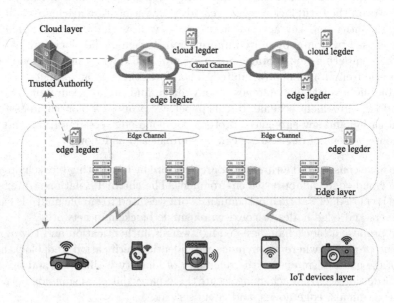

Fig. 1. System model

(2) *CS*. Cloud servers are trusted entities and serve as peer entities of the blockchain. They are members of two channels of the blockchain, one with other cloud servers and another with edge nodes. The ledger maintained by the channel consisting of multiple cloud servers in our scheme is referred to as the cloud ledger. Smart contracts deployed on trusted cloud server nodes are responsible for verifying the identity of smart terminals and edge nodes in the authentication and key agreement steps.

(3) *EN*. As a peer node in a blockchain network, an edge node participates in maintaining an edge ledger, which is a ledger maintained by multiple edge nodes and a cloud server in the same channel. It acts as a data collection node for IoT smart terminals and also facilitates the addition of data from smart terminals to the blockchain, which is then verified during the authentication and key agreement phases. The edge node provides identity verification messages between *ST* and *CS* and establishes a shared key among *ST*, *EN*, and *CS*.

(4) *ST*. The smart terminal is an IoT terminal device with certain computing capabilities, which sends data or requests services to the nearest edge node. It first registers with *TA* and then saves the authentication credentials to the cloud ledger and edge ledger via API for identity verification during the session key agreement phase.

(5) *BC*. The blockchain platform is built using the Hyperledger Fabric framework for consortium blockchains. It contains pseudo-identities, identities, and other validation parameters related to the smart terminals and edge nodes, and provides distributed access to all participating cloud servers and edge nodes. Smart contracts deployed on the platform verify entity identities during the key agreement process.

3 Blockchain-Assisted Lightweight Authentication and Key Agreement Protocol

The blockchain-assisted lightweight authentication and key agreement protocol for cloud-edge collaboration mainly includes two processes: the registration process and the authentication and key agreement process. Notice that cloud servers do not need to register separately because when building the blockchain network, the cloud servers will configure the corresponding private key $SK_{CS} = k \in Z_p^*$ and public key $PK_{CS} = k \cdot G$, and publish their public key PK_{CS} throughout the network. The system defines an elliptic curve $E : y^2 = x^3 + ax + b$ over a finite field F_p, where $a, b \in Z_p^*$. A cyclic additive group G is selected over the elliptic curve E with a generator P and prime order q. The relevant parameters and symbols used in this protocol are defined as shown in Table 1.

3.1 Registration Process

The registration process refers to the process in which edge nodes and smart terminals become legitimate entities in the cloud-edge collaborative environment.

Table 1. Notation decription

Notation	Description
ST_i	the i-th smart terminal
EN_j	the j-th edge node
CS	cloud server
ID	the identity identifier of the entity
G	the generator of elliptic curve E
SK_{CS}	private key of cloud server
PK_{CS}	public key of cloud server
h_0	$\{0,1\}^* \times \{0,1\}^* \to Z_p^*$
h_1	$0,1^* \times E_p \times \{0,1\}^* \to Z_p^*$
h_2	$E_p \times E_p \to Z_p^*$
h_3	$E_p \times E_p \times \{0,1\}^* \times \{0,1\}^* \times \{0,1\}^* \times \{0,1\}^* \to Z_p^*$
h_4	$E_p \times E_p \times E_p \times \{0,1\}^* \to Z_p^*$
h_6	$E_p \times E_p \times \{0,1\}^* \times \{0,1\}^* \to Z_p^*$
h_6	$E_p \times E_p \times \{0,1\}^* \times \{0,1\}^* \times \{0,1\}^* \to Z_p^*$
CTR	counter of smart terminal, edge node and cloud server

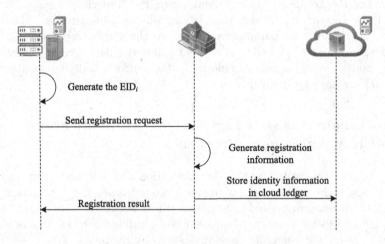

Fig. 2. Edge node registration process

(1) *Edge node registration.* Edge device ED registering to TA refers to the process in which network edge device entities with certain computing capabilities in the cloud-edge collaborative environment become legitimate entities. The specific process is shown in Fig. 2.

1) Generate the EID_i and send registration request. Edge node EN_j first selects random data $n_j \in Z_p^*$ and computes $EID_j = h_0(ID_{EN,j}\|n_0)$, and then sends a registration request of EID_j to TA.

2) Generate registration information and store it in the cloud ledger. When TA receives the registration request from EN_j, it first chooses a random number $s_j \in Z_p^*$ and computes $DID_j = h_1(EID_j||SK_{CS}||s_j)$ and $SID_j = EID_j \oplus PK_{CS}$. Then, it initializes a counter $CTR_{EN,j} = 0$. $CTR_{EN,j}$ is used to keep track of the number of login or authentication errors by EN. If $CTR_{EN,j}$ exceeds a certain threshold n, the current communication will be terminated. Finally, TA saves $\{s_j, EID_j, CTR_{EN,j}\}$ to the cloud ledger and returns $\{DID_j, SID_j\}$ to EN_j.

3) Respond to the registration result. After receiving $\{DID_j, SID_j\}$, EN_j first calculates $ET = DID_j \oplus EID_j$. Then EN_j stores $\{ET_j, SID_j, CTR_{EN,j}\}$ in the edge ledger.

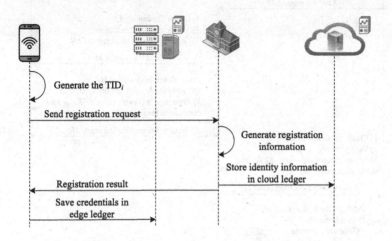

Generate the TID_i

Send registration request

Generate registration information

Store identity information in cloud ledger

Registration result

Save credentials in edge ledger

Fig. 3. Smart terminal registration process

(2) *Smart terminal registration.* Smart terminal ST registering with TA refers to the process in which the IoT device entity in the edge-cloud collaborative environment becomes a legitimate user. The specific process is shown in Fig. 3.

1) Generate the TID_i and send registration request. Smart terminal ST_i first selects a random number m_i, calculates $TID_i = h_0(ID_{ST,i}||m_i)$, and then sends TID_i registration request to TA.

2) Generate registration information and store it in the cloud ledger. When TA receives the registration message from ST_i, it first chooses a random number $s_i \in Z_p^*$, then calculates $CID_i = h_1(TID_i||SK_{CS}||s_i)$ and $SID_i = TID_i \oplus PK_{CS}$, and stores the $\{TID_i, s_i\}$ in the cloud ledger. Finally, TA returns $\{CID_i, SID_i\}$ to ST_i.

3) Respond to the registration result and save the registration credential to the edge ledger. After receiving $\{CID_i, SID_i\}$, ST_i first calculates $TT_i = CID_i \oplus TID_i$ and $RID_i = h_1(ID_{ST,i}||m_i)$. Then, it initializes a counter $CTR_{ST,i} = 0$ and saves $\{TID_i, RID_i, CRT_{ST,i}\}$ to the edge ledger by interacting with the nearest edge node and keep $\{TT_i, SID_i, m_i\}$.

3.2 Mutual Authentication and Key Agreement Process

In this section, ST, EN, and CS first perform identity authentication and then agreement the session key. EN and CS verify ST's credentials through the edge ledger and cloud ledger, respectively. The specific process is shown in Fig. 4.

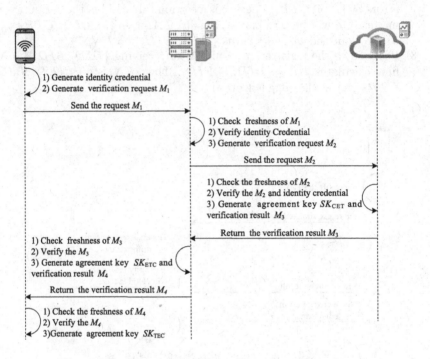

Fig. 4. Mutual authentication and key agreement process

(1) ST_i performs mutual authentication and key agreement with the nearest edge node in the cloud-edge collaborative environment. ST_i first selects a random number m_1, then calculates $RID_i^* = h_1(ID_{ST,i}\|m_0)$, $A_1 = m_1 \cdot G$, $A_2 = m_1 \cdot PK_{CS}$, $APD_i = ID_{ST,i} \oplus h_2(A_1\|A_2)$, $AND_i = h_3(A_1\|A_2\|ID_i\|T_1\|TID_i)$, where T_1 is the current timestamp. Finally, ST_i sends $M_1 = \{A_1, APD_i, AND_i, T_1, RID_i, TID_i\}$ to the edge node ED_j.

(2) After receiving the authentication message from ST_i, EN_j first checks the freshness $|T_1^* - T_1| < \Delta T$ of the received message, where ΔT is the freshness threshold set. If the inequality holds, EN_j queries the edge ledger to obtain RID_i and verifies whether $RID_i = RID_i^*$ holds or not. If not, EN_j aborts the process. Then, EN_j selects a random number $n_1 \in Z_p^*$ and current timestamp T_2, calculates $B_1 = n_1 \cdot G$, $B_2 = n_1 \cdot PK_{CS}$, $EID_j^* = h_0(ID_{EN,j}\|n_0)$, $B_3 = n_1 \cdot A_1$, $BND_j = h_3(B_1\|B_2\|ID_{EN,j}\|T_2\|DID_j)$ and $BPD_j = ID_{EN,j} \oplus h_2(B_1\|B_2)$. Finally, the edge node EN_j sends $M_2 = \{A_1, B_1, B_3, EID_j^*, APD_i, AND_i, BPD_j, BND_j, T_2\}$ to the cloud

server CS. Notice that if the freshness check or RID_i verification fails at this stage, the current session will be terminated.

(3) Upon receiving a message from ED_j, CS first checks the freshness $|T_2^* - T_2| < \Delta T$ of the message, where T_2^* is the current timestamp of the received message. If the inequality holds, CS verifies whether EID_j obtained from the cloud ledger matches the received EID_j^*. If it matches, CS calculates $A_2^* = SK_{CS} \cdot A_1$, $B_2^* = SK_{CS} \cdot B_1$, $ID_i^* = APD_i \oplus h_2 (A_1 \| A_2^*)$, $ID_j^* = BPD_j \oplus h_2 (B_1 \| B_2^*)$, $AND_i^* = h_3 (A_1 \| A_2^* \| ID_i^* \| T_1 \| TID_i)$ and $BND_j^* = h_3 (B_1 \| B_2^* \| ID_j^* \| T_2 \| DID)$, and then verifies whether AND_i^* and BND_j^* match those in the received message AND_i and BND_j. If all the verifications pass, CS chooses a random number $s_2 \in Z_p^*$ and calculates $C_1 = s_2 \cdot G, C_2 = s_2 \cdot A_1, C_3 = s_2 \cdot B_1, C_4 = s_2 \cdot B_3$. Then generate the session key $SK_{CET} = h_4 (C_4 \| A_1 \| B_1 \| C_1 \| PK_{CS})$ between the cloud and the edge, and calculate $CDM_j = h_5 (B_1 \| B_2^* \| ID_j^* \| T_3)$ and $CDM_i = h_6 (A_1 \| A_2^* \| ID_i^* \| T_3)$. Finally, CS returns $M_3 = \{C_1, C_2, C_3, CDM_i, CDM_j\}$ to ED_j. If any of the verifications fail or the message freshness is invalid, the session is terminated.

(4) ED_j receives a message from CS, it first checks the freshness $|T_3^* - T_3| < \Delta T$ of the message, where T_3^* is the current timestamp. If the inequality does not hold, ED_j aborts the process. Then, ED_j calculates $CMD_j^* = h_5 (B_1 \| B_2 \| ID_j \| T_3)$ and verifies whether CDM_j^* is the same as CDM_j in the returned message. If they match, ED_j computes $ETC = n_1 \cdot C_2$ and session key $SK_{ETC} = h_4 (ETC \| A_1 \| B_1 \| C_1 \| PK_{CS})$, and returns $M_4 = \{B_1, C_1, C_3, CDM_3, T_3\}$ to the ST_i, otherwise the current session is terminated.

(5) ST_i first checks the freshness $|T_4^* - T_3| < \Delta T$ of the message, where T_4^* is the current timestamp. If the inequality holds, ST_i calculates $CDM_i^* = h_6 (A_1 \| A_2 \| ID_i \| T_3)$, then ST_i verifies whether $CDM_i^* = CDM_i$ holds or not. if not ST_i terminates the current process. Otherwise, ST_i calculates $TEC = m_1 \cdot C_3$ and session key $SK_{TEC} = h_4 (TEC \| A_1 \| B_1 \| C_1 \| PK_{CS})$.

4 Security Analysis

In this section, we will conduct a security analysis of the proposed scheme.

(1) *Perfect Forward Secrecy.* Assuming that an adversary $\mathcal{A}$ obtains the registration information $\{TT_i, SID_i, m_i\}$ held by the smart terminal ST_i and also obtains b transmitted in the secure channel. When $\mathcal{A}$ wants to obtain the negotiated session key $SK_{TEC} = h_4 (TEC \| A_1 \| B_1 \| C_1 \| PK_{CS})$ of the ST_i, due to the $TEC = n_1 \cdot m_1 \cdot s_2 \cdot G$ in SK_{TEC}, obtaining the random number n_1, m_1 and s_2 are Diffie-Hellman hard problem, so adversary A cannot obtain the agreement key of SK_{TEC}. Therefore, our proposed scheme achieves perfect forward secrecy.

(2) *Replay Attack.* Since the messages M_1, M_2, M_3, and M_4 all contain the timestamp at the time of message transmission, the freshness of the message is checked first upon receiving the message. Therefore, our proposed scheme is secure against replay attacks.

(3) *Identity Anonymity.* During the registration phase, the ST_i stores the ID_i in the cloud ledger and edge ledger as anonymized TID_i and RID, respectively. Attackers cannot obtain the identity information of the smart terminal through CS, which ensures the anonymity of users in the registration phase. Furthermore, in the authentication and agreement phase, the ID_i is anonymized as $APD_i = ID_i \oplus h_2 (A_1 \| A_2)$, and even if an attacker obtains APD_i, they cannot calculate ID_i because they cannot obtain the random number m_1 and SK_{CS} to calculate A_1 and A_2. Similarly, it can be proved that the IDj of the edge node ED_j is also anonymized in the same way.

(4) *Impersonation Attack.* Assuming the CS private key SK_{CS} is leaked, even if the adversary $\mathcal{A}$ obtains the ST_i registration information ET_i, SID_i, m_0 and APD_i, due to the existence of random number m_1, $\mathcal{A}$ cannot obtain the correct AND_i, making it difficult to generate a valid M_1. Similarly, $\mathcal{A}$ cannot impersonate an edge node EN_j. In addition, in the registration phase, the identity ID_{CS} of the CS is bound to the registration information of the edge node and the smart terminal, and $\mathcal{A}$ cannot impersonate the CS because it cannot obtain ID_{CS}.

(5) *Man-in-the-middle Attack.* Given that the adversary $\mathcal{A}$ can obtain M_1, it will still be difficult for them to access the random number M_1, ID_i of ST_i, and A_2 in M_1. Therefore, even if $\mathcal{A}$ forces a tampering of the message M_1, it cannot be verified by ED_j. Similarly, since the adversary cannot easily obtain SK_{CS} and compute B_2, any tampering of messages M_2 and M_3 will result in illegal messages. Therefore, our proposed solution is secure against man-in-the-middle attacks.

(6) *Untraceability.* ST_i, EN_j, and CS set timestamps in the messages of the authentication agreement process, and the time of each phase is dynamically changing. In addition, ST_i, EN_j, and CS add random numbers n_1, m_1, and s_2 to the calculated A_1, B_1, and C_1, respectively, and these are randomly changing and uncontrollable. Therefore, our proposed solution can satisfy untraceability.

(7) *Session key leakage attack.* Taking the example of the session key held by CS, each session key $SK_{CS} = h_4 (C_4 \| A_1 \| B_1 \| C_1 \| ID_{CS})$ contains a C_4 as well as random numbers n_1, m_1, and s_2. Therefore, each session key negotiated has randomness, even if one of the session keys is leaked, it will not affect the agreement of other session keys.

5   Performance Analysis

In this section, we present the functional comparison and experimental analysis to demonstrate the performance of our scheme.

5.1   Functional Comparison

In this section, we will analyze the security features of the proposed scheme. At the same time, we also compare our scheme with existing schemes.

Table 2. Functional comparison

Function	Jia [11]	Sahoo [19]	Wu [12]	our scheme
Perfect Forward Secrecy	✓	✓	✓	✓
Resist Replay Attack	✗	✗	✓	✓
Identity Anonymity	✗	✓	✓	✓
Resist Man-in-the-middle Attack	✓	✓	✓	✓
Resist Insider Attacks	✗	✓	✗	✓
Untraceability	✓	✗	✓	✓
Resist Impersonation Attack	✗	✓	✓	✓
Resist Session key leakage attack	✗	✓	✗	✓

Table 3. Comparison of computational time

Scheme	Smart terminal	Edge node	Cloud server	Time (ms)
Jia [11]	$6T_h + 2T_{sm} + T_{bp}$	$4T_h + 2T_{sm} + T_{bp}$	$11T_h + 3T_{sm} + T_{bp}$	109.567
Sahoo [19]	$8T_h + 2T_{sm} + 2T_{se}$	$4T_h + 2T_{sm} + 2T_{se}$	$3T_h + 2T_{sm} + 2T_{se}$	84.405
Wu [12]	$5T_h + 3T_{sm} + T_{bp}$	$4T_h + 3T_{sm} + T_{bp}$	$4T_h + 2T_{sm} + T_{bp}$	130.015
our scheme	$4T_h + 3T_{sm}$	$4T_h + 4T_{sm}$	$7T_h + 6T_{sm}$	79.912

As shown in Table 2, the security of scheme Jia et al. [11], Sahoo et al. [19], Wu et al. [12] and our proposed scheme are compared. Jia et al. [11] scheme did not achieve mutual authentication and anonymity, and cannot resist impersonation attacks. In the registration stage, the identity IDs of the smart terminal ST and edge node EN were not anonymized. If the attacker steals the registration table on the cloud server, internal attacks and impersonation attacks can be launched. In addition, the identity ID of ST is not verified in the key agreement phase. Sahoo et al. [19] scheme has a replay attack and does not achieve untraceability. In Wu et al. [12] scheme, the identity ID is directly transmitted in plaintext to the cloud server for registration in the registration stage. Due to the same reason as the Jia et al. [11] scheme, there are impersonation attacks and internal attacks. In addition, in the session key agreement of Wu et al. [12] scheme, all other related parameters except for the random number can be easily obtained in the public channel. If the random number is leaked, it will lead to specific session attacks on the temporary session key.

5.2   Computing Performance Comparison

Taking into account the differences in computing capabilities among cloud servers, edge nodes, and intelligent terminals, we simulated them on the Alibaba Cloud platform. Specifically, cloud services and edge nodes were configured with Intel (R) Xeon (R) CPU E5-26300@2.30 GHz and 1 GB RAMi, with both operating systems being 64-bit Ubuntu 14.04. Intelligent terminals were simulated using a Google Nexus One smartphone with a configuration of 2 GHz ARM

CPU armeabi-v7a, 300 MiB RAM, and running Android 4.4.2 operating system. Notice that we select an elliptic curve group with Type A: $y^2 = x^3 + x$ and the order of the group is 160bits. In addition, We evaluated blockchain operations using Hyperledger Fabric v2.0, where a basic blockchain business network was deployed to a single organization Fabric network instance running on the Alibaba Cloud platform, equipped with an Intel (R) Xeon (R) CPU E5-26300@2.30 GHz, 1 GB RAMi, and Ubuntu 14.04.

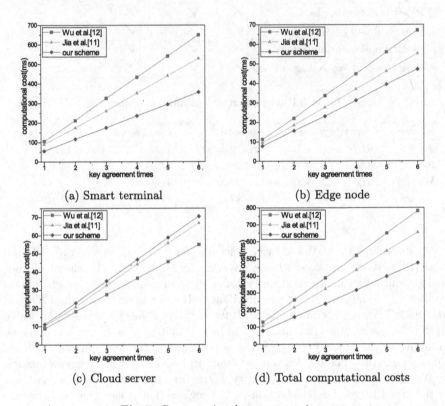

(a) Smart terminal   (b) Edge node

(c) Cloud server   (d) Total computational costs

Fig. 5. Computational cost comparison

We measured the runtime of basic cryptographic operations on the simulation platform. The double bilinear pairing (T_{bp}), scalar multiplication (T_{sm}), point addition (T_{pa}) in elliptic curve, hash function (T_h), modular exponentiation (T_{me}) in finite field, and symmetric encryption (T_{se}). Among them, the double bilinear pairing had the highest computational cost, with a cost of 48.66 ms on smart terminals, and 5.257 ms on edge nodes and cloud servers. The scalar multiplication in elliptic curve was also computationally expensive, with a cost of 19.919 ms on intelligent terminals, and 1.97 ms on edge nodes and cloud servers. The hash function had the smallest computational cost, with a cost of only 0.089 ms on intelligent terminals. Therefore, it can be seen that in order to achieve lightweight goals, the use of double bilinear pairing should be minimized.

As shown in Table 3, our proposed scheme has certain advantages in the total time cost of authentication and key agreement processes. The computation cost of identity authentication and session key agreement stages is only 79.912 ms. In comparison, the Jia et al. [11] and Wu et al. [12] have higher computation costs. Additionally, our proposed scheme only uses hash algorithm and elliptic curve point multiplication on the smart terminal, while the Jia et al. [11] and Wu et al. [12] employ more bilinear pairing and symmetric encryption operations, resulting in higher computation costs for these schemes. Therefore, our scheme is more suitable for resource-limited smart terminals.

The computational costs of the authentication and key establishment process on smart terminals, edge nodes, and cloud services are compared in Fig. 5. As shown in Fig. 5a, our scheme has the lowest computational cost on smart terminals. Figure 5d indicates that our scheme has a significantly better total time cost for key agreement than the other schemes, achieving the goal of lightweight key agreement on resource-limited smart terminals.

6   Conclusion

In this article, we propose a blockchain-assisted lightweight authentication and key agreement protocol. By leveraging blockchain technology and cloud-edge collaborative computing, we create a three-layer architecture to achieve better scalability and reduce dependence on a single trusted authority. The reliability of identity information is ensured by deploying smart contracts for anonymous identity verification at edge nodes and cloud services. Additionally, lightweight operations such as XOR and hash are utilized for entity authentication and key agreement, further reducing the computational burden on resource-constrained IoT devices by offloading complex computing tasks to edge nodes and cloud services. A comparative analysis of security and performance with several similar protocols demonstrates that our protocol not only exhibits more secure characteristics but also has low computational costs, making it more suitable for resource-constrained IoT devices.

Acknowledgments. This work was supported in part by the National Natural Science Foundation of China (62162018, 61861013); The Natural Science Foundation of Guangxi (2019GXNSFGA245004); Guilin Science and Technology Project (20210226-1); The Innovation Project of Guangxi Graduate Education (YCSW2022296).

References

1. Wang, C., Wang, D., Tu, Y., Xu, G., Wang, H.: Understanding node capture attacks in user authentication schemes for wireless sensor networks. IEEE Trans. Dependable Secure Comput. **19**(1), 507–523 (2020)
2. He, Q., Song, J., Wang, S., Liu, P., Jiang, B.: A secure authentication approach for the smart terminal and edge service. In: Wang, L., Segal, M., Chen, J., Qiu, T. (eds.) WASA 2022, Part III. LNCS, vol. 13473, pp. 419–430. Springer, Cham (2022). https://doi.org/10.1007/978-3-031-19211-1_35

3. Ding, W., Feifei, W., et al.: Multi-factor user authentication scheme for multi-gateway wireless sensor networks. Chin. J. Comput. **43**(4), 683–700 (2020)

4. Das, A.K., Wazid, M., Kumar, N., Vasilakos, A.V., Rodrigues, J.J.: Biometrics-based privacy-preserving user authentication scheme for cloud-based industrial Internet of Things deployment. IEEE Internet Things J. **5**(6), 4900–4913 (2018)

5. Wang, D., Li, W., Wang, P.: Crytanalysis of three anonymous authentication schemes for multi-server environment. Ruan Jian Xue Bao. J. Softw. **29**(7), 1937–1952 (2018)

6. Wu, T.-Y., Guo, X., Yang, L., Meng, Q., Chen, C.-M.: A lightweight authenticated key agreement protocol using fog nodes in social internet of vehicles. Mob. Inf. Syst. **2021**, 1–14 (2021)

7. Amin, R., Kumar, N., Biswas, G., Iqbal, R., Chang, V.: A light weight authentication protocol for IoT-enabled devices in distributed cloud computing environment. Future Gener. Comput. Syst. **78**, 1005–1019 (2018)

8. Wazid, M., Bagga, P., Das, A.K., Shetty, S., Rodrigues, J.J., Park, Y.: AKM-IoV: authenticated key management protocol in fog computing-based internet of vehicles deployment. IEEE Internet Things J. **6**(5), 8804–8817 (2019)

9. Ma, M., He, D., Wang, H., Kumar, N., Choo, K.-K.R.: An efficient and provably secure authenticated key agreement protocol for fog-based vehicular ad-hoc networks. IEEE Internet Things J. **6**(5), 8065–8075 (2019)

10. Eftekhari, S.A., Nikooghadam, M., Rafighi, M.: Security-enhanced three-party pairwise secret key agreement protocol for fog-based vehicular ad-hoc communications. Veh. Commun. **28**, 100306 (2021)

11. Jia, X., He, D., Kumar, N., Choo, K.-K.R.: Authenticated key agreement scheme for fog-driven IoT healthcare system. Wireless Netw. **25**, 4737–4750 (2019). https://doi.org/10.1007/s11276-018-1759-3

12. Wu, T.-Y., Wang, T., Lee, Y.-Q., Zheng, W., Kumari, S., Kumar, S.: Improved authenticated key agreement scheme for fog-driven IoT healthcare system. Secur. Commun. Netw. **2021**, 1–16 (2021)

13. Xu, H., Hsu, C., Harn, L., Cui, J., Zhao, Z., Zhang, Z.: Three-factor anonymous authentication and key agreement based on fuzzy biological extraction for industrial Internet of Things. IEEE Trans. Serv. Comput. **16**(4), 3000–3013 (2023)

14. Androulaki, E., et al.: Hyperledger fabric: a distributed operating system for permissioned blockchains. In: Proceedings of the Thirteenth EuroSys Conference, pp. 1–15 (2018)

15. Zhang, Y., Deng, R.H., Bertino, E., Zheng, D.: Robust and universal seamless handover authentication in 5G HetNets. IEEE Trans. Dependable Secure Comput. **18**(2), 858–874 (2019)

16. Guo, S., Hu, X., Guo, S., Qiu, X., Qi, F.: Blockchain meets edge computing: a distributed and trusted authentication system. IEEE Trans. Ind. Inf. **16**(3), 1972–1983 (2019)

17. Cheng, G., Chen, Y., Deng, S., Gao, H., Yin, J.: A blockchain-based mutual authentication scheme for collaborative edge computing. IEEE Trans. Comput. Soc. Syst. **9**(1), 146–158 (2021)

18. Wang, J., Wu, L., Choo, K.-K.R., He, D.: Blockchain-based anonymous authentication with key management for smart grid edge computing infrastructure. IEEE Trans. Ind. Inf. **16**(3), 1984–1992 (2019)

19. Sahoo, S.S., Mohanty, S., Majhi, B.: A secure three factor based authentication scheme for health care systems using IoT enabled devices. J. Ambient. Intell. Human. Comput. **12**, 1419–1434 (2021). https://doi.org/10.1007/s12652-020-02213-6

Towards Efficient and Privacy-Preserving Hierarchical Federated Learning for Distributed Edge Network

Ningyu An[1], Xiao Liang[1], Fei Zhou[1], Xiaohui Wang[1], Zihan Li[2], Jia Feng[3], and Zhitao Guan[2(✉)]

[1] State Grid Laboratory of Grid Advanced Computing and Applications, State Grid Smart Grid Research Institute Co.Ltd, Beijing 100209, China
[2] School of Control and Computer Engineering, North China Electric Power University, Beijing 102206, China
guan@ncepu.edu.cn
[3] State Grid Zhejiang Electric Power Company.Ltd, Hangzhou 310007, China

Abstract. Federated learning is a promising paradigm that utilizes widely distributed devices to jointly train a machine learning model while maintaining privacy. However, when oriented to distributed resource-constrained edge devices, existing federated learning schemes still suffer from heterogeneity challenge. Hierarchical federated learning divides devices into clusters based on their resources to enhance training efficiency. In addition, there are also security concerns such as the risk of privacy leakage during the interactions intra and cross the layers. In this paper, we propose PHFL, a Privacy-Preserving Hierarchical Federated Learning Scheme, which includes a personalized task assignment protocol and a heterogeneous-friendly aggregation scheme, so as to achieve an efficient and low-cost training for resource-constrained edge devices. To address the heterogeneity challenge, we combine synchronous and asynchronous aggregation, and design different aggregation weights for device differences. On top of that, a privacy-preserving scheme based on threshold homomorphic encryption is designed to accommodate the privacy requirements of the proposed hierarchical federated learning scenario. The security analysis and performance evaluation demonstrate that this approach improves model generalizability and learning efficiency with acceptable overhead, while also providing privacy protection.

Keywords: Federated Learning · Privacy-preserving · Edge Computing · Resource-constraint · Optimization

1 Introduction

With the proliferation of edge devices and the vast amount of data derived from them, federated learning is considered as a potentially viable solution to train a globally shared model collaboratively with these edge devices [1, 2]. No raw data need to be pooled together, which helps to protect the sensitive data to some extent. However, there are still

J. Chen et al. (Eds.): BlockSys 2023, CCIS 1896, pp. 91–104, 2024.
https://doi.org/10.1007/978-981-99-8101-4_7

several major challenges when it applied to distributed edge network. Firstly, there is with high heterogeneity between edge devices, including the unbalance network environment, unbalance computational power and the non-Independent-identical distribution (non-IID) data [3].

To this end, several pertinent works have devoted to solve the data heterogeneity issue. FedProx is proposed to address the challenges of heterogeneity by improving the local objective function and adding a Proximal Term [4]. Wang et al. try to eliminate objective inconsistency and propose FedNova, which can achieve a normalized averaging while preserving fast error convergence [5]. Unfortunately, the huge communication and computation overhead may be expensive for the resource-constrained device [6]. Furthermore, the interaction between edge devices and remote server may be unstable and slow, pulling down the learning efficiency.

Hierarchical Federated learning (HFL) is a novel learning paradigm for edge computing, which can achieve an efficient learning by dividing all the devices into clusters based on their resources. Abad et al. propose a hierarchical federated learning framework for heterogeneous cellular network, devices send local gradient estimate to small cell base station and a periodic averaging is performed by parameter server to establish a global consensus [7]. Gong et al. design an adaptive clustered federated learning scheme which classify clients into corresponding clusters according to their data distribution. Moreover, an automatic search mechanism of optimal cluster number is added for better model accuracy and low communication cost [8]. Wang et al. first design a resource-efficient federated learning mechanism with hierarchical aggregation, which combine the synchronous and asynchronous aggregation and achieve a significant resource reduction. They also extend to re-clustering the edge nodes to adapt to the dynamic scenario [9].

However, the second challenge in distributed edge network is not addressed in the above approaches, which is the security risk for middle parameters during the training process [10, 11]. Wainakh et al. try to fill this part of gap and analyze that several characteristics of HFL can naturally serve as some privacy enhancements, such as Sampling strategy, multiple levels of aggregation [12]. Despite the protections on data privacy of HFL, the semi-honest participants or adversaries can still infer the sensitive information from the interaction of the intermediate models. To this end, Shi et al. add the noise to the shared model parameters before uploading and propose a local-differential-privacy-based privacy-preserving scheme, which achieve a balance between privacy and utility [13]. Whereas, they fail to take the consider of the limited resource and the heterogeneity of devices.

In this work, we design a privacy-preserving Hierarchical Federated Learning Scheme based on threshold-paillier mechanism which can improve training efficiency and achieve a stable and fast convergence while preserving privacy. The main contributions of this work are as follows:

1. We propose a personalized task assignment protocol to evaluate and layering the devices based on their learning capacities, so as to balance the training task according to the constrained resource of devices.

2. We design a heterogeneous-friendly aggregation scheme for federated learning which includes Intra-layer synchronous aggregation and Cross-Layer asynchronous aggregation, where the factor affecting aggregation weight varies with the process. The experimental results show that the proposed method can achieve faster and more stable convergence.
3. We adopt a threshold-paillier-encryption-based privacy-preserving scheme for the hierarchical federated learning, which can defend against the security threat from semi-honest adversaries.

2 Preliminaries

2.1 Threshold-Paillier

Threshold-Paillier algorithm is a threshold variant of the classic additive homomorphic encryption scheme, Paillier [14]. The main operations of Threshold-Paillier are as follows:

$KeyGen() \rightarrow \{Pub = n, Pri = s_i | i \in \{1, 2, \cdots n_r\}\}$: Pick an integer $n = pq$, then $m = p'q'$ where $p = 2p' + 1, q = 2q' + 1$. Pick $d = 0 \bmod m, d = 1 \bmod n$ and select a_i from $\{0, \cdots n \times m - 1\}$ and construct the polynomial $f(X) = \sum_{i=0}^{t-1} a_i X^i \bmod nm$, where $a_0 = d, 0 < i < t, t < n/2$ is the decryption threshold. If there are n_r decryption entities, then the key share of entity i is $s_i = f(i)$. The public key is n, g, where $g = n+1$.

$Encrypt_{Pub}(m) \rightarrow c = g^M r^n \bmod n^2$: pick a random $r \in Z_{n^2}^*$, use the public key Pub to encrypt and thus the plaintext space will be Z_{n^2}.

$Decrypt(c) \rightarrow M = \dfrac{L(\prod_{i \in S} c_i^{2\lambda_{0,i}^S} \bmod n^2)}{L(g^{4\Delta^2} \bmod n^2)} \bmod n$: each decryption entity calculates decryption share $SubDe_{s_i}(c) \rightarrow c_i = c^{2\Delta s_i}$ by using their private key share, where $\Delta = n_r!$. If there are more than t decryption shares are collected, we define the set of the decryption shares is S, then $c' = \prod_{i \in S} c_i^{2\lambda_{0,i}^S} \bmod n^2$, where $\lambda_{0,i}^S = \Delta \prod_{i' \in S \setminus i} \frac{-i'}{i-i'} \in Z$.

According to the Secret Share Algorithm:

$$c' = \prod_{i \in S} c^{4\Delta s_i \lambda_{0,i}^S} = c^{4\Delta \sum_{i \in S} s_i \lambda_{0,i}^S} = c^{4\Delta^2 f(0)} = c^{4\Delta^2 d} = (1+n)^{4\Delta^2 M} \bmod n^2 = g^{4\Delta^2 M} \bmod n^2.$$

Let $L(u) = \frac{u-1}{n}$, then $M = \dfrac{L(c' \bmod n^2)}{L(g^{4\Delta^2} \bmod n^2)} \bmod n = \dfrac{L(\prod_{i \in S} c_i^{2\lambda_{0,i}^S} \bmod n^2)}{L(g^{4\Delta^2} \bmod n^2)} \bmod n$, where $\lambda_{0,i}^S = \Delta \prod_{i' \in S \setminus i} \frac{-i'}{i-i'} \in Z$.

The homomorphism of the algorithm is proved as follow, let the plaintext m_1, m_2:

$$\begin{aligned} Decrypt(E(m_1) \times E(m_2)) &= Decrypt(g^{m_1} r_1^n \cdot g^{m_2} r_2^n \bmod n^2) \\ &= Decrypt(g^{m_1+m_2} \cdot (r_1 r_2)^n \bmod n^2) \\ &= m_1 + m_2 \end{aligned}$$

3   Model and Design Goals

3.1   System Model and Threat Model

System Model. We consider a lot of distributed mobile edge devices to form a federated learning network. These devices are data owners who do not want to expose sensitive information about local data during the learning process. Considering the actual situation, on the one hand, these devices have strong heterogeneity, which is mainly reflected in the differences in sample size, sample distribution, and communication and computing capabilities. The first two differences are a very common challenge in federated learning, non-IID problem. On the other hand, these devices are poorly reliable and have limited resources, which leads to a potential straggler problem, in which some client training processes have significant delays or drop calls. Therefore, as illustrated in Fig. 1, we layer many devices (called workers) according to their learning ability, select Layer Head from them, and then combine the parameter server responsible for aggregation to build a hierarchical federated learning framework. Workers send the updated model to the nearby Layer Head rather than server, reducing the communication overhead. And due to the similar learning ability, the staleness within the Layer is approximate, so as to improve the training efficiency. The main entities of the framework are as follows:

- Worker: Each worker $P_k, k = 1, 2, \cdots N_P$ trains the downloaded global model upon the local dataset D_k which follows distribution $\mathcal{P}_k$, and submit the updated model.
- Layer Head (LH): Assume that all workers are divided into N_c clusters $\{L_i, i = 1, 2, \cdots N_L\}$, and the workers in layer L_i is represented as $\{P_k^i, k = 1, 2, \cdots N_P^i, i = 1, 2, \cdots N_L\}$. Layer Heads are elected from the workers within a layer according to the reliability, and are responsible for aggregating the updated local model in a synchronous way. Then the obtained layer model is sent to the server. We always let P_1^i to represent layer head of layer L_i.
- Server: A parameter server takes charge of aggregating the layer models in an asynchronous manner.
- Key management Center (KMC): The trusty third party is responsible for generating the key pairs for encryption. Each layer is assigned a unified pair of keys, where the private key is pre-segmented into shares and the split way vary from layer to layer. The Worker owns the public key and the private key share.

The learning process is trying to optimize a global model whose parameters are represented by $w \in \mathbb{R}^d$, and the optimization problem to be solved can be expressed as:

$$\min_{w \in \mathbb{R}^d} \left[F(w) := \sum_{k=1}^{N} \frac{n_k}{\sum n_k} f_k(w) \right] \tag{1}$$

where $n_k = |D_k|$ indicates the sample size of P_k, f_k indicates the local objective function of P_k. The local model maintained by P_k is w_k, and the local empirical risk on P_k is defined as $f_k(w_k) = \frac{1}{n_k} \sum_{i \in D_k} \ell_i(x_i, y_i; w_k)$, where ℓ denotes the loss function.

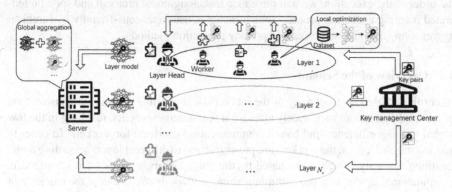

Fig. 1. System model

Threat Model. We adopt an honest-but-curious threat model for workers in the system. All the workers, including LH, keep their data locally, but are curious about others' data or model. Workers participate in learning in the hope of obtaining information that is not available locally through collaborative training, so as to obtain a more generalized model. In addition, considering of the sunk cost of the training process, we can infer that the more a worker makes contributions to the global training, the less likely he is to jeopardize the global process.

In terms of the server, they can be more threatening than workers because they have access to all the local models. They perform the aggregation protocol correctly but try their best to infer useful information from the submitted local model, such as Member inference attack.

3.2 Design Goals

- **Efficiency.** Provided that the edge devices have limited resources, the proposed federated learning framework can improve global training efficiency reduce the communication and computational cost of devices to a certain extent.
- **Heterogeneous friendly.** By addressing the problem of stragglers, PHFL aims to accommodate the high heterogeneity of edge devices and achieve a faster and more stable convergence without compromising model performance.

– **Privacy preservation.** Our framework can ensure the confidentiality of sensitive local information of workers. Individual workers, especially Layer Heads, are unable to infer the information of other workers from the local model update. The server can correctly execute the federated training process without knowing anything about the data in the sample set.

4   Details of the Proposed Scheme

In this section, we will develop our description according to the full training cycle of federated learning. We first introduce overview of the proposed scheme. Then, according to the order of the execution, we will introduce task assignment protocol and specific federated learning execution process, which includes heterogeneous-friendly hierarchical aggregation strategies and threshold privacy protection methods.

4.1   Overview of the Scheme

According to high heterogeneity of the workers, it is possible that the submission time of the local update can vary widely after local optimization process, resulting in the low global training efficiency and heavy communication overhead for workers. In order to address the challenges, the workers are pre-organized to different layers according to the Learning Capacity, which is evaluated by the multi factors, such as local sample size, computational power, and the communication bandwidth. We evaluate the capacity of all the workers, and divide them into different layers before learning.

The workers within a layer have the similar learning capacity, which helps them to have a greater tendency to synchronize throughout the learning process. On basis of that, the federated learning process are conducted hierarchically, the local model updates within the layer are aggregated by Layer Head synchronously to generate the layer model, while the layer models are then aggregated asynchronously by server, thus improve the communication efficiency.

Even if keeping the data locally, benefit from the characteristic of the federated learning, attackers still can infer sensitive data from the processed model. For the purpose to defend against the security threat faced by the local sensitive data, we introduce the threshold-additive homomorphic encryption to ensure the confidentiality of the local model. Moreover, the maintenance of the private key is distributed to all the workers in a layer, which helps to prevent the security threat from private key misuse and create a decentralized trust environment.

Overall, the process of PHFL is as follows, these steps will be executed cyclically until the global model converges: Step 1:Worker Assessment and Layering. This step includes the system initialization and the election of Layer Head. Step 2: Keys Assignment and Global Model Broadcast. Step 3: Local Optimization and Encryption. Step 4: Intra-layer Synchronous Aggregation in Ciphertext level. Step 5: Cross-Layer Asynchronous Aggregation in Ciphertext level. Step 6: Share Decryption.

4.2 Task Assignment Protocol

The personalized task assignment protocol is designed based on the core idea of the Load Balancing strategies, i.e. the task of each worker should be adaptive to his resources, so as to improve the data processing efficiency and to reduce the load on devices. We consider local optimization of the model as TASKs, and the hardware capacity of devices as RESOURCEs. Under the above assumptions, our goal is to assign the corresponding local training tasks according to the capacity of specific worker.

Learning Capacity. To quantify the RESOURCEs, a definition of Learning Capacity is given to measure the capacity that workers can contribute to federated learning process by $LC_k = n_k / (s + 1)$, where n_k denotes sample size of the worker P_k before the learning process, and s denotes the potential staleness of P_k. Actually, the staleness is related to two types of metrics: computational power and communication bandwidth. The computational power is related to the total CPU cycles, RAM, and the power available. However, these metrics are usually time-varying and heterogeneous [15], so in our protocol we directly find the average latency in the last few federated learning tasks for this worker to evaluate his learning capacity.

Nevertheless, we offer an available formula for calculate the staleness for the system initialization, which helps to make an initial prediction of the learning capability of a device that has just joined the system:

$$s(P_k) = \frac{k_1 \cdot \log(B)}{1 + e^{-k_2 \cdot \log(P_A) - k_3 \cdot \log(R) + k_4 \cdot \log(C)}} \tag{2}$$

where B is the communication bandwidth, P_A is the power available, R is the memory of the device and C is the total CPU cycles.

After evaluating the learning capability of each device, we divide them into multiple layers based on the centralized distribution of learning capability, and next we initiate the election of layer heads, which is also decided by learning capacity. Inspired by the Proof-of-Stake mechanism of Blockchain, the concept of Learning Age based on the learning capacity is given: $LA_k = (R_A + 1) \times LC_k$, where R_A denotes the number of times the worker participated in the federated learning process. After being divided into the layers, the election of the Layer Head is triggered and the worker with the oldest learning age will be elected.

Personalized Task Assignment. Based on the learning capacity, we assign the corresponding TASKs, which is quantified by the number of local iterations ρ to approximate the amount of work required per round for a device. The TASKs of the workers within a layer are floating above and below a baseline task volume. Assume the baseline local iteration of layer L_i is ρ_b^i, then the other workers in the layer could calculate their own iteration rounds $\rho_k^i = \left\lceil \rho_b^i \times \frac{LC_k \times N_P^i}{\sum LC_k} \right\rceil, k = 1, 2, \cdots, N_P^i$.

The baseline local iterations ρ_b of all the layers could be the same at the very first time, and the Layer Head takes charge of adjusting the baseline local iterations when the staleness of its layer model is always too large to participant the global aggregation:

$$\rho_{new}^i = \left\lfloor \rho_{old}^i \times \frac{\overline{\tau}_{ini}}{\overline{\tau}} \right\rfloor \tag{3}$$

where $\overline{\tau}_{ini}$ denotes the average delayed rounds in the first ω global iterations, and $\overline{\tau}$ denotes the average delayed rounds in the nearby ω global iterations, and ω is a constant. Overall, unlike those frameworks that all devices perform the same training, we assign personalized training tasks to different workers, which can significantly reduce the burden of the resource-constrained devices.

4.3 Privacy-Preserving Heterogeneous-Friendly Aggregation

We introduce the details of the execution of PHFL which includes two main contributions, heterogeneous friendly hierarchical aggregation strategy and threshold-homomorphic-encryption-based privacy protection methods. Hierarchical aggregation strategy relies on the divided layer structure and the core idea is aggregating the local model of workers with similar learning capacities synchronously in a layer and aggregating the layer models of layers with large heterogeneity asynchronously.

Following the layering, KMC generates the key pairs by calling $KeyGen() \rightarrow \{Pub = n, Pri = \{Pri^i = \{s_k^i, k = 1, 2, \cdots N_P^i\}, i = 1, 2, \cdots n_L\}\}$. Especially, the same private key Pri is split in many different ways for different layers and the public key Pub is in common. Then KMC broadcast Pub and randomly distributes the key shares in a set of private key shares Pri^i to workers in layer L_i. The threshold of decryption is t.

As shown in Algorithm 1, the federated learning process starts after the initial global model is broadcast to all the workers in the system. In round $T = 1, 2, \cdots$, the LH P_1^i in L_i downloads the newest global model from server and distributed to the workers in the layer. Except for the first round of downloading the global model in plaintext, the global model is in ciphertext in other rounds. So once P_1^i receives the encrypted model, he records the current number of iteration rounds between server as $\tau = T$ and organizes the Share Decryption which we will explain in detail later.

As shown in algorithm 1–2 (line 3–6), the worker $P_k, k = 1, 2, \cdots, N_P^i$ takes the decrypted global model as the initial model of this iteration. According to the assigned training task, P_k performs ρ_k^i local iterations based on the local dataset D_k, and obtains the local model update w_i^k. He then encrypts the model update with his public key $C_k^i \leftarrow Encrypt_{pub}(w_k^i)$ and send it to LH.

LH P_1^i collects the ciphertexts of local models in the layer L_i and performs Intra-layer Synchronous Aggregation (Line 8) based on FedAvg algorithm:

$$C^i = \prod_{k=1}^{N_P^i} \frac{n_k^i}{\sum n_k^i} C_k^i \tag{4}$$

where $\frac{n_k^i}{\sum n_k^i}$ is the relative sample size of worker P_k^i, and n_k^i is size of his local dataset. Taking the advantages of Layering, the time cost of collecting can not be too high and thus avoiding wasted computing power due to model discard. According to Eq. (1), the correctness of the aggregation relies on the homomorphism additivity of encryption algorithm:

$$Decrypt(\prod_{k=1}^{N_P^i} \frac{n_k^i}{\sum n_k^i} C_k^i) = \sum_{k=1}^{N_P^i} \frac{n_k^i}{\sum n_k^i} C_k^i \tag{5}$$

Then P_1^i packages the aggregated layer model with τ and sends them to server.

Server performs the Cross-Layer Asynchronous Aggregation (Algorithm 1–1) as soon as it receives the layer model C^i, τ. In round T, asynchronous aggregation weight of each layer is adjusted depending on the staleness $T - \tau$ and their task assignment baseline ρ_b^i, This allows for a combination of both factors: the heterogeneity and their training contribution: $C_{T+1} = (1 - \beta)C_T \times \beta C_T^i$, where $\beta = \beta_s \times (\frac{e}{2})^{-\frac{(T-\tau)}{\rho_b^i}}$. β_s is a constant indicating the aggregation ratio between the old global model and the newly received local model. Similarly, according to the characteristic of threshold-paillier: $Decrypt((1 - \beta)C_T \times \beta C_T^i) = (1 - \beta)C_T + \beta C_T^i$. In this case, if the staleness of layer model is large, it will be aggregated to global model in a little ratio and thus weakening its influence on the direction of the global optimization, while layers with larger local training baselines have layer models that are considered more likely have high generalizability and therefore have higher aggregation weights.

The new global model C_T together with the current round T will be shared to L_i, and the Shared Decryption process within the layer is triggered. The layer head P_1^i organizes at least $N_D \geq t$ workers to participant in the decryption. Worker P_k^i who wants to participant in performs share decryption to obtain decryption share c_k: $SubDe_{s_k^i}(C_T) \rightarrow c_k = C_T^{2\Delta s_k^i}$ and broadcast within the layer. Once more than t decryption shares are collected, any worker within the layer can decrypt to obtain a new global model for training:

$$Decrypt(C_T) \rightarrow w^i = \frac{L(\prod_{i \in S} c_k^{2\lambda_{0,i}^S} \bmod n^2)}{L(g^{4\Delta^2} \bmod n^2)} \bmod n \tag{6}$$

where the set of the decryption shares is S. If the required number of decryption shares is not collected, it can be presumed that the current device offline rate of the layer is high and it is not suitable to participate in the next training round.

Algorithm 1: Hierarchical aggregation strategy	
1-1 Cross-Layer Asynchronous Aggregation (Server) Input: C^i, τ Output: C	1-2 Intra-layer Synchronous Aggregation Input: (In layer L_i): C_T, T, Pub Output: C^i, τ
1: for $T = 1, 2, \cdots$	1: if $\lvert Pri^i \rvert \geq t$
2: Once the layer model C^i, τ received	2: $w^j \leftarrow Decrypt_{Pri^i}(C_T)$
3: $C_{T+1} = (1 - \beta)C_T + \beta C_T^i$, where $\beta = \beta \times (\frac{e}{2})^{-\frac{(T-\tau)}{\rho_b}}$	3: Worker $P_k^i : w_{k,0}^j \leftarrow w^j$
	4: for $j \in [1, \rho_k^i]$:
4: $T \leftarrow T + 1$	5: $w_{k,j}^j \leftarrow w_{k,j-1}^j - \eta \nabla f_k(w_{k,j-1}^j)$
5: return C_T, T	6: $w_k^j \leftarrow w_{k,\rho_k^i}^j$
	7: $C_k^i \leftarrow Encrypt_{pub}(w_k^j)$, send $C_k^i, n_k^i = \lvert D_k^i \rvert$ to LH
	8: Layer Head $P_1^i : C^i = \prod_{k=1}^{N_p^i} \frac{n_k^i}{\sum n_k^i} C_k^i$
	9: return $C^i, \tau = T$

5   Security Analysis

In this section, we analyze the security of proposed PHFL aimed at the adversaries under honest-but-curious threat model.

Definition 1: Chosen Plaintext Attack (CPA): If for all the probabilistic polynomial time adversary $\mathcal{A}$, there exists a negligible function $\varepsilon(\cdot)$ such that the encryption scheme Π satisfies: $\left\lvert Pr[Exp_{\mathcal{A},\Pi}^{CPA}(\mathcal{K}) = 1] - \frac{1}{2} \right\rvert \leq \varepsilon(\mathcal{K})$, where Pr is the advantage of adversary, Exp is the Indistinguishable experiment, and $\mathcal{K}$ is the security parameter. Then encryption scheme Π is IND-CPA security.

Lemma 1: It is safe for workers to execute local optimization (Algorithm 1–2, line 3–7) locally.

Lemma 2: Threshold-paillier homomorphic encryption is IND-CPA security [15]. The operations following threshold-paillier homomorphic encryption are considered to be secure.

Theorem 1: Under the honest-but-curious threat model, even if there exists the threat of semi-honest adversary, The proposed PHFL is secure.

Proof: If the identity of a semi-honest adversary is an ordinary worker, he only has access to the ciphertext of the global model, according to Lemma 2, he cannot infer any sensitive information from the ciphertext with one private key share. Also, he cannot threaten other workers in the local calculation process based on Lemma 1. And if he is a LH, he could additionally receive the ciphertexts of other local models and compute the aggregated layer model. The security of the former is similarly to the previous statement, and the latter is also an effective ciphertext by the nature of homomorphic encryption, so its security can reduce to Lemma 2. As for a semi-honest server, he only has access to the layer model and the aggregated global model, the two types of models are both computed from the homomorphic property in the ciphertext state, so as to be secure under lemma 2.

6 Performance Evaluation

6.1 Hierarchical Federated Learning Performance Assessment

Simulation Settings. In our experiments, we use the GPU configuration parameters as NVIDIA GEFORCE RTX 3060, the CPU configuration parameters as 12th Gen Intel(R) Core(TM) i7-12700F 2.10 GHz, and the memory of the computer device we use as 16GB. In addition, the Python version is 3.8.0 and the torch version is 1.9.0.

- *Benchmarks.* In order to evaluate the impact of local iterations ρ and basic weight of asynchronous aggregation β_s on the communication cost of device, we choose the PHFL algorithm with fixed constant ρ and β_s as a benchmark, for convenience, we name this algorithm as HFL. In addition, we compare the PHFL algorithm with two other federated learning algorithms. To verify the superiority of our proposed algorithm, we contrast PHFL with purely synchronous and asynchronous methods. Therefore, one of the baseline algorithms is FedAvg introduced in [17], which implements synchronous federated optimization. At the same time, we also use the FedAsync introduced in [17] as another baseline.
- *Models and Datasets.* We conduct the experiments over two realworld datasets (e.g., MNIST [18] and CIFAR10 [19]) on a Convolutional Neural Network (CNN) model.
- *Data Distribution.* To evaluate the impact of data imbalance on simulation experiment performance, we primarily focus on the label distribution skew to represent the non-IID problem of the data and the labels of each edge dataset are distributed as Dirichlet [20].
- *Simulation Parameters.* The simulation experiments set up with 15 edge devices, they are divided into three groups according to their Learning Capacities. In all simulations, the learning rate η is 0.01. The initial values of the local iterations ρ and basic weight of asynchronous aggregation β_s are 5 and 0.6, respectively. The maximum client delay $T - \tau$ during asynchronous training is set to 9.

Simulation Results. In our first set of experiments, we name the PHFL algorithm that dynamically adjusts the local iterations ρ as PHFL-epoch, and the PHFL algorithm that dynamically adjusts the basic weight of asynchronous aggregation β_s is named PHFL-beta. The test results of HFL, PHFL-epoch and PHFL-beta on different datasets are shown in Fig. 2.

We can observe that the convergence rate of PHFL-epoch and PHFL-beta is faster compared to HFL in Fig. 2 a), b). In the previous training process, the accuracy of PHFL-epoch and PHFL-beta on the test set is significantly higher.

Based on our analysis of two cases, the personalized task assignment and the strategy of the basic weight of asynchronous aggregation β_s can reduce communication costs and the burden of the resource-constrained devices.

In the second part of the experiment, the test results of FedAvg, FedAsync and PHFL on different datasets are shown in Fig. 3. First of all, it can be obviously observed in

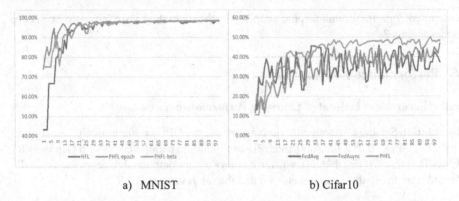

a) MNIST   b) Cifar10

Fig. 2. Performance of HFL, PHFL-epoch and PHFL-beta on different datasets

Fig. 3 a) that HFL has the fastest convergence rate, achieving 98% accuracy in round 20, while FedAvg and FedAsync achieve the same accuracy in round 42 and 70, respectively. In addition, we can observe the training situation on the CIFAR10 dataset in Fig. 3 b), after 47 rounds, the accuracy of PHFL on the test set is significantly higher than that of FedAvg and FedAsync.

Based on our analysis of two cases, it can be concluded that the proposed federated learning framework accelerates the convergence of the learning and improves the global model performance.

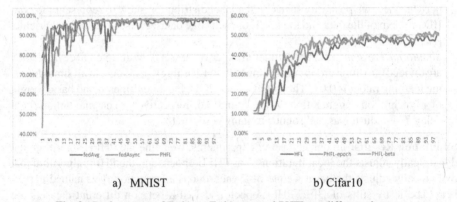

a) MNIST   b) Cifar10

Fig. 3. Performance of FedAvg, FedAsync and PHFL on different datasets

6.2 Overhead of Homomorphic Encryption

We evaluate the additional overhead of privacy protection in terms of the four processes involved in threshold homomorphic encryption: Share decryption, Encryption, Synchronous ciphertext aggregation of Layer Head and Asynchronous ciphertext aggregation of Server. With the same parameters, we repeat the experiment 5 times and take the average. The test results are shown in Table 2. After analysis, we believe that the time cost of homomorphic encryption is acceptable, but we can provide better privacy protection effect. As a result, it is feasible to incorporate threshold homomorphic encryption into our framework to reduce the risk of privacy leakage during joint training (Table 1).

Table 1. Overhead of homomorphic encryption

Process	Share decryption	Encryption	Synchronous aggregation	Asynchronous aggregation
Time cost(s)	52.77847731	11.95364105	8.66005801	6.451267421

7 Conclusion

In this paper, we propose PHFL, a hierarchical federated learning framework for widely distributed edge devices. To mitigate the negative effect caused by heterogeneity between devices, we first draw on the idea of load balancing and design a personalized task assignment protocol to layering and assigning tasks to devices according to their learning capacity. This also leads to a reduction of communication and computational burden that the device needs to consume. We also design the strategy of heterogeneous-friendly aggregation for federated learning that combine Intra-layer synchronous aggregation and Cross-Layer asynchronous aggregation. In addition, we incorporate threshold homomorphic encryption into our framework to mitigate the risk of privacy leakage during the training process. It has been proven that PHFL can achieve a more stable convergence and while training efficiently.

Acknowledgments. This work is supported by the science and technology project of State Grid Corporation of China "Research on demand-side flexible resources characterization analysis and collaborative optimization techniques based on privacy computing." (Grand No. 5108-202218280A-2-43-XG).

References

1. McMahan, B., et al.: Communication-efficient learning of deep networks from decentralized data. In: Artificial Intelligence and Statistics. PMLR (2017)
2. Qiao, C., Brown, K.N., Zhang, F., Tian, Z.: Federated adaptive asynchronous clustering algorithm for wireless mesh networks IEEE Trans. Knowl. Data Eng.https://doi.org/10.1109/TKDE.2021.3119550
3. Yang, W., et al.: A practical cross device federated learning framework over 5G networks. IEEE Wirel. Commun. **20**(6), 128–134 (2022)
4. Li, T., et al.: Federated optimization in heterogeneous networks. Proc. Mach. Learn. Syst. **2**, 429–450 (2020)
5. Wang, J., et al.: Tackling the objective inconsistency problem in heterogeneous federated optimization. Adv. Neural. Inf. Process. Syst. **33**, 7611–7623 (2020)

6. Wang, N., et al.: A blockchain based privacy-preserving federated learning scheme for Internet of Vehicles. Digit. Commun. Netw. **99** (2022)
7. Abad, M.S.H., et al.: Hierarchical federated learning across heterogeneous cellular networks. In: ICASSP 2020–2020 IEEE International Conference on Acoustics, Speech and Signal Processing (ICASSP). IEEE (2020)
8. Gong, B., et al.: Adaptive clustered federated learning for heterogeneous data in edge computing. Mob. Netw. Appl. **27**(4), 1520–1530 (2022)
9. Wang, Z., et al.: Resource-efficient federated learning with hierarchical aggregation in edge computing. In: IEEE INFOCOM 2021-IEEE Conference on Computer Communications. IEEE (2021)
10. Tian, Z., Wang, Y., Sun, Y., Qiu, J.: Location privacy challenges in mobile edge computing: classification and exploration. IEEE Network **34**(2), 52–56 (2020)
11. Li, M., Sun, Y., Lu, H., Maharjan, S., Tian, Z.: Deep reinforcement learning for partially observable data poisoning attack in crowdsensing systems. IEEE Internet Things J. **7**(7), 6266–6278 (2020)
12. Wainakh, A., et al.: Enhancing privacy via hierarchical federated learning. In: 2020 IEEE European Symposium on Security and Privacy Workshops (EuroS&PW). IEEE (2020)
13. Shi, L., et al.: HFL-DP: hierarchical federated learning with differential privacy. In: 2021 IEEE Global Communications Conference (GLOBECOM). IEEE (2021)
14. Damgård, I., Jurik, M.: A generalisation, a simplification and some applications of paillier's probabilistic public-key system. In: Kim, K. (eds.) Public Key Cryptography, PKC 2001. Lecture Notes in Computer Science, vol. 1992, pp. 119–136. Springer, Berlin (2001). https://doi.org/10.1007/3-540-44586-2_9
15. Wang, S., et al.: Device sampling for heterogeneous federated learning: theory, algorithms, and implementation. In: IEEE INFOCOM 2021-IEEE Conference on Computer Communications. IEEE (2021)
16. McMahan, B., Moore, E., Ramage, D., Hampson, S., et al.: Communication-efficient learning of deep networks from decentralized data. arXiv:1602.05629 (2016)
17. Xie, C., Koyejo, S., Gupta, I.: Asynchronous federated optimization. arXiv:1903.03934 (2019)
18. Shalev-Shwart, S., Ben-David, S.: Understanding Machine Learning: From Theory to Algorithms. Cambridge Unix. Press, Cambridge (2015)
19. LeCun, Y., Bottou, L., Bengio, Y., Haffner, P.: Gradient-based learning applied to document recognition. Proc. IEEE **86**(11), 2278–2324 (1998)

Blockchain System Security

Securing Blockchain Using Propagation Chain Learning

Shifeng Jin[1], Yijun Zhai[2(✉)], Yuxuan Zhong[3], Jifu Cui[4], Lei Xu[5],
Hongxia Sun[6], and Yan Lei[1]

[1] School of Big Data and Software Engineering, Chongqing University,
Chongqing 400044, China
[2] College of Computer Science, Chongqing University, Chongqing 400044, China
yjzhai@stu.cqu.edu.cn
[3] School of Pre-school Education, Chongqing College of International Business
and Economics, Chongqing 401520, China
[4] Qingdao Penghai Software Co., Ltd., Qingdao 266000, China
[5] Haier Smart Home Co., Ltd., Qingdao 266000, China
[6] Qingdao Haidacheng Purchasing Service Co., Ltd., Qingdao 266000, China

Abstract. Smart contract vulnerabilities are the most common and
severe type of blockchain vulnerability, which may result in very serious
economic and property losses. Vulnerability detection and repair are necessary to ensure the security of the blockchain. Currently, the-state-of-art
smart contract vulnerability detection methods (e.g. Oyente and Securify) use heuristics based on human-designed algorithms, which have certain shortcomings in different application scenarios. Therefore, this paper
proposes a smart contract vulnerability detection method, i.e. CuVuD,
which uses Propagation Chain Learning to solve the current vulnerability detection problem. This method first parses the source code, then
obtains and trims the propagation chain of smart contracts, and finally
detects vulnerabilities in smart contracts. To verify the effectiveness of
CuVuD, this paper compares the CuVuD method with seven the-state-
of-art smart contract vulnerability detection methods on a large-scale
smart contract dataset based on the Solidity language. The experimental
results show that CuVuD's effectiveness in detecting smart contract vulnerabilities is significantly higher than seven the-state-of-art smart contract vulnerability detection methods, significantly improving the ability
to detect vulnerabilities.

Keywords: Blockchain · Smart Contract · Vulnerability Detection ·
Propagation Chain · Graph Learning

1 Introduction

Smart contracts are computer programs that automatically execute contract
terms based on blockchain technology, enabling decentralized transactions and
data management. The development of smart contracts can be traced back to

J. Chen et al. (Eds.): BlockSys 2023, CCIS 1896, pp. 107–118, 2024.
https://doi.org/10.1007/978-981-99-8101-4_8

1994 when Nick Szabo proposed the concept of "smart contracts" [23]. However, it was not until 2009, with the emergence of Bitcoin [21], that smart contracts began to receive widespread attention. In recent years, with the development and popularization of blockchain technology, smart contracts have further developed and been applied. For example, smart contracts on the Ethereum blockchain have supported the development of numerous decentralized applications (dApps) that can automatically execute specific operations [7]. Smart contracts have enormous potential in decentralized transactions and data management, but there are also some security issues. Typical loss events due to vulnerabilities include the 2017 Parity freeze event [2] that resulted in all funds in the smart contract library being frozen. Moreover, in 2018, malicious attackers exploited vulnerabilities in the BEC contract on the Meituan Chain to infinitely duplicate tokens, resulting in the BEC token's value evaporating to zero.

Blockchain vulnerabilities include smart contract vulnerabilities, 51% attacks, double-spending attacks, etc. [29]. Among them, smart contract vulnerabilities are the most common and severe type of blockchain vulnerability, which may result in very serious economic and property losses. According to statistics from Bcsec and Slowmist [3,4], economic losses caused by smart contract security vulnerabilities have exceeded billions of US dollars. As smart contracts are pieces of program code, it is inevitable for them to have code security issues during design and development. Additionally, smart contracts deployed on public chains are usually exposed to open network environments, which further makes them vulnerable to attacks. These statistics suggest that conducting vulnerability detection and security audits on smart contracts before deployment is crucial, as it can reduce security vulnerabilities in smart contracts and protect the security of digital assets. So far, researchers have developed many tools for detecting smart contract vulnerabilities, such as those based on program static analysis (e.g. SmarkCheck [25] and Slither [8]), formal methods (e.g. ZEUS [15] and Securify [27]), fuzz testing (e.g. ContractFuzzer [14]), and symbolic execution (e.g. Oyente [18], Osiris [26], Mythri [20] and Manticore [19]). However, these methods for detecting smart contract vulnerabilities have some shortcomings because these methods require manual summarization of vulnerability rules and patterns in advance, which cannot be applied to the explosively growing number of smart contracts today.

Currently, many scholars have joined the research in this field. Among them, SmartEmbed [10] uses a deep learning model to calculate the similarity with known vulnerabilities in smart contracts to detect whether there are vulnerabilities. Sgram [16] uses Oyente [18] for labeling and combines N-gram language modeling and lightweight static semantic labeling to predict vulnerabilities. Zhuang et al. [33] constructed a correlation graph to represent the syntactic and semantic features of smart contracts and used graph neural networks for learning and calculation. Huang et al. [13] based on a manually labeled dataset, first converted the smart contract bytecode into RGB colors, and then used a convolutional neural network to train and predict smart contract security vulnerabilities. Tann et al. [24] used MAIAN to label smart contract security issues and used LSTM to predict potential vulnerabilities.

In order to improve the vulnerability detection effect on this basis, this paper proposes CuVuD to solve the current vulnerability detection problem. The CuVuD method parses the source code into an abstract syntax tree [5] (AST) to determine the variable sequence, then generates a contract propagation chain and performs trimming, and finally detects vulnerabilities in smart contracts. This paper conducted a comparative experiment on vulnerability detection using the SmartBugs Wild Dataset [9], a large-scale smart contract dataset based on the Solidity language. The experimental results show that CuVuD's effectiveness in detecting smart contract vulnerabilities is significantly higher than seven the-state-of-art smart contract vulnerability detection methods, with an average relative improvement of 58%, 54%, and 65%.

The rest of this paper is organized as follows. Section 2 presents related works of this research. Section 3 illustrates the overview and details of our approach. Section 4 presents experimental results and case studies to evaluate the efficiency of the approach. Finally, we briefly make a conclusion of this paper in Sect. 5.

2   Related Work

In order to improve the security of smart contracts, many researchers have invested in the field of smart contracts [6]. As a result, a lot of smart contract vulnerability detection techniques have emerged, including program analysis-based technologies, symbolic execution-based technologies and machine learning-based technologies. Program analysis aims to obtain the characteristics and attributes of a program by automatically analyzing it. Representative smart contract vulnerability detection technologies based on program analysis include Smartcheck [25], SASC [32] and Slither [8]. Symbolic execution is a traditional automatic program vulnerability mining technology that is now widely used in smart contract vulnerability detection. This technology explores program branches by continuously solving constrained paths through abstracting the input of the program with symbolic values that are not fixed. Representative smart contract vulnerability detection technologies based on symbolic execution include Osiris [26] and Manticore [19].

However, the above-mentioned smart contract vulnerability detection methods are designed based on expert knowledge. With the explosive growth of the number of smart contracts, it is becoming increasingly difficult to summarize all the vulnerability patterns that exist in smart contracts. Therefore, in order to overcome this deficiency, researchers have placed their hopes on machine learning, attempting to automatically learn the characteristics of smart contract vulnerabilities by utilizing code big data methods, thereby assisting in vulnerability detection. Therefore, in the field of program defect detection, there are also many deep learning-based detection methods. CNN-FL [30] uses convolutional neural networks to learn from program dynamic execution coverage information to locate program defects. Zhang et al. [31] comprehensively use multiple deep neural networks to learn from program spectra to assist in detecting defects in real large-scale programs. DeepBugs [22] uses word2vec to represent source code and detect name-based program vulnerabilities. Although the focus is different, these deep learning-based program defect detection works can provide reference for smart contract vulnerability detection.

3   Methodology

The workflow of the CuVuD method in this paper has four stages: parsing the source code into an AST; obtaining the propagation chain of smart contracts; trimming the propagation chain; and detecting vulnerabilities in smart contracts. The following will introduce these four stages in detail through the example of a real smart contract vulnerability code to the vulnerability propagation chain in Fig. 1.

3.1   Parsing Source Code into an AST

Zhuang et al. [33] constructed smart contracts as contract graphs. However, the information structure in the graph is too complex and not conducive to the generalization of the model [12]. To overcome this shortcoming, this paper adopts a more concise method to represent graph information, thereby improving the generalization of the model.

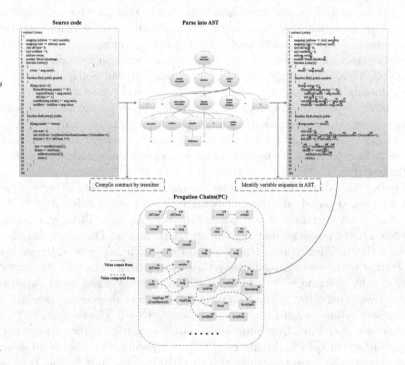

Fig. 1. The procedure of extracting propagation chains from given a source code

CuVuD uses treesitter to parse a source code represented as $C = \{C_1, C_2, \ldots, C_n\}$ into an abstract syntax tree [5] (AST). Due to the lack of support for the Solidity language in Tree-sitter, it has been improved based on JoranHonig's grammar rules [1] to enable parsing of the Solidity language. The AST contains the syntactic information of the source code, and its leaf nodes can be used to determine the variable sequence. The variable sequence can be represented as $V = \{v_1, v_2, \ldots, v_k\}$. For example, the owner variable in line 7 and line 11 of the Identify variable sequence in Fig. 1, although their variable names are the same, they have different variable numbers and therefore represent different variables.

3.2   Obtaining the Propagation Chain of Smart Contracts

A propagation chain refers to a sequence of code between two specified program code segments [11]. In this sequence, there is a direct or indirect data or control dependency relationship between any two adjacent code segments. For a given code segment a and code segment b, there may be multiple propagation chains between a and b, and their collection can be called the propagation chain set of a and b. Each code segment may be associated with several vulnerability propagation chains. In this paper, CuVuD uses data flow relationships to construct smart contract propagation chains. Data flow relationships are the same under different abstract syntaxes of the same function source code, making it easier for deep learning models to understand and learn.

Each variable in the variable sequence is a node in the propagation chain. The graph $CH(C) = (V, E)$ represents the propagation chain of source code C, where the nodes are V and the edges are $E = \{e_1, e_2, \ldots, e_1\}$. Suppose edge $e = \langle v_i, v_j \rangle$ indicates that v_j in the variable sequence comes from v_i or is calculated from v_i. In Fig. 1's Identify variable sequence, v_j coming from v_i is represented by a green solid line (Value comes from), and v_j calculated from v_i is represented by a red dashed line (Value computed from). For example, in the expression $owner^{32} = msg^{34} \cdot sender^{36}$ on line 11, $owner^{32}$, msg^{34}, and $sender^{36}$ are all added as nodes to the propagation chain, while $msg^{34} \rightarrow owner^{32}$ and $sender^{36} \rightarrow owner^{32}$ are added as value computed from type edges to the propagation chain.

3.3   Trimming the Propagation Chain

As shown in Fig. 2, the CuVuD model consists of six parts: the input layer, the connection layer, the multi-head attention layer, the Layer Normalization layer, several transformation layers, and the linear layer. The input layer of CuVuD includes six input units: the token set of the source code, the variable set, the position set of the source code tokens, the variable position set, the smart contract propagation chain, and key information. The first four input units represent the source code. The token set CT and variable set V of source code C are concatenated into a sequence I_1. The position set of source code tokens and variable position set are linked into another sequence I_2. I_1 and I_2 are transformed into an input vector X^0 as the representation vector of source code C. The fifth input

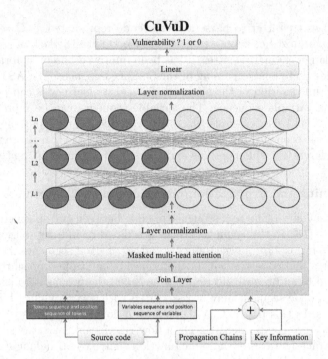

Fig. 2. Architecture of CuVuD

unit is the smart contract propagation chain, represented as $CH(C) = (V, E)$. The sixth input unit is a set of key information $V' = \{v'_1, v'_2, \ldots, v'_n\}$ obtained from source code C for vulnerabilities, where v'_i represents variables on the same line as key information for vulnerabilities (block.timestamp, block.number, now, etc.). The input layer refines the smart contract propagation chain according to the fifth and sixth input units. Specifically, in the propagation chain $CH(C)$, corresponding nodes are found according to $v'_i (i \in \{1, 2, \ldots, n\})$ in the key information set and edges not associated with v'_i are trimmed to obtain a new edge set E'. Then isolated nodes (nodes in $CH(C)$ that do not have edges in E' passing through them) are trimmed to obtain a refined vulnerability propagation chain $CH_1(C)$ related to vulnerabilities.

3.4   Detecting Vulnerabilities in Smart Contracts

As shown in Fig. 2, in the Join Layer, I_1, I_2 and $CH_1(c)$ are transformed into input vector X^0. The input vector X^0 will go through the Masked multi-head attention Layer, Layer Normalization layer, and several transformer layers (n=12) to generate a specific context representation. $X^n = transformer_n(X^{n-1})$, $n \in [1, 12]$. Where, as shown in formula (1), after each transformer layer's vector X^{n-1} goes through a multi-head attention operation, it will generate a vector H^n [28], and then output vector X^n according to the calculation of formula (2).

$$H^n = LN\left(\text{MHSA}\left(X^{n-1}\right) + X^{n-1}\right) \tag{1}$$

$$X^n = LN\left(FFN\left(H^n\right) + H^n\right) \tag{2}$$

In formula (1), $MHSA$ represents a multi-head self-attention operation, FFN is a two-layer forward network, and LN represents a Layer Normalization operation. For the nth transformer layer, the output is X^n, and the calculation process of $MHSA(X^{n-1})$ is shown in formulas (3), (4) and (5). In order to enable the transformer layer to learn the graph structure, a mask matrix M is used to implement graph-guided masked attention to establish the association relationship between tokens in smart contracts [12]. In formula (4), $M \in R^{|I| \times |I|}$ is a mask matrix. If the ith token and the jth token are related, then $M_{ij} = 0$, otherwise it is $-\infty$. The calculation of the mask matrix M is shown in formula (7). For the propagation chain set $CH_1(C)$, E_1 is the edge set, E_1' represents the set of relationships between tokens in smart contracts and variables in the propagation chain. $\langle v_i, ct_j \rangle \langle ct_j, v_i \rangle \in E_1'$ if and only if variable v_i is determined by ct_j in source code tokens and node v_i's query is related to c_j's node-key. If there is a directed edge between node v_i and node $v_j (\langle v_i, v_j \rangle \in E_1)$ or they are the same node $(i = j)$, then query q_{vj} and node-key k_{vi} are related. Otherwise, the attention value will be assigned $-\infty$, and after being calculated by $softmax$ in formula (4), it will be assigned 0. In formula (5), m is the number of heads in multi-head attention. d_k is the dimension of head. $W_n^O \in R^{d^h \times d^h}$ is a model parameter.

$$Q_i = X^{n-1}W_i^Q, K_i = X^{n-1}W_i^K, V_i = X^{n-1}W_i^v \tag{3}$$

$$\text{head}_i = \text{softmax}\left(\frac{Q_i K_i^{\mathrm{T}}}{\sqrt{d_k}} + M\right) V_i \tag{4}$$

$$X^n = [\text{head}_1; \dots, \text{head}_m] W_n^Q \tag{5}$$

After the nth transformer layer, a Layer Normalization layer is used for normalization, and then a Linear Layer and Sigmoid function are used to output the probability y of the contract containing vulnerabilities.

$$y = \text{Sigmoid}\left(X^n\right) \tag{6}$$

$$M_{ij} = \begin{cases} 0 \text{ if } : q_i \in \{[\text{CLS}], [\text{SEP}]\} \\ \quad \text{or} : q_i, k_j \in CT \\ \quad \text{or} :< q_i, k_j >\in E_1 \cup E_1' \\ -\infty \quad \text{otherwise} \end{cases} \tag{7}$$

The goal of the entire task is to find potential vulnerabilities in smart contracts by learning from the model. During the learning process, the CuVuD model takes a large number of smart contract source codes and their propagation chains, as well as their corresponding labels as input. When predicting smart contract vulnerabilities, the source code of smart contracts in the test set is used as test data. The source code and propagation chain are input into the trained model to finally obtain the predicted value of whether the smart contract contains vulnerabilities.

4 Experiment

4.1 Experiment Setup

Dataset. The experiment is based on the SmartBugs Wild Dataset [9]. The dataset contains 47,398 smart contracts extracted from the Ethereum network. It was analyzed using SmartBugs and each smart contract was labeled by professionals to indicate whether it contains vulnerabilities [17]. It has been made open-source online[1].

Comparison Method. This paper compares CuVuD with seven state-of-the-art smart contract vulnerability detection methods. These include 3 traditional expert knowledge-based smart contract vulnerability detection methods (Manticore [19], Osiris [26], Slither [8]) and 4 deep learning-based smart contract vulnerability detection methods (GCN [17], Vanilla-RNN [17], LSTM [17], GRU [17]).

Experimental Environment. The experimental environment is a computer containing an Intel I7-9700 CPU and 64 GB of physical memory, with a 12 GB NVIDIA TITAN X Pascal GPU. The operating system is Ubuntu 18.04 and data analysis is performed using MATLAB R2016b.

Parameter Settings. CuVuD uses the Adam optimizer and attempts to find the optimal hyperparameter settings: learning rate is 2e-5, training batch size is 2, validation batch size is 32, gradient accumulation step is 1, and Adam epsilon is 1e-8. For the division of the original dataset, the experiment randomly selects 20% as the training set, 10% as the validation set, and the remaining 70% as the test set according to reference [33].

4.2 Evaluation Metrics

This paper uses widely used evaluation metrics in the field of smart contract vulnerability detection, namely Precision, Recall and F1-score [25,33]. In order to reflect the overall performance of CuVuD, this paper chooses the macro method (i.e., calculating the indicators for vulnerable and non-vulnerable smart contracts separately and then averaging) to calculate the indicators. The calculation method is shown below:

$$Precision = \frac{TruePositive}{(TruePositive + FalsePositive)} \tag{8}$$

$$Recall = \frac{TruePositive}{(TruePositive + FalseNegative)} \tag{9}$$

$$F1 = \frac{Precision \times Recall}{2 \times (Precision + Recall)} \tag{10}$$

---

[1] https://github.com/zz8477/Scruple.

4.3   Experimental Results

The experiment compared CuVuD with seven state-of-the-art methods. Table 1 and Fig. 3 show the comparison results and distribution of their Recall, Precision and F1 values.

As can be seen from Table 1 and Fig. 3, the highest Recall of the first 3 traditional smart contract vulnerability detection methods (Manticore, Osiris, Slither) when detecting vulnerabilities is 0.78 for Slither, the lowest is 0.50 for Manticore, with an average of 0.60; the highest Precision is 0.82 for Slither, the lowest is 0.53 for Osiris, with an average of 0.64; the highest F1-score is 0.84 for Slither, the lowest is 0.50 for Manticore; with an average of 0.62. Compared with them, CuVuD's Recall has a maximum relative increase of 92%, a minimum relative increase of 23%, and an average relative increase of 60%; Precision has a maximum relative increase of 70%, a minimum relative increase of 10%, and an average relative increase of 41%; F1-score has a maximum relative increase of 86%, a minimum relative increase of 11%, and an average relative increase of 50%.

Table 1. Performance comparison of related methods in Recall, Precision and F1-score

Method	Vulnerability Detection		
	Recall	Precision	F1-score
Manticore	0.50	0.57	0.50
Osiris	0.51	0.53	0.52
Slither	0.78	0.82	0.84
GCN	0.76	0.68	0.72
Vanilla-RNN	0.45	0.52	0.46
LSTM	0.59	0.50	0.54
GRU	0.59	0.49	0.54
CuVuD	**0.96**	**0.90**	**0.93**

The last 4 deep learning-based smart contract vulnerability detection methods (GCN, Vanilla-RNN, LSTM, GRU) when detecting vulnerabilities have a highest Recall of 0.76 for GCN, a lowest of 0.45 for Vanilla-RNN, with an average of 0.60; the highest Precision is 0.68 for GCN, the lowest is 0.49 for GRU, with an average of 0.55; the highest F1-score is 0.72 for GCN, the lowest is 0.46 for Vanilla-RNN; with an average of 0.57. Compared with deep learning-based smart contract vulnerability detection methods, CuVuD's Recall has a maximum relative increase of 113%, a minimum relative increase of 26%, and an average relative increase of 60%; Precision has a maximum relative increase of 84%, a minimum relative increase of 32%, and an average relative increase of 64%; F1-score has a maximum relative increase of 102%, a minimum relative increase of 29%, and an average relative increase of 63%.

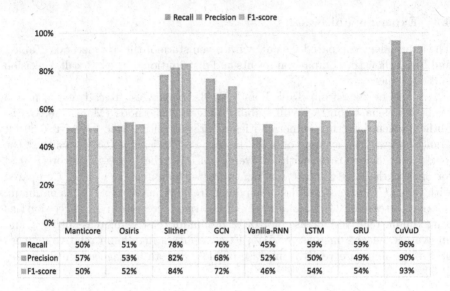

Fig. 3. Recall, Precision and F1-score promotion of CuVuD over 7 baselines

Overall, compared with 7 smart contract vulnerability detection methods, CuVuD's Recall has an average relative increase of 58%; Precision has an average relative increase of 54%; F1-score has an average relative increase of 65%. Therefore, the experiment concluded that CuVuD's effectiveness in detecting smart contract vulnerabilities is significantly higher than that of 7 the-state-of-art smart contract vulnerability detection methods, significantly improving the vulnerability detection results.

5   Conclusion

To overcome the shortcomings and improve the effectiveness of smart contract vulnerability detection, this paper proposes a smart contract vulnerability detection method called CuVuD based on propagation chain learning. This method can learn from the source code of smart contracts as features through program propagation chains. Experimental results show that the vulnerability detection effect of this method is significantly better than 7 the-state-of-art smart contract vulnerability detection methods, greatly improving the performance of vulnerability detection. However, attention should also be paid to the validity threats of the experiment. The main threats include the existence of more unknown factors in reality than in the experimental dataset of this paper and the potential errors that may be included when implementing different comparison methods and CuVuD. In future work, we plan to study the contribution of different modules of CuVuD to the model and optimize the CuVuD method.

Acknowledgments. This work is partially supported by the National Key Research and Development Project of China (No. 2020YFB1711900).

References

1. tree-sitter-solidity. https://github.com/joranhonig/tree-sitter-solidity
2. Parity multisig bug (2017). https://hackingdistributed.com/2017/07/22/deep-dive-parity-bug/
3. Bcsec (2018). https://bcsec.org/
4. Slowmist (2018). https://hacked.slowmist.io/
5. Lua, G.T., et al.: tree-sitter. https://tree-sitter.github.io/tree-sitter/
6. Atzei, N., Bartoletti, M., Cimoli, T.: A survey of attacks on Ethereum smart contracts (SoK). In: Maffei, M., Ryan, M. (eds.) POST 2017. LNCS, vol. 10204, pp. 164–186. Springer, Heidelberg (2017). https://doi.org/10.1007/978-3-662-54455-6_8
7. Buterin, V.: A next generation smart contract & decentralized application platform (2015)
8. Feist, J., Grieco, G., Groce, A.: Slither: a static analysis framework for smart contracts. In: 2019 IEEE/ACM 2nd International Workshop on Emerging Trends in Software Engineering for Blockchain (WETSEB), pp. 8–15 (2019)
9. Ferreira, J.F., Cruz, P., Durieux, T., Abreu, R.: Smartbugs: a framework to analyze solidity smart contracts. In: 2020 35th IEEE/ACM International Conference on Automated Software Engineering (ASE), pp. 1349–1352 (2020)
10. Gao, Z., Jayasundara, V., Jiang, L., Xia, X., Lo, D., Grundy, J.C.: Smartembed: a tool for clone and bug detection in smart contracts through structural code embedding. In: 2019 IEEE International Conference on Software Maintenance and Evolution (ICSME), pp. 394–397 (2019)
11. Guo, A., Mao, X., Yang, D., Wang, S.: An empirical study on the effect of dynamic slicing on automated program repair efficiency. In: 2018 IEEE International Conference on Software Maintenance and Evolution (ICSME), pp. 554–558. IEEE (2018)
12. Guo, D., et al.: Graphcodebert: pre-training code representations with data flow. ArXiv abs/2009.08366 (2020)
13. Huang, T.H.D.: Hunting the ethereum smart contract: color-inspired inspection of potential attacks. ArXiv abs/1807.01868 (2018)
14. Jiang, B., Liu, Y., Chan, W.K.: Contractfuzzer: fuzzing smart contracts for vulnerability detection. In: 2018 33rd IEEE/ACM International Conference on Automated Software Engineering (ASE), pp. 259–269 (2018)
15. Kalra, S., Goel, S., Dhawan, M., Sharma, S.: Zeus: analyzing safety of smart contracts. In: Network and Distributed System Security Symposium (2018)
16. Liu, H., Liu, C., Zhao, W., Jiang, Y., Sun, J.: S-gram: towards semantic-aware security auditing for Ethereum smart contracts. In: 2018 33rd IEEE/ACM International Conference on Automated Software Engineering (ASE), pp. 814–819 (2018)
17. Liu, Z., Qian, P., Wang, X., Zhuang, Y., Qiu, L., Wang, X.: Combining graph neural networks with expert knowledge for smart contract vulnerability detection. IEEE Trans. Knowl. Data Eng. **35**, 1296–1310 (2021)
18. Luu, L., Chu, D.H., Olickel, H., Saxena, P., Hobor, A.: Making smart contracts smarter. In: Proceedings of the 2016 ACM SIGSAC Conference on Computer and Communications Security (2016)

19. Mossberg, M., et al.: Manticore: a user-friendly symbolic execution framework for binaries and smart contracts. In: 2019 34th IEEE/ACM International Conference on Automated Software Engineering (ASE), pp. 1186–1189 (2019)
20. Mueller, B.: Mythril-reversing and bug hunting framework for the ethereum blockchain (2017)
21. Nakamoto, S.: Bitcoin: a peer-to-peer electronic cash system (2008)
22. Pradel, M., Sen, K.: Deepbugs: a learning approach to name-based bug detection. Proc. ACM Program. Lang. **2**, 1–25 (2018)
23. Szabo, N.: Smart contracts : building blocks for digital markets (2018)
24. Tann, W.J.W., Han, X.J., Gupta, S.S., Ong, Y.: Towards safer smart contracts: a sequence learning approach to detecting security threats. arXiv: CryptographyandSecurity (2018)
25. Tikhomirov, S., Voskresenskaya, E., Ivanitskiy, I., Takhaviev, R., Marchenko, E., Alexandrov, Y.: Smartcheck: static analysis of ethereum smart contracts. In: 2018 IEEE/ACM 1st International Workshop on Emerging Trends in Software Engineering for Blockchain (WETSEB), pp. 9–16 (2018)
26. Torres, C.F., Schütte, J., State, R.: Osiris: hunting for integer bugs in ethereum smart contracts. In: Proceedings of the 34th Annual Computer Security Applications Conference (2018)
27. Tsankov, P., Dan, A.M., Drachsler-Cohen, D., Gervais, A., Buenzli, F., Vechev, M.T.: Securify: practical security analysis of smart contracts. In: Proceedings of the 2018 ACM SIGSAC Conference on Computer and Communications Security (2018)
28. Vaswani, A., et al.: Attention is all you need. ArXiv abs/1706.03762 (2017)
29. Yang, X., Chen, Y., Chen, X.: Effective scheme against 51% attack on proof-of-work blockchain with history weighted information. In: 2019 IEEE International Conference on Blockchain (Blockchain), pp. 261–265 (2019)
30. Zhang, Z., Lei, Y., Mao, X., Li, P.: CNN-FL: an effective approach for localizing faults using convolutional neural networks. In: 2019 IEEE 26th International Conference on Software Analysis, Evolution and Reengineering (SANER), pp. 445–455 (2019)
31. Zhang, Z., Lei, Y., Mao, X., Yan, M., Xu, L., Zhang, X.: A study of effectiveness of deep learning in locating real faults. Inf. Softw. Technol. **131**, 106486 (2021)
32. Zhou, E., et al.: Security assurance for smart contract. In: 2018 9th IFIP International Conference on New Technologies, Mobility and Security (NTMS), pp. 1–5 (2018)
33. Zhuang, Y., Liu, Z., Qian, P., Liu, Q., Wang, X., He, Q.: Smart contract vulnerability detection using graph neural network. In: International Joint Conference on Artificial Intelligence (2020)

Privacy Protection Multi-copy Provable Data Possession Supporting Data Reliability

Feng Zhang[1,2,3], Bin Wen[1,2,3](✉), Yifei Yan[1,2,3], Zhaowu Zeng[1,2,3], and Wei Zhou[1,2,3]

[1] School of Information Science and Technology, Hainan Normal University, Haikou 571158, China
1171941649@qq.com, binwen@hainnu.edu.cn
[2] Cloud Computing and Big Data Research Center, Hainan Normal University, Haikou 571158, China
[3] Key Laboratory of Data Science and Smart Education, Ministry of Education, Hainan Normal University, Haikou 571158, China

Abstract. With the development of technology, a massive amount of data continues to emerge, and there is still a strong demand for data storage. Outsourcing data to cloud service providers has become a common practice. Although cloud storage offers the advantage of location-independent data access and reduces burdens such as hardware and software maintenance, this service still faces some challenges in terms of privacy and data reliability. To address this issue, we present Privacy-preserving Multi-copy Provable Data Possession supporting data Reliability (PMPDP-R). Our proposal ensures the integrity, reliability, and freshness of data by designing Timestamp-based Double-layer Merkle Hash Tree (TD-MHT), a novel dynamic structure for multicopy storage. Furthermore, our approach uses random masking techniques to develop unique replica blocks and safeguard privacy. We've also ensured data reliability by enabling PMPDP-R to locate damaged data blocks to aid recovery. The experimental analysis proves that our scheme is both practical and effective.

Keywords: Data integrity audit · Third party audit · Cloud storage · Privacy preserving · Trustworthy audit

1 Introduction

With the integration and innovation of technologies like 5G, AI, cloud computing, and the Internet of Things, the surge in demand for data storage has sparked a transformation. Since users have rather limited local storage and computing capabilities that cannot match their needs, more organizations or individuals are choosing to outsource their data to remote cloud service providers. However, since the user's data is stored on remote cloud servers, the cloud server is

© The Author(s), under exclusive license to Springer Nature Singapore Pte Ltd. 2024
J. Chen et al. (Eds.): BlockSys 2023, CCIS 1896, pp. 119–132, 2024.
https://doi.org/10.1007/978-981-99-8101-4_9

actually the one implementing operations on the data. Therefore, the security of user data and the trustworthiness of computation are entirely dependent on the reputation of the cloud service provider. Neverthelesss, Cloud service providers may cause data leaks or losses due to hardware failures, space saving measures, employee abuse, or hacker attacks. They may not necessarily disclose the information truthfully to the data owners. This poses a huge challenge to the security of user data.

Traditional techniques for ensuring data integrity, such as hash functions and digital signatures, are ineffective in the cloud due to the unavailability of local copies of data. Additionally, resource constraints for users make it practically unfeasible to download complete data for integrity verification. The situation is even worse for mobile users. As a result, due to the abundance of outsourced data and resource constraints, users may be unable to perform effective periodic integrity audits on their data and therefore rely on third-party auditing.

1.1   Related Work

To ensure data integrity in cloud systems, Ateniese et al. [1] proposed the first concept of the public provable data possession (PDP). To alleviate the burden of users, a trusted Third-party auditor (TPA) is assigned the responsibility of performing data integrity auditing. Unfortunately, the PDP model does not support dynamic data updates. Afterwards, Herway et al. [2] proposed the first PDP scheme to leverage RASL to fully support data dynamics, but their framework is only suitable for private auditing and not applicable for public auditing. Wang et al. [3] developed a way to support public audits and full dynamics through MHT. However, if the block index is not properly validated, malicious CSS is able to trick the cloud user by choosing another block and its valid proof. More importantly, insertion and deletion operations would alter the sequence numbers of all blocks located behind the operation, resulting in significant computational costs due to the recalculation of their tags.

As for protecting data privacy, Wang et al. [4] proposed the first scalable privacy-preserving public storage audit, but it is vulnerable to malicious CSS and external attackers. Yu et al. [5] enhances the privacy of integrity audit protocols by using zero-knowledge proof systems, but it introduces additional computing and communication costs. Zhou et al. [6] employed random masking techniques to produce unique replica blocks, but their scheme was unable to pinpoint exactly which replica had been compromised. Liu et al. [7] has designed a data integrity auditing scheme based on disinfectable digital signatures, which utilizes the properties of disinfectable digital signatures to conceal private information and protect user data privacy. However, this scheme introduces a new role called the sanitizer, which must be trusted. Liang et al. [8] proposed a privacy protection scheme based on consortium blockchain, in which the consortium chain improves data transmission efficiency and guarantees user privacy. Zhang et al. [9] proposed a privacy-preserving public auditing scheme based on distributed data storage blockchain to prevent malicious behavior from TPA. Nonetheless, both schemes lack support for batch auditing and data updating.

To improve data reliability, Curtmola et al. [10] proposed the first RSA signature-based multi-copy solution. As long as one copy of the original file remains intact, the corrupted data can be fully recovered. In addition, user data is encrypted before being uploaded to CSS to protect data privacy. However, it only applies to static files. To identify corrupted replicas, Barsoum et al. [11] developed a multi-copy solution that does not support update operations. In follow-up work, Barsoum et al. [12] proposed the first dynamic multicopy PDP based on improved MHT, called TB-PMDDP. Unfortunately, the proposed scheme is not resistant to substitution attacks, as neither the value of the block nor the location of the block is validated. To solve this problem, Liu et al. [13] designed a multi-copy public audit structure called MuR-DPA, which contains a dynamic structure of data based on MHT. Compared to previous work, MuR-DPA has less communication overhead to update verification under cloud storage. However, TPA requires verification of all replicas one by one, resulting in the computational cost of MuR-DPA increasing linearly and inefficient as the number of replicas increases.

1.2   Contributions

This section gives the contributions of the proposed scheme in the field of data integrity auditing protocols for cloud computing.:

1. TD-MHT not only guarantees the integrity and freshness of data but also identifies damaged data blocks. Moreover, the root hash signature of TD-MHT is generated using a secret timestamp, file name, and root hash, which ensures the correlation between the file and TD-MHT, as well as the freshness of the signature. This prevents the generation or replacement of the root hash signature, ensuring its authenticity.
2. Our scheme uses random masking techniques to generate replica blocks of blocks, guaranteeing data privacy so that only those with secret parameters can access the data. In addition, to ensure data availability, our solution also supports data recovery, which when a data block is corrupted, it can find the damaged data block and restore it through a full redundant copy.
3. Our formal security analysis indicates that PMPDP-D is provably secure in random oracle mode. In addition, experimental evaluation shows that proof generation and verification phase in our protocol do not increase with the number of replicas.
4. The protocol is effectively designed to support public auditing of data and data dynamics.

1.3   Paper Organization

The rest of paper is organized as follows. Section 2 presents the system model and the threats model. Section 3 gives details of the proposed scheme and Sect. 4 indicates support for data dynamics and data reliability. Section 5 gives a detailed security analysis of the PMPDP-R scheme. Section 6 evaluates the performance of the PMPDP-R scheme. Conclusions is drawn in Sect. 7.

2   System and Threat Model

2.1   System Model

The system model of proposed data integrity auditing protocol is illustrated in Fig. 1. This auditing model possess three entities defined as follows:

1. Data owner (DP): An individual, company, or business organization that has a large number of data files, but is an entity with limited resources.
2. Cloud Service Provider (CSP): An entity that has sufficient computing power resources and unlimited storage space. The CSP is responsible for keeping outsourced data. CSPs are considered untrusted entities.
3. Third-Party Auditor (TPA): An entity that performs an integrity audit of DP data. TPAs are trustworthy but curious entities. TPA can reduce the computational pressure of data audit on DP.

Fig. 1. system modele

2.2   Threat Model

As mentioned earlier, TPAs are trusted but curious entities, while CSPs are untrusted entities. However, both TPA and CSP pose some threats to DP's data [14] as follows:

1. Threats posed by TPA: DP relies on TPA for data integrity. However, there is always the possibility that TPA is curious about DP's data. Therefore, in public audit agreements, TPAs may compromise the privacy of data. Therefore, in addition to data integrity protection, privacy maintenance is also required to prevent TPA from obtaining any information from DP's data.
2. Threats posed by CSP: Some of the threats posed by CSP to DP data are as follows:
   (a) CSP may intentionally delete rarely accessed data to save server space without notifying the DP.
   (b) CSP may cause some data processing errors, which may permanently corrupt DP's data.

2.3   Scheme Outline

Our PMPDP-R scheme consists of seven algorithms: *keyGen,copyGen, sigGen, authGen, chalGen, proofGen, verifyProof*. In particular, these seven algorithms are described detailedly as below.

1. $keyGen(1^\lambda)$: This algorithm is executed by DP. Here λ denotes a security parameter, and the output is a key pair $(pubkey, seckey) \leftarrow (\eta, \kappa)$.
2. $copyGen(F, \kappa)$: The algorithm is run by DP to create m differentiable replicas. On inputting the data file F and the key κ, all data blocks with m different replicas F_i are created.
3. $sigGen(D, \kappa, m, n, fname, u)$: This algorithm is run by the DP and generates signatures for the file and each block of data. On Inputting the data replicas $D = \{F_i\}_{1 \le i \le m}$ and key κ, the signature set of the data block is represented as $\theta = \{\psi_{ij}\}_{1 \le i \le m, 1 \le j \le n}$. Additionally, this file signature is represented as sig_F.
4. $authGen(id, fname, \kappa)$: This algorithm is run by the DP to create authorization information for the TPA. On inputting the TPA's identity id and DO's private key κ, and calculate the authorization signature sig_{auth} to prevent the illegal TPA from conducting integrity audits.
5. $chalGen(sig_{auth}, k, \eta)$: The algorithm is executed by TPA to generate a random challenge C for CSPs after DP authorization audits. On inputting the authorization information $auth$, the number of challenged blocks k, and the public key eta to generate a challenge message C.
6. $proofGen(C, auth, D, \theta, \eta)$: The algorithm is executed by the CSP to generate a validation proof P_f. On inputting data replicas D, signature set θ, and challenge message C are entered, the CSP generates proof P_f for verification.
7. $verifyProof(C, P_f, h, \eta)$: The algorithm is run by the TPA to verify the receiving proof. On inputting the challenge message C, proof P_f, and public key eta. If validation is successful, the algorithm outputs "TRUE", otherwise it outputs "FALSE".

3   The Proposed Scheme

3.1   Notations

We present some notations used in this paper in Table 1

3.2   Preliminaries

Bilinear Pairings. Consider three multiplicative cyclic groups G_1, G_2 and G_T of order p, where p is prime. A pairing is a map defined as $e : G_1 \times G_1 \to G_T$ satisfying the properties as follows:

1. Bilinear: $\forall P \in G_1, \forall Q \in G_2, \forall a, b \in Z_p$, a map 'e' is said to be bilinear if $e(P^a, Q^b) = e(P, Q)^{ab}$
2. Non-degenerate: $\forall P, Q \in G_1, e(P, Q) \ne 1$
3. Computable: There is an effective algorithm that can calculate $e(P, Q)$, where $\forall P \in G_1, \forall Q \in G_2$

Table 1. Notations and descriptions

Notations	Descriptions
$H(\cdot)$	$\{0,1\}^* \to G_1$ defining a cryptographic hash function
$H_1(\cdot)$	$G_1 \to Z_q$ mapping group element of G_1 uniformly to Z_q
$H_2(\cdot)$	$\{0,1\}^* \to Z_q$ mapping arbitrary length string uniformly to Z_q
$fname$	The file name
m	The replica number
n	The block number of a replica
s_t	The date and time of tree creation or modification
F_i	The ith replica
d_{ij}	The jth block in ith replica
ψ_{ij}	A signature of the jth block in ith replica
D	The replicas set
θ	The signature set
R	The root of the master tree
r_j	The root of the subtree of replicas produced by the jth data block
k	Number of challenged blocks
C	Challenge message sent by TPA
$auth$	The authorization information of a valid TPA
a_t	The authorization deadline
P_f	Proof of data possession
sig_R	The signature of the master root
sig_F	The signature of the file F
sig_{auth}	The signature of the authorization information $auth$

TD-MHT. To maintain consistency and freshness among multiple replicas, while providing block index verification, we designed TD-MHT based on the classic Merkle tree. Each node P in TD-MHT contains three pieces of information: hash value, relative index, and position information. The relative index indicates the number of leaf nodes in P's subtree. If P is a leaf node, its relative index is 1. The position information indicates whether P is the left child (0) or right child (1) of its parent node. TD-MHT consists of two layers, with the bottom layer containing multiple Merkle trees. The hash value of each leaf node in a Merkle tree is composed of different replica blocks derived from the same data block, as well as a timestamp. For example, in Fig. 2, data block $d[1]$ corresponds to two replica blocks, d_{11} and d_{21}, which are concatenated with the timestamp st_1 to calculate their hash values $h_1 = H(d_{11}\|st_1)$ and $h_2 = H(d_{21}\|st_1)$ using a digest algorithm. The upper layer has only one Merkle tree, whose leaf nodes are the hash values of the root nodes of the bottom layer Merkle trees. Additionally, TD-MHT's root node is associated with the date and time of tree creation to ensure the freshness of the data. Most importantly, TD-MHT supports dynamic operations for multi-replica blocks at the block level and can locate erroneous replica blocks.

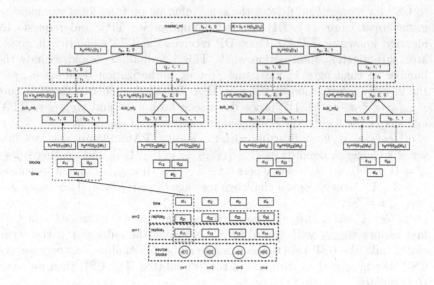

Fig. 2. Timestamp-based Double-layer Merkle Hash Tree(TD-MHT)

3.3   The Concrete PMPDP-R Scheme

Consider the file 'F' is split into 'n' data blocks $(d_1, d_2, ..., d_n)$. Let G_1, G_2, and G_T be three multiplicative groups of the same order q, where q is some large prime. Let $e : G_1 \times G_2 \rightarrow G_T$, where g selected as a generator of G_2. The proposed scheme is described in detail as follows:

1. $keyGen(1^\lambda)$: The algorithm first chooses a random element $\kappa \in Z_p$ as a secret key and produces $\eta = g^\kappa$ as the public key.
2. $copyGen(F, \kappa)$: DP generates a random value $\lambda \in Z_p$ and a random element $u \in G_2$. it then computes $w = u^\kappa$ and creates m different replicas $D = \{F_i\}_{1 \leq i \leq m}$, where $F_i = \{d_{ij}\}_{1 \leq j \leq n}$ and $d_{ij} = d_j + H_1(w^\lambda) + \lambda H_2(i) \in Z_q$.
3. $sigGen(D, \kappa, m, n, fname, u)$:DP generates the system date and time, denoted as s_t, and generates the BLS signature of block d_{ij} for each file F_i as $\psi_{ij} = (H(d_{ij}||s_t) \cdot u^{d_{ij}})^\kappa$. The set of signatures is represented as $\theta = \{\psi_{ij}\}_{1 \leq i \leq m, 1 \leq j \leq n}$. DP then generates n subtrees using $H(d_{ij}||s_t)_{\{1 \leq i \leq m\}}$ as the leaf, to get the root nodes of the subtrees $\{r_j\}_{\{1 \leq j \leq n\}}$. DP uses $\{r_j\}_{\{1 \leq j \leq n\}}$ as the leaves to generate a main root node R. DP computes $H_R = H(R||fname||s_t)$ and obtains the signature of the root, denoted as $sig_R = Sig_\kappa(H_R)$. After generating the root signature sig_R, DP also needs

to generate the file F signature. DP concatenates $fname, n, m, u,$ and s_t to form the string $h = (fname||n||m||u||s_t)$, and obtains the file signature $sig_F = Sig_\kappa(h)$. DP stores the concatenated string 'h' locally for future verification of the file signature. DP sends the information $\{D, \theta, sig_R, sig_F\}$ to CSP for storage and deletes the same information from local storage.

4. $authGen(id, fname, \kappa)$: DP selects an appropriate TPA and requests its identity, known as TPA_{id}. Once DP receives the TPA's identity, it generates authorization information $auth$. This information should include the number of challenges k, file name $fname$, authorization deadline a_t, and the identity information of DP and TPA. DP then calculates the signature $sig_{auth} = Sig_\kappa(auth)$. DP proceeds to send both $auth$ and sig_{auth} to TPA, and shares the file details h using secure and trusted channels.

5. $chalGen(sig_{auth}, k, \eta)$: Starting with the audit, TPA randomly selects a subset of k elements, denoted as $P = \{v_1, v_2, ..., v_k\} \subset [1, n]$, and another subset $Q = \{c_j\} \subset [1, m]$ is chosen where $\forall j \in P$, TPA chooses a random k-element $b_j \in Z_p$. TPA then sends a challenge message $C \leftarrow \{(j, b_j, c_j)\}_{j \in P}$, $auth$ and sig_{auth} to CSP.

6. $proofGen(C, auth, D, \theta, \eta)$: Upon receiving the challenge message C, the CSP first verifies sig_{auth} with $(auth, TPA_{id}, a_t)$ using the pubkey η. If the verification fails, the CSP rejects the message and emits "failure". Otherwise, the CSP searches for the c_jth node in the jth subtree. The CSP then proceeds to calculate:

$$\psi \leftarrow \prod_{j=v_1}^{v_k} \psi_{c_j j}^{b_j} \in G \tag{1}$$

$$\mu \leftarrow \sum_{j=v_1}^{v_k} b_j d_{c_j j} \in Z_p \tag{2}$$

After computing ψ and μ, CSP will respond to TPA by providing the proof of possession: $P_f = \{\psi, \mu, (d_{c_j j}, AI_{sub_j}(c_j), AI_{master}(j))_{j \in P}, sig_R, sig_F\}$ Here $AI_{sub_j}(c_j)$ refers to the auxiliary information of the c_jth element in the jth subtree, which contains information about siblings of the c_jth element on the path from the root node r_j to $H(d_{c_j j})$. Similarly, $AI_{master}(j)$ refers to the auxiliary information of the jth element in the master tree, which contains information about siblings of jth on the path from the root node R to $H(r_j)$. For example, if $j = 2$ and $c_j = 1$, then $AI_{sub_2}(1) = \{(h_4, 1, 1)\}$ and $AI_{master}(2) = \{(r_1, 1, 0), (h_y, 2, 1)\}$ (as shown in Fig. 2)

7. $verifyProof(C, P_f, h, \eta)$: The input to this algorithm comprises of the challenge message C, the proof P_f and the public key η, If the verification is successful, the algorithm outputs "TRUE", otherwise it outputs "FALSE". Before the actual verification process begins, TPA verifies the file signature sig_F as follows:

   (a) Prepare the file signature hash h from DP and the file signature sig_F from CSP.
   (b) Verify $e(h, \eta) \stackrel{?}{=} e(sig_F, g)$

(c) Outputs "TRUE" if validation is successful and restores u and s_t. Otherwise send a "failure" message to DP

After that, TPA verifies the MHT root. TPA begins the process by utilizing $(H(d_{c_jj}\|s_t), AI_{sub_j}(c_j))$ to generate the root of each subtree r_j. Next, TPA uses $(r_j, AI_{master}(j))$ to generate a root of the master tree R, TPA concatenates $fname$ and s_t fields with H_r and denotes it as H_R. Finally, TPA verifies the root using the following equation:

$$e\left(H_R, \eta\right) \overset{?}{=} e(sig_R, g) \tag{3}$$

If sig_R is incorrect, the above verification will fail. On verification failure, TPA stops the audit process and reports authentication failure to DP. On successful authentication verification, the TPA continues the audit process and verifies the following equation:

$$e\left(\prod_{j=v_1}^{v_k} H(d_{c_jj}\|s_t)^{b_j} \cdot u^\mu, \eta\right) \overset{?}{=} e(\psi, g) \tag{4}$$

Therefore, it is apparent that the proposed agreement is precise only if the CSP provides an honest response to P_f. However, if any file block has been removed or if any modifications to the file block were incomplete, the aforementioned verification formula will not apply.

4 Supporting Data Reliability

4.1 Data Dynamic Procedures

Enabling data dynamics is a crucial aspect of data integrity auditing protocols, which many existing protocols do not possess. In this section, we describe how PMPDP-R supports dynamic data processes, including data modification. In the following explanation, we assume that the server has already stored the data file F, the file block signature set ϕ and the root sig_R.

Modification. For the file $F = \{d_j\}_{1 \leq j \leq n}$, we modify d_j to d'_j at system time s_{t_j}'. The DP performs the following operations.

1. DP first generates m differential blocks $d_{ij}' = d'_j + H_1\left(w^\lambda\right) + \lambda H_2(i)_{1 \leq i \leq m}$, and corresponding signatures $\psi_{ij}' = \left(H(d_{ij}'\|s_{t_j}') \cdot u^{d_{ij}'}\right)^\kappa_{1 \leq i \leq m}$. It then generates the jth new subtree and sends a request $\{M, j, s_{t_j}', \{d_{ij}', \psi_{ij}'\}_{1 \leq i \leq m}\}$ to CSP. Here, M specifies "modification".
2. CSP performs the following actions:Replaces d_{ij} with d_{ij}', replaces ψ_{ij} with ψ_{ij}', replaces $H(d_{ij})$ with $H(d_{ij}')$, generates the jth new subtree, and generates a new root hash R' of the master tree. The CSP replies to DP with $P_f = \{r_j, AI_{master}(j)), R, sig_R\}$.

3. After DP receives P_f, it uses $\{P_f, fname, s_t\}$ to authenticate the root's signature by Eq. 3. Upon successful authentication, DP uses $\{r_j', AI_{master}(j)\}$ to calculate a new root R' and generates $sig_R' = H(R'||fname||s_{t_j}')^\kappa$. DP then produces a new file signature $sig_F' = Sig_\kappa(fname||n||m||u||s_{t_j}')$. The new signature associates the date and time of modification to ensure data freshness. DP sends $\{sig_F', sig_R'\}$ to CSP. Finally, DP runs the default integrity auditing protocol for new blocks. If result is TRUE, DP can delete $\{d_{ij}', sig_F', sig_R'\}$ from its local system.

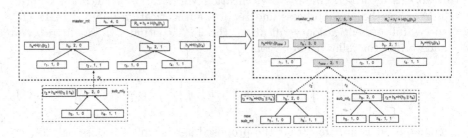

Fig. 3. Insert the new data block d_2'.

Insertion. Assume DP wants to insert a new data block d_j' at system time s_{t_j}', it must perform the following steps:

1. First, DP produces m copy blocks as $d_{ij} = d_j' + H_1\left(w^\lambda\right) + \lambda H_2(i)_{1 \leq i \leq m}$ along with its corresponding signature $\psi_{ij}' = \left(H(d_{ij}'||s_{t_j}') \cdot u^{d_{ij}}\right)^\kappa_{1 \leq i \leq m}$. DP then generates the new subtree of the new block to obtain the new root r_j' and sends a request $\{I, j, s_{t_j}', \{d_{ij}', \psi_{ij}'\}_{1 \leq i \leq m}\}$ to CSP. Here I specifies "insertion".
2. next, CSP generates the new subtree of the new block to obtain the new root r_j'This new root, combined with the root r_j from the original jth position, becomes a pair of sibling leaf nodes. Then, the CSP generates a new root hash R' for the master tree as shown in Fig. 3. Finally, the CSP sends a reply $P_f = \{r_j, AI_{master}(j)), R, sig_R\}$ to DP.
3. After DP receives P_f, it uses $\{P_f, fname, s_t\}$ to authenticate the root's signature by using Eq. 3. If the authentication is successful, DP calculates a new root R' using $\{r_j, r_j', AI_{master}(j))\}$ and generates $sig_R' = H(R'||fname||s_{t_j}')^\kappa$. DP then produces a new file signature $sig_F' = Sig_\kappa(fname||n||m||u||s_{t_j}')$ which associates the modification date and time to ensure the freshness of data. DP then sends $\{sig_F', sig_R'\}$ to CSP. Finally, DP runs the default integrity auditing protocol for new blocks. If result is TRUE, DP can delete $\{d_{ij}', sig_F', sig_R'\}$ from its local system.

Deletion. For the file $F = \{d_j\}_{1 \leq j \leq n}$, we want to remove d_j at system time s_{t_j}'. The DP performs the following operations. Initially, the first few steps of deletion are similar to those of insertion. The structure of a deletion message is (D, j, s_{t_j}'), where D specifies "deletion". The jth subtree is then removed from the master tree, and the relative index value and hash value of the parent node are updated accordingly. The remaining steps of the deletion process are similar to those of insertion and are therefore omitted here.

4.2 Data Recoverability

Assuming that DP is implementing the integrity auditing protocol and finds corrupted data blocks, resulting in $P_f = \{\psi, \mu, d_{ij}, AI_{sub_j}(i), AI_{master}(j),$ $sig_R, sig_F\}$, these corrupted blocks can be recovered through redundant replicas. Let d_{ij} is corrupted, but $d_{(i+1)j}$ is intact, the following steps can be taken to recover:

1. DP requests $d_{(i+1)j}$;
2. Compute $part = \lambda(H_2(i) - H_2(i+1))$;
3. Recovery $d_{ij}^* = d_{(i+1)j} + part$ and send d_{ij}^* to CSP;
4. DP implements the integrity auditing protocol again.

5 Security Analysis

Theorem 1. (Correctness of PMPDP-R). In the PMPDP-R scheme, provided that the DP, authorized TPA, and CSP behave honestly throughout the integrity audit process, the TPA can verify the integrity of the data that has been uploaded. Proof: To demonstrate the correctness of our PMPDP-R scheme, it is necessary to prove that Eq. 4 holds. Let us now consider the left-hand side of Eq. 4.

$$e\left(\prod_{j=v_1}^{v_k} H(d_{c_jj}\|s_t)^{b_j} \cdot u^{\mu}, \eta\right)$$

$$= e\left(\prod_{j=v_1}^{v_k} H(d_{c_jj}\|s_t)^{b_i} \cdot u^{b_i d_{c_jj}}, g^{\kappa}\right)$$

$$= e\left(\prod_{j=v_1}^{v_k} \left(H(d_{c_jj}\|s_t) \cdot u^{d_{c_jj}}\right)^{b_i}, g^{\kappa}\right) \tag{5}$$

$$= e\left(\prod_{j=v_1}^{v_k} \left(H(d_{c_jj}\|s_t) \cdot u^{d_{c_jj}}\right)^{b_i\kappa}, g\right)$$

$$= e\left(\prod_{j=v_1}^{v_k} \left(\left(H(d_{c_jj}\|s_t) \cdot u^{d_{c_jj}}\right)^{\kappa}\right)^{b_i}, g\right) = e\left(\prod_{j=v_1}^{v_k} \psi_i^{b_i}, g\right)$$

$$= e(\psi, g) = R.H.S$$

Thus, the proposed PMPDP-R can ensure the correctness for public verifiability.

Theorem 2. (Privacy preserving). In the PMPDP-R scheme, unauthorized entities are unable to access any data content of the DP from the information collected during the auditing process.

Case 1: A CSP may try to obtain the data content d_j from the uploaded information d_{ij}. But during CopyGen phase, $d_{ij} = d_j + H_1 \left(w^\lambda\right) + \lambda H_2(i) \in Z_q$, where $w = u^\kappa$ and $\lambda \in Z_q$ is chosen randomly by the DP and remains unknown to the CSP. Thus, the CSP cannot access the second component $H_1(w^\lambda)$ or $\lambda H_2(i) \in Z_q$,and therefore cannot obtain the content d_j.

Case 2: A authorized TPA could be an unauthorized party with the purpose to drive the data content from the retrievable information $\{\psi, \mu\}$.

Firstly, it is impossible to deduce information about d_j from μ. Even though the TPA can easily obtain d_{ij} by solving a group of linear equations using enough Eq. 2 during auditing, it cannot derive the content of the data from it. The proof process remains the same as in Case 1. Secondly, there is no way to gain knowledge about d_j from ψ concerning the Eq. 1 assumed by CDH. Finally, even with access to both $\{\psi, \mu\}$, TPA still cannot infer the d_j.

6   Performance Analysis

We carry out our experiments using the Pairing Based Cryptography (PBC) library version 0.5.14 for "Type A" pairing and cryptographic library OpenSSL version 3.0.2 for implementing hash operations (SHA256) to simulate all cryptographic operations. The user, CSP, and TPA roles were all run on the same PC, using the Ubuntu 22.04.2 LTS operating system, an Intel(R) Core(TM) CPU i7-7700HQ with a clock speed of 2.80 GHz, and 16GB of RAM.

To ensure a detection probability of corrupted data greater than 0.99 [1], we set n = 5000 and k = 460 for each challenge in our experiments. We did not consider the system's preprocessing time for preparing various file replicas and generating signature sets in the experiments, as this preprocessing is only done once during the system's lifetime. Additionally, most of the computational overhead in PDP schemes is concentrated in the proof generation and verification phases, which involve expensive operations such as power exponential operations, multiplication, and hashing operations. The results presented in this study are an average of 10 trials. The block sizes used in the experimental demonstration range from 1 KB to 210 KB. Figure 4 illustrates the change in computational cost for different block sizes as the number of copies m increases. According to the 3-2-1 backup rule for data backup, we set the parameter m to 3. Figure 5 illustrates the change in computational cost for integrity audits as the number of challenged blocks increases. Our results indicate that in our scheme, the computational cost increases with the number of challenged blocks rather than the block size.

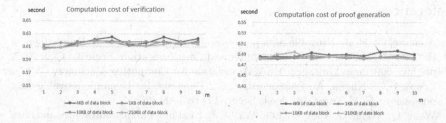

(a) Computational cost for proof generation with varying m.

(b) Computational cost for verification with varying m.

Fig. 4. Computational costs for different block sizes with varying m

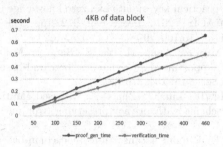

Fig. 5. Computation cost for ver Number of challenged blocks.

7 Conclusions

This paper proposes a cloud data integrity auditing protocol, PMPDP-R, based on an improved MHT structure. The unique feature of this protocol is its ability to locate and recover a damaged data block through a full redundant copy. Our construct associates timestamp fields with blocks of data, ensuring that the data is an up-to-date copy. Moreover, the root hash is combined with the timestamp field and file name, guaranteeing freshness and correspondence between the file and root hash, which is lacking in most existing schemes. PMPDP-R effectively ensures data privacy protection, data public auditing, data dynamic processing, data freshness, and data reliability. Furthermore, our formal security analysis showed that PDP-D is provably secure. The results of experiments demonstrates that PMPDP-R is a reliable auditing scheme.

Acknowledgment. This research has been supported by Hainan Provincial Natural Science Foundation of China (No.623RC485; No.620RC605) and Postgraduates' Innovative Research Projects of Hainan Province (No.Qhys2022-266).

References

1. Ateniese, G., et al.: Provable data possession at untrusted stores. In Proceedings of the 14th ACM Conference on Computer and Communications Security, CCS 2007, pp. 598–609, New York, NY, USA, Association for Computing Machinery (2007)
2. Erway, C.C., Küpçü, A., Papamanthou, C., Tamassia, R.: Dynamic provable data possession. ACM Trans. Inf. Syst. Secur. **17**(4), 1–29 (2015)
3. Wang, Q., Wang, C., Ren, K., Lou, W., Li, J.: Enabling public auditability and data dynamics for storage security in cloud computing. IEEE Trans. Parallel Distrib. Syst. **22**(5), 847–859 (2011)
4. Wang, B., Li, B., Li, H.: Oruta: privacy-preserving public auditing for shared data in the cloud. IEEE Trans. Cloud Comput. **2**(1), 43–56 (2014)
5. Yu, Y., Li, Y., Au, M.H., Susilo, W., Choo, K.-K.R., Zhang, X.: Public cloud data auditing with practical key update and zero knowledge privacy. In: Liu, J.K., Steinfeld, R. (eds.) ACISP 2016. LNCS, vol. 9722, pp. 389–405. Springer, Cham (2016). https://doi.org/10.1007/978-3-319-40253-6_24
6. Zhou, L., Fu, A., Mu, Y., Wang, H., Yu, S., Sun, Y.: Multicopy provable data possession scheme supporting data dynamics for cloud-based electronic medical record system. Inf. Sci. **545**, 254–276 (2021)
7. Liu, Z., Ren, L., Li, R., Liu, Q., Zhao, Y.: Id-based sanitizable signature data integrity auditing scheme with privacy-preserving. Comput. Secur. **121**, 102858 (2022)
8. Liang, W., et al.: PDPchain: a consortium blockchain-based privacy protection scheme for personal data. IEEE Trans. Reliab. 1–13 (2022)
9. Zhang, X., Zhao, J., Xu, C., Li, H., Wang, H., Zhang, Y.: CIPPPA: conditional identity privacy-preserving public auditing for cloud-based WBANs against malicious auditors. IEEE Trans Cloud Comput **9**(4), 1362–1375 (2021)
10. Curtmola, R., Khan, O., Burns, R., Ateniese, G.: MR-PDP: multiple-replica provable data possession. In: 2008 The 28th International Conference on Distributed Computing Systems, pp. 411–420 (2008)
11. Barsoum, A,F., Hasan, M.A.: Integrity verification of multiple data copies over untrusted cloud servers. In: 2012 12th IEEE/ACM International Symposium on Cluster, Cloud and Grid Computing (CCGRID 2012), pp. 829–834 (2012)
12. Barsoum, A.F., Hasan, M.A.: Provable multicopy dynamic data possession in cloud computing systems. IEEE Trans. Inf. Forensics Secur. **10**(3), 485–497 (2015)
13. Liu, C., Ranjan, R., Yang, C., Zhang, X., Wang, L., Chen, J.: MUR-DPA: top-down levelled multi-replica Merkle hash tree based secure public auditing for dynamic big data storage on cloud. IEEE Trans. Comput. **64**(9), 2609–2622 (2015)
14. Garg, N.: Bawa, Seema: Comparative analysis of cloud data integrity auditing protocols. J. Netw. Comput. Appl. **66**, 17–32 (2016)

Research on Comprehensive Blockchain Regulation and Anti-fraud System

Shaoxuan Zhuo[1], Weigang Wu[1], Yongzhang Zhou[4,5], Rong Cao[1], and Jing Bian[1,2,3(✉)]

[1] School of Data and Computer Science, Sun Yat-sen University, Guangzhou 510006, China
{zhuoshx3,caor37}@mail2.sysu.edu.cn, {wuweig,mcsbj}@mail.sysu.edu.cn
[2] Guangdong Province Key Laboratory of Computational Science, Sun Yat-sen University, Guangzhou 510006, China
[3] Science and Technology on Parallel and Distributed Processing Laboratory (PDL), Guangzhou 510006, China
[4] School of Earth Science and Engineering, Sun Yat-sen University, Zhuhai 519082, China
zhouyz@mail.sysu.edu.cn
[5] Guangdong Provincial Key Laboratory of Geological Processes and Mineral Resources Exploration, Zhuhai 519082, China

Abstract. The blockchain technology has attracted attention due to its characteristics of anonymity, openness, decentralization, traceability, and tamper-resistance. However, with the development of the blockchain industry, various financial fraud activities have also emerged on the blockchain. Effective regulation is a necessary condition for the healthy development of the blockchain ecosystem. A comprehensive blockchain anti-fraud prototype system is a system that combines multiple technologies to achieve fraud detection and anti-fraud techniques, aimed at addressing the existing fraud issues in the blockchain field. In this paper, we design and implement an anti-fraud system prototype based on a graph database platform and neural network model. The prototype system has the characteristics of fast, accurate, and reliable, and can effectively combat blockchain fraud activities by identifying blockchain transaction patterns and detecting illegal transaction behavior using new heuristic learning methods and graph neural network methods to detect frequent frauds. The system monitors and detects fraudulent activities such as phishing, ICO, price manipulation, money laundering, and illegal fundraising. The research results of this paper can provide an effective solution for anti-fraud work in the blockchain field and provide technical support for future wider applications.

Keywords: Blockchain · Transaction Supervision · Transaction Anti-fraud · Blockchain Regulatory Platform · Machine Learning

J. Chen et al. (Eds.): BlockSys 2023, CCIS 1896, pp. 133–146, 2024.
https://doi.org/10.1007/978-981-99-8101-4_10

1   Introduction

The current blockchain technology has attracted wide attention and is regarded as one of the important foundational information technologies that can trigger a new round of technological revolution and industrial transformation [9]. Blockchain has also become a crucial strategic technology for the development of our country's science and technology [5]. However, fraudulent and malicious activities such as scams and money laundering occur frequently in blockchain systems, posing significant challenges to social governance and market regulation [14]. As shown in the Fig. 1, blockchain fraud caused over 600 million dollars in financial losses in August 2020 [15]. Effective regulation of blockchain is a necessary condition for the healthy development of the blockchain ecosystem, but currently, there is a lack of effective technical means [8]. The characteristics of anonymity, decentralization, openness, and diversity in blockchain systems present a series of technical challenges for effective regulation. Detecting abnormal transactions and illegal activities in blockchain systems are technical problems that require further research and resolution. There are two main scientific problems to be addressed. Firstly, how to monitor the status of various blockchain systems comprehensively and in real-time. Secondly, how to accurately identify illegal and malicious behavior in blockchain transactions. To solve these two problems, research needs to be conducted on the technical challenges specific to blockchain systems. Diversity refers to the significant differences among different blockchain systems in terms of technical implementation, transaction models, application areas, and scenarios [4]. This poses great difficulties for data analysis and monitoring of multi-chain systems. Openness refers to the ability of blockchain, especially public chains, for users to join and leave autonomously. A user can have multiple accounts and addresses within the system, which adds dynamism to entities in the blockchain and increases the difficulty of data analysis [17, 18].

In response to the aforementioned challenges, the project will research the following key technologies: 1)Blockchain information fusion and management technology, integrating data from different blockchain systems to form a comprehensive knowledge base of illegal activities. 2) Blockchain transaction monitoring and detection technology, enabling the recognition of various transaction patterns in blockchain systems and further analyzing and detecting illegal transaction behavior. Based on research on key technologies, we will develop a comprehensive blockchain monitoring and anti-fraud prototype system. This system will provide real-time situational awareness for various types of blockchain systems and enable monitoring of illegal and fraudulent activities such as phishing, ICO scams, illegal fundraising, price manipulation, and money laundering [10, 16].

2   Background and Related Work

In this section, we introduce some background related to cryptocurrency market, blockchain regulatory platform and existing works on regulatory systems.

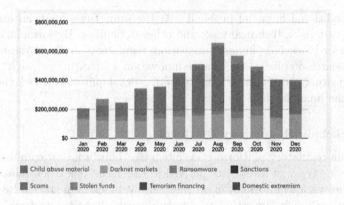

Fig. 1. Total cryptocurrency value received by illicit entities in 2020

2.1 Cryptocurrency Market

Blockchain technology is a decentralized distributed ledger technology that ensures the security and trustworthiness of data through cryptography and consensus mechanisms [3]. It was initially introduced as the underlying technology for Bitcoin but has now been widely adopted in various fields [6]. The distributed nature of blockchain eliminates the need for centralized authorities to verify and record transactions [2]. Instead, transaction verification and ledger maintenance are achieved through consensus algorithms among multiple nodes in the network. Blockchain technology offers several advantages [1]. Firstly, it provides higher security as data is stored across multiple nodes in the network, reducing the risk of single points of failure. Secondly, blockchain has transparent and traceable characteristics, allowing all transaction records to be publicly viewed, thereby increasing trust. Additionally, blockchain enables smart contracts [19], which are computer programs that automatically execute contract conditions and provide automation and programmability for various business and financial transactions. Despite the potential applications of blockchain technology, it also faces challenges, including issues related to regulation and compliance with laws and regulations [11–13]. Zhang et al. elaborated on the regulatory and legal requirements that need to be improved for Blockchain Finance innovation. The main purpose of law and regulation is to establish an appropriate regulatory system to encourage and promote positive factors of innovation, avoid and prevent negative factors, and maintain long-term stability of investor rights and financial market order [28]. Wang et al. need to establish an environmental data center and carbon emission data center to promote the application of blockchain technology in green finance; ensure the quality of basic data; build green financial information infrastructure to reduce application costs; formulate technology innovation policies and talent policies to promote the industrialization of blockchain; improve laws and regulations, and strengthen supervision of blockchain and blockchain finance [29]. Lu et al. pointed out that the innovative application of blockchain technology in the financial field provides some new solutions for traditional financial problems. At the same time, financial innovation also faces trust risks, technical risks and other difficulties. By formulating regulatory laws for blockchain finance innovation, regulatory sandbox system, implementing research on blockchain finance innovation, cultivating research technical talents and other strategies to achieve better development of blockchain technology in the financial field [30].

2.2   Blockchain Regulatory Platform

A blockchain regulatory platform is an integrated platform that combines detection of various types of fraudulent activities. Etherscan is a blockchain explorer that provides various information on the relevant blockchain status. Its features include the ability for investors to use Etherscan's monitoring tools to track ongoing airdrops, check smart contracts, and set custom alerts to track asset changes. Additionally, blockchain analysis researchers can obtain tags for corresponding transaction accounts on Etherscan for data analysis.

2.3   Regulatory Systems

Existing regulatory systems mainly analyze and monitor blockchain transactions based on community reports and statistical information on abnormal behavior in transaction accounts, without considering specific fraudulent activities. There is a lack of systematic research on identifying and disposing of fraudulent activities in the entire chain of supervision from regulatory recognition to fraud detection based on neural network models in blockchain. Furthermore, most scholars have only conducted theoretical and conceptual research on identifying fraudulent behavior based on neural networks, with many designing systems for fraudulent accounts but lacking implementation and feasibility studies.In this context, this project aims to study blockchain regulatory technology and build a comprehensive blockchain transaction situation awareness and illegal behavior monitoring system based on chain data, to achieve transaction monitoring and illegal behavior detection and identification in various blockchain scenarios. The implementation of this project will make a breakthrough in key blockchain regulatory technologies, fill technical gaps at home and abroad, and promote the development and application of blockchain technology.

3   Comprehensive Blockchain Supervision and Anti-fraud System Construction

3.1   Overall Technical Approach of Blockchain Regulatory System

The overall approach of system design is to integrate existing mature blockchain data into a data platform, analyze and explore fraudulent activities that are prevalent across different chains, and achieve efficient and accurate recognition of blockchain transaction patterns as well as detection and monitoring of various illegal behaviors.Based on preliminary research and accumulated studies, illegal activities related to blockchain can be classified into the following five categories:

- Phishing: malicious actors spread false information through various channels to induce users to transfer funds to specified blockchain addresses [23, 24].
- Illegal fundraising: unlawful individuals use the guise of blockchain to attract funds through the issuance of so-called virtual currencies, digital assets, digital tokens, and other means, thereby infringing on the legitimate rights and interests of the public [31].
- Price manipulation: insiders, fraudsters, and large players manipulate the prices of various cryptocurrencies through illegal price manipulation, rather than being driven by market fundamentals [27].
- Initial Coin Offerings (ICOs): providing virtual currency trading services domestically or serving as a service channel for overseas virtual currency trading platforms, including drainage, proxy trading, and issuing tokens ICOs in various names to raise funds in cryptocurrencies such as Bitcoin and Ether [32].
- Money laundering: the act of legitimizing illegal proceeds using characteristics of virtual currencies like Bitcoin, such as anonymity and decentralization [33, 34].

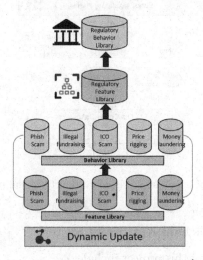

Fig. 2. Blockchain behavior library

The behavior information repository constructed based on these five types of fraudulent activities is illustrated in the Fig. 2. By researching the highly relevant characteristic information of various types of fraud and incorporating it into the regulatory system's behavior information repository, it becomes possible to detect high-risk fraudulent activities.

The overall technical roadmap and key points are shown in the Fig. 3. At the system's functional level, mainstream blockchain data from Bitcoin [6], Ethereum

[7], and other platforms are integrated using blockchain fusion management technology to build the information repository. Various data mining and analysis algorithms are applied to the constructed data platform for real-time analysis. This enables the detection of illegal transactions such as money laundering and black market activities, monitoring of Ponzi schemes and price manipulation, and surveillance of illegal information dissemination. In addition, through blockchain transaction trend detection, various activity indicators (such as transaction volume, amount of currency exchanged, number of smart contracts) and health indicators (such as fraudulent address count, illegal transaction count, illegal information count) of the blockchain ecosystem are computed and measured. The public opinion monitoring system primarily discloses the status of public opinion information stored in the blockchain public chain, and performs public opinion early warning by analyzing statistics such as relevant frequencies and high-frequency words. And the main function of the situational awareness subsystem is to perform regular and recent address detection on various links and analyze and report any abnormal situations in different blockchains.

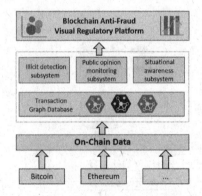

Fig. 3. Blockchain supervision system technical proposal

3.2   Design of Blockchain Anti-fraud System

The main components of this project include:

Data Platform System: This part primarily provides data support for upper-level business and model research, achieving unified deployment and management of the system's complete data. And different blockchain systems have significant differences in their technical implementation and transaction models. The current data of this system mainly originates from the Ethereum and Bitcoin public blockchains, and there are plans to incorporate data from other blockchains in the future. In Ethereum, the transaction model follows an account-based approach, where each transaction address corresponds to a specific account. The parties of transaction are represented as account nodes in the graph database, and the transactions form the edges between the two account nodes. On the other hand, Bitcoin follows the UTXO (Unspent Transaction Output) transaction model. To align with the Ethereum account-based transaction model, it is necessary to scan all UTXO tables to extract the balances and transaction relationships for each Bitcoin transaction account. The data collection module serves as the data input module for the data platform system, consisting of the data acquisition layer and data distribution layer. Its main functionalities include:

- Real-time tracking of mainstream blockchain platforms to obtain various transaction information on the blockchain, enabling real-time parsing to form various on-chain transaction databases and on-chain content repositories.
- Utilizing web scraping techniques to gather diverse digital currency transaction information and create a comprehensive transaction market database.
- Integrating various cross-chain data from blockchain platforms and high-risk data in the system to provide unified structured data input for modules such as transaction detection, public sentiment monitoring, and situational supervision.

Anti-fraud Model System: This part focuses on utilizing the support of the data platform to identify various frauds related to blockchain addresses and monitor newly added account addresses. The challenge in detecting illegal transactions on the blockchain lies in extracting illegal transaction features. The following are the methods for identifying the five types of fraudulent activities in the blockchain regulatory platform:

- Phishing: using the statistical and topological characteristics of the original Ethereum transaction network, including inDegree, outDegree, inValue, outValue, totalTx, minTimestamp, maxTimestamp, numberofNeighbors, and frequencyofTransactions, as input to the graph neural network. Training the network through unsupervised learning to obtain node embeddings. Performing down-sampling based on the Phishing label to reduce the impact of data imbalance. Employing the LightBGM classifier for scam detection.
- Illegal fundraising: mainly targeting Ponzi Scams for fraud detection. Analyzing the calling relationships between smart contracts on the Ethereum platform using seven key features for data analysis, including knownRate, balance, numberofInvestments, numberofPayments, differenceIndex, paidRate, and numberofMaximumPayments. Utilizing the XGBoost classifier for identifying abnormal patterns.
- Price manipulation: this system focuses on mining the Mt.Gox trading network. Employing static network analysis methods to characterize the activities of different accounts. Applying singular value decomposition (SVD) to analyze daily snapshots, studying price manipulation mechanisms, and storing corresponding addresses in the data platform.
- Initial Coin Offerings (ICOs): this system targets RugPull scams detection, especially for ICO scams involving non-valuable tokens. Computing token-related features, including fluctuations in price or liquidity and activity denoting the maximum drop, which calculates the greatest drop in liquidity or

price during token activity. Additionally, considering the difference in blocks between token creation and the pool. The effectiveness of this feature is that a lower block difference between token and pool creation implies negative SHAP values, which correspond to malicious tokens. Using the original transaction features and token-specific design features as inputs to the graph neural network. Employing XGBoost for binary classification to detect ICO scams and alleviate class imbalance issues.

- Money laundering: each node has 166 features, where the first 94 features represent local information about the node's original transaction information (number of inputs/outputs, transactionFee, etc.). The remaining 72 features are based on aggregating features of the first-order neighbors, including calculating maximum, minimum, standard deviation, and correlation coefficient of various local information. These features are input into the graph neural network.

The majority of scam detection methods in this system employ deep learning graph neural networks, the transaction data is modeled as a graph, and complex network embedding algorithms and graph analysis algorithms are introduced to analyze the constructed transaction network, extract transaction behavior features, and build a knowledge base of transaction behavior. This is achieved by extracting transaction information such as Parties, Amount, Timestamp, etc., from the raw data of the blockchains during the ETL process. Additionally, statistical features data such as in-out degree, Number of neighbors, Frequency, etc., are derived from the original data. The main process of fraud identification by the model is illustrated in the Fig. 4.

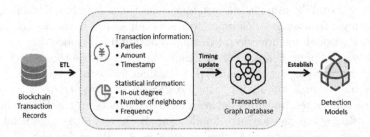

Fig. 4. Technical scheme of transaction monitoring and illegal behavior inspection

For illegal activities based on account transactions, it is necessary to establish feature information capture based on multiple perspectives to identify abnormal transaction accounts. By delving into their complexity and substructure information, a model for identifying illegal transaction accounts is constructed. The basic architecture of the graph neural network is shown in the Fig. 5. Initially, the raw transaction graph data undergoes preprocessing operations, obtaining global perspective data containing global information through graph clustering

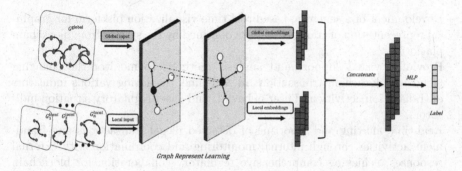

Fig. 5. Graph neural network model anomaly detection technology scheme

algorithms [26], and obtaining local perspective data containing local information through random neighbor sampling. The preprocessed data is then input into the graph neural network [22] (e.g., GCN [21], GAT [20]). Every neural network layer can written as a non-linear function

$$H^{(l+1)} = f(H^{(l)}, A)$$

with $H^{(l)} = X$ and $H^{(L)} = Z$, L being the number of layers. The specific models then differ only in how $f(\cdot, \cdot)$ is chosen and parameterized. And spectral convolution function is formulated as

$$f(H^{(l)}, A) = \sigma(\tilde{D}^{-\frac{1}{2}} \tilde{A} \tilde{D}^{-\frac{1}{2}} \tilde{H}^{(l)} W^{(l)})$$

with $\tilde{A} = A + I$, where A refers to the adjacency matrix, I is the identity matrix and $\tilde{D}$ is the diagonal node degree matrix of $\tilde{A}$. $W^{(l)}$ denotes the layer-specific trainable weight matrix, and $\sigma(\cdot)$ denotes the activation function. $H^{(l)} \in R^{n \times k}$ means the matrix of activation in l layer, while n and k refer to the number of nodes and output dimensions of layer l. And models are trained by reconstructing the network structure [25]. And reconstruction loss function is formulated as

$$L_{recon} = \frac{\|A - \bar{A}\|_F^2}{n}$$

where $\|\|_F^2$ denotes the square of F-norm. $\bar{A} = ZZ^T$ is an operation that reconstructing the original graph structure with Z. This process yields global perspective embedding and local perspective embedding, which are concatenated to obtain the final node embedding representation. Finally, the node embedding is applied to various fraud identification inspection tasks.

Regulatory Data Analysis System: This part focuses on statistics and analysis of recent data from the data platform and high-risk account addresses, enabling visualization of system monitoring and anti-fraud functionalities. The real-time visualization monitoring module serves as the visual terminal module of the prototype system and includes the following key elements:

- Development of a semantic-based real-time visualization platform for graphical representation of transaction data obtained by the system from blockchain platforms.
- Providing visual support and analysis methods to monitor the changing trends of blockchain transactions in real-time, displaying various indicators of transaction activity and user behavior, and other regulatory situation indicators.
- Real-time alerting and reporting of detected illegal transactions and fraudulent activities through internal monitoring and coordination with external responses, achieving comprehensive regulatory collaboration for blockchain digital asset transactions.

4   Implementation of Blockchain Supervision System Based on Data Platform

4.1   Implementation of Data Platform

The concrete implementation of the data platform is as follows:

- The data is distributed to the upper-level core business modules responsible for providing real-time data analysis of illegal transactions and blockchain trends, using streaming data processing platforms such as Kafka and Spark for real-time analysis and processing.
- The data is distributed to offline data processing and analysis modules using platforms such as HDFS, MySQL, and MongoDB, for the analysis and storage of blockchain regulatory sample data.
- The data platform of this system adopts the Hugegraph graph database platform, which synchronously constructs on-chain data and builds index functionality based on business requirements. The system has fast average response time and supports large-scale deployment.

4.2   Implementation of Anti-fraud Model

The anti-fraud model system primarily utilizes graph neural network models based on DGL to identify and monitor various types of fraud, including phishing scams, Ponzi schemes, money laundering fraud, RugPull scams, and illegal arbitrage on the blockchain. Real-time computation of various situational awareness indicators is performed using the data provided by the data collection module. The system utilizes various behavioral samples and patterns accumulated in the integrated information repository to train and update relevant data mining and artificial intelligence algorithms, enabling real-time monitoring and detection of illicit on-chain activities. Additionally, the computed results are fed back to the information repository and provided as data flow support to the visualization monitoring platform through APIs.

4.3   Implementation of Regulatory Analysis System

The regulatory data analysis system is built using the Flask framework and follows a browser-server architecture, greatly enhancing the convenience of system deployment and maintenance. At the software architecture level, the entire system is designed using a microservices architecture, with each service module hosted in containers and uniformly scheduled and orchestrated using Kubernetes. To achieve microservice architecture for all services, the system is divided into control plane and data plane using the Service Mesh pattern. Technically, the Kubernetes-based Service Mesh framework, Istio, can be used to achieve microservice architecture in a Kubernetes environment. Istio's built-in control plane provides features such as load balancing, service-to-service authentication, and monitoring for microservices, while its data plane, based on the Envoy proxy, enables efficient communication and data forwarding between services. Within Kubernetes, each service module is composed of a container and an Envoy traffic proxy container, forming a Pod that shares network resources at the network layer. As the Envoy proxy container handles all network traffic for the microservice containers, Istio-based microservice containers can communicate across languages and environments solely through the Envoy proxy container within the Pod, enabling functionalities such as cross-language service requests and service discovery (Fig. 6).

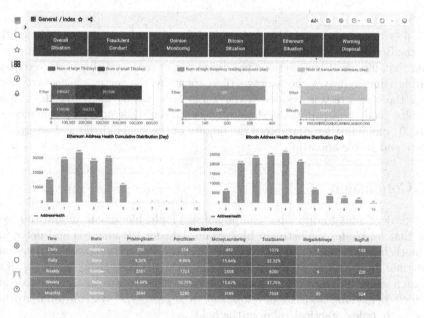

Fig. 6. Blockchain monitoring system overall situation interface

4.4 Stress Testing

Stress testing is a type of software testing that can verify the effectiveness and stability of software applications. The purpose of stress testing is to evaluate the robustness and error-handling capabilities of software under extreme heavy load conditions, ensuring that the software does not crash in emergency situations. It primarily measures the performance of the server by simulating a certain number of concurrent user requests. For the blockchain anti-fraud regulatory system, the number of client terminals in a typical regulatory agency is within 500, while in large regulatory agencies is within 1000. Therefore, this stress testing of system only needs to achieve a concurrent user count of 1000 to meet the requirements for normal user experience. The stress testing results are shown in the Table 1.

Table 1. Stress Testing Results

# Total Requests	# Concurrency	Throughput Rate	Avg Request Waiting Time/(ms)
1000	500	380.82	2.626
10000	500	678.30	1.474
100000	500	667.89	1.497
1000	1000	216.64	4.616
10000	1000	353.30	2.830
100000	1000	402.01	2.487

The stress testing of the blockchain anti-fraud regulatory system utilized the Apache Bench performance testing tool. The throughput rate in the table represents the number of transactions processed per second, and the average request waiting time indicates the average time spent by the server on each request. From the stress testing results in the Table 1, it can be seen that the system exhibits good throughput and short request waiting time at a user concurrency of 1000, which further guarantees the quality of the system itself and ensures its secure and stable operation.

5 Conclusion

This project aims to develop a comprehensive multi-blockchain monitoring system that integrates mainstream blockchain data for the analysis and detection of blockchain transactions, focusing on the core key technologies of detecting abnormal transactions and illicit activities in multi-blockchain scenarios. The research scope of the project includes transaction pattern analysis, detection of illicit behaviors, and the development of a prototype system, among other aspects. It holds practical value in the field.

Acknowledgments. This work is supported by the Key-Area Research and Development Program of Guangdong Province (No.2020B0101090005), the National Natural Science Foundation of China and Guangdong Provincial Joint Fund (No.U1911202) ,

Guangdong Province Key Laboratory of Computational Science at the Sun Yat-sen University (No.2020B1212060032), Science & Technology on Parallel and Distributed Processing Laboratory (PDL), the State Key Program funded by the National Natural Science Foundation of China (No.U1911202) and Guangdong Provincial Key Research Program funded by Guangdong Provincial Department of Science and Technology (No.2020B111137001)

References

1. Szalachowski, P., Reijsbergen, D., Homoliak, I., Sun, S.: StrongChain: transparent and collaborative proof-of-work consensus[C]. In: 28th USENIX Security Symposium (USENIX Security 19). USENIX Association, Santa Clara, CA (2019)
2. Yu, H., et al.: OHIE: blockchain scaling made simple[C]. In: 2020 IEEE Symposium on Security and Privacy (SP). IEEE (2020)
3. Liu, Z., et al.: HyperService: interoperability and programmability across heterogeneous blockchains[C]. In: Proceedings of the 2019 ACM SIGSAC Conference on Computer and Communications Security. Association for Computing Machinery, New York, NY, USA (2019)
4. Su, L., et al.: Evil under the sun: understanding and discovering attacks on Ethereum decentralized applications[C]. In: 30th USENIX Security Symposium (USENIX Security 21). USENIX Association (2021)
5. The 14th Five-Year Plan for National Economic and Social Development of the People's Republic of China and the Outline of the Long-term Goals for 2035 [M]. People's Publishing House, Beijing (2021)
6. Nakamoto, S.: Bitcoin: a peer-to-peer electronic cash system[J]. Decentralized Bus. Rev. (2008)
7. Wood. Ethereum: a secure decentralised generalised transaction ledger. Ethereum project yellow paper (2014)
8. Dai, C., et al. A survey of research on blockchain technology [J]. Comput. Sci. (2021)
9. Shen X., Pei, Q., Liu, X.-F.: A survey of blockchain technology [J]. J. Netw. Inf. Secur. (2016)
10. Wang. F., Zhu, M.: Bibliometric analysis of domestic blockchain research hotspots [J]. J. Intell. (2017)
11. He, P., et al.: A survey on blockchain technology and application prospect [J]. Comput. Sci. (2017)
12. Song, K., Cheng, J., Zhu, Y.: Research progress of international blockchain - based on content analysis of SCI/SSCI journal papers [J]. Inf. Sci. (2021)
13. Sheng, S.: Research on the Construction of supply chain information resource sharing model based on blockchain technology [J]. Inf. Sci. (2021)
14. The slow fog technology. The fog: block chain ecological safety review in 2021, the global loss exceeds $9.8 billion [EB/OL] (2021)
15. Chainalysis. 2021-Crypto-Crime-Report. Accessed February (2021)
16. Zheng, Z., Xie, S., Dai, H.-N., Chen, X., Wang, H.: Blockchain challenges and opportunities: a survey. Int. J. Web Grid Serv. (2018)
17. Marc, P.: Blockchain technology: principles and applications[J]. Res. Handbook Digit. Trans. (2016)
18. Chen, H., et al.: A survey on ethereum systems security: vulnerabilities, attacks and defenses[J]. ACM Comput. Surv. (2019)

19. Wang, Z., et al.: Ethereum smart contract security research: survey and future research opportunities[J]. Front. Comput. Sci. (print) (2021)
20. Velikovi, P., et al.: Graph attention networks. In: Proceeding of the 6th International Conference on Learning Representations, ICLR (2017)
21. Kipf, T.N., Welling, M.: Semi-supervised classification with graph convolutional networks. In: Proceeding of the 5th International Conference on Learning Representations, ICLR (2016)
22. Zhang, D., Chen, J., Lu, X.: Blockchain phishing scam detection via multi-channel graph classification. In: Proceeding of the International Conference on Blockchain and Trustworthy Systems, Blocksys (2021)
23. Chen, W., et al.: Phishing scam detection on Ethereum: towards financial security for blockchain ecosystem[C]. In: International Joint Conference on Artificial Intelligence. International Joint Conferences on Artificial Intelligence Organization (2020)
24. Wu, J., et al.: Who are the phishers? Phishing scam detection on Ethereum via network embedding[J]. IEEE Trans. Syst. Man Cybernet. Syst. (2020)
25. Kipf, T.N., Welling, M.: Variational graph auto-encoders[J]. Comput. Res. Repository, CoRR (2016)
26. Chiang, W.L., et al.: Cluster-GCN: an efficient algorithm for training deep and large graph convolutional networks[J]. ACM (2019)
27. Chen, W., et al. Market manipulation of bitcoin: evidence from mining the Mt. Gox transaction network[C]. In: Proceeding of the IEEE Conference on Computer Communications, INFOCOM (2019)
28. Zhang, Q.: Blockchain finance: innovation, law and regulation [J]. Fintech Era (2022)
29. Wang, Y.L.: Research on blockchain solving the "Greenwashing" problem of green finance under the background of double carbon [J]. Fintech Era (2022)
30. Xie, T.: Professor Gao Jin Hu Jie of Shanghai Jiaotong University: The rapid development of blockchain needs to improve the level of supervision [N]. National Business Daily (2022)
31. Chen, W., et al.: Detecting Ponzi schemes on Ethereum: towards healthier blockchain technology[C]. In: The 2018 World Wide Web Conference (2018)
32. Mazorra, B., Adan, V., Daza, V.: Do not rug on me: zero-dimensional Scam Detection[J]. ArXiv papers (2022)
33. Lorenz, J., et al.: Machine learning methods to detect money laundering in the Bitcoin blockchain in the presence of label scarcity[J]. ArXiv papers (2020)
34. Weber, M., et al.: Anti-money laundering in bitcoin: experimenting with graph convolutional networks for financial forensics. In: The 25th SIGKDD Conference on Knowledge Discovery and Data Mining (2019)

Analysis of Peeling Chain Model
in Bitcoin Mixing Service

Yi Li[1,2], Xiancheng Lin[1,2], Lu Qin[1,2], and Ziqiang Luo[1,2(✉)]

[1] School of Information Science and Technology, Hainan Normal University,
Haikou 571158, China
306003057@qq.com
[2] Key Laboratory of Data Science and Smart Education of Ministry of Education,
Haikou 571158, China

Abstract. In Bitcoin, users often use mixing services to conceal the true information of transactions and protect their privacy. In these services, the peeling chain is a common mixing method that distributes funds to users through multiple consecutive transactions connected by change addresses. This paper investigates the peeling chain model in Bitcoin mixing services, categorizing it into three parts: user input transactions, merge transactions, and distribution transactions. Additionally, a peeling chain search algorithm is proposed to detect distribution transactions in the chain, and its validity is demonstrated through experiments. The findings of this study have implications for other Bitcoin mixing services.

Keywords: Bitcoin · Mixing Service · BitcoinFog · Peeling Chain · Data Analysis

1 Introduction

Bitcoin's introduction [1] pioneered blockchain technology, solidifying its position as the foremost global cryptocurrency. Its decentralized structure and tamper-proof characteristics, ensured by shared ledger technology, make it authentic and reliable, solving the trust crisis issue. Security is further bolstered by asymmetric encryption. Bitcoin's anonymity, facilitating transactions without disclosing personal information, presents both allure and concern. This feature complicates tracing transactions to individuals, making it popular among cybercriminals and illicit financial activities.

To combat illicit Bitcoin transactions, many researchers have focused on de-anonymizing Bitcoin, revealing its pseudo-anonymity. Despite its supposed anonymity, Bitcoin transactions are transparent and open to public scrutiny, with every transaction process visible. Bitcoin addresses can be linked to entities through transaction analysis using three heuristic clustering methods: the multi-input heuristic clustering method proposed by Reid et al. [2], the change address finding heuristic clustering [3,4], and the mining transaction heuristic clustering [5]. These methods have been widely accepted in the academic community and have been shown to be effective in de-anonymizing Bitcoin.

© The Author(s), under exclusive license to Springer Nature Singapore Pte Ltd. 2024
J. Chen et al. (Eds.): BlockSys 2023, CCIS 1896, pp. 147–160, 2024.
https://doi.org/10.1007/978-981-99-8101-4_11

However, the rise of mixing services like CoinJoin, MixCoin [6], BitLaundry, and Bitmix can reduce entity clustering accuracy and make tracking challenging. When users seek to launder money through a mixing service, they typically send the illicit funds to a designated address and receive "cleaned" bitcoins at another address. The mixing process is usually a black box with no visible connection between the sender and receiver, making it hard to determine the entities involved in the mixing service.

The aim of this paper is to examine the common occurrence of peeling chains in mixing services. Section 2 outlines the background information, including the format of Bitcoin transactions and the identification and definition of peeling chains. Section 3 delves into the transaction pattern of the BitcoinFog mixing service and proposes a peeling chain search algorithm to determine the entire peeling chain by recognizing the change address in distribution transactions. The paper concludes with a summary and outlook.

2   Relevant Work

Indeed, the literature in the related field contains limited references to peeling chain. However, the following literature acknowledges the presence and particularity of peeling chain.

Möser et al. [7] conducted experiments on the popular Bitcoin coin mixing service in 2013, revealing that a significant number of UTXOs were used as inputs in the same transaction, combining multiple small amounts of bitcoins into a few addresses and then separating them for payment. This payment structure takes the form of a long single input chain with multiple small payments made to different bitcoin addresses in sequence. This split payment model is used by coin mixing services to provide "cleaned" bitcoins to users and for the distribution of large amounts of illicit funds.

Meiklejohn et al. [3] studied a list of bitcoin thefts reported on bitcoin forums to analyze the flow of stolen funds in four ways: aggregation, folding, splitting, and peeling. "Peeling" refers to the process of gradually removing large amounts of bitcoins from addresses through multiple transactions.

Balthasar et al. [8] researched Bitcoin mixing services and introduced the peeling-chain concept, involving repeated division of amounts. They discovered that these services utilize the peeling-chain method to fund their customers, typically beginning with a large sum of bitcoins received at an address. From there, the bitcoins are sent to two (or more) addresses, one of which belongs to the service, and this process continues until the funds are depleted.

Wu et al. [9] conducted a study on various types of bitcoin mixing services in recent years and classified these mixing mechanisms into two categories: obfuscation and swap. Obfuscation mechanisms hide the user's output by creating one or more anonymous sets of the same amount. The correspondence between input and output is broken. The swap mechanism means that the mixing service provider uses the input of different users as the output of other users to ensure the anonymity of the relationship. The authors define peeling chain specifically in the paper, but there is no mention of how to accurately locate peeling chain or any experimental study on this topic.

This paper focuses on the peeling chain phenomenon in mixing services and the process of finding peeling chain. Building on the findings of literature [9], this paper provides clearer and more comprehensive description of the peeling chain: all transactions in the peeling chain are considered chain nodes and a complete peeling chain can be divided into three parts - user input transactions, merge transactions, and distribution transactions. Figure 1 displays a diagram of a complete peeling chain, encompassing three different transaction types in the peeling chain. These three components are analyzed and distinguished accordingly below.

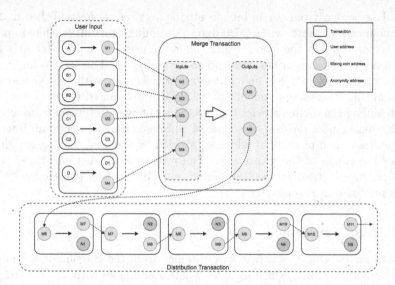

Fig. 1. Diagram of peeling chain

- **User input transaction**
  The User Input Transaction, as its name suggests, is a transaction where a user sends bitcoins to a mixing service and is typically the starting point of the peeling chain. This type of transaction can take various irregular forms, with four types listed in Fig. 1. To correctly identify a transaction as a user-input transaction for a mixing service, it must be determined that one of the output addresses belongs to the mixing service.
- **Merge transaction**
  We observed that some transactions in mixing service aggregate amounts from multiple bitcoin addresses into one or two addresses, referred to as Merge Transaction (MT). The input address of transaction is typically the address used to receive the user's input transaction or the change address of distribution transaction, and the output address is used as the input address for a subsequent distribution transaction to distribute the funds.

– **Distribution transaction**

As the most crucial part of the peeling chain, the Distribution Transaction (DT) serves to distribute funds to users through the peeling chain model. A distribution transaction has one input (referencing the previous distribution transaction) and two outputs (one for the user's output and one for the change address for future distribution transactions), referred to as the one-input-two-output transaction model. Each distribution transaction is linked through the change address, forming a chain, hence the term "peeling chain".

3   BitcoinFog Transaction Analysis

BitcoinFog, an early pioneer in bitcoin mixing services, was established in 2011 but announced its shutdown in 2020 due to declining demand. It offered anonymous access through the Tor network, allowing users to deposit bitcoins into up to 5 addresses and withdraw to up to 20 addresses. The service imposed a random mixing fee of 1–3% and processed transactions within 6–96 hours. A minimum total transaction amount of 0.2 BTC was required for service usage.

BitcoinFog is a mixing service that provides anonymous bitcoin transactions. It uses transfer pool technology to transfer bitcoins from a user to an intermediate address, then to a target address provided by the user, making it difficult to trace the origin of the transaction. The process is divided into three parts: user input transaction, merge transaction, and distribution transaction, which will be analyzed in this chapter.

3.1   Merge Transaction

The data analyzed in this article was obtained from the BitcoinFog tag on the WalletExplorer website, which includes 244,975 addresses with 227,178 (92.7%) having a prefix of '1' and 17,797 addresses having a prefix of '3'. The next analysis is based on 2890 transactions labeled as BitcoinFog transactions prior to 2020, which had 10 or more input addresses and only one or two output addresses, typical characteristics of merge transactions.

In our investigation of 2890 merge transactions (available at https://github. com/L0re1ei/Peeling-Chain), the input addresses were found to be associated with the coin mixing service, including user input addresses and change addresses in distribution transactions. Analysis of previous transactions revealed three prominent patterns: one-input-two-output, two-input-two-output, and one-input-one-output, accounting for 65% of the total transactions. Out of the 142,882 UTXOs, they originated from 87,924 different addresses, with 68,071 addresses being used only once as output. These addresses are considered disposable and may be reused if a user sends bitcoins to the same address multiple times from the mixing service provider.

For a deeper understanding of the 2890 merge transactions, we sorted them based on the number of output addresses and conducted an experiment. Results showed that the bitcoins from 2855 merge transactions were concentrated in 13 addresses. We sorted the list of addresses receiving large amounts of bitcoins in ascending order based on the block height where they first appeared, as shown in Table 1. The number of transactions and all amount values in the table refer specifically to those observed in the merger transactions, and the values are retained to two decimal places only.

Table 1. Address specific information

	Address	Frist block height	Last block height	Number of trans-action	Max value	Average value
A1	1YZJKaAx2HRWvcbCXDBtQbBZcRU46WJqw	152678	172897	18	2825.53	1440.62
A2	1F9kYDpu2CqwR18ovineZr8Y88NQfW1bzR	173193	211293	19	10612.46	6497.61
A3	1BPgf9qGD5emvf154XAwNSrJu667S9H9j	184808	210500	27	20366.30	10118.41
A4	1JmQN8NvX3XXWWrJW3rEEcKQMQd5DUgkH3	211293	231939	39	11653.54	3582.53
A5	1MsmThtteKPu6fWxwn2SMDEnmJex3vKSBk	232302	258815	84	942.88	829.59
A6	15U5NjgAbKqKyGKwayS648WwJoiCCvGnTG	258909	268295	61	603.0	522.40
A7	1Cwb33nqn4S2uDsXwhNrUNy7FPdiRYhyM8	268298	279208	123	889.33	130.09
A8	1P5pMkN1wr3ozHXwCXtRmv6kJBYLyPPMzc	279208	285171	74	252.71	81.42
A9	19owvByG9J8WVkM6wDUykgnchBLvjnFggW	285206	285299	2	136.27	115.12
A10	16FgQXGzSLRtdwuwCN7mcaPUtbJ6JFTkVw	285310	309000	567	130.58	14.68
A11	17gH1u6VJwhVD9cWR59jfeinLMzag2GZ43	292595	327148	1826	13.88	13.79
A12	15CLUub6yaov3yMZtmxPQ4pSeR22PuDSLT	327148	345921	14	112.27	36.85
A13	1AxCPXytzSpoKjBKCmoDJv6VbQhjhSs7pB	392912	460206	1	468.59	468.59

Out of the 2890 merge transactions, only 6% (176 transactions) have single output address. In the majority of these transactions, the bitcoins were consolidated into addresses A1, A4–A13. Our findings are as follows:

1. In 64 merge transactions with an output value greater than 30BTC, all subsequent transactions at the output address were in the one-input-two-output transaction mode.
2. There were 33 transactions with an output value of 13.88 BTC, and their output address was either A10 or A11.
3. There were 69 transactions with an output value of 1.25452BTC, and their output address was consistently A10.

Out of the 2890 merge transactions, 94% (2714 transactions) had two output addresses, with most bitcoins being consolidated into addresses A1-A12. Assuming Address A and Address B as the two output addresses, with Address A having a larger output value. Our findings are as follows:

1. Our findings showed that 2657 transactions (97.9%) had an output value for Address B within the range of 0.01 ± 0.001 BTC and had only one output transaction, indicating that these were disposable addresses.
2. There were 371 transactions where the output value of Address A was greater than 30BTC, and the subsequent transactions at this address were in the form of one-input-two-output transactions.

3. There were 1701 transactions with an output value of 13.88 BTC, and their output address was either A10 or A11.
4. There were 331 transactions with an output value of 1.25452BTC, and their output address was consistently A10.

Our analysis of the block heights of these addresses, shown in Fig. 2, revealed that the blue portion of the figure represents the block height range of each address and the red portion shows their overlap. There was little overlap between the block height ranges of addresses A2 and A3, A10 and A11, except for a minor overlap. The intervals between these addresses were also found to be very close.

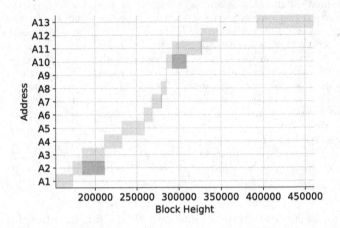

Fig. 2. Visualization of the block height of addresses

Therefore, we suspect that BitcoinFog typically uses specific addresses in stages during merge transactions to collect inputs from users. The outputs from these transactions can be broadly categorized into three types: addresses with larger amounts use a one-input-two-output format for fund distribution, creating the peeling-chain effect. There are also two fixed amounts (13.88 BTC and 1.25452 BTC) for smaller outputs, but their formats are not fixed. Among the merge transactions with two outputs, there is an output address with all amounts concentrated within the range of 0.01 ± 0.001 BTC, which are disposable and not be reused.

3.2 Distribution Transaction

In the previous phase of the study, we collected merge transactions labeled with the BitcoinFog tag and compiled 13 commonly used output addresses. The transaction block heights of these addresses range from 152678 to 460206 and the time frame is from November 10, 2011 to April 3, 2017, when the BitcoinFog coin mixing service was active. By analyzing the pattern and regularity of input transactions at these addresses, we can understand the mixing process of the BitcoinFog mixing coin service.

BitcoinFog uses a peeling chain approach for user output, as reflected in the one-input-two-output transaction pattern. Figure 3 show the percentage of transaction patterns for these 13 addresses as input addresses. Most of the input transactions for addresses A1-A11 use the one-input-two-output transaction mode. But it decreases for addresses A12 and A13 as the block height increases, suggesting a shift away from the peeling chain approach later.

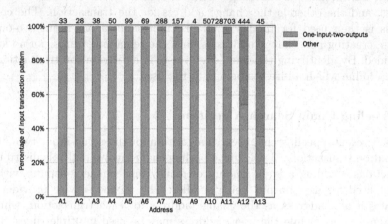

Fig. 3. Address input transaction pattern percentage chart. The number above each bar represents the total number of transactions for these addresses as input addresses.

Next, we analyze the transactions that use these 13 addresses as input addresses. We focus on two types of transactions: large value distribution transactions and special constant value distribution transactions. The large value distribution transactions are 654 transactions in the one-input-two-output mode with a transaction value greater than 20BTC. We refer to these transactions as "initial distribution transactions". The total value of these transactions was 783976BTC, with the largest transaction being 20366BTC.

We found that two constant values (13.88BTC and 1.25452BTC) appeared repeatedly in the merge transactions, with addresses A10 and A11 both receiving these values. There were 6829 UTXOs of 1.25452 BTC and 540 UTXOs of 13.88 BTC received by A10, while A11 received 8181 UTXOs of 13.88 BTC. These subsequent transactions can be divided into three categories: (1) 3456 one-input-two-output transactions with 1.25452 BTC input, with A10 as the input address; (2) 7900 one-input-two-output transactions with 1.25452BTC input, with 511 from A10 and 7389 from A11; and (3) N-input-2-output transactions with 1220 transactions, some of which used A10 and A11 together as the input address.

After analyzing the 1220 transactions with multiple inputs and two outputs, we found a common characteristic: one of the two output addresses is usually a disposable address, which can be treated as a change address with a smaller output value. However, there are three exceptions with evenly distributed output values. This suggests that the disposable address acts as the change address, while the other output address belongs to the user. Multiple input addresses are used to provide enough inputs for the desired output.

For the remaining 11,356 small-input distribution transactions and the 654 large-input distribution transactions screened out before, all of them are one-input-two-output distribution transactions. We perform a follow-up analysis on these 12,010 initial distribution transactions.

Each transaction has two output addresses, one address is the user's output address, and the other is the change address for the transaction. The change address is then used for further fund distribution in a one-input-two-output pattern, creating new change addresses until the remaining funds can no longer be divided. By identifying the change addresses in a distribution transaction, we can determine which addresses belong to the user.

3.3   Peeling Chain Search Algorithm

We now present a peeling chain search algorithm for those one-input-two-output distribution transactions. Typically, a peeling chain involve multiple distribution transactions, dividing a large amount of money into smaller outputs, with the amount used for user output being smaller. The mixing service provider also generates a new address as the change address for each transaction, which is usually used once, while the user's address may be used multiple times. These characteristics allow for more accurate identification of the change address in the distribution transaction.

We propose the peeling search algorithm for the one-input-two-output initial distribution transactions, as shown in Algorithm 1. The algorithm determines the change address in the transaction by considering if the output address is new and if subsequent transactions at this address follow the one-input-two-output pattern. The output amount and number of transactions at the output address are used as supporting conditions to track the distribution transactions in the peeling chain. The steps of the algorithm are described as follows:

1. For a one-input-two-output distribution transaction, first check whether the two output addresses have previously participated in a transaction.
2. If only one address appears for the first time and the subsequent transaction at that address is a one-input-two-output transaction pattern, then that address is the change address.
3. If both output addresses appear for the first time and one has fewer transactions, check the address with fewer transactions first to see if the subsequent transaction follows the one-input-two-output pattern. If the number of transactions is equal, check the address with larger output first. If it follows the pattern, it's the change address, otherwise check the other address.
4. If both output addresses are not newly generated or do not satisfy the above conditions, the peel chain search ends.

Algorithm 1. Peeling chain search algorithm

Input: tx: a distribution transaction with one-input-two-output.

    Fuction FindNextDistribution(tx)

1: $k \leftarrow 0$
2: **for** output **in** tx **do**
3:    **if** $output\_address.first\_tx.hash = tx.hash$ **then**
4:       $k += 1, first\_tx \leftarrow 1$
5:    **else**
6:       $first\_tx \leftarrow 0$
7:    **end if**
8:    $tx\_output[5] \leftarrow \{output\_address, output\_value,$
9:       $address\_transaction\_number, next\_transaction, first\_tx\}$
10: **end for**
11: **if** $k = 0$ **then**
12:    **return** False
13: **elseif** $k = 1$ **then**
14:    $index \leftarrow tx\_output[4].index(1)$
15:    $next\_tx \leftarrow tx\_output[3][index]$
16:    **if** $next\_tx.input\_count = 1$ **and** $next\_tx.output\_count = 2$ **then**
17:       **FindNextDistribution**($next\_tx$)
18:    **end if**
19: **elseif** $k = 2$ **then**
20:    $index \leftarrow tx\_output[2].index(min(tx\_output[2]))$
21:    $next\_tx \leftarrow tx\_output[3][index]$
22:    **if** $next\_tx.input\_count = 1$ **and** $next\_tx.output\_count = 2$ **then**
23:       **FindNextDistribution**($next\_tx$)
24:    **end if**
25:    **if** $tx\_output[2][index] = tx\_output[2][index]$ **then**
26:       $index \leftarrow tx\_output[1].index(max(tx\_output[1]))$
27:       $next\_tx \leftarrow tx\_output[3][index]$
28:       **if** $next\_tx.input\_count = 1$ **and** $next\_tx.output\_count = 2$ **then**
29:          **FindNextDistribution**($next\_tx$)
30:       **end if**
31:    **end if**
32: **end if**

3.4 Experimental Data Analysis

Comparative Analysis of Different Input Values. We employed the peeling chain search algorithm to analyze 654 large and 11,356 small initial distribution transactions, with constant values of 1.25452 BTC (3456 transactions) and 13.88 BTC (7900 transactions) filtered out. This led to the discovery of a total of 12,010 peeling chains, and a subsequent detailed comparison of the relevant data was conducted.

For the remaining 11,356 small value input and the 654 large value input distribution transactions, we perform a subsequent analysis. The first factor to consider is the number of distribution transactions in a peeling chain. The length of a peeling chain depends on the number of distribution transactions in the chain. Figure 4 shows the distribution of the number of distribution transactions in peeling chains formed by initial distribution transactions of different input amounts. As we can see, the larger the input value of the peeling chain, the greater the number of distributed transactions.

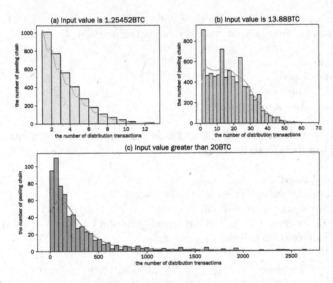

Fig. 4. Distribution of the number of distribution transactions in peeling chain with different input values

In BlockSci [10], the bitcoin parsing tool we use, the "age" field in the transaction input class gives information on the number of blocks between the creation of a UTXO and its usage. This lets us examine the time elapsed between the creation of distribution transactions in peeling chains. Our analysis of 345,048 distribution transactions showed that only 2.29% (7890 transactions) had an "age" value greater than 10 blocks. The majority of transactions (63%) had "age" values of 0 or 1, indicating they were quickly executed by the mixing service. This suggests that BitcoinFog likely used a list of user output addresses and amounts, and rapidly executed distribution transactions using the peeling chain model in a short period of time.

With our peeling chain search algorithm, we identified change addresses and determined user addresses in distribution transactions. Our experiment compiled a list of 40,848 user output addresses from peeling chains with initial distribution transactions over 20 BTC. Only 8841 of these addresses appeared once, showing a lack of awareness of address anonymity protection at the time. Some addresses appeared multiple times in the output addresses of distribution transactions with substantial output values. We sorted these addresses by output amount and listed the top ten addresses with the largest output values in Table 2. The output transactions and value in this table represent observed transaction distribution in our experiments, while the total transactions refer to the overall number of transactions associated with this address. This indicates that certain users use the coin mixing service quite frequently and often use the same address to receive mixing bitcoins.

Table 2. List of top ten addresses with largest output values

Address	Number of output transaction	Output values	Total number of transactions
1AV4KGCsvtPZ9tG7hvwgb85wJyFd9xdpFv	388	8516.7170508	467
1Q5RLJ864z8YiFHAS37hDVAv3bdPXTe3M9	185	6065.41910167	246
1GRSR869UvoR5inVxVj9tGegH9ZUafLzyj	57	4463.62526429	106
1KTthyJv8KfjqCgpKzPsWvK343taKVxutT	56	3455.90217618	101
18bdtURDuXaa5QSPuJr2BHQgiSxuPvm1C9	481	3195.70103078	712
1KLxHfmgWbifqD6LwiroELyqMKFReoQXzd	38	2778.7631225	70
1KQZkyyVTWna1QVeodXx3SVCYLMzM77TqM	9	2726.27	18
15a5nVrmGCyvjN81Fqtadrtjn3GwgcuWUi	87	2689.30309806	208
1AcaFH3VsQuxUvDkB2v8Tyc9uDDsz13Bff	43	2607.49491199	69
14BdkzEbx6SR8QinbQ3D5A6dp2nqk9AzZ1	42	2517.48132789	68

Next, we examined the details of the final distribution transactions in 12,010 peeling chains to understand why the peeling chain search algorithms stopped querying. Our analysis found that only 74 of the 12,010 final distribution transactions had neither output address as a newly generated address. 9118 transactions had a unique newly generated output address, while 11,141 transactions had 2 transactions with a unique output address (one for input and one for output) and more than 2 transactions with another output address. Based on our understanding of change addresses, we believe that the latter case, where there is a unique output address in a transaction with a total of 2 transactions, is likely to be the change address for that transaction.

We investigated the subsequent transactions of 11,141 transactions with 2 outputs. We found that these 11,141 UTXOs went to 7126 different transactions, with 2740 transactions repeated, the most frequent one occurring 39 times. We sorted these 7126 transactions by the number of output addresses, and 287 transactions had input addresses greater than 10. Among these, there are 274 transactions with output addresses of 1 or 2. Through observation, it was found that the form of these transactions conforms to the characteristics of merged transactions described earlier, and we also observed addresses A8, A10, and A11 from Table 1 in some transaction output addresses. The remaining 6839 transactions had input addresses less than 10, and 6764 of them had output addresses of 2. We observed that there is always one output address among these addresses that is newly generated and has a total of 2 transactions, and its amount is smaller than the other output address. We believe that these multiple (less than 10) -input-two-output transactions also belong to the transactions distributed to users by the mixing coin service and that, since each peeling chain has less money left at the end, multiple UTXOs must be aggregated before they are used for money distribution.

Detailed Transaction Analysis. Möser et al. [7] conducted an interaction experiment with BitcoinFog, in 2013 and provided IDs for six transactions, as shown in Table 3, which included two user-input transactions and four user-output transactions. Figure 5 shows the details of these six transactions in the peeling chain.

Table 3. Interaction experiment specific transaction information (Cited in Literature [7])

	Time	Type	Value	Transaction hash
t1	2013-04-29	in	0.3	97e723ded27cd1e4f9954689c503d092fe5a1b79747d6c45b18ad8f90bf61c62
t2	2013-04-30	out	0.2052473	56a4f35b4a2fb5eb15549befdb1285e831a5dd67bc1b559c1b2ef8e145627856
t3	2013-04-30	out	0.08804699	8f4bf3e95c00025d42fc2c6a9f28e66c7ed75eb08560b7675c712accb1d75b2c
t4	2013-05-07	in	0.3141593	ac8d82b3c3088a633fc4b48562e8c5794f502acbfbec360b406958e0acc92451
t5	2013-05-14	out	0.1104155	18ee1ea93a9c84dd5f1e7bd758410368e545a45a989aafcd78584f51c3da4566
t6	2013-05-15	out	0.1019295	a95e2fea5498dae5ec3419d8d5c62dea23b09d69923eb15e829a562a6975a962

The user sends 0.3 BTC and 0.3131593 BTC to the mixing service via transactions t1 and t4, respectively, and these two UTXOs are aggregated into address A7 through two merge transactions, which demonstrates the phenomenon of users entering transactions into merge transactions that we described.

During the peeling chain search algorithm, we detect the transaction IDs of t2, t3, t5, and t6. Transactions t2 and t3 are both on peeling chain 1, which has an initial distribution transaction of DT1 with an initial amount of 6013 BTC and 1491 distribution transactions. Transactions t2 and t3 are located on the 1443rd and 1445th of this peeling chain, respectively. Transactions t5 and t6 are on peeling chain 2, which has an initial distribution transaction of DT2 with an initial amount of 942.883004 BTC and 496 distribution transactions. Transactions t5 and t6 are located on the 180th and 482nd distribution transactions of this peeling chain, respectively.

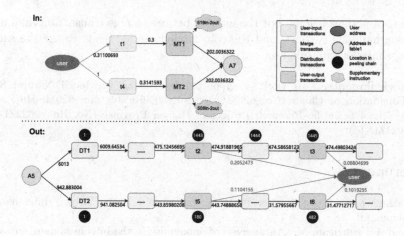

Fig. 5. Details of user-input and user-output transactions

4   Conclusion

This paper studies the widespread occurrence of peeling chains in Bitcoin mixing services and examines the operation of BitcoinFog as the research subject. The process of BitcoinFog mixing coins was found to consist of three parts: user input transactions, merge transactions, and distribution transactions. User input transactions exhibit an indeterminate transaction pattern, thereby posing challenges in accurate assessment. In user input transactions, accurately determining them is challenging due to the absence of a fixed transaction pattern. Merged transactions consolidate a significant number of user input bitcoins into a limited number of addresses. Analyzing 2890 merge transactions, we identified 13 output addresses that concentrate the majority of the merged transaction values. These output addresses can be classified into three types based on the handled amounts: a large amount address using a one-input-two-output format, and two types with fixed amounts (13.88 BTC and 1.25452 BTC), but with variable transaction formats.

Distribution transactions, with one input and two outputs, are used to distribute user funds and form a chain called a peeling chain through change addresses. We propose a peeling-chain search algorithm for one-input-two-output distribution transactions to find the change addresses by determining if the output address is new and if subsequent transactions match the pattern. With this algorithm, we obtained 12010 peeling chain data and analyzed the number of distribution transactions, time intervals, user outputs, and endpoint transactions. Generally, larger initial distribution amounts lead to longer peeling chains, and time intervals between distribution transactions are short. Some users use the same address frequently to receive mixing bitcoins. Most endpoint transactions in the peeling chain are multiple-input-two-output, but it's unclear if they are user outputs or merge transactions. Our algorithm was verified by analyzing 6 interaction experiments and we found that the interval between user-input and merge transactions is long, but the interval between merge transactions and distribution handoffs is short, and the coin mixing service tends to use the same peeling chain for multiple user outputs.

Acknowledgments. This work is supported by Hainan Provincial Natural Science Foundation of China (No. 620MS045, No. 3620RC605, No. 620MS046), and Higher School Scientific Research Project of Hainan Province (No. Hnky2022ZD-7, Hnjg2021ZD-15).

References

1. Nakamoto, S.: A peer-to-peer electronic cash system (2008). https://bitcoin.org/bitcoin.pdf
2. Reid, F., Harrigan, M.: An analysis of anonymity in the bitcoin system. In: Altshuler, Y., Elovici, Y., Cremers, A., Aharony, N., Pentland, A. (eds.) Security and Privacy in Social Networks, pp. 197–223. Springer, New York (2013). https://doi.org/10.1007/978-1-4614-4139-7_10
3. Meiklejohn, S., et al.: A fistful of bitcoins: characterizing payments among men with no names. In: Proceedings of the 2013 Conference on Internet Measurement Conference, pp. 127–140 (2013)
4. Androulaki, E., Karame, G.O., Roeschlin, M., Scherer, T., Capkun, S.: Evaluating user privacy in bitcoin. In: Sadeghi, A.-R. (ed.) FC 2013. LNCS, vol. 7859, pp. 34–51. Springer, Heidelberg (2013). https://doi.org/10.1007/978-3-642-39884-1_4
5. Zhao, C., Guan, Y.: A graph-based investigation of bitcoin transactions. In: Peterson, G., Shenoi, S. (eds.) DigitalForensics 2015. IAICT, vol. 462, pp. 79–95. Springer, Cham (2015). https://doi.org/10.1007/978-3-319-24123-4_5
6. Bonneau, J., Narayanan, A., Miller, A., Clark, J., Kroll, J.A., Felten, E.W.: Mixcoin: anonymity for bitcoin with accountable mixes. In: Christin, N., Safavi-Naini, R. (eds.) FC 2014. LNCS, vol. 8437, pp. 486–504. Springer, Heidelberg (2014). https://doi.org/10.1007/978-3-662-45472-5_31
7. Möser, M., Böhme, R., Breuker, D.: An inquiry into money laundering tools in the bitcoin ecosystem. In: 2013 APWG eCrime Researchers Summit, pp. 1–14. IEEE (2013)
8. de Balthasar, T., Hernandez-Castro, J.: An analysis of bitcoin laundry services. In: Lipmaa, H., Mitrokotsa, A., Matulevičius, R. (eds.) NordSec 2017. LNCS, vol. 10674, pp. 297–312. Springer, Cham (2017). https://doi.org/10.1007/978-3-319-70290-2_18
9. Wu, L., et al.: Towards understanding and demystifying bitcoin mixing services. In: Proceedings of the Web Conference 2021, pp. 33–44 (2021)
10. Kalodner, H., et al.: BlockSci: design and applications of a blockchain analysis platform. In: 29th USENIX Security Symposium (2020)

A Blockchain-Based On-Chain and Off-Chain Dual-Trusted Carbon Emission Trading System with Reputation Mechanism

Chenxu Wang[✉] ⓘ and Xinxin Sang

School of Software Engineering, Xi'an Jiaotong University, Xi'an, China
cxwang@mail.xjtu.edu.cn

Abstract. Traditional centralized carbon emission trading systems suffer from data falsification, which is not conducive to the goal of carbon reduction. This paper proposes a blockchain-based on-chain and off-chain dual-trusted carbon emission trading system with reputation mechanism (BoodCET). We employ the Internet of Things technology, BigchainDB storage, and supervision by the Ministry of Ecology Environment for the "collection - storage - calculation - supervision" of carbon data to ensure the authenticity and credibility of carbon emission data off the chain. The Hyperledger Fabric is used to build a consortium blockchain network formed by enterprises and government regulated exchanges. BoodCET provides two trading modes, one-way auction, and agreement transfer. Enterprises get reputations by participating in trading and reducing carbon emissions, and enterprises with high reputation value have a high priority in carbon emission trading. To ensure that BoodCET does not disrupt carbon markets, we introduce a trading rationality review mechanism to review the rationality of carbon emission trading on the consortium chain. In this work, we implement a prototype of BoodCET and conduct a case study to evaluate the performance of the proposed system.

Keywords: Carbon emission trading · On-chain and off-chain dual-trusted · Reputation mechanism · Authority supervision

1 Introduction

The Kyoto Protocol introduced the concept of carbon emissions trading (CET), which monetizes carbon dioxide emissions in the hope of controlling them

The research presented in this paper is supported in part by National Natural Science Foundation of China (No. 62272379), National Key R&D Program of China (2021YFB1715600), Natural Science Basic Research Plan in Shaanxi Province (2021JM-018), and the Fundamental Research Funds for the Central Universities (xzy012023068).

through market mechanisms [1]. Countries are allowed to emit carbon dioxide as long as they do not exceed their carbon allowances and can trade carbon allowances with other countries [2]. The International Carbon Action Partnership (ICAP)'s 2022 Status report highlights the success of carbon trading, and the current carbon trading system is playing an increasing role in addressing the change of climate [3]. However, from October to December 2021, the Ministry of Ecology and Environment of China conducted a special supervision and on-site inspection on the quality of carbon emission reports and found that Beijing Zhongchuang Carbon Investment Technology Co., Ltd. had falsified test reports and distorted report conclusions [4]. These companies falsified key data to obtain carbon quota surpluses and gain improper benefits through carbon trading. In addition, a centralised emissions trading system risks data falsification. Data falsification will reduce the willingness of enterprises to participate in emissions trading, which is not conducive to the achievement of carbon reduction targets. Therefore, it is extremely important to ensure the authenticity of carbon emission data provided by enterprises and the authenticity of data in the process of carbon emission trading between enterprises.

Many researchers have proposed using blockchain to solve the problem of data falsification in carbon emissions trading. Blockchain technology has the characteristics of decentralization, transparent and traceable data, and untameable, which ensures the authenticity and credibility of the carbon emission data of enterprises on the blockchain [5]. However, it cannot ensure that the carbon emission data provided by enterprises is authentic and trustworthy. Some scholars proposed using Ethereum to store carbon emission data generated by enterprises to ensure that the carbon emission data cannot be tampered with. However, the efficiency of Ethereum to store Internet of Things data is low. Some scholars have proposed carbon emission trading based on the reputation mechanism. However, they fail to provide a clear measurement method of reputation. Most of the solutions do not limit the trading price, and the trading of carbon emissions on the consortium chain could disrupt the carbon market.

This paper proposes a blockchain on-chain and off-chain dual-trusted carbon emission trading with reputation mechanism to ensure that the on-chain and off-chain data of the blockchain are authenticated and credible in the process of carbon emission trading. This system uses BigchainDB to store carbon emission data to ensure the authenticity and reliability of carbon emission data off-chain. BigchainDB has high throughput, decentralized control, and immutable data storage, which can be used to store a large amount of Internet of Things data [6]. This system uses consortium blockchain to trade carbon emission rights to ensure the authenticity and traceability of the data on-chain. The premise of the dual trusted carbon emission trading system is that local ecological environment departments install and deploy Internet of Things devices for enterprises to ensure the authenticity and credibility of data collected by Internet of Things devices, and that enterprises themselves do not have malicious data tampering in the process of carbon emission data transmission. The main contributions of this paper are as follows:

- The Internet of Things (IoT) and BigchainDB technologies are used to collect and store massive IoT data in the process of carbon emission, which solves the problem of low efficiency of data storage in Ethereum. A hierarchical computing process is proposed to calculate carbon emission, which solves the problem of off-chain carbon emission data fraud.
- In the BigchainDB network, we introduce a node of the Ministry of Ecology Environment to supervise the carbon emission data of enterprises. The digital certificates of trusted carbon emissions are issued for the signature of enterprises, which are used for carbon emission trading.
- We optimize the query of BigchainDB based on MongoDB and implement BigchainDB fuzzy query. The consortium blockchain trading network will set up exchange nodes under the jurisdiction of the government, and the exchange develops a smart contract for transaction rationality verification mechanism to verify the rationality of the enterprise's trusted carbon emission digital certificate and trading request.
- We provide two kinds of trading, including one-way auction and agreement transfer. We propose a novel reputation mechanism to calculate the reputation of enterprises based on the proportion of carbon emissions over the total carbon quota and the number of times that enterprises participate in carbon emission trading. Enterprises with high reputation value have high trading priority, which encourages enterprises to reduce carbon emissions and participate in carbon emission trading.

The rest of this paper is organized as follows: Sect. 2 introduces the related work. Section 3 describes the detailed design of BoodCET. Section 4 analyzes a case of carbon emission trading. Section 5 concludes the work.

2   Related Work

Since the proposal of carbon emission trading, many countries and regions in the world have implemented their carbon emission trading systems. The European Union Emission Trading Scheme (EU ETS) is the first carbon emission trading system with the participation of many countries [7]. The most influential ETS in North America are the Regional Greenhouse Gas Initiative (RGGI) and the California ETS [8]. California's carbon trading system is one of the core measures for the North American carbon market to achieve the emission reduction target [9]. Quebec in Canada established a carbon trading system in 2012, which covers a variety of greenhouse gases such as CO2 emitted by fossil fuel combustion, industry and so on [10]. China has formulated a series of policies for the construction of the carbon market. In 2011, local pilot carbon emission trading was launched in Beijing, Tianjin, Shanghai, and other provinces.

The above traditional carbon emission trading system has problem of data fraud. To solve this problem, many researchers have proposed a series of feasible schemes based on blockchain. Pan et al. [11] explained the application of blockchain in carbon emission trading. Blockchain technology can realize decentralized point-to-point trading, lower the threshold of access to the carbon trading market. However, it cannot guarantee the authenticity of carbon emission data provided by enterprises. Niya et al. [12] proposed a distributed system based on the IoT and blockchain for measuring, storing, and monitoring water and air quality in environments. Using Ethereum to store IoT data ensures the authenticity and credibility of enterprise carbon emission data [13–16]. However, it does not provide a carbon emission trading system based on blockchain. Moreover, the Internet of Things data is huge, and using Ethereum to store the process is inefficient and not feasible. Khaqqi et al. [17] implemented a reputation-based carbon emission trading system based on blockchain technology. Reputation determines different alternative transactions seen by enterprises in the trading system. However, this scheme cannot guarantee the authenticity of the carbon emission data of enterprises and does not provide a clear measurement method of reputation values. Liang et al. [18] proposed a double blockchain architecture based on reputation. The confirmation chain and financial chain improve efficiency and ensure security and privacy. However, it lacks the collection process of carbon emission data off the chain. Sadawi et al. [19] proposed a three-phase layered blockchain framework for carbon trading and carbon budget in the public chain. However, they failed to implement and verify the architecture. It is inefficient to use the blockchain for IoT data storage and calculation. Muzumdar et al. [20] proposed a carbon emission trading system based on the Fabric consortium chain and a reputation mechanism. Enterprises with high reputation have the priority to participate in the auction transaction, but the authenticity of enterprise's carbon emission data off chain cannot be guaranteed.

3 Our Solution

3.1 Blockchain On-Chain and Off-Chain Dual-Trusted Structure

This paper presents a blockchain-based on-chain and off-chain dual-trusted carbon emission trading system with reputation mechanism. Figure 1 shows the physical architecture of BoodCET.

Each enterprise in the carbon emission trading network shall be equipped with humidity testers, velocity testers, pressure testers, temperature testers, and carbon dioxide analyzers to collect carbon data in the production process according to the Technical Specifications for Continuous Monitoring of Flue Gas Carbon Dioxide Emissions of Heat-engine plants issued by the National Energy Administration of China [21]. The data is then transferred via MQTT to the carbon data center and then uploaded to the BigchainDB network [22], which consisting of the generator set Carbon Data Center and the Ministry of Ecology Environment carbon Data Center. The carbon emission data is calculated by hierarchy. The Ministry of Ecology Environment issues carbon emission digital certificates to trusted enterprises. The system uses the Fabric consortium chain to build a carbon emission trading network composed of enterprises and exchanges [23]. Fabric CA manages enterprise identity certificates and is responsible for enterprise identity authentication. Enterprises in the consortium chain can obtain carbon emission value and trusted carbon emission digital certificates on the BigchainDB storage network through the interactive gateway. Then enterprises that have passed the identity authentication can initiate transaction requests, and the exchange develops smart contracts for transaction rationality verification mechanism, which will check the enterprises' trusted carbon emission digital certificates and rationality of trading applications. The approved transactions will be published in the trading network, and the transaction smart contract will match the transactions of enterprises according to the reputation mechanism. Finally, enterprises' transactions are cleared. The transactions will end.

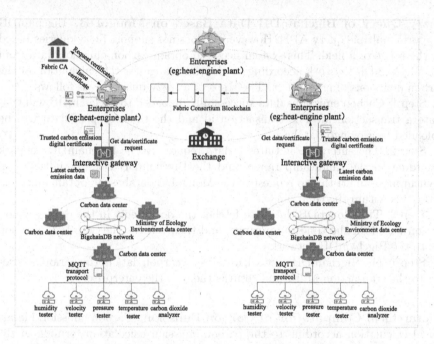

Fig. 1. The physical architecture diagram of our BoodCET scheme.

3.2 Off-Chain Trusted Carbon Emission Data Management Scheme

Carbon Data Collection and Storage. The BoodCET system uses the measurement method to calculate the carbon emissions. IoT devices continuously monitor and collect carbon data during the production process of enterprises. MQTT transport protocol is used to transmit carbon data. The MQTT transport protocol is based on the message publish/subscribe mode of client-server architecture. In BoodCET, IoT devices and carbon data centers are MQTT clients. To ensure the security of carbon emission data, the collected data are encrypted, then published to the MQTT server. The carbon data center subscribes to the topic of the carbon emission data, and then gets the data from the MQTT server, and then decrypts the data.

BoodCET uses BigchainDB to store the carbon emission data. BigchainDB has the data tamper-proof feature to ensure the authenticity and credibility of the carbon emission data off the chain. If a transaction is successfully generated, it will be uploaded to the BigchainDB network. If the transaction fails to be generated, the data will be stored in the cache and the transaction will be generated again. If the transaction is successfully uploaded to BigchainDB, the transaction id, and timestamp will be stored in a MongoDB database. If the transaction upload fails, the transaction will be uploaded again.

Fuzzy Query of BigchainDB Data Based on MongoDB. BigchainDB supports multiple query APIs. However, it does not support fuzzy queries based on the range of a field. This system needs to obtain carbon emission data from the BigchainDB network according to the time range for the calculation of the carbon emissions of enterprises. The steps of a fuzzy query are as follows:

Step 1: Carbon emissions data successfully uploaded to BigchainDB will generate a transaction id. The transaction id and the timestamp of data will be uploaded to a mongo database.

Step 2: The enterprise initiates a data request to the BigchainDB network according to the timestamp range, and the BigchainDB network initiates an asynchronous multi-thread request to the MongoDB database to obtain all transaction ids within the time range.

Step 3: The MongoDB database fetches the documents in the database collection based on the timestamp range, and then returns the list of transaction ids to the BigchainDB network.

Step 4: The BigchainDB network obtains all carbon data in the period according to the transaction id list and returns them to the enterprise.

Hierarchical Computation of Carbon Emission. Carbon emission hierarchical calculation according to the carbon emission calculation formula in the Technical Specifications for Continuous Monitoring of Flue Gas Carbon Dioxide Emissions of Heat-engine plants issued by the National Energy Administration of China [21].

Real-time carbon emission data storage: After the real-time data of carbon emission is successfully stored in the BigchainDB network, the transaction id and timestamp are stored in RealtimeCol of a MongoDB database.

Minutely carbon emissions data calculation: It calculates the average carbon dioxide volume concentration, average carbon dioxide mass concentration, average flue gas velocity, average flue gas temperature, average flue gas static pressure, and average flue gas humidity per minute and uploads the average values and minute timestamps of these parameters to BigchainDB. The txid and timestamp of the successful data are stored in MinTimeCol in MongoDB.

Hourly carbon emission calculation: The system needs multiple threads to obtain the minute carbon data of all generator sets in that hour. The enterprise includes multiple generating units to produce carbon emissions. Therefore, the calculation formula is expanded, and the carbon emissions of multiple generating sets of the enterprise are calculated as follows:

$$G_h = c_d \times Q_{Sn} \times 10^{-6} \tag{1}$$

$$G_H = \sum_{n=1}^{n} G_{hn} \tag{2}$$

In formula 1, G_h is the mass flow rate of flue gas carbon dioxide emission. c_d is the dry base mass concentration of carbon dioxide under standard condition. Q_{Sn} Wet flue gas flow under actual working conditions. In formula 2, G_H is the mass flow rate of accumulated flue gas carbon dioxide emission from all engine units of the enterprise. G_{hn} is the mass flow rate of flue gas carbon dioxide emission from Group n generating units of the enterprise. The enterprise has n sets of generating units. The calculated carbon emissions and hour timestamps are uploaded to BigchainDB, and then the txid and timestamp are stored in HourTimeCol of MongoDB.

The daily carbon emission is the cumulative sum of the hourly carbon emission of the enterprise; the monthly carbon emission is the cumulative sum of the daily carbon emission of the enterprise in a month; and the annual carbon emission of the enterprise is the cumulative sum of the daily carbon emission of the enterprise in a year. The calculated carbon emissions are uploaded to BigchainDB, which stores txid and timestamp to DayTimeCol, MonthTimeCol, and YearTimeCol of MongoDB, respectively.

Credible Carbon Emission Data Certificates Management for Enterprises. The Ministry of Ecology Environment first examines whether enterprises are equipped with a complete set of IoT devices to monitor carbon emissions, then examines whether enterprises are equipped with the BigchainDB storage network to store carbon emission data, and finally examines whether enterprises are equipped with carbon emission hierarchical calculation. If all the verification passes, the enterprises will be issued with credible certificates. If any process fails to pass the examination, the enterprises will not be issued credible certificates. The steps for the Ministry of Ecology and Environment to issue a trusted carbon emission digital certificate to an enterprise are as follows:

Step 1: The enterprise generates a public key and a private key, and then consolidates information to generate X500Name. The enterprise assembles the basic information and public key, and uses the private key to sign the request information and generate the CSR request file.

Step 2: The Ministry of Ecology Environment generates a public key and a private key. The X509CertificateUtils invokes the root certificate creation method to generate the root certificate, which is used to issue the trusted carbon emission digital certificate for enterprises.

Step 3: The Ministry of Ecology Environment reads the CSR file of an enterprise, and then issues the enterprise certificate with the root certificate and own private key. The private key is used to sign the enterprise certificate. The Subject information of an enterprise trusted digital certificate is as follows: "CN = manageA, L = xi'an, OU = HEP1". The Issue information is as follows: "CN = EnvironmentAdmin, L = xi'an, OU = Environment".

3.3   On-Chain Trusted Carbon Emission Trading Scheme

Identity Authentication and Transaction Rationality Review. Before carbon trading, enterprises are required to pass identity authentication and a reasonableness review by auditing smart contract.

Enterprises that pass the identity authentication can access the carbon emission trading system and initiate trading requests. Enterprises that fail the identity authentication cannot access the carbon emission trading system. It is used to ensure that enterprises participating in carbon emission rights trading have real and credible carbon emissions off the chain, ensuring the authenticity and credibility of carbon emission data of enterprises in the consortium chain network.

Exchange nodes are set up on the consortium chain network to develop smart contracts for transaction rationality verification mechanism, which will check enterprises' trusted carbon emission digital certificates and the rationality of trading applications. Taking the average transaction value of carbon emission trading on the National Carbon Emission Exchange as the baseline, the floating price from the lowest transaction value to the highest transaction value is used to examine the rationality of the transaction. BoodCET offers one-way auction and agreement transfer transactions. For a one-way auction, auditing smart contract examines the reasonableness of the selling reserve price and the purchase reserve price. If the selling reserve price is at a reasonable floating price, the audit is approved. Otherwise, the transaction initiation fails. Agreement transfer reviews the seller's sales volume and selling unit price, and reviews the buyer's purchase unit price. If the selling unit price and the purchase unit price are at a reasonable floating price, the review passes. Otherwise, the enterprise transaction rationality audit failed.

Reputation Mechanism. BoodCET employs the enterprise reputation mechanism to encourage enterprises to actively achieve carbon reduction and actively participate in carbon emission trading.

The reputation of the enterprise is determined based on the number of the enterprise's participation in carbon emission trading and the proportion of the enterprise's latest used carbon emission over the total quota. In the case of the same price, enterprises with high reputation value have the high priority trading right in carbon emission trading. In the process of transaction matching, enterprises are ordered from high to low according to their reputation, and those with high reputation values have 100% purchase right. The reputation of an enterprise R_{score} is calculated as follows:

$$R_{score} = T_{nums} + CE_{proportion} \tag{3}$$

T_{nums} is the reputation value of enterprises participating in carbon emission trading number, which is used to encourage enterprises to participate in carbon emission trading. If the enterprise's transaction is successful, the reputation value is added by 1. If the enterprise's transaction is failure, the reputation value is added by 0.5.

The $CE_{proportion}$ value is calculated as follows. The system calculates the proportion of the latest used carbon emissions to the total quota of the participating enterprises and ranks enterprises proportionally from lowest to highest at zero point each month. The reputation value of the top 25% of enterprises with the lowest proportion will be increased by 1. For enterprises between 25% and 75% reputation value after the transaction, 0.5 is added. The enterprises with the highest proportion, namely the last 25%, will not get the reputation value.

Carbon Emission Trading. BoodCET constructs a Fabric consortium chain network between enterprises and exchanges. Data related to carbon emission trading is stored on the blockchain to ensure that transaction data is tamper-proof. It ensures that the data on the chain is real, reliable, and traceable. Bood-CET offers one-way auction and agreement transfer two trading ways. Figure 2 shows the carbon emission trading process. The steps of the carbon emission trading process are as follows:

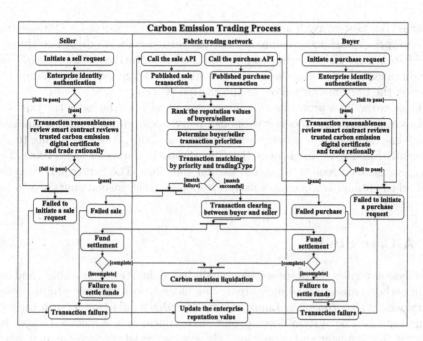

Fig. 2. The carbon emission trading process.

Step 1: The seller initiates a sale request. It then needs to pass the identity authentication. Transaction reasonableness review smart contract checks the enterprise's trusted carbon emission digital certificate and transaction rationality. After the verification is passed, calls the sale API to publish the sale transaction.

Step 2: The buyer initiates a purchase request. It also needs to pass identity authentication. Transaction reasonableness review smart contract checks the enterprise's trusted carbon emission digital certificate and transaction rationality. After the verification is passed, and then calls the purchase API to publish the purchase transaction.

Step 3: Take the seller selling and multiple buyers buying as an example to introduce the transaction process. Firstly, the enterprises' credit value is sorted and the transaction is matched according to the purchase price. If the purchase price is the same, the buyers with high credit value have the priority to deal. Secondly, the carbon emission rights that can be purchased by buyers follow the ranking result of enterprise reputation value. Enterprises with the top 25% credit value have 100% purchase right, enterprises with 25% to 75% credit value have 75% purchase right, and enterprises with the bottom 25% credit value have 50% purchase right. Then, the transaction matching is carried out. If the transaction matching succeeds, the enterprise carbon emission value will be updated, and the credit value of the enterprises participating in the transaction is increased by 1. If the match fails, the credit value is increased by 0.5. Finally, the enterprise credit value is updated. The carbon emission trading is over.

Interactive Gateway. The interactive gateway is responsible for transmitting the enterprise's carbon emission and trusted carbon emission digital certificate. The system uses gRPC technology to realize the interactive gateway [24]. This section takes the carbon emissions of transmission enterprises as an example to describe the implementation of the interaction process.

First, we write a proto file. The message request body includes the txid and URL parameters. The message response body is enterprise's carbon emission value. Then, the system generates the grpc class of the service according to the proto file. Finally, we implement the Client and the Server of the service. The enterprise sends a request to obtain carbon emissions. The Server side calls the method to obtain carbon emissions and responds to the carbon emissions to the enterprise.

4   A Case Study

This section verifies the proposed blockchain-based dual trusted on-chain and off-chain carbon emission trading system. The blockchain nodes are run in docker containers, which run on a Linux server. The BigchainDB nodes run on four Linux servers. The system development environment is a Windows 11 host for program development and debugging. The system initializes 5 heat-engine plant nodes and 1 exchange node, and the heat-engine plant enterprise BigchainDB storage network initializes 3 generator set carbon data centers and 1 Ministry of Ecology Environment carbon data center.

Taking one-way auction trading as an example, the process of carbon emission rights trading is analyzed. After the seller passes the identity authentication and the government-affiliated exchange's review, the seller makes public the sale transaction information. In the key information of sale transaction, sellId is sell10, hepId is HEP1, latestRemainCep is 4.2 million tons, sellNum is 100,000 tons, and sellPrice is 39 yuan/ton, tradingType is One-way auction, tradingTime is 2023-02-25-08-00–2023-02-25-10-00, and reputationValue is 3.

The buyer launches the auction within the auction time, to prevent malicious auction, the sealed auction method is adopted, and the buyer encrypts the purchase price and publishes it on the consortium chain network. After the auction time, the one-way auction smart contract decrypts the purchase price. Table 1 shows all buyers' auction transaction information.

Table 1. All buyers auction transaction information.

Buyers	Purchase price	Purchase volume	Reputation value	Purchase right
HEP2	42 yuan/ton	100000 tons	3	75%
HEP3	48 yuan/ton	80000 tons	4	100%
HEP4	40 yuan/ton	100000 tons	1	50%
HEP5	45 yuan/ton	60000 tons	2	75%

Smart contracts first rank heat-engine plants according to the purchase price, from highest to lowest HEP3, HEP5, HEP2, and HEP4. The four heat-engine plants participating in the auction transaction are sorted according to the reputation value: HEP3, HEP2, HEP5, and HEP4. According to the order of reputation value, HEP3 has 100% purchase right, HEP2 and HEP5 have 75% purchase right, and HEP4 has 50% purchase right. The transaction matching results are shown in Table 2.

Table 2. Transaction matching results.

Participator	Transaction price	Trading volume	proportion of used	New reputation value
HEP1	39 yuan/ton	100000 tons	16%	5
HEP3	48 yuan/ton	80000 tons	24.85%	5
HEP5	45 yuan/ton	20000 tons	22.50%	3.5
HEP2	42 yuan/ton	0 ton	23.08%	4
HEP4	40 yuan/ton	0 ton	23.88%	1.5

HEP3 has the highest purchase price and 100% purchase right, so the HEP3 transaction price is 48 yuan and the transaction volume is 8 tons. HEP5 has the second purchase price and 75% purchase right, so HEP5 can buy 45000 tons, HEP1 can sell 100000 tons, HEP3 can buy 80000 tons, and HEP5 can trade 20000 tons. The participation of HEP2 and HEP4 in this auction transaction failed. According to the proportion of used carbon emissions in the total carbon emissions of the heat-engine plant at zero point and the success of the heat-engine plant trading, the heat-engine plant's reputation value is determined. HEP1's reputation of successful trading is increased by 1. HEP1 proportion ranked first, so the reputation value is added 1. HEP1's final reputation value is 5. According to the calculation method of HEP1 reputation value, HEP3's final reputation value is 5. HEP5's final reputation value is 3.5. HEP2's final reputation value is 4. HEP4's final reputation value is 1.5. The system transaction result interface is shown in Fig. 3.

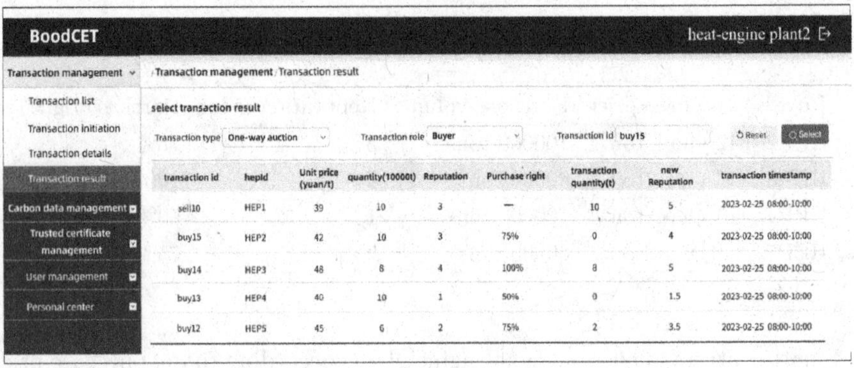

Fig. 3. The system transaction result interface.

This paper tests the data storage synchronization performance of BigchainDB storage network, the fuzzy query performance of BigchainDB and the interactive gateway processing performance. According to the requirements, 200 users are simulated to initiate 20,000 requests for 10 rounds of performance tests. The system performance test results are shown in Table 3. The test results show that the data storage performance of Ethereum is much lower than that of BigchainDB storage network, and the BoodCET system can meet the performance requirements of users using the system. Since the traditional carbon emission trading system requires carbon emission enterprises to have access rights, this paper does not compare the traditional carbon emission trading system.

Table 3. Performance test results.

Test item	Number of requests	Average tps	Ethereum	Requirement
BigchainDB storage	20000	8529	18	5000
BigchainDB fuzzy query	20000	19523	–	8000
interactive gateway	20000	4634	–	3000

5   Conclusion

This paper proposes a blockchain-based dual trusted on-chain and off-chain carbon emission trading framework. To realize the authenticity and credibility of carbon emission data provided by enterprises under the chain, BoodCET uses the BigchainDB storage network and IoT devices to collect and store carbon emission data. Moreover, BoodCET introduces the Ministry of Ecology Environment to supervise the carbon emission data. It also uses the Fabric consortium chain technology and government regulated exchanges to build a trusted carbon emission trading network. Fabric CA is employed to authenticate enterprises accessing the consortium network, ensuring the security of the carbon emission trading network. To encourage enterprises to reduce carbon emissions and participate in carbon emission trading, a reputation mechanism is proposed. Enterprises obtain reputation value by participating in carbon emission trading and reducing carbon emissions and have advantages in trading. Finally, BoodCET is implemented and verified. This paper uses a one-way auction as an example to analyze and test the process and results of enterprises participating in carbon emission trading.

BoodCET ensures dual-trusted carbon emission trading in the process of carbon emission trading and has a wide range of application prospects and practical value in the future carbon emission trading market.

References

1. Protocol, K.: Kyoto protocol. UNFCCC Website (1997). http://unfccc.int/kyoto_protocol/items/2830.php. Accessed 1 Jan 2011
2. Abrell, J.: Regulating CO2 emissions of transportation in Europe: a CGE-analysis using market-based instruments. Transp. Res. Part D: Transp. Environ. **15**(4), 235–239 (2010)
3. Emissions Trading Worldwide: ICAP Status Report 2022. https://icapcarbonaction.com/en/publications/emissions-trading-worldwide-icap-status-report-2022. Accessed 24 Mar 2023
4. The Ministry of Ecology and Environment notified four institutions of data fraud in carbon emission reporting. http://finance.people.com.cn/n1/2022/0315/c1004-32375033.html. Accessed 20 Mar 2023
5. Patsonakis, C., Terzi, S., Moschos, I., Ioannidis, D., Votis, K., Tzovaras, D.: Permissioned blockchains and virtual nodes for reinforcing trust between aggregators

and prosumers in energy demand response scenarios. In: 2019 IEEE International Conference on Environment and Electrical Engineering and 2019 IEEE Industrial and Commercial Power Systems Europe (EEEIC/I&CPS Europe), pp. 1–6. IEEE (2019)

6. McConaghy, T., et al.: BigchainDB: a scalable blockchain database. White paper, BigChainDB (2016)

7. Skjærseth, J.B., Wettestad, J.: EU Emissions Trading: Initiation, Decision-Making and Implementation. Ashgate Publishing, Ltd. (2008)

8. Haines, A., et al.: Public health benefits of strategies to reduce greenhouse-gas emissions: overview and implications for policy makers. Lancet **374**(9707), 2104–2114 (2009)

9. Cushing, L., et al.: Carbon trading, co-pollutants, and environmental equity: evidence from California's cap-and-trade program (2011–2015). PLoS Med. **15**(7), e1002604 (2018)

10. Kim, S.K., Huh, J.H.: Blockchain of carbon trading for un sustainable development goals. Sustainability **12**(10), 4021 (2020)

11. Pan, Y., et al.: Application of blockchain in carbon trading. Energy Procedia **158**, 4286–4291 (2019)

12. Niya, S.R., Jha, S.S., Bocek, T., Stiller, B.: Design and implementation of an automated and decentralized pollution monitoring system with blockchains, smart contracts, and LoRaWAN. In: NOMS 2018-2018 IEEE/IFIP Network Operations and Management Symposium, pp. 1–4. IEEE (2018)

13. Ashley, M.J., Johnson, M.S.: Establishing a secure, transparent, and autonomous blockchain of custody for renewable energy credits and carbon credits. IEEE Eng. Manage. Rev. **46**(4), 100–102 (2018)

14. Tang, Q., Tang, L.M.: Toward a distributed carbon ledger for carbon emissions trading and accounting for corporate carbon management. J. Emerg. Technol. Account. **16**(1), 37–46 (2019)

15. Hartmann, S., Thomas, S.: Applying blockchain to the Australian carbon market. Econ. Pap.: J. Appl. Econ. Policy **39**(2), 133–151 (2020)

16. Hua, W., Sun, H.: A blockchain-based peer-to-peer trading scheme coupling energy and carbon markets. In: 2019 International Conference on Smart Energy Systems and Technologies (SEST), pp. 1–6. IEEE (2019)

17. Khaqqi, K.N., Sikorski, J.J., Hadinoto, K., Kraft, M.: Incorporating seller/buyer reputation-based system in blockchain-enabled emission trading application. Appl. Energy **209**, 8–19 (2018)

18. Liang, X., Du, Y., Wang, X., Zeng, Y.: Design of a double-blockchain structured carbon emission trading scheme with reputation. In: 2019 34rd Youth Academic Annual Conference of Chinese Association of Automation (YAC), pp. 464–467. IEEE (2019)

19. Al Sadawi, A., Madani, B., Saboor, S., Ndiaye, M., Abu-Lebdeh, G.: A comprehensive hierarchical blockchain system for carbon emission trading utilizing blockchain of things and smart contract. Technol. Forecast. Soc. Chang. **173**, 121124 (2021)

20. Muzumdar, A., Modi, C., Vyjayanthi, C.: A permissioned blockchain enabled trustworthy and incentivized emission trading system. J. Clean. Prod. **349**, 131274 (2022)

21. National Energy Administration of China: Technical Specifications for Continuous Monitoring of Flue Gas Carbon Dioxide Emissions of Heat-Engine Plants, 2nd edn. China Electric Power Press (2021)

22. Hunkeler, U., Truong, H.L., Stanford-Clark, A.: MQTT-s-a publish/subscribe protocol for wireless sensor networks. In: 2008 3rd International Conference on Communication Systems Software and Middleware and Workshops (COMSWARE 2008), pp. 791–798. IEEE (2008)
23. Androulaki, E., et al.: Hyperledger fabric: a distributed operating system for permissioned blockchains. In: Proceedings of the Thirteenth EuroSys Conference, pp. 1–15 (2018)
24. Wang, X., Zhao, H., Zhu, J.: GRPC: a communication cooperation mechanism in distributed systems. ACM SIGOPS Oper. Syst. Rev. **27**(3), 75–86 (1993)

Empirical Study and Surveys

Smart Contract Vulnerability Detection Methods: A Survey

GuoJin Sun[1], Chi Jiang[2], JinQing Shen[1], and Yin Zhang[1,2](✉)

[1] Shenzhen Institute for Advanced Study, UESTC, University of Electronic Science and Technology of China, 518000 Shenzhen, China
zhangyin123@uestc.edu.cn
[2] School of Information and Communication Engineering, University of Electronic Science and Technology of China, Chengdu 610000, China

Abstract. Blockchain technology has gained widespread attention due to its decentralized nature. With the combination of smart contracts, the application of blockchain technology has expanded into more complex business scenarios, including digital collectibles, financial trades, and metaverses. However, the security vulnerabilities in smart contracts not only pose significant risks to their applications but also undermine the credibility of the blockchain system. As a result, research on smart contract vulnerability detection methods has attracted global attention. This paper introduces common smart contract vulnerabilities and summarizes the research on smart contract vulnerability detection methods and commonly used datasets. The progress of smart contract vulnerability detection research is reviewed from the perspectives of static analysis methods and dynamic analysis methods. A comparison and analysis are conducted on the input code categories, vulnerability types, and classification output formats of each method. Finally, based on the summary of existing research on smart contract vulnerability detection, the challenges in the field of smart contract vulnerability detection are discussed, and future research directions are proposed.

Keywords: Blockchain · Smart Contract · Ethereum · Smart Contract Datasets · Vulnerability Detection

1 Introduction

The concept of blockchain was proposed by S. Nakamoto in 2008, and later, the early representative blockchain platform, Bitcoin [1], was established, which significantly accelerated the development of blockchain technology. Blockchain technology represents a fully distributed public ledger and peer-to-peer platform that leverages cryptographic knowledge to store various data, including applications, digital currencies, and more. The advent of the Ethereum Zone [2] blockchain platform marked the beginning of the 2.0 era for blockchain technology. Smart contracts, which are executable code on the blockchain, have greatly expanded the range of applications for blockchain technology, extending beyond the initial financial sector to include areas such as the industrial

J. Chen et al. (Eds.): BlockSys 2023, CCIS 1896, pp. 179–196, 2024.
https://doi.org/10.1007/978-981-99-8101-4_13

Internet of Things [3], medical [4], and energy [5]. In contrast to Bitcoin, the Ethereum platform allows for the execution of smart contracts. Smart contracts are a core component of Ethereum, enabling developers to create their own applications at a lower cost using the blockchain structure. Since smart contracts are enforced automatically by the blockchain's consensus mechanism and do not rely on trusted authorities, they are both open and immutable. The bytecode, or open-source source code, of smart contracts on the blockchain can be accessed by anyone. However, due to their openness and close association with blockchain account assets, smart contracts have become a prime target for hackers. Exploiting vulnerabilities in smart contracts can lead to significant financial losses. For instance, the infamous DAO vulnerability [6] resulted in economic losses exceeding $60 million in June 2016. Additionally, the integer spill error during the BEC activity caused losses of $900 million.

Hence, smart contract user groups typically have the following two requirements: (1) As developers and deployers of the contract, they face the challenge that once the contract is deployed on the blockchain, it becomes immutable and cannot be updated or modified in situ. Therefore, to ensure the contract's security and the rights and interests of its user groups, there is an urgent need for methods that can accurately and swiftly detect vulnerabilities in the contract. This information would provide a reference for developers, enabling them to modify the contract before deployment and ensure its security without vulnerabilities. (2) As users of the contract, they encounter difficulties in verifying the security of the called contract, as smart contracts deployed on the blockchain often lack source code and their bytecode is difficult to comprehend for most users. Manual review alone is insufficient to guarantee the security of the contract. Consequently, these user groups are in need of a tool that can detect vulnerabilities in the contract based on its bytecode information. This would enable them to obtain contract vulnerability information even after deployment, thereby safeguarding the security of the contract caller's account.

In response to the aforementioned user needs, numerous researchers have investigated and summarized methods for detecting vulnerabilities in smart contracts from various perspectives. Among them, Xu et al. [7] conducted an analysis of tools capable of identifying contract vulnerabilities through smart contract bytecode files, categorizing the types of vulnerabilities. Zhou et al. [8] examined 13 vulnerabilities in Ethereum smart contracts, along with their corresponding countermeasures, and studied nine security analysis tools. Purathani Praitheeshan et al. [9] conducted an investigation into vulnerabilities, with a focus on identifying key vulnerabilities in Ethereum's smart contracts based on internal mechanisms and software security vulnerabilities. M. Saad et al. [10] delved into smart contract attacks and defenses. N. Atzei et al. [11] discussed security vulnerabilities in Ethereum smart contracts within the context of common programming problems, highlighting specific security vulnerabilities and associated real-world attacks. However, these investigations and studies did not delve into comprehensive classification research on currently known smart contract vulnerability detection methods and lacked a comparative analysis of the detection capabilities of relevant methods.

Therefore, the main contributions of this paper are as follows:

– Introduction of several common contract vulnerabilities and statistical analysis of the presently known common contract vulnerabilities.

- A categorized survey of existing smart contract detection methods was conducted, comparing the functionalities of these detection methods and summarizing some of the existing datasets.
- Identification of existing issues in current smart contract detection methods and a discussion on future research goals and directions in the field of smart contract detection.

2   Common Contract Loopholes

2.1   Reentrancy Vulnerability

The reentrancy vulnerability [11] enables an attacker to execute recursive calls to request and receive funds from a susceptible contract. In this scenario, the attacker continuously withdraws funds by invoking a smart contract with vulnerabilities before updating the smart contract's account. They achieve this by recursively invoking the fetch function of the target contract until the contract balance reaches zero. Specifically, the attacker embeds the recall function within the fallback function of the attack contract. The fallback function serves as the default function in Ethereum smart contracts and can be declared without an explicit function name. As the fallback function is automatically triggered whenever an attacker receives funds, the smart contract effectively invokes the embedded withdrawal function. This arrangement allows the attacker to recursively invoke the recall function prior to updating the user's balance. Notable instances of such attacks include the DAO (Decentralized Autonomous Organization) incidents [12] (Fig. 1).

```solidity
1  pragma solidity ^0.8.0;
2  contract EtherStore {
3      mapping(address => uint) public balances;
4      function deposit() public payable {
5          balances[msg.sender] += msg.value;
6      }
7      function withdraw() public {
8          uint bal = balances[msg.sender];
9          require(bal > 0);
10         (bool sent,) = msg.sender.call{value: bal}("");
11         require(sent, "Failed to send Ether");
12         balances[msg.sender] = 0;
13     }
14     function getBalance() public view returns (uint) {
15         return address(this).balance;
16     }
17 }
```

Fig. 1. Reentrant Vulnerability Code Case (A malicious contract can empty the contract account by calling the withdraw function in a loop until the contract executes balance [msg.sender] = 0)

Exploiting reentrancy vulnerabilities involves several steps:

Step 1: The attacker initiates the transaction by calling the victim's exit function.
Step 2: The victim transfers funds and invokes the attacker's fallback function.
Step 3: The fallback function recursively calls the exit function, thereby establishing a reentrant process.
Step 4: Within the iteration range, additional funds are transferred to the attacker multiple times.

2.2 Timestamp Dependency Vulnerability

Blocks in Ethereum are created during the mining process, where miners can arbitrarily decide the timestamp of the entire block within a 900-s range. However, after the Ethereum upgrade [2], this range has been reduced to a few seconds. All transactions recorded in a block share the same timestamp. Since miners have control over the timestamp, certain applications that rely on time constraints can be vulnerable to malicious miners. Additionally, timestamps are often used as seeds for generating random numbers. Hence, an attacker can exploit a smart contract by manipulating the timestamp of a block. For instance, if a feature is designed to allow each user access once per hour, an attacker can modify their system clock or manipulate server communication to make it appear as if an hour has passed. This enables the attacker to bypass restrictions and access the feature multiple times.

2.3 Integer Overflow Vulnerability

Integer overflow vulnerabilities encompass both underflow and overflow situations, occurring when the execution requires storing data outside the range of a fixed-size variable. The Ethereum Virtual Machine (EVM) [2] specifies that integers have fixed-size data types, limiting the number of values that can be represented by an integer variable. Attackers can exploit this vulnerability by leveraging smart contract code to create unexpected logical flows. To address integer overflow vulnerabilities, Ethereum provides the SafeMath library for developers. This library detects integer overflow behavior and throws an exception when an overflow occurs.

2.4 Delegate Call Vulnerability

In Solidity, there are two commonly utilized built-in variables: msg.sender and msg.data. The former represents the address of the contract caller, while the latter represents the data passed in by the caller. Additionally, in Solidity, methods that invoke other contracts can be implemented using the delegatecall() method through delegates, apart from the call() method. Unlike call() invocations, delegatecall() modifies the caller's storage, and upon its invocation, msg.sender always retains the address of the original caller [13]. Exploiting the context of their own contract, attackers employ delegate calls to execute the code of other contracts. By setting the delegate call parameter to msg.data, attackers typically construct msg.data to execute any function that invokes the victim's contract. Notably, it was due to this hazardous vulnerability in delegated calls that the Parity contract suffered a loss of 30 million dollars' worth of ether [14].

2.5 Access Control Vulnerabilities

The Ethereum contract developer (Owner) has super authority over the contract, including freezing tokens, issuing additional tokens, burning tokens, minting new tokens, and terminating contract operations. If the contract permissions are stolen by an attacker, it will have a serious impact [15]. Access control vulnerabilities arise because the writers of smart contracts fail to accurately check the access rights of functions in the contract, such as indiscriminate or undefined permissions for some functions that should be set to private, defaulting to the public type. These functions should be inaccessible to ordinary users, so attackers have sufficient privileges to access functions or variables that they should not access.

In addition to the above five common contract vulnerabilities, smart contracts may also contain vulnerabilities such as block information dependence, insecure delegated calls, suicidal contracts, and short address attacks [16], as shown in Table 1.

With the development of blockchain technology, some original loopholes will be avoided in future development, and new loopholes will gradually enter the public's field of vision. Therefore, the study of how to find vulnerabilities and fix them will be accompanied by the development of blockchain technology.

Table 1. Other Common Smart Contract Vulnerabilities.

Vulnerability Name	Basic Description
block information dependency [17]	Malicious miners may manipulate block information to manipulate the behavior of smart contracts
unsafe delegate call [18]	Malicious external contracts can directly control the behavior of the caller contract and modify the state of the caller contract
suicide contract [19]	Solidity provides a self-destruct interface to destroy contracts, but due to missing or insufficient access controls, malicious parties can destroy contracts
short address attack [20]	When an attacker maliciously packs address data with a length less than 20 bytes, it will cause transaction data parsing errors
transaction-ordering dependent [21]	If the business logic of the smart contract uses the order of transactions as a decision-making condition or the execution of the current transaction has an impact on the results of subsequent transactions, an attacker can attack the contract by manipulating transaction packaging
Unchecked call return value [22]	Some external function call interfaces do not throw exceptions but display them in the form of return values. Therefore, developers need to verify the return value of these interfaces to determine whether the call was successful

3   Contract Detection Method

3.1   Static Analysis Method

Static analysis is a methodology used for analyzing computer programs or compiled code in a non-runtime environment. It involves examining programming code without executing the program, aiming to identify all possible code behaviors, vulnerable patterns, and potential runtime flaws. This section presents the main static analysis methods for detecting vulnerabilities in smart contracts, focusing on non-deep learning methods and deep learning methods.

Non-deep Learning Methods. SmartCheck [23]. SmartCheck is a source code-level vulnerability detection tool that utilizes static analysis. It converts the Abstract Syntax Tree (AST) into an intermediate representation in the form of an XML parse tree. Then, it checks for predefined vulnerability patterns in this intermediate representation.

Securify [24]. Securify is a lightweight and scalable Ethereum smart contract security verifier. It is a static analysis tool based on symbolic abstraction and pattern matching. Securify defines compliance patterns and violation patterns for each security attribute. It then matches contracts against these patterns to detect vulnerabilities. Securify is capable of detecting vulnerabilities such as frozen tokens, transaction-ordering dependence (TOD), exception handling errors, and more (Fig. 2).

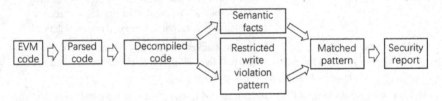

Fig. 2. Securify contract verification process.

Oyente [25]. Oyente is a symbolic execution-based static analysis tool that operates directly on EVM bytecode without relying on high-level languages like Solidity. It constructs a control flow graph (CFG) from the bytecode of a smart contract and applies symbolic execution to the CFG to identify predefined vulnerable patterns. Oyente is capable of detecting vulnerabilities such as transaction-ordering dependence (TOD) and exception handling errors.

Slither [26]. Slither is a static analysis framework for Ethereum smart contract analysis. It combines data flow analysis and taint analysis to provide comprehensive information. The tool converts smart contract source code into an intermediate representation called SlithIR, which utilizes static single allocation (SSA) form and a reduced instruction set to simplify the analysis process while retaining the semantics lost during the conversion to EVM bytecode. Slither can detect common vulnerabilities in smart contracts and offer suggestions for code optimization.

Mythril [27]. Mythril is an Ethereum contract security analysis tool that employs symbolic execution and taint analysis. It disassembles the EVM bytecode and initializes the contract account's state. Mythril explores the state space of the contract using two transactions. If an undesired state is encountered, Mythril employs Z3-Solver to prove or disprove its reachability under specific assumptions. When a vulnerable state is discovered, Mythril computes the transactions necessary to reach that state and verifies the existence of the vulnerability.

Deep Learning Method. RecChecker [28]. RecChecker is a deep learning-based method primarily used for detecting reentrancy vulnerabilities in smart contracts. This approach captures fundamental semantic information and control flow dependencies by converting contract source codes into contract fragments. RecChecker utilizes a bidirectional long-short-term memory (BLSTM) with an attention mechanism to automatically detect reentrancy vulnerabilities.

DR-GCN [29] and TMP [29]. The DR-GCN method explores the contract graph for smart contract vulnerability detection and employs a graph convolutional neural network (GCN) to transform the smart contract into a contract graph structure with highly semantic representation. It constructs a vulnerability detection model and analyzes smart contracts on the Ethereum and VNT Chain platforms, targeting three types of vulnerabilities: reentrancy, timestamp dependency, and infinite loops. TMP is a deep learning-based source-level vulnerability detection tool that utilizes graph representation and a graph neural network (GNN). It converts contracts into normalized graphs and employs a deep learning model called the Time Message Propagation Network (TMP) for vulnerability detection. TMP is an advanced version that incorporates contract graphs for smart contract vulnerability detection. By constructing the contract graph, key functions and variables are transformed into core nodes with high semantic information, while the execution mode is reflected in the directed edges based on control dependency and data dependency. TMP consists of three phases, and it also considers time information at the edge of the contract graph and constructs the time message propagation graph neural network (Fig. 3).

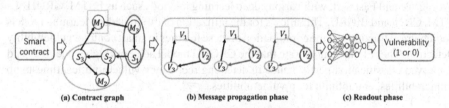

| (a) Contract graph | (b) Message propagation phase | (c) Readout phase |

Fig. 3. Contract diagram generation and TMP architecture diagram.

CGE [30]. CGE is the first to explore the fusion of traditional expert mode and graph neural networks for extracting features in smart contract vulnerability detection. It proposes representing contract function source code as a contract graph. CGE explicitly normalizes the graph to emphasize key variables and calls. Finally, it employs a novel temporal information propagation network to automatically capture semantic graph features and combine them with the designed expert patterns to obtain the final detection results.

AME [31]. AME is a novel system that goes beyond pure neural networks to automatically detect vulnerabilities and incorporate expert patterns into the network in an interpretable manner. Firstly, AME extracts vulnerability-specific expert patterns from function code. Secondly, AME utilizes graph construction and normalization modules to transform function codes into code-semantic graph vectors. Finally, AME combines local expert patterns and global graph features for vulnerability detection and produces interpretable weights. AME serves as an essential tool for explainable and accurate contract vulnerability detection.

Peculiar [32]. This method is based on key data flow graphs and Graph-CodeBERT, a deep learning-based source code-level vulnerability detection tool proposed by Guo et al. It converts contracts into key data flow graphs and employs graph-codeBERT models for vulnerability detection.

LSTM [33]. This method employs long short-term memory (LSTM) in deep learning to learn the sequence of smart contract weaknesses, allowing for the timely detection of new attack trends and the enhancement of smart contract security. LSTM classifies three types of contracts: greed, suicide, and squandering.

WBL-ATT [34]. This study proposes a method that combines Bi-LSTM and attention mechanisms for detecting multiple vulnerabilities in smart contract opcodes. Firstly, the data is preprocessed to convert opcodes into feature matrices suitable for neural network input. Then, the Bi-LSTM model with attention mechanism is employed to test smart contracts for reentrancy, integer overflow, transaction-ordering dependence (TOD), and timestamp dependency vulnerabilities, enabling their classification.

CBGRU [35]. CBGRU, as illustrated in Fig. 4 below, is a hybrid deep learning model proposed by Lejun, Zhang, et al. It integrates different word embeddings, namely Word2Vec and FastText, with various deep learning methods such as LSTM, GRU, BiLSTM, CNN, and BiGRU. This allows for the utilization of different deep learning models for feature extraction and the combination of these features in smart contract vulnerability detection. The results demonstrate that the CBGRU model achieves higher accuracy and improved classification performance in detecting reentrancy vulnerabilities, timestamp vulnerabilities, and infinite loop vulnerabilities.

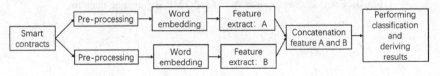

Fig. 4. CBGRU hybrid network architecture diagram.

MANDO [36]. MANDO is a novel heterogeneous graph representation method proposed in this study. It aims to learn multi-level embeddings of different types of nodes and their metapaths in heterogeneous contract graphs. This method is the first learning-based approach capable of identifying vulnerabilities at the fine-grained line level. It enables a more accurate capture of the code semantics of smart contracts, facilitating fine-grained line-level and coarse-grained contract-level vulnerability detection.

SPCBIG-EC [37]. This study presents SPCBIG-EC, a string convolution method suitable for hybrid models. It can extract features from input sequences, considering multivariate combinations while preserving temporal structure and position information. To enhance the model's robustness, the authors utilize an ensemble classifier during the classification stage. Experimental results demonstrate that SPCBIG-EC achieves superior performance in detecting reentrancy, timestamp dependence, and infinite loop vulnerabilities.

SCVDIE [38]. SCVDIE is a smart contract detection method based on ensemble learning (EL) and an infographic. It utilizes seven different neural networks, each pre-trained using an infographic(IG) consisting of a source dataset. These neural networks are integrated into an ensemble model, referred to as SCVDIE. The effectiveness of the model is verified using a dataset composed of infographics, and the method exhibits higher accuracy and robustness compared to other data-driven approaches.

3.2 Dynamic Analysis Method

Dynamic analysis is a method of examining a program while it is executing or running. It behaves similarly to an attacker searching for vulnerabilities in vulnerable code segments by providing malicious code or anonymous input to required functions in the program. Some vulnerabilities will have false negatives in static analysis but can be successfully identified by dynamic analysis methods. Usually, dynamic analysis methods are used to verify the accuracy of the results of static analysis methods.

ContractFuzzer [39]. The ContractFuzzer tool combines ABI and bytecode static analysis with fuzzing techniques to explore smart contract vulnerabilities. It utilizes an offline EVM to create an Ethereum testnet for monitoring the execution of smart contracts and extracting information from the execution process. By analyzing the ABI and bytecode, ContractFuzzer computes the function selector (the first four bytes of the function signature hash) and maps each ABI function to the set of function selectors used. Subsequently, an input generation algorithm is created based on the obtained information to obfuscate each function.

Sereum [40]. Sereum focuses on detecting reentrancy vulnerability types, including cross-functional reentrancy, delegation reentrancy, and creation-based reentrancy. It serves as an important tool for contract vulnerability detection.

Table 2. Comparison of Smart Contract Vulnerability Detection Methods.

Method Name	Type	Two-classification/multi-classification	Input	Detected Vulnerabilities
SmartCheck [23]	static/intermediate representation	Two-classification	source code	TOD, timestamp, dependencies, reentrancy and exception handling errors, etc.
Securify [24]	static/formal verification	Two-classification	bytecode	Exception handling, transaction- -ordering, call stack depth limit, unlimited writes, unlimitedtransfers, unvalidated parameters, etc.
Oyente [25]	static/symbolic execution	Two-classification	bytecode	Reentrancy, exception handling, transaction ordering, timestamp dependency, call stack depth limit
Slither [26]	static/intermediate representation	Two-classification	source code	Reentrancy, unprotected variables, incorrect ERO20 interface, multiple calls in loops, etc.
Mythril [27]	static/symbolic execution/deep learning	Two-classification	bytecode	Reentrancy, integer overflow, exception handling, etc.
RecChecker [28]	static/deep learning	Two-classification	source code	reentrant vulnerability
DR-GCN [29]	static/deep learning	Two-classification	source code	Reentrancy, timestamp dependencies, and infinite loops
TMP [29]	static/deep learning	Two-classification	source code	Reentrancy, timestamp dependencies, and infinite loops
CGE [30]	static/deep learning	Two-classification	source code	Reentrancy, timestamp dependencies, and infinite loops
AME [31]	static/deep learning	Two-classification	source code	Reentrancy, timestamp dependencies, and infinite loops
Peculiar [32]	static/deep learning	Two-classification	source code	reentrant vulnerability
LSTM [33]	static/deep learning	Two-classification/multi-classification	bytecode	Greed, suicide and profligacy

(*continued*)

Table 2. (*continued*)

Method Name	Type	Two-classification/multi-classification	Input	Detected Vulnerabilities
WBL-ATT [34]	static/deep learning	Two-classification/multi-classification	bytecode	Reentrancy, integer overflow, TOD and tires tamp dependencies
Contract Fuzzer [39]	dynamic	Two-classification/multi-classification	bytecode	Exceptions handle errors, reentrancy, predictable nonces, freeze fags,and etc.
Sereum [40]	dynamic	Two-classification/multi-classification	bytecode	reentrant vulnerability
sFuzz [41]	dynamic	Two-classification/multi-classification	ABI	Reentrancy, arithmetic problems, delegate calls tounsafe contracts, self-destruction, exception handling errors, ether freezing, timestamp dependencies
CBGRU [35]	deep learning	Two-classification/multi-classification	source code	Callstack Depth Attack, Integer overflow, Integer Underflow, Reentry, Timestamp Dependency, and Transaction Order Dependency
MANDO [36]	deep learning/Heterogeneous mapping methods	Two-classification/multi-classification	source code	Access control, arithmetic, denial of service, pre-run retracking, time manipulation, and unchecked low-level calls
SPCBIG-EC [37]	deep learning	Two-classification/multi-classification	source code	Reentrant vulnerabilities, timestamp dependencies, infinite loops, call stack depth attack vulnerabilities, integer overflow, and integer underflow
SCVDIE [38]	deep learning	Two-classification/multi-classification	bytecode	Reentrant vulnerability, arithmetic vulnerability, contract contains unknown address

sFuzz [41]. The sFuzz tool is an adaptive fuzzer that combines policies from the AFL fuzzer [42] and other adaptive policies based on Aleth [43]. It implements three additional components: runner, libfuzzer, and liboracles. The runner program configures the options for testing the network environment, while the other two components, libfuzzer and liboracles, execute the contract on the testnet. Libfuzzer selectively generates test cases using a feedback-guided adaptive fuzzing strategy, and liboracles monitors the execution of test cases and corresponding stack events to detect vulnerabilities.

RLF [44]. RLF is an emerging method based on reinforcement learning for vulnerability-guided fuzzing. It aims to generate a sequence of vulnerability transactions for the detection of complex vulnerabilities in smart contracts. Su et al. initially developed a reinforcement learning framework, modeling the process of contract fuzzing as a Markov decision-making process. To effectively guide the fuzzer in generating a specific transaction sequence to uncover vulnerabilities, particularly those related to multiple functions, a reward function was designed, taking into account vulnerabilities and code coverage. RLF represents a novel vulnerability detection method that outperforms many dynamic detection methods.

4   Function Comparison of Smart Contract Detection Methods

This section presents a comparison of the types, input data forms, and covered vulnerabilities among the aforementioned smart contract detection methods, as shown in Table 2. Bytecode-based methods primarily focus on static symbol execution, intermediate representation, formal verification, and dynamic techniques. On the other hand, source code-based vulnerability detection methods for smart contracts mainly emphasize deep learning approaches. However, there is a scarcity of detection methods that combine bytecode and deep learning techniques. Additionally, non-deep learning-based methods generally exhibit lower efficiency and accuracy in detecting contract vulnerabilities compared to deep learning-based approaches [8]. Existing methods often rely on fixed rules established by experts, which suffer from limitations such as single detection types, limited scalability, and high false-positive rates.

5   Future Directions and Open Issues

While numerous smart contract vulnerability detection methods have shown promising results in recent years, there are still several challenges that require attention in future research:

The first challenge lies in smart contract security. Although current research focuses on employing either a single AI method or a dynamic method for contract defect detection, future work should integrate the syntax, semantic information, and characteristics of smart contracts to conduct a comprehensive analysis. For instance, an integrated approach combining deep learning methods and automated auditing techniques can be explored to target specific contract defect characteristics and obtain contract information.

The second challenge pertains to vulnerability categorization. Smart contracts encompass various vulnerability types, including well-known ones like integer overflow and timestamp vulnerabilities. However, there are still numerous unknown category vulnerabilities that have implications for Ethereum's asset security. Existing detection methods often lack generalization capability and sufficient accuracy when it comes to detecting these unknown category vulnerabilities. Addressing this challenge is crucial for the further development of vulnerability detection methods.

Table 3. Smart Contract Datasets.

No.	Kinds	Label	Size	Description	URL
1	source code	no label	440 MB	The dataset consists of more than 40K real-life smart contracts of Ethereum	https://github.com/ Messi-Q/Smart-Contract-Dataset
2	bytecode/source code	with label	15.8 MB	This dataset involves four types of vulnerabilities: reentrancy, timestamp dependence, integer overflow, and dangerous delegate calls	https://github.com/ Messi-Q/Smart-Contract-Dataset
3	source code	with label	54.1 MB	The dataset contains more than 12K Ethereum smart contracts, including inheritance contracts, involving eight types of vulnerabilities including Reentrancy, Timestamp Dependency, and Block Number Dependency	https://github.com/ Messi-Q/Smart-Contract-Dataset
4	source code	with label	–	Smart contract vulnerability classification and test cases	https://github.com/ SmartContract
5	source code	with label	5.24 MB	This dataset contains more than 600 smart contract data, including 104 contracts with ether leakage and suicide vulnerabilities	https://github.com/ kupl/VeriSmart-benchmarks

(*continued*)

Table 3. (*continued*)

No.	Kinds	Label	Size	Description	URL
6	source code	no label	1.01 GB	The dataset contains 47,398 smart contracts extracted from the Ethereum network	https://github.com/smartbugs/smartbugs-wild
7	bytecode	with label	2.05 GB	The dataset has 148,384 contracts after cleaning,including 30 vulnerabilities such as integer overflow or underflow, unchecked call return value, unprotected ether withdrawal, etc	https://github.com/huangjing2021/SmartContract_Data
8	bytecode	with label	–	The dataset contains 93,497 samples, and each contract may contain multiple vulnerabilities, including eight smart contract vulnerabilities such as Callstack Depth, Reentrancy, and Multiple Sends	https://github.com/sss-wue/smarter-contracts
9	bytecode/source code	with label	292 MB	The dataset contains 6498 smart contracts on Ethereum, of which 318 are marked as Ponzi contracts annually and the rest are marked as non-Ponzi contracts per year	http://xblock.pro/#/dataset/25
10	bytecode/source code	no label	5.02 GB	Smart contract properties dataset, containing approximately 14,000 open source smart contracts	http://xblock.pro/#/dataset/17

The third challenge concerns the availability of datasets. Smart contract vulnerability detection heavily relies on substantial data support, whether employing static analysis methods or dynamic analysis methods. Experimental data constitutes a vital component of the research process. As the application of deep learning technology in smart contract vulnerability detection becomes increasingly extensive, there is a growing demand for standardized datasets related to smart contract vulnerabilities. However, obtaining and processing data poses certain difficulties due to the unique nature of smart contracts. Additionally, there is currently a lack of a recognized standard sample library for smart contract vulnerabilities, and no standard dataset exists for the same vulnerability, making it difficult to compare detection results with the latest models. In order to assist researchers dedicated to smart contract vulnerability detection, we have compiled and summarized existing datasets in Table 3.

The fourth challenge pertains to interpretability. The explainability of smart contract vulnerability detection is crucial, as the root cause of a vulnerability determines how it can be fixed and detected. However, some methods struggle to provide interpretable results due to complex data processing and algorithms, thereby making it challenging to comprehend and accept the detection results.

The fifth challenge involves solving the multi-classification detection problem. Although there is a considerable amount of research on smart contract vulnerability detection methods, most of them can only determine the presence or absence of vulnerabilities, without identifying the specific types of vulnerabilities. Therefore, future work in smart contract vulnerability detection should focus on classifying different types of vulnerabilities to achieve better method performance.

6   Conclusion

Due to the decentralized nature of blockchain technology and the immutability of smart contracts, the blockchain ecosystem is susceptible to security vulnerabilities and malicious activities. Numerous vulnerable contracts have been deployed on the Ethereum blockchain, and their functionality cannot be modified unless the blockchain undergoes a fork. While there have been some research efforts in the field of smart contract vulnerability detection, detecting all vulnerabilities within a contract remains highly challenging due to the wide variety of vulnerability types and the scarcity of labeled data. In this paper, we first introduce several commonly encountered contract vulnerabilities. Then, we conducted a comprehensive analysis and summary of some representative and recently proposed smart contract vulnerability detection methods. Finally, we highlight the challenges encountered in current research on smart contract vulnerability detection and outline some potential future directions for improving smart contract vulnerability detection. By addressing these research challenges and exploring new avenues for improvement, researchers can work towards mitigating the risks associated with smart contract vulnerabilities and enhancing the overall security of blockchain systems.

Acknowledgments. This research is funded by the National Key R&D Program of China (No. 2020YFB1006002).

References

1. Nakamoto, S.: Bitcoin: a peer-to-peer electronic cash system. Decentralized Bus. Rev. 21260 (2008)
2. Home—ethereum.org. https://ethereum.org/en/. Accessed 13 Apr 2023
3. Christidis, K., Devetsikiotis, M.: Blockchains and smart contracts for the internet of things. IEEE Access **4**, 2292–2303 (2016)
4. Azaria, A., Ekblaw, A., Vieira, T., Lippman, A.: MedRec: using blockchain for medical data access and permission management. In: 2016 2nd International Conference on Open and Big Data (OBD), pp. 25–30. IEEE (2016)
5. Knirsch, F., Unterweger, A., Eibl, G., Engel, D.: Privacy-preserving smart grid tariff decisions with blockchain-based smart contracts. In: Rivera, W. (ed.) Sustainable Cloud and Energy Services, pp. 85–116. Springer, Cham (2018). https://doi.org/10.1007/978-3-319-62238-5_4
6. CoinDesk: Bitcoin, Ethereum, Crypto News and Price Data. https://www.coindesk.com/. Accessed 13 Apr 2023
7. Xu, J., Dang, F., Ding, X., Zhou, M.: A survey on vulnerability detection tools of smart contract bytecode. In: 2020 IEEE 3rd International Conference on Information Systems and Computer Aided Education (ICISCAE), pp. 94–98. IEEE (2020)
8. Zhou, H., Milani Fard, A., Makanju, A.: The state of Ethereum smart contracts security: vulnerabilities, countermeasures, and tool support. J. Cybersecurity Priv. **2**(2), 358–378 (2022)
9. Praitheeshan, P., Pan, L., Yu, J., Liu, J., Doss, R.: Security analysis methods on Ethereum smart contract vulnerabilities: a survey. arXiv preprint arXiv:1908.08605 (2019)
10. Saad, M., et al.: Exploring the attack surface of blockchain: a systematic overview. arXiv preprint arXiv:1904.03487 (2019)
11. Atzei, N., Bartoletti, M., Cimoli, T.: A survey of attacks on Ethereum smart contracts (SoK). In: Maffei, M., Ryan, M. (eds.) POST 2017. LNCS, vol. 10204, pp. 164–186. Springer, Heidelberg (2017). https://doi.org/10.1007/978-3-662-54455-6_8
12. Manning, A.: Comprehensive list of known attack vectors and common antipatterns (2018)
13. Lu, N., Wang, B., Zhang, Y., Shi, W., Esposito, C.: Neucheck: a more practical Ethereum smart contract security analysis tool. Softw. Pract. Experience **51**(10), 2065–2084 (2021)
14. Fu, M., Wu, L., Hong, Z., Feng, W.: Research on vulnerability mining technique for smart contracts. J. Comput. Appl. **39**(7), 1959 (2019)
15. Zhao, W., Zhang, W., Wang, J., Wang, H., Wu, C.: Smart contract vulnerability detection scheme based on symbol execution. J. Comput. Appl. **40**(4), 947 (2020)
16. Cai, J., Li, B., Zhang, J., Sun, X., Chen, B.: Combine sliced joint graph with graph neural networks for smart contract vulnerability detection. J. Syst. Softw. **195**, 111550 (2023)
17. Wang, D., Jiang, B., Chan, W.: WANA: symbolic execution of wasm bytecode for cross-platform smart contract vulnerability detection. arXiv preprint arXiv:2007.15510 (2020)
18. Ma, F., et al.: Security reinforcement for Ethereum virtual machine. Inf. Process. Manag. **58**(4), 102565 (2021)
19. Salmerón-Manzano, E., Manzano-Agugliaro, F.: The role of smart contracts in sustainability: Worldwide research trends. Sustainability **11**(11), 3049 (2019). https://doi.org/10.3390/su111113049
20. Ferreira Torres, C., Iannillo, A.K., Gervais, A., State, R.: The eye of horus: spotting and analyzing attacks on Ethereum smart contracts. In: Borisov, N., Diaz, C. (eds.) FC 2021. LNCS, vol. 12674, pp. 33–52. Springer, Heidelberg (2021). https://doi.org/10.1007/978-3-662-64322-8_2
21. Alharby, M., Van Moorsel, A.: Blockchain-based smart contracts: a systematic mapping study. arXiv preprint arXiv:1710.06372 (2017)

22. Staderini, M., Palli, C.: An analysis on Ethereum vulnerabilities and further steps. In: 27th Ph.D. Minisymposium of the Department of Measurement and Information Systems, pp. 21–24. Budapest University of Technology and Economics (2020)
23. Tikhomirov, S., Voskresenskaya, E., Ivanitskiy, I., Takhaviev, R., Marchenko, E., Alexandrov, Y.: Smartcheck: static analysis of Ethereum smart contracts. In: Proceedings of the 1st International Workshop on Emerging Trends in Software Engineering for Blockchain, pp. 9–16 (2018)
24. Tsankov, P., Dan, A., Drachsler-Cohen, D., Gervais, A., Buenzli, F., Vechev, M.: Securify: practical security analysis of smart contracts. In: Proceedings of the 2018 ACM SIGSAC Conference on Computer and Communications Security, pp. 67–82 (2018)
25. Luu, L., Chu, D.-H., Olickel, H., Saxena, P., Hobor, A.: Making smart contracts smarter. In: Proceedings of the 2016 ACM SIGSAC Conference on Computer and Communications Security, pp. 254–269 (2016)
26. Feist, J., Grieco, G., Groce, A.: Slither: a static analysis framework for smart contracts. In: 2019 IEEE/ACM 2nd International Workshop on Emerging Trends in Software Engineering for Blockchain (WETSEB), pp. 8–15. IEEE (2019)
27. GitHub - ConsenSys/mythril: Security analysis tool for EVM bytecode. Supports smart contracts built for Ethereum, Hedera, Quorum, Vechain, Roostock, Tron and other EVM-compatible blockchains. https://github.com/ConsenSys/mythril. Accessed 13 Apr 2023
28. Qian, P., Liu, Z., He, Q., Zimmermann, R., Wang, X.: Towards automated reentrancy detection for smart contracts based on sequential models. IEEE Access **8**, 19685–19695 (2020)
29. Zhuang, Y., Liu, Z., Qian, P., Liu, Q., Wang, X., He, Q.: Smart contract vulnerability detection using graph neural network. In: IJCAI, pp. 3283–3290 (2020)
30. Liu, Z., Qian, P., Wang, X., Zhuang, Y., Qiu, L., Wang, X.: Combining graph neural networks with expert knowledge for smart contract vulnerability detection. IEEE Trans. Knowl. Data Eng. 3 (2021)
31. Liu, Z., Qian, P., Wang, X., Zhu, L., He, Q., Ji, S.: Smart contract vulnerability detection: from pure neural network to interpretable graph feature and expert pattern fusion. arXiv preprint arXiv:2106.09282 (2021)
32. Wu, H., et al.: Peculiar: smart contract vulnerability detection based on crucial data flow graph and pre-training techniques. In: 2021 IEEE 32nd International Symposium on Software Reliability Engineering (ISSRE), pp. 378–389. IEEE (2021)
33. Tann, W.J.-W., Han, X.J., Gupta, S.S., Ong, Y.-S.: Towards safer smart contracts: a sequence learning approach to detecting security threats. arXiv preprint arXiv:1811.06632 (2018)
34. Qian, S., Ning, H., He, Y., Chen, M.: Multi-label vulnerability detection of smart contracts based on bi-LSTM and attention mechanism. Electronics **11**(19), 3260 (2022)
35. Zhang, L., et al.: CBGRU: a detection method of smart contract vulnerability based on a hybrid model. Sensors **22**(9), 3577 (2022)
36. Nguyen, H.H., et al.: Mando: multi-level heterogeneous graph embeddings for fine-grained detection of smart contract vulnerabilities. arXiv preprint arXiv:2208.13252 (2022)
37. Zhang, L., et al.: SPCBIG-EC: a robust serial hybrid model for smart contract vulnerability detection. Sensors **22**(12), 4621 (2022)
38. Zhang, L., et al.: A novel smart contract vulnerability detection method based on information graph and ensemble learning. Sensors **22**(9), 3581 (2022)
39. Jiang, B., Liu, Y., Chan, W.K.: Contractfuzzer: fuzzing smart contracts for vulnerability detection. In: Proceedings of the 33rd ACM/IEEE International Conference on Automated Software Engineering, pp. 259–269 (2018)
40. Rodler, M., Li, W., Karame, G.O., Davi, L.: Sereum: protecting existing smart contracts against re-entrancy attacks. arXiv preprint arXiv:1812.05934 (2018)

41. Nguyen, T.D., Pham, L.H., Sun, J., Lin, Y., Minh, Q.T.: sFuzz: an efficient adaptive fuzzer for solidity smart contracts. In: Proceedings of the ACM/IEEE 42nd International Conference on Software Engineering, pp. 778–788 (2020)

42. Page not found—vyagers. https://vyagers.com/2018/12/15/technicalwhitepaperfor-afl-fuzz/. Accessed 13 Apr 2023

43. GitHub - ethereum/aleth: Aleth – Ethereum C++ client, tools and libraries. https://github. com/ethereum/aleth/. Accessed 13 Apr 2023

44. Su, J., Dai, H.-N., Zhao, L., Zheng, Z., Luo, X.: Effectively generating vulnerable transaction sequences in smart contracts with reinforcement learning-guided fuzzing. In: 37th IEEE/ACM International Conference on Automated Software Engineering, pp. 1–12 (2022)

Who Needs the Most Research Effort? Investigating the Importance of Smart Contract Weaknesses

Shijian Chen, Yanlin Wang(✉), and Zibin Zheng

School of Software Engineering, Sun Yat-sen University, Zhuhai 519000, China
wangylin36@mail.sysu.edu.cn

Abstract. Smart contracts have witnessed widespread adoption across various industries since the introduction of Ethereum. Also, smart contracts' vulnerabilities have gradually attracted academic attention, e.g., Oyente was developed to detect security bugs in contracts. However, it remains unclear which smart contract vulnerabilities require more research attention. To fill the gap, we recruit eight researchers to collect 281 Ethereum-related security events from SlowMist and Rekt, and analyze the root causes (e.g., the code weakness) behind each occurrence based on SWC Registry. Our results reveal that only 10 SWC weaknesses lead to security events, causing a total loss of USD 74 Billion. Moreover, *Reentrancy* exhibits the highest frequency. Our results provide guidance for research efforts allocated in the academic community.

Keywords: Smart contract weakness · SWC Registry · Blockchain security · Empirical study · Smart contract audit

1 Introduction

In the decentralized world, smart contracts are programmed contracts that automatically execute on the blockchain (e.g., Ethereum) when pre-defined conditions are met, enabling a decentralized trust mechanism. They have received widespread attention since Ethereum became the first platform for users to develop and deploy smart contracts. By 2022, more than 44 million smart contracts have been deployed on Ethereum [22], while their market capitalization is expected to reach USD 1,515.4 million in the next decade [14]. However, to some extent, smart contract development still remains enigmatic due to its unique design and application. As an example from a security perspective, Zou et al. [28] discovered that there is no effective way to guarantee the security of smart contract code, with code vulnerability being one of the issues. For example, hackers took advantage of *Reentrancy* to steal a large portion of ETH from THE DAO smart contract [20]. Fortunately, a number of tools have emerged to assist in the security of smart contracts. Luu et al. built Oyente [19] (a symbolic execution tool) to detect potential security bugs. Kalra et al. presented Zeus, a

J. Chen et al. (Eds.): BlockSys 2023, CCIS 1896, pp. 197–210, 2024.
https://doi.org/10.1007/978-981-99-8101-4_14

framework to verify the accuracy and validate fairness of smart contracts [16]. Moreover, smart contract tools for weaknesses detection (teEther [17], Securify [25], Harvey [27], etc.) have been developed one after another and enhanced in different ways, e.g., coverage and accuracy.

Nevertheless, the weaknesses reported in previous works are of differing importance, meaning that the weaknesses with low severity may need less research effort, and vice versa. For example, contracts with *Reentrancy* can lead to huge financial losses [9], whereas the weakness known as *Use of a Deprecated Solidity Function* may only reduce the code quality and increase the difficulty of code reuse. Thus, *Reentrancy* may require more research efforts than *Use of a Deprecated Solidity Function*. Consequently, there is room for a new discussion of smart contract weaknesses.

To fill this gap, we conduct analyses on the security events caused by smart contract weaknesses listed on SWC Registry (a standardized system for classifying the 37 kinds of smart contract weaknesses). We first recruit five master's researchers and three Ph.D. researchers to collect 148 and 149 security events that happened in relation to Ethereum up to July 2022 from SlowMist and Rekt (both of them are teams for blockchain security), respectively. They then manually analyze the key reasons (e.g., the weakness) underlying these security issues. Eventually, we find that 42 security events are caused by SWC weaknesses, corresponding to 10 kinds of SWC weaknesses and a total loss of around USD 74 billion. For the other 27 kinds of weaknesses, we could not find any related security events. In this sense, researchers should spend more effort detecting those 10 weaknesses. Specifically, *Reentrancy* (18 times) and *Integer Overflow and Underflow* (6 times) are among the most commonly occurring weaknesses, leading to losses of USD 0.3 and 1.1 billion, respectively.

The contribution of this paper can be summarized as follows.

- We recruit eight researchers to help collect and analyze 281 security events, discovering that only 10 kinds of SWC weaknesses lead to financial losses. We will make our dataset public in the future.
- To the best of our knowledge, this work is the first to conduct research on the importance of 37 smart contract weaknesses. We provide pointers to the types of weaknesses detected and the research effort allocated to the many smart contract vulnerability detection tools.

2   Background

2.1   Ethereum

Ethereum is an improved version of Bitcoin, introducing the 'Ether Virtual Machine (EVM)' that allows for the execution of smart contracts. Ethereum allows developers to use programming languages (e.g., Solidity) to write smart contracts and deploy them to the Ethereum network. Smart contracts on Ethereum can execute any pre-programmed logic, including asset trading, voting, and more. As a result, many decentralized applications (DApps), digital assets, blockchain games, and financial applications have been created.

2.2 Smart Contract Weakness

After a smart contract is deployed on Ethereum, it cannot be modified again. An attacker could exploit a logic or code weakness to achieve unintended behavior of smart contracts, which could cause financial loss and other unpredictable damage. For example, Listing 1 is a smart contract weakness that leads to *Reentrancy*. Specifically, the attacker can create a smart contract (see an example in Listing 2) that contains a malicious fallback function, which includes the message call of withdraw() in the target contract. Then, they send a certain amount of Ether to the target contract. When it comes to line 3 in Listing 1, the target contract will call the fallback function in the attacker contract, and thus, withdraw() is called again in it. Therefore, the attacker can repeatedly withdraw funds from the target contract through *Reentrancy*.

```
1:function withdraw(uint amount) public {
2:   if (balances[msg.sender] >= amount) {
3:       require(msg.sender.call.value(amount)());
4:       balances[msg.sender] -= amount;
5: }
6:}
```

Listing 1. Withdraw function of the victim contract

```
1:function attack() public {
2:   victim.withdraw(1);
3:}
4:function() public payable {
5:   victim.withdraw(1);
6:}
```

Listing 2. An example of the attacker contracts

2.3 SWC Registry

The SWC Registry[1] stands for 'Smart Contract Weakness Classification and Test Cases', a standardized system for classifying and managing smart contract vulnerabilities. The SWC Registry currently contains over 200 smart contract vulnerabilities with detailed descriptions, sample codes, test cases, and suggestions. These include common smart contract vulnerabilities such as *Reentrancy*, *Integer Overflows*, and more. Auditors can use the SWC Registry to inspect smart contracts and refer to the weakness descriptions and corrective solutions to improve their code. In our research, we only focus on the 37 smart-contract-related weaknesses listed on the SWC Registry. For example, the *Reentrancy* is marked as **SWC-107** in SWC Registry.

---

[1] https://swcregistry.io/.

2.4 SlowMist and Rekt

SlowMist [6] and Rekt [5] are two teams related to Ethereum smart contract security. Their main business is smart contract auditing and security research, helping smart contract developers to find and fix vulnerabilities and ensure the security and reliability of smart contracts. As of April 10, 2023, SlowMist and Rekt have reported 988 and 223 security events, respectively. Notably, not all of these hacks are against Ethereum and its applications.

3 Motivation

The presence of some SWC weaknesses in a smart contract does not mean that it will be attacked or lose Ethers. For example, the SWC-120 weakness (*Weak Sources of Randomness from Chain Attributes*) indicates that using block timestamp to generate a random number is not safe, as miners can control the timestamp of a block in a few seconds. It is true that malicious miners can attack smart contracts through this weakness; however, this kind of attack may be rare in real-world situations. Nowadays, most miners choose to join a mining pool [3,4], which collects a large amount of mining power. Thus, it is not easy for a single miner to mine a block on the Ethereum network with Proof-of-Work mechanism [2]. Miners in the mining pool should follow some protocols and share the rewards based on their contributions. There is a low probability for these mining pools to change their strategy to attack some contracts, as misbehaving behavior could damage their reputation and lead to more losses than they earned. Furthermore, generating a random number is not easy on the blockchain. Although some blockchain oracles provide safe methods to generate random numbers, e.g., Chainlink [1], the service is usually expensive. Thus, although some developers may be aware that their contracts could be exploited by misbehaving minors, it is also hard to find a better way to generate a secure and free random number.

Thus, it is worth investigating whether there are real security events on Ethereum based on SWC weaknesses. It might be more valuable if we contribute more research efforts to analyzing the SWC weaknesses that can lead to huge financial losses.

4 Methodology

This section introduces how we recruit students for data collection and data analysis, as seen in Fig. 1.

4.1 Participant Recruitment

We recruit five students with master's degrees in software engineering and three Ph.D. students with professional knowledge of blockchain and smart contracts. The following information is their detailed background and responsibilities in this work.

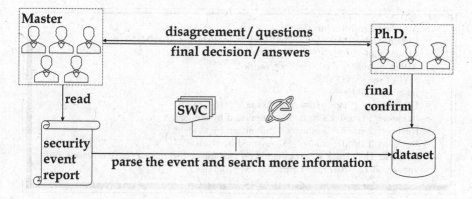

Fig. 1. The workflow of our methodology

- Master's students. **Background:**These five master's students have good knowledge of smart contract programming but have not yet published any academic works. Before conducting data collection and analysis, they are required to participate in specially designed training, which includes: 1)detailed information of each SWC weakness; 2)identification of each SWC weakness example. 3)the ability to independently analyze a blockchain security event. 4)the content they should submit to our dataset. **Functionality:**They are responsible for reading security events, parsing the key information (e.g., the financial loss and the related SWC type), and searching for additional information (e.g., the attacker and victim addresses).
- Ph.D. students. **Background:**These three Ph.D. students have grasped the details of SWC registry and each SWC weakness. Notably, they have already published smart-contract-related works at top venues. **Functionality:**They are responsible for answering master's students' questions and finally confirming the information submitted.

4.2   Data Collection

Two well-known security teams, i.e., SlowMist and Rekt, have already collected blockchain security events. Thus, we first crawl the security events reported by these two teams. By July 2022, we totally collect 148 and 149 security events from SlowMist and Rekt, respectively. To ensure the completeness of our dataset, we also collect 5,269 blockchain-related news articles from search engines.

4.3   Data Analysis

Understanding the key reasons for a security event is difficult because it does not contain detailed descriptions of the corresponding SWC weaknesses, i.e., what is the smart contract weakness behind each security event, and what role does the smart contract weakness play? In this sense, the five masters are required to search for more information about the security event, i.e., the name of the

- Attacked Project: Quixotic
- Victim Address: 0x065e8A87b8F11aED6fAcf9447aBe5E8C5D7502b6
- Attack Time: 2022/7/1
- Attack Summary: signature not verified
- SWC_Type: SWC-122
- Lost: $119,000
- URL: https://www.jinse.com/lives/307708.html
- Reviewer 1 (master's student): Submitted by student A
- Reviewer 2 (master's student): Submitted by student B
- Reviewer 3 (Ph.D. student): Confirmed by student C
- Remark: The attack was conducted on Optimism. See http://caibao.3news.cn/yaowen/2022/0703/72278.html for more details.

Fig. 2. An example of at least information we collect for each security event.

exploited project, the financial loss, the exploited time, a summary of the security event, and a reference to the event. After understanding the attacks, they are required to identify whether the event was caused by an SWC weakness and a related SWC type. To ensure the correctness of their results, each security event is checked by two masters independently. Then, they compare their results and discuss the differences. If they could not reach an agreement, the Ph.D. students help reach a final decision. Eventually, all the information submitted to the dataset by masters will be confirmed by the Ph.D. students. Figure 2 is an example in our dataset containing at least information we collect and students' review process for an attack in the project *Quixotic*.

Notably, we only focus on security events on Ethereum. Although we collected 5,269 news articles, most of them were not related to attacks. Moreover, there is a large amount of repeated information, as most security events were reported by multiple platforms. All of the irrelevant and repeated information is removed during our manual analysis process.

5   Result

In this section, we introduce the results of our data analysis and discuss the working mechanism and security events related to the SWC weaknesses.

5.1   Result Overview

After removing irrelevant and repeated information, we finally collect 281 security events on Ethereum. These events lead to a financial loss of USD 73,943,943,-552 in total. Among them, 42 events (14.9%) are caused by SWC weaknesses, leading to a loss of USD 7,285,504,180. Detailed information on these security events is listed in Table 1. Specifically, only 10 kinds of SWC weaknesses lead to 42 security events on Ethereum. For the other 27 kinds of SWC weaknesses, we could not find any related security events. Since our finding has proved that smart contracts with these 27 kinds of SWC weaknesses might not be attacked in real security events, more research efforts need to be devoted to the 10 SWC weaknesses listed in Table 1.

Table 1. Security events caused by SWC Weaknesses on Ethereum

SWC-ID	Title	#Times	Total Lost	Loss/Event
107	*Reentrancy*	18	308,720,000	17,151,111
101	*Integer Overflow and Underflow*	6	1,145,700,000	190,950,000
104	*Unchecked Call Return Value*	4	645,200,000	161,300,000
122	*Lack of Proper Signature Verification*	4	326,242,000	81,560,500
105	*Unprotected Ether Withdrawal*	3	7,833,900	2,611,300
112	*Delegatecall to Untrusted Callee*	2	182,211,000	91,105,500
100	*Function Default Visibility*	2	3,137,800	1,568,900
128	*DoS With Block Gas Limit*	1	4,558,859,480	4,558,859,480
129	*Typographical Error*	1	80,000,000	80,000,000
111	*Use of Deprecated Solidity Functions*	1	27,600,000	27,600,000
Total	/	42	7,285,504,180	/

5.2 Result of SWC-107 (*Reentrancy*)

SWC-107. *(Reentrancy)* has the highest frequency of leading to attacks. About 42.86% SWC-related security events are caused by *Reentrancy*, with a total financial loss of USD 0.3 billion. However, neither the total financial loss nor the average loss per event (the last column in Table 1) is the most serious for *Reentrancy* attacks. *Reentrancy* attacks are one of the famous attacks on Ethereum. This weakness allows hackers to call the victim contract several times in a single transaction. The first *Reentrancy* attack, the notorious DAO attack [9], happened in 2016. Although the vulnerable code example of the DAO attack has been widely publicized by blogs, books, and journals today, *Reentrancy* events still happen almost every year. Many new kinds of *Reentrancy* attack methods are born with this event. For example, the flash loan [26] strategy has been widely used in *Reentrancy* attacks as it can reduce the risk of the attack. Furthermore, the birth of the EIP-777 standard [15] introduces a new weakness to smart contracts. Specifically, transferFrom() of EIP-777 has a callback mechanism, which may lead to a *Reentrancy* attack if a *Reentrancy* lock is missing. In summary, we consider that SWC-107 *(Reentrancy)* should be the most noteworthy smart contract weakness, and researchers should spare more effort in identifying and avoiding such weakness.

5.3 Result of SWC-101 (*Integer Overflow and Underflow*)

SWC-101. *(Integer Overflow and Underflow)* has the second highest attack frequency. It also has the second-highest total loss per attack among all the

SWC attacks. In Solidity programming, each value type has a maximum size. For example, the type *uint8* can only store an 8-bit unsigned number ranging from 0 to 255. For the case of a *uint8* variable 0 minus 1, the value will become 255, which is called *Integer underflow*. *Integer overflow/underflow* can lead to serious security issues. The latest SWC-101 attack happened on March 20, 2022. A project named the Umbrella network has an underflow in its withdraw function, which allows attackers to withdraw an arbitrary amount of tokens from the smart contract [7]. The SWC-101 weakness can be avoided by using the SafeMath library [21].

5.4 Result of SWC-104 (*Unchecked Call Return Value*)

SWC-104. *(Unchecked Call Return Value)* lead to four security events in our dataset, accounting for USD 645.2 million. SWC-104 happens when the return value of a message call is not checked, which might be used by attackers and thus lead to unexpected behavior in the subsequent program logic. For example, one of the security events caused by *Unchecked Call Return Value* through our review is the attack on the Force DAO (a DeFi project) on Apr. 4, 2021. Force DAO supports investors to pledge FORCE tokens, after which investors receive xFORCE tokens. The vulnerability displays in line 43 in ForceProfitSharing.sol as seen in Listing 3, the partial code of Force DAO's smart contracts. The lack of processing of the return value of transferFrom() allows attackers to receive xFORCE tokens even if an error occurs when they deposit FORCE. Then, attackers destroy the xFORCE and replace it with FORCE, making a profit.

```
28:function deposit(uint256 amount) external nonReentrant {
   ...
42:// Lock the Force in the contract
43:force.transferFrom(msg.sender, address(this), amount);

45:emit Deposit(msg.sender, amount);
46:}
```

Listing 3. ForceProfitSharing.sol [10]

5.5 Result of SWC-122 (*Lack of Proper Signature Verification*)

In terms of **SWC-122** (*Lack of Proper Signature Verification*), it leads to 4 security events, accounting for USD 326,242,000. Take the attack of NBA NFT on April 21, 2022, as an example. The project owner uses an off-chain signature and on-chain verification to save gas. However, the verify function in its smart contract 0xDD5A64 [11] does not validate the sender address (msg.sender), resulting in non-whitelisted users being able to mint the NFT by copying the whitelisted users' signatures. It suggests that off-chain message signing comes with a certain risk of financial loss, and more researchers should pay more attention to related vulnerability to avoid such a tragedy.

5.6   Result of SWC-105 (*Unprotected Ether Withdrawal*)

SWC-105. *Unprotected Ether Withdrawal* typically occurs when access control or authentication is not properly set up in a smart contract, where malicious users could extract Ether. For example, the contract in Listing 4 suffers from *Unprotected Ether Withdrawal* because it does not authenticate or control access to the user invoking the withdraw() function, indicating that attackers could extract Ether from other users. Listing 5 is an example of the attackers, where the attacker creates an attack() function with the parameter that specifies the victim address, and then he obtains the balance of the victim stored in SWC105example.sol and extracts and transfers all the Ethers.

```
1: contract SWC105example {
2:   mapping(address => uint256) public balances;
3:   function withdraw(uint256 amount) public {
4:     require(balances[msg.sender] >= amount);
5:     msg.sender.transfer(amount);
6:     balances[msg.sender] -= amount;
7: }
8: }
```

Listing 4. SWC105example.sol

```
1: contract AttackSWC105 {
2:   SWC105example victim;
3:   address payable attacker;
4:
5:   constructor(address _victim, address payable _attacker)
     public {
6:       victim = SWC105example(_victim);
7:       attacker = _attacker;
8: }
9:
10: function attack(address _victimAddress) public {
11:     uint256 victimBalance = victim.balances(
    _victimAddress);
12:     victim.withdraw(victimBalance);
13:     attacker.transfer(victimBalance);
14: }
15:
16: function() payable external {
17:     revert();
18: }
19: }
```

Listing 5. AttackSWC105.sol

In our dataset, SWC-105 leads to three security events, causing a total loss of USD 7,833,900. For example, Multichain was attacked on Jan. 18, 2022 due to the fact that the validity of the token parameter was not checked. Therefore, attackers transferred WETH from victim's account to their own accounts by easily bypassing various checks.

5.7   Result of SWC-112 (*Delegatecall to Untrusted Callee*)

SWC-112. (*Delegatecall to Untrusted Callee*) refers to calling into untrusted contracts by *delegatecall* (a type of message call in Solidity), and thus changing the content (e.g., variable values) of the current smart contracts. *Delegatecall to Untrusted Callee* leads to two security events in our dataset, i.e., an attack on Beanstalk (April 17, 2022) and an attack on dYdX (Nov. 27, 2021), causing a total loss of USD 182,211,000.

5.8   Result of SWC-100 (*Function Default Visibility*)

SWC-100. (*Function Default Visibility*) means that malicious users may attack the smart contracts (e.g., making unauthorized state changes) if developers haven't constrained functions' visibility. Fortunately, fixing *Function Default Visibility* is easy because developers can specify each function as external, public, internal, or private based on different requirements, reducing the possibility of being taken advantage of. Our result also proves that SWC-100 is uncommon in real scenarios, i.e., it only leads to two security events, causing a total loss of USD 3,137,800.

5.9   Result of SWC-128 (*DoS with Block Gas Limit*)

Although **SWC-128** *(DoS with Block Gas Limit)* only leads to one security event, it causes the highest financial loss. On Ethereum, the maximum gas consumption of a block is fixed. The execution of a function exceeding the maximum gas consumption of a block will lead to the denial of service. The only project exploited by SWC-128 is a game contract named Fomo3D [24]. In the Fomo3D game, users can transfer Ethers to the contract, and the latter user should pay more than the previous one. The last user, when the timer runs out, is declared the winner and receives all the Ethers. The hacker uses a contract to exhaust the gas in a block to raise the DoS attack when he becomes the last person. This attack might be regarded as a special case for the exploitation of the SWC-128 weakness, as raising this attack is not easy. First, the hacker should be able to monitor the price function of the contract. Second, the hacker's contract can exhaust the gas in a block, which is the most important step. In this security event, the hacker set a high gas price in order to make miners execute their transactions first. However, this method is risky as a miner may discover the malicious intent and execute other transactions.

5.10   Result of SWC-129 (*Typographical Error*)

SWC-129. (*Typographical Error*) refers to the incorrect operator in smart contracts. For example, the incorrect use of = + (initializes the variable) instead of + = (sums a number to a variable). Moreover, as reported by Rekt, the attacked project COMP lost USD 80 million just because of a tiny error, misuse of '>' instead of '>=', and this is the only case leading to the financial loss we find related to *Typographical Error* in Solidity. We suppose the research on the detection of SWC-129 is relevant, but also difficult due to the need to truly understand the intentions of smart contract developers.

5.11   Result of SWC-111 (*Use of Deprecated Solidity Functions*)

Solidity's initial version is 0.1.0, released in August 2015, and has now evolved to 0.8.x (April. 2023). With each version update, some features of Solidity will change. For example, version 0.7.x introduces try-catch exception handling. **SWC-111** (*Use of Deprecated Solidity Functions*) refers to using old-version functions, causing side effects. In our dataset, although SWC-111 leads to only one security event, it proves that this weakness is a potential for financial loss. However, to the best of our knowledge, there is currently no SWC-111-related identification process in the major smart contract tools (e.g., Oyente, Zeus, Securify, Smartdagger, and eTainter) that can detect vulnerabilities. Since it has been exploited in history, academics should spend a certain effort on SWC-111.

6   Discussion

6.1   Threats to Validity

Threats to Internal Validity. For security events, we only collected security events reported on SlowMist, Rekt, and Blockchain News. However, these websites usually only report security events for famous projects or those which lead to huge financial losses. Thus, we may have missed some security events, which could affect the results. However, it may be impossible to collect information on all security events. We collected 281 security events and 5,296 news in this study. It can also indicate the importance of some SWC weaknesses due to their frequency of involvement in security events.

Threats to External Validity. Since our research focuses on the major security events in history, possibly, those 27 kinds of SWC weaknesses, that are not related to financial loss, will lead to new and different security events in the future. In other words, several of them might also likely require more effort from academics later. To this end, we will continue to update our dataset.

6.2   Implications

Some SWC weaknesses have attracted too much research attention. For example, SWC-116 (*Block Values as a Proxy for Time*) and SWC-120 (*Weak Sources of Randomness from Chain Attributes*) are two weaknesses that can be exploited by malicious miners. As we mentioned in Sect. 3, there may be a low probability of being attacked by miners using these two weaknesses on Ethereum. As expected, no security events are found to have been caused by them.

This is our advice for allocating research efforts to smart contract weaknesses. *Reentrancy* is the most widespread weakness (18 times) that leads to security events in our datasets. Fortunately, many tools are able to detect this weakness, and subsequent research should pay more attention to how to improve detection accuracy. The second most serious weakness is *Integer Overflow and Underflow*. 66.7% of its related security events happened in 2018, and as time goes on, the frequency decreased. However, as this weakness can easily cause significant financial damage, researchers should focus more on it. *DoS With Block Gas Limit* is the weakness that causes the hugest financial loss in a single security event, and it is meaningful to design better ways to prevent it. In addition to detecting these weaknesses, we think that research efforts should also be focused on promptly alerting developers. For example, vulnerabilities like *Typographical Error* and *Use of Deprecated Solidity Functions* are just tiny errors when writing the code. For the remaining 27 SWC weaknesses that do not lead to any security events, researchers could reduce their efforts on them to some extent.

7   Related Work

Many researchers have already focused on identifying and mitigating vulnerabilities in smart contracts. Twenty related tools have been developed since the launch of Oyente [19] (the first symbolic execution tool to detect smart contract vulnerabilities) in 2016. For example, Choi et al. [8] made smart contracts fuzzy using static and dynamic analysis to find weaknesses without needing source code. So et al. [23] presented VeriSmart to ensure the arithmetic safety of smart contracts. Frank et al. [12] conducted a large-scale analysis of around 2.2 million accounts and found 5,905 valid inputs that could trigger a vulnerability. Ghaleb [13] presented eTainter to detect gas-related vulnerabilities based on the bytecode of smart contracts. Nevertheless, the importance of smart contract weaknesses has still not been considered. Lee et al. [18] listed five metrics of SWC weaknesses for Ethereum developers to refer to when writing code, but they were designed to assist developers, e.g., how to minimize the cost. Therefore, our work is the first to guide the current research efforts on SWC weaknesses.

8   Conclusion and Future Work

8.1   Conclusion

Our aim is to investigate the importance of different smart contract weaknesses and provide guidance for the distribution of further research efforts. We collect

281 Ethereum security events in total and find that 42 events are caused by SWC weaknesses. We analyze the working mechanism and some related topics (e.g., its financial loss) of the SWC weaknesses involved in security events. Our results provide guidance for further research on smart contract analysis.

8.2   Future Work

In the future, we will expand our research into more platforms (e.g., EOS, TRON, Polygon), and collate a larger dataset and identify more security events corresponding to SWC weaknesses. Furthermore, in addition to security event frequency and financial losses, we would like to quantify additional metrics to guide academic efforts in smart contract weakness research, such as whether the weakness will have an impact on the stability of blockchain systems and whether the weakness will cause additional financial losses in the future.

Acknowledgments. This work is partially supported by fundings from the National Key R&D Program of China (2022YFB2702203).

References

1. Chainlink (2022). https://docs.chain.link/docs/get-a-random-number/
2. Ethereum.org (2022). https://www.ethereum.org/
3. Miner info on etherscan (2022). https://etherscan.io/blocks
4. Mining pool stats (2022). https://miningpoolstats.stream/ethereum
5. Rekt (2022). https://rekt.new
6. Slowmist hacked (2022). https://hacked.slowmist.io/
7. Umbrella network hacked: $700k lost (2022). https://medium.com/uno-re/umbrella-network-hacked-700k-lost-97285b69e8c7
8. Choi, J., Kim, D., Kim, S., Grieco, G., Groce, A., Cha, S.K.: Smartian: enhancing smart contract fuzzing with static and dynamic data-flow analyses. In: 2021 36th IEEE/ACM International Conference on Automated Software Engineering (ASE), pp. 227–239. IEEE (2021)
9. CoinDesk: The DAO attack: Understanding what happened (2022). https://www.coindesk.com/learn/2016/06/25/understanding-the-dao-attack/
10. Etherscan: Forceprofitsharing.sol. https://etherscan.io/address/0xe7f445b93eb9cdabfe76541cc43ff8de930a58e6#code
11. Etherscan: Victim address of NBA NFT (2023). https://etherscan.io/address/0xDD5A649fC076886Dfd4b9Ad6aCFC9B5eb882e83c. Accessed 10 Apr 2023
12. Frank, J., Aschermann, C., Holz, T.: ETHBMC: a bounded model checker for smart contracts. In: Proceedings of the 29th USENIX Conference on Security Symposium, pp. 2757–2774 (2020)
13. Ghaleb, A., Rubin, J., Pattabiraman, K.: eTainter: detecting gas-related vulnerabilities in smart contracts. In: Proceedings of the 31st ACM SIGSOFT International Symposium on Software Testing and Analysis, pp. 728–739 (2022)
14. Insights, F.M.: Smart contract market outlook (2022 to 2032) (2022). https://www.futuremarketinsights.com/reports/smart-contracts-market
15. Jacques, D., Jordi, B., Thomas, S.: Eip-777: Token standard (2022). https://eips.ethereum.org/EIPS/eip-777

16. Kalra, S., Goel, S., Dhawan, M., Sharma, S.: Zeus: analyzing safety of smart contracts. In: Ndss, pp. 1–12 (2018)
17. Krupp, J., Rossow, C.: teEther: gnawing at ethereum to automatically exploit smart contracts. In: 27th {USENIX} Security Symposium ({USENIX} Security 18), pp. 1317–1333 (2018)
18. Lee, J.H., Yoon, S., Lee, H.: SWC-based smart contract development guide research. In: 2022 24th International Conference on Advanced Communication Technology (ICACT), pp. 138–141 (2022). https://doi.org/10.23919/ICACT53585.2022.9728898
19. Luu, L., Chu, D.H., Olickel, H., Saxena, P., Hobor, A.: Making smart contracts smarter. In: Proceedings of the 2016 ACM SIGSAC Conference on Computer and Communications Security, pp. 254–269 (2016)
20. Mehar, M.I., et al.: Understanding a revolutionary and flawed grand experiment in blockchain: the DAO attack. J. Cases Inf. Technol. (JCIT) 21(1), 19–32 (2019)
21. OpenZepplelin: Openzepplelin safemath library (2022). https://github.com/OpenZeppelin/openzeppelin-contracts/blob/master/contracts/utils/math/SafeMath.sol
22. Rowden, S.: How many smart contracts on ethereum? how do ethereum smart contracts work? (2022). https://bitkan.com/learn/how-many-smart-contracts-on-ethereum-how-do-ethereum-smart-contractswork-8989
23. So, S., Lee, M., Park, J., Lee, H., Oh, H.: VeriSmart: a highly precise safety verifier for ethereum smart contracts. In: 2020 IEEE Symposium on Security and Privacy (SP), pp. 1678–1694. IEEE (2020)
24. Team, S.: How the winner got fomo3d prize - a detailed explanation (2022). https://medium.com/coinmonks/how-the-winner-got-fomo3d-prize-a-detailed-explanation-b30a69b7813f
25. Tsankov, P., Dan, A., Drachsler-Cohen, D., Gervais, A., Buenzli, F., Vechev, M.: Securify: practical security analysis of smart contracts. In: Proceedings of the 2018 ACM SIGSAC Conference on Computer and Communications Security, pp. 67–82 (2018)
26. Wang, D., et al.: Towards understanding flash loan and its applications in defi ecosystem. arXiv preprint arXiv:2010.12252 (2020)
27. Wüstholz, V., Christakis, M.: Harvey: a greybox fuzzer for smart contracts. In: Proceedings of the 28th ACM Joint Meeting on European Software Engineering Conference and Symposium on the Foundations of Software Engineering, pp. 1398–1409 (2020)
28. Zou, W., et al.: Smart contract development: challenges and opportunities. IEEE Trans. Software Eng. 47(10), 2084–2106 (2019)

A Survey on Blockchain Abnormal Transaction Detection

Shuai Liu, Bo Cui$^{(\boxtimes)}$, and Wenhan Hou

Inner Mongolia Key Laboratory of Wireless Networking and Mobile Computing,
College of Computer Science, Inner Mongolia University, Hohhot 010021, China
cscb@imu.edu.cn

Abstract. Blockchain technology has undergone rapid development in recent years, transactions on Blockchains, represented by prominent examples such as Bitcoin and Ethereum, are rapidly increasing in number. However, with the large volume of transactions, a variety of scams such as phishing and Ponzi schemes have become more prevalent and are often hidden among legitimate transactions. To combat these anomalies and fraudulent activities, it is necessary to adopt anomaly detection methods. In this article, we conduct an extensive survey of the current body of research in the area of blockchain anomaly transaction detection and analyze the current state of research by examining the key point involved in detection, including data imbalance, feature extraction, and classification algorithms. Additionally, we discuss the potential of applying graph convolutional networks (GCN) to the domain of blockchain anomaly detection and predict that GCN will likely become a mainstream approach in the near future.

Keywords: Blockchain · Abnormal Transaction · Ponzi · Phishing · GCN

1 Introduction

Blockchain is a decentralized ledger technology that securely, verifiably and permanently records information about both sides of a transaction [1]. With its core advantages of transparency and decentralization, blockchain has gained widespread use across various industries, including politics, finance, and science. A particularly critical application of blockchain technology is in the realm of *cryptocurrency*, where individual accounts can issue and trade directly via network protocols, without the need for central organization [2,3].

However, the lack of regulation on these transactions has made them an attractive target for criminals seeking to steal cryptocurrencies. Phishing scams, scam wallets, and Ponzi schemes are just a few examples of illegal activities in the cryptocurrency space [4]. According to the SAFEIS Security Institute's 2022 Crimes Involving Virtual Currency Research Report [5]. Compared with 2021, the amount of virtual currency cases in 2022 rose from 11.791 billion yuan to 34.849 billion yuan, an increase of nearly 3 times. Compared with 2021, the amount of virtual currency crimes in 2022 increased from 11.791 billion yuan to

© The Author(s), under exclusive license to Springer Nature Singapore Pte Ltd. 2024
J. Chen et al. (Eds.): BlockSys 2023, CCIS 1896, pp. 211–225, 2024.
https://doi.org/10.1007/978-981-99-8101-4_15

34.849 billion yuan, an increase of nearly three times, and the average amount of each case increased from 3.64 million yuan to 28.45 million yuan, an increase of nearly eight times. This indicates that the trend of organizing and scaling up crimes involving virtual currencies is becoming increasingly serious.

Several studies have been conducted to mitigate the risk of abnormal transactions on blockchains. Wu et al. [6] proposed a network embedding algorithm called Tran2Vec, which uses One-Class support vector machine (SVM) to classify phishing addresses in the Ethereum transaction graph and achieved an precision of 0.972. Zheng et al. [7] built a larger dataset on Ponzi schemes and extracted numerous features from multiple perspectives to identify such schemes through machine learning methods. The proposed method is capable of detecting Ponzi schemes during smart contract creation.

To conduct a comprehensive review of the existing literature in this field, we collected 40 representative papers from various sources such as ACM Digital Library, DBLP, Web of Science, IEEE Xplore, Springer, etc., published in the last five years. These papers were categorized into three groups: data imbalance, feature extraction, and classification algorithms. Our review summarizes the methods for detecting Ponzi schemes and phishing activities, and concludes by discussing the future trends and challenges in this area (Table 1).

2   Background

Blockchain abnormal transaction refers to any transaction that deviates from the expected normal transaction behavior in a blockchain network. These transactions may indicate fraudulent activities, security vulnerabilities, or other unusual activities that violate the normal operation of the blockchain network. The identification of anomalous transactions is vital for preserving the security and stability of blockchain networks and for guaranteeing the accuracy of the data stored on the blockchain. Common unusual transactions in blockchain are phishing as well as Ponzi schemes.

In the context of blockchain technology, network phishing refers to a type of malicious activity where an attacker poses as a trustworthy entity and tricks users into revealing their sensitive information, such as private keys or login credentials, or into sending cryptocurrency to the attacker's address. This type of fraud can occur through various means, such as email phishing, fake websites or apps, and even through social engineering [41]. In essence, network phishing in the blockchain context is similar to other forms of phishing, with the goal of stealing sensitive information or cryptocurrency.

A Ponzi scheme is a fraudulent investment strategy that promises high returns with low risk to investors. In the blockchain context, this can take the form of a fake cryptocurrency or token being created and marketed to potential investors, with the promise of high profits. The returns promised to early investors are usually paid out of funds obtained from later investors, rather than from any legitimate business activities. As more people invest, the scheme attracts new investors, allowing the operator to collect more funds. However,

Table 1. The classifications and major contributions of related papers.

Category	Focus	Paper	Year	Major contribution
Data imbalance		[8]	2021	Random undersampling is used to reduce the majority of samples
		[9]	2020	Define data cleanup steps for sample sifting
		[10]	2022	Random repetitive collection to generate a few classes of samples
		[11]	2022	Balanced data using SMOTE.
		[12]	2022	
		[13]	2020	
		[14]	2021	
		[15]	2020	Evaluate the effectiveness of SMOTE and GAN to generate blockchain transaction data
		[6]	2020	Detect abnormal transaction with OCC.
		[16]	2020	
Feature Extraction	non-graph data	[17]	2021	Manual extraction of account features and network features for phishing detection.
		[10]	2022	Propose a novel voting-based technique to select the most significant features.
		[18]	2018	Extracted code features and account features for Ponzi detection.
		[19]	2021	
		[20]	2021	Used deep learning algorithms for feature extraction.
		[21]	2020	Analyze features with XGBoost.
		[22]	2021	Word extraction for bytecodes.
	graph data	[9]	2020	Propose a graph-based cascade feature extraction.
		[23]	2020	Extract features using the graph embedding method.
		[23]	2020	
		[24]	2022	
		[25]	2021	
		[26]	2020	Learn the features with GCN.
		[27]	2022	
		[28]	2021	
		[29]	2022	
		[30]	2022	Use temporal information about the behavior of the transactions.
		[31]	2022	Extract code-level and transaction-level features for Ponzi detection.
		[32]	2020	Propose a one-class graph deep learning framework for anomaly detection.
		[33]	2021	Propose a subgraph-based anomaly detection method.
Classification Algorithm		[23]	2020	For classification of phishing nodes.
		[6]	2020	
		[27]	2022	
		[26]	2020	
		[34]	2022	
		[17]	2021	
		[10]	2022	
		[18]	2018	Classifying Ponzi scheme contracts.
		[21]	2020	
		[19]	2021	
		[35]	2018	
		[36]	2021	
		[14]	2021	
		[11]	2022	
		[37]	2020	For the classification of illegal entities.
		[12]	2022	
		[38]	2019	
		[39]	2022	
		[40]	2019	

when fewer people are willing to invest or when too many people want to withdraw their funds, the scheme collapses, resulting in many investors losing their money [42].

3 Methodology

This section provides a comprehensive overview of the current research on the detection of anomalous transactions in blockchain, with a specific focus on phishing and Ponzi schemes. The primary steps involved in blockchain abnormal transaction detection include data collection and processing, feature extraction, and identification algorithm classification. To provide a comprehensive overview, this research state is summarized from three key points: data imbalance, feature extraction, and classification algorithm.

3.1 Data Imbalance

A vast amount of transaction data has been accumulated in blockchains, particularly public chains, but the amount of marked abnormal data is relatively small. For instance, Bitcoin and Ether have accumulated massive transaction data, but only a small proportion of it is marked as abnormal. According to statistics from Watcher.Guru [43], Tokenview [44] and, Reddit [45] as of 2022, the total number of Bitcoin addresses has surpassed one billion, and the number of held addresses exceeds 53.02 million. Moreover, the total number of Bitcoin transactions and non-zero addresses in 2022 has exceeded 93.1 million and 44 million, respectively, with only about 8,000 marked as anomalous addresses. Etherscan [46], a prominent platform for blockchain exploration and analysis, reports that the total number of addresses and transactions in Ethereum exceeds 500 million and 3.8 billion, respectively. However, the total number of tagged anomalous addresses is only about 5,000. The unbalanced data distribution between normal and abnormal transactions poses a significant challenge to detection models, which are susceptible to overfitting.

A common approach to addressing the issue of data imbalance is the use of resampling techniques, which involve adjusting the data to balance the distribution of classes [47]. Resampling can be divided into two categories: undersampling and oversampling. Undersampling creates a subset of the original dataset by reducing the majority of samples, as demonstrated by Agarwal et al. [8], who performed random undersampling to uniformly sample 697,000 benign accounts from 79 million Ethereum accounts. However, this technique is rarely used in blockchain anomaly detection because it is more convenient to construct a new subset of samples. Chen et al. [9] obtained 43,783,194 accounts, among which phishing addresses controlled 1,683 accounts. They set three data cleaning steps, which involved filtering transaction records involving a smart contract address, eliminating addresses with fewer than 10 or more than 1,000 transaction records, and ignoring all transactions that appeared before block height 2 million. The data cleaning resulted in a new dataset containing 534,820 addresses, with 323 of them being flagged as phishing addresses. Li et al. [34] and Wen et al. [17] used the same data cleaning steps. While the data cleansing steps may filter out some phishing accounts, focusing on the more important parts is highly beneficial to building an effective detection framework. The second resampling technique is oversampling, which involves increasing the number of instances in the minority class by replicating or generating new instances from the existing ones. This creates a superset of the original dataset. Kabla et al. [10] used random duplication of the phishing scam samples in order to increase their proportion in the dataset to over 40%. The Synthetic Minority Over-sampling Technique (SMOTE) is an oversampling approach that generates new minority class instances instead of applying a simple replication. SMOTE works by synthesizing new minority class samples based on the existing minority class samples. It randomly selects a minority class sample and finds its k nearest neighbors. It then creates synthetic samples along the line segments connecting the minority sample and its neighbors. By doing so, SMOTE effectively increases the number of minority class samples in the dataset, balancing the class distribution. Several researchers have used SMOTE to balance the data in blockchain anomaly detection, such as He et al. [11] in Ponzi scheme identification and Ashfaq et al. [12] in Bitcoin network fraud and anomalies detection. Fan et al. [13,14] employed the Borderline-SMOTE 2 [48] oversampling technology to enhance the presence of smart Ponzi schemes on the boundary and bring newly generated contracts closer to real ones. This is due to the fact that nodes on the boundary line and near it are more susceptible to misclassification than nodes that are far from the boundary. Generative Adversarial Networks(GAN) model generates new data instances based on the existing data. GAN also seem to be able to handle data imbalances, but the results from Han et al. [15] showed that SMOTE performed better than GAN-based frameworks in imbalanced data.

Another approach to avoid the problem of imbalanced data is One-class Classification (OCC) algorithm. In OCC, the algorithm is trained on a single class, referred to as the normal class. The purpose of this algorithm is to identify instances that do not belong to this class, referred to as anomalies. The imbalance problem is inherently addressed in one-class classification as the focus is on identifying instances that are different from the majority of the data, regardless of their minority or majority status. This approach can lead to accurate results, even in cases where the data distribution is heavily skewed towards one class, effectively avoiding the problem of imbalanced data [49]. For instance, Wu et al. [6] employed a one-class SVM method to differentiate between phishing and non-phishing nodes and achieved an precision of 0.972. This result outperformed the logistic regression, Bayesian, and isolated forest algorithms using the same set of features. Demertzis et al. [16] addressed the problem of imbalanced data by using the OCC methodology with a Deep Learning Autoencoder, and their experiments showed that the Deep Autoencoder performed better than the One-class SVM.

3.2   Feature Extraction

Feature extraction plays a crucial role in blockchain abnormal transaction detection. It is the process of selecting and transforming relevant information from the raw data into a condensed and informative representation that can be used for further analysis and modeling. It is essential for identifying key characteristics of normal and abnormal transactions and constructing accurate and effective detection models.

Non-graph Data Feature Extraction. Non-graph data is typically processed by manually extracting features using traditional feature engineering methods.

Wen et al. [17] extracted both account features and network features from transaction records. Account features describe the status and activity of Ethereum accounts, and Network features describe adjacency information from the perspective of the network. As only a small number of contracts provide source code, Chen et al. [18] used the Ethereum client to obtain the bytecode, disassembled it to obtain Opcode, and calculated the frequency of operating codes to generate code features. Account features are extracted on the basis of the transaction history. Zhang et al. [19] used similar features, including 7 account features and 64 code features.

Different from manual analysis, Kabla et al. [10] proposed a novel voting-based technique for feature selection using ranking methods. They used CorrelationAttributeEval, PairwiseCorrelationAttributeEval, and ClassifierAttributeEval methods in feature selection to vote on features. Chen et al. [20] proposed a MTCformer method, which uses deep learning algorithms for source code feature extraction combined with TextCNN for feature learning and an attention encoder in Transformer. MTCformer achieved higher precision, recall, and F-score values than [18]. Farrugia et al. [21] used the XGBoost decision-treeensemble Machine Learning algorithm to detect illicit accounts in the Ethereum community. They concluded that the top three features with the largest impact on the final model output were "Time diff between first and last (Mins)", "Total Ether balance", and "Min value received".

The aforementioned studies are generally able to provide effective features for classification tasks, but they lack consideration of the correlations between different blockchain accounts.

Graph Data Feature Extraction. Blockchain transactions records have a graphical structure, which has prompted researchers to utilize graph data for detecting anomalous transactions.

Table 2. Graph data feature extract methods in phishing.

paper	methods	Precision	Recall	F1	AUC
[9]	Features only	0.8196	0.8050	0.8122	0.8097
[23]	Deepwalk, Node2vec	0.8710	0.8220	0.8460	-
[6]	Tran2vec	0.9270	0.8930	0.9080	-
[27]	hop directed ego-graph	0.8132	0.8271	0.8199	-
[26]	E-GCN	0.7294	0.1453	0.2357	0.5725
[30]	MP-GCN	0.9350	0.9040	0.9190	-
[34]	TTAGN	0.7770	0.8590	0.8160	0.9280

Table 2 shows the number of related papers for phishing detection. Chen et al. [9] proposed a graph-based cascade feature extraction method where only the node attributes are considered to extract 219-dimensional statistical features from the 1-order and 2-order neighbors of nodes and analyzed why some of these features are important. This approach treats phishing detection as a node classification task, but it incurs high memory costs due to the requirement of loading a full-size graph. To address this issue, some studies have processed the task from a graph classification perspective and extracted subgraphs of accounts for representation [50], but this approach is also limited by insufficient data, such as transaction amount, quantity, and direction, in Ethereum transaction-related fields. Graph embedding, a graph-based approach, has received significant attention due to its ability to convert nodes in the network into low-dimensional embeddings while preserving structural information. Yuan et al. [23] applied the Node2vec algorithm, a random walk-based network embedding method, to extract features, and compared its performance to Deepwalk and non-embedding methods. Wu et al. [6] used the Trans2vec algorithm to extract features from the large-scale Ethereum transaction network, which balances the weights between amount and timestamp. Xia et al. [27] proposed a novel attribute-based ego-graph embedding method that learns both structural and attributed features of the Ethereum transaction networks. GCN have shown great potential in detecting anomalous transactions in blockchain. GCN can model the transaction graph as a network and capture the structural information and features of each node and edge. By propagating information through the graph, GCNs can learn node embeddings that represent the local and global structural information of each node. Chen et al. [26] make statistics on the edge information of each node as the node's features. Then, they utilized GCN to learn the structural features of the transaction network. This is the first time that GCN has been introduced in Ether phishing detection. They collected a very large graph, sampled datasets with 30,000, 40,000, 50,000 nodes in the same random step, and had the highest recall compared to feature only, Deep walk , Node2vec, LINE methods. Yu et al. [30] designed the MP-GCN method to obtain information from the surrounding neighboring nodes and neighboring edges. The vector representation of nodes is obtained by transforming nodes, edges, and features into vector space through GCN. MP-GCN has higher accuracy, recall, and F1 than graph embedding algorithms, such as Deepwalk, Node2vec, and Tran2vec. However, these works rarely use temporal information about the behavior of the transactions, and thus they cannot capture the complete edge representation. In addition, the node representation uses only manually designed features, leading to a weak node representation for these detection methods. Li et al. [34] proposed the Temporal Transaction Aggregation Graph Network (TTAGN) as a solution to improve the performance of phishing scams detection on Ethereum. TTAGN captures the temporal relationships between historical transaction records of nodes and aggregates the effective edge representations to incorporate the interactive topological relationships into nodes.

In the area of detecting abnormal smart contracts on Ethereum, Jin et al. [31] proposed a Ponzi-Warning framework that utilizes dual channels, namely the code-aware channel and the transaction-aware channel. Liu et al. [24] constructed a Heterogeneous Information Network (HIN) for smart contracts by extracting features and used a transformer network to obtain the relationship matrix, which was then input into a convolution network. Patel et al. [32] presented a one-class graph deep learning framework for anomaly detection in the Ethereum blockchain. The framework collected external transactions from the blockchain and extracted 34 statistical features for each node based on the transaction ledger. The data was manually labeled as anomalies and the desired features were extracted. This approach avoids the issue of imbalanced labeled data, but it ignores network structure information in the Ethereum-based transaction graph. Tan et al. [25] considered both the behavioral characteristics of user transactions and the structural characteristics of the transaction network, reconstructed the transaction network based on the publicly available transaction ledger, and constructed an amount-based network embedding framework to extract node features to identify fraudulent transactions. They designed an amount-based Node2vec network embedding method to better capture the feature of the transaction amount in the transaction network. Morishima et al. [33] presented a subgraph-based anomaly detection approach for blockchain with the goal of reducing processing time. They designed a subgraph structure that is optimized for GPU processing, which enables acceleration of anomaly detection through parallel processing. The target transaction is used to identify the final subgraph for anomaly detection. Patel et al. [29] proposed a novel GCN-based novel learning framework for anomaly detection in dynamic transaction networks. A temporal feature aggregation mechanism was designed to model the evolutionary properties of nodes, and temporal and structural features were computed at each time step to add knowledge about the transaction patterns of nodes. The transaction trends and relationships between nodes and neighboring nodes were captured by graph features, enhancing robustness and performance for highly dynamic datasets. Yu et al. [28] applied the GCN to combine structural information with account features and achieved decent classification performance compared to network embedding methods, such as Node2vec, DeepWalk, and LINE.

In the field of anomaly detection, it is evident that since 2020, GCN-based automatic feature extraction has gradually replaced traditional feature engineering methods. This is due to GCN's ability to identify outliers in a graph by comparing the learned embeddings of each node with those of its neighboring nodes, which enables it to detect anomalous transactions that deviate from normal patterns in the transaction graph. Furthermore, GCN can be enhanced with attention mechanisms and other techniques to improve its performance in detecting complex anomalies in blockchain transactions, such as those associated with Ponzi and phishing schemes. In summary, GCN technology provides a promising approach to enhancing the accuracy and efficiency of anomaly detection in blockchain transactions.

3.3   Classification Algorithm

Once the features have been extracted, they must be inputted into a classifier for classification to identify anomalous nodes. The selection of the classifier in the detection framework is a factor that can impact detection performance. Table 3 summarizes the classifiers used in the blockchain anomaly detection articles in the field.

Table 3. Classification algorithm.

task	paper	classifier	Precision	Recall	F-score	AUC	Comparative approaches	Major contribution
phishing Scams	[6,23]	One-class SVM	0.927	0.893	0.908	-	Logistic regression, naïve-bayes, Isolation forest	Resolve data imbalance problems
	[27]	DT	0.8132	0.8271	0.8199	-	-	Resolve data imbalance problems
	[26,34]	LightGBM	0.928	0.859	0.777	0.816	-	Beneficial training effect and difficult over-fitting
	[17]	AdaBoost	0.83	0.66	0.74	0.9276	SVM,KNN	Identifies better and is relatively robust in the face of phishing hidden strategy attacks.
	[10]	KNN	0.98	0.98	0.98	0.9811	C4.5 DT, Naïve Bayes Tree, J48 Consolidated, Fast DT, PART Decision List, JRip, OneR	The highest detection accuracy
Ponzi Schemes	[18,21]	XGBoost	0.94	0.81	0.86	-	-	Hight accuracy
	[19]	LightGBM	0.967	0.967	0.967	0.983	-	Enhance the recognition effect
	[36]	CatBoost	0.97	0.97	0.97	-	-	Avoid over-fitting and significantly improve test efficiency.
	[14]	AI-SPSD	0.95	0.96	0.96	-	LightGBM, GBDT, Chen-XGBoost, Adaboost, Chen-RF, SVM, DT, KNN, LSTM	Avoid over-fitting and performs well on all metrics.
	[11]	CTRF	0.928	0.891	0.909	-	KNN, CNN, DT, SVM, XGBoost	Significantly improved recall.
Illicit Entities	[37]	Ensemble Decision Trees	0.66	-	-	-	DT, RF	Excellent in parameters other than accuracy.
	[12]	XGBoost, RF	-	-	-	0.92	-	Combination of XGboost and RF construction
	[38]	-	-	-	-	-	XGBoost, SVM, RF	Results of three classifiers compared.
	[39]	K-means	-	-	-	-	-	Novel method.
	[40]	One-class SVM, K-means	0.93	-	-	-	-	High performance results on accuracy

For phishing scams, Wu et al. [6,23] utilized a one-class SVM to classify phishing and non-phishing addresses, in order to overcome the problems of data imbalance and network heterogeneity. To address the same imbalance issue, Xia et al. [27] used a Decision Tree(DT), which is considered efficient for classification tasks with class imbalance. Chen et al. and Li et al. [26,34] selected

LightGBM, a GBDT (Gradient Boosting Decision Tree) algorithm that supports efficient parallel training. Wen et al. [17] manually extracted features from phishing accounts and fed them into three classifiers: SVM, K-NearestNeighbor (KNN) and AdaBoost, with the latter performing the best and being relatively robust against hidden phishing strategy attacks. Eight classifiers, different from those used in the previous related work, were experimentally applied by Kabla et al. [10]. For the evaluation of the performance of each classifier, two test approaches are in use: Supplied Set Test and Cross-Validation. Based on the experimental results, the KNN classifier was found to be the best for optimization of detection.

For Ponzi schemes, the majority of studies have used the gradient boosting method for classification. Chen et al. and Farrugia et al. [18,21] chose XGBoost and Zhang et al. [19] chose LightGBM, both with good detection performance. However, these classical gradient boosting algorithms have an over-fitting problem caused by gradient deviation, which affects the model's generalization ability [35]. This is because the loss function in each iteration uses the same data points on which the current model is based to find the gradient, which affects the generalization ability of the training model. To solve this problem, Zhang et al. [36] selected the CatBoost algorithm. CatBoost, developed by Yandex [35], is a type of boosting algorithm that has been improved upon the gradient boosting decision tree (GBDT) algorithm. It is similar to other boosting algorithms such as XGBoost and LightGBM, but has a distinct feature of using Oblivious DT as its base model. This ensures symmetry in tree partitioning at the same level, which helps in preventing overfitting and enhances the testing efficiency. Fan et al. [14] proposed a novel boosting method, referred to as Al-SPSD. Al-SPSD constructs a model with unbiased residuals based on the ordered target statistics and ordered boosting idea, using the DT as the base predictor. The results show that Al-SPSD achieves a high recall rate while retaining a relatively high precision rate and has the highest F-score, compared to other methods. He et al. [11] combined the RF (Random Forest) algorithm with smart contract properties to propose the CTRF (Code and Transaction Random Forest) algorithm to identify Ponzi schemes.

Nerurkar et al. [37] proposed a supervised learning approach for detecting categories of illicit bitcoin users by estimating the most discriminative features. Ashfaq et al. [12] applied XGboost and RF for data classification into fraudulent or non-fraudulent. Ostapowicz et al. [38] evaluated the performance of RF, SVM, and XGBoost classifiers for identifying accounts in a dataset of over 300,000 accounts. Shayegan et al. [39] presented a K-means based method to detect anomalous behavior of Bitcoin with more suitable efficiency, designing a method that can check user behavior instead of wallet address, which can be more efficient. Sayadi et al. [40] proposed a new model for anomaly detection over bitcoin electronic transactions. They used two machine learning algorithms, namely the One-class SVM algorithm to detect outliers and the K-Means algorithm in order to group the similar outliers with the same type of anomalies.

Based on the performance of the classifiers mentioned above, it can be concluded that classifiers have shown promising results in detecting abnormal transactions in the blockchain domain. The different studies applied various classifiers such as One-class SVM, DT, LightGBM, XGBoost. Overall, these classifiers perform better in detecting abnormal transactions in the blockchain domain.

4   Future Trend and Challenges

Blockchain technology has rapidly evolved and its applications have become widespread. However, with the increasing use of blockchain technology, fraud and security vulnerabilities are also on the rise. As a result, the detection of abnormal transactions in blockchain networks has become a crucial aspect to ensure the stability and security of blockchain networks, and to enhance the trust and value of blockchain technology.

Data mining techniques play a crucial role in the detection of abnormal transactions in blockchain networks. Through analyzing and mining the transaction data in blockchain networks, data mining techniques can identify suspicious abnormal transaction behavior. For instance, analyzing the time, amount, geographical location, and other features of the transaction data can reveal the presence of abnormal transactions. Moreover, data mining techniques can predict abnormal transaction behavior through pattern recognition of transaction data in blockchain networks, such as identifying the characteristic patterns of abnormal transactions through association rule mining. Furthermore, data mining techniques can solve the issue of data imbalance that is prevalent in the detection of abnormal transactions in blockchain by using feature engineering techniques, such as the SMOTE, to synthesize new samples of abnormal transactions.

Deep learning is a machine learning technique that has gained attention for its ability to identify patterns in data. It is also important for the detection of abnormal transactions in blockchain networks. Deep learning can identify complex anomalous transaction patterns by learning from large amounts of historical transaction data. Additionally, deep learning can adapt to changing anomalous transaction patterns by continuously learning new data and functions. Over the past few years, researchers have explored the use of GCN in blockchain anomalous transaction detection and have seen promising results.

According to recent studies, detecting abnormal transactions in blockchain technology has become a hot topic in the field of blockchain research in recent years. However, there are still several issues with current research efforts both domestically and internationally:

- Data imbalance is a key issue in the current research on blockchain anomaly transaction detection. Existing solutions primarily use undersampling and oversampling techniques, which are at risk of information loss and overfitting.
- Existing feature extraction methods mainly include traditional feature engineering methods and graph-based learning methods. Traditional feature engineering lacks consideration of the relationship between blockchain accounts, while graph-based methods tend to ignore some implicit features.

- Current research mainly considers blockchain anomaly transaction detection as a binary classification problem, and commonly used classifiers are often employed to solve binary classification problems. However, due to the influence of upstream tasks, there is still significant room for improvement in the classification performance of these classifiers.

5   Conclusion

In this paper, we provide a comprehensive review of the current approaches for detecting anomalous transactions in blockchain technology. We analyze the existing techniques for processing blockchain data, extracting features, and using classification algorithms in the field of blockchain anomaly transaction detection. Our results indicate that addressing the data imbalance issue and utilizing GCN for efficient feature extraction have a substantial impact in this area and are likely to play a critical role in future studies. Therefore, we aim to further explore and underscore the importance of solving the data imbalance problem and using GCN in the realm of blockchain abnormal transaction detection in our future research.

Acknowledgments. This paper is supported by the National Natural Science Foundation of China (61962042) and Science and Technology Program of Inner Mongolia Autonomous Region (2020GG0188), and Natural Science Foundation of Inner Mongolia (2022MS06020), and the Central Government Guides Local Science and Technology Development Fund (2022ZY0064), and the University Youth Science and Technology Talent Development Project (Innovation Group Development Plan) of Inner Mongolia A. R. of China (Grant No. NMGIRT2318).

References

1. Wang, S., Ouyang, L., Yuan, Y., Ni, X., Han, X., Wang, F.Y.: Blockchain-enabled smart contracts: architecture, applications, and future trends. IEEE Trans. Syst. Man, Cybern. Syst. **49**(11), 2266–2277 (2019)
2. Crosby, M., Pattanayak, P., Verma, S., Kalyanaraman, V.: Blockchain technology: beyond bitcoin. Appl. Innovation **2**(6–10), 71 (2016)
3. Trozze, A.: Cryptocurrencies and future financial crime. Crime Sci. **11**(1), 1–35 (2022)
4. Chen, H., Pendleton, M., Njilla, L., Xu, S.: A survey on ethereum systems security: Vulnerabilities, attacks, and defenses. ACM Comput. Surv. (CSUR) **53**(3), 1–43 (2020)
5. SAFEIS: 2022 crimes involving virtual currency research report (2023). https://safeis.cn/
6. Wu, J., et al.: Who are the phishers? phishing scam detection on ethereum via network embedding. IEEE Trans. Syst. Man, Cybern. Syst. **52**, 1156–1166 (2020)
7. Zheng, Z., Chen, W., Zhong, Z., Chen, Z., Lu, Y.: Securing the ethereum from smart ponzi schemes: identification using static features. ACM Trans. Softw. Eng. Methodology **32**, 1–28 (2022)

8. Agarwal, R., Barve, S., Shukla, S.K.: Detecting malicious accounts in permissionless blockchains using temporal graph properties. Appl. Netw. Sci. **6**(1), 1–30 (2021)
9. Chen, W., Guo, X., Chen, Z., Zheng, Z., Lu, Y.: Phishing scam detection on ethereum: towards financial security for blockchain ecosystem. In: IJCAI, pp. 4506–4512 (2020)
10. Kabla, A.H.H., Anbar, M., Manickam, S., Karupayah, S.: Eth-PSD: a machine learning-based phishing scam detection approach in ethereum. IEEE Access **10**, 118043–118057 (2022)
11. He, X., Yang, T., Chen, L.: CTRF: ethereum-based ponzi contract identification. Secur. Commun. Netw. 2022 (2022)
12. Ashfaq, T., et al.: A machine learning and blockchain based efficient fraud detection mechanism. Sensors **22**(19), 7162 (2022)
13. Fan, S., Fu, S., Xu, H., Zhu, C.: Expose your mask: smart ponzi schemes detection on blockchain. In: 2020 International Joint Conference on Neural Networks (IJCNN), pp. 1–7. IEEE (2020)
14. Fan, S., Fu, S., Xu, H., Cheng, X.: AL-SPSD: anti-leakage smart ponzi schemes detection in blockchain. Inf. Process. Manag. **58**(4), 102587 (2021)
15. Han, J., Woo, J., Hong, J.W.K.: Oversampling techniques for detecting bitcoin illegal transactions. In: 2020 21st Asia-Pacific Network Operations and Management Symposium (APNOMS), pp. 330–333. IEEE (2020)
16. Demertzis, K., Iliadis, L., Tziritas, N., Kikiras, P.: Anomaly detection via blockchained deep learning smart contracts in industry 4.0. Neural Comput. Appl. **32**(23), 17361–17378 (2020)
17. Wen, H., Fang, J., Wu, J., Zheng, Z.: Transaction-based hidden strategies against general phishing detection framework on ethereum. In: 2021 IEEE International Symposium on Circuits and Systems (ISCAS), pp. 1–5. IEEE (2021)
18. Chen, W., Zheng, Z., Cui, J., Ngai, E., Zheng, P., Zhou, Y.: Detecting ponzi schemes on ethereum: Towards healthier blockchain technology. In: Proceedings of the 2018 World Wide Web Conference, pp. 1409–1418 (2018)
19. Zhang, Y., Yu, W., Li, Z., Raza, S., Cao, H.: Detecting ethereum Ponzi schemes based on improved lightGBM algorithm. IEEE Trans. Comput. Soc. Syst. **9**(2), 624–637 (2021)
20. Chen, Y., Dai, H., Yu, X., Hu, W., Xie, Z., Tan, C.: Improving ponzi scheme contract detection using multi-channel textCNN and transformer. Sensors **21**(19), 6417 (2021)
21. Farrugia, S., Ellul, J., Azzopardi, G.: Detection of illicit accounts over the ethereum blockchain. Expert Syst. Appl. **150**, 113318 (2020)
22. Hara, K., Takahashi, T., Ishimaki, M., Omote, K.: Machine-learning approach using solidity bytecode for smart-contract honeypot detection in the ethereum. In: 2021 IEEE 21st International Conference on Software Quality, Reliability and Security Companion (QRS-C), pp. 652–659. IEEE (2021)
23. Yuan, Q., Huang, B., Zhang, J., Wu, J., Zhang, H., Zhang, X.: Detecting phishing scams on ethereum based on transaction records. In: 2020 IEEE International Symposium on Circuits and Systems (ISCAS), pp. 1–5. IEEE (2020)
24. Liu, L., Tsai, W.T., Bhuiyan, M.Z.A., Peng, H., Liu, M.: Blockchain-enabled fraud discovery through abnormal smart contract detection on ethereum. Futur. Gener. Comput. Syst. **128**, 158–166 (2022)
25. Tan, R., Tan, Q., Zhang, P., Li, Z.: Graph neural network for ethereum fraud detection. In: 2021 IEEE International Conference on Big Knowledge (ICBK), pp. 78–85. IEEE (2021)

26. Chen, L., Peng, J., Liu, Y., Li, J., Xie, F., Zheng, Z.: Phishing scams detection in ethereum transaction network. ACM Trans. Internet Technol. (TOIT) **21**(1), 1–16 (2020)
27. Xia, Y., Liu, J., Wu, J.: Phishing detection on ethereum via attributed ego-graph embedding. IEEE Trans. Circuits Syst. II Express Briefs **69**(5), 2538–2542 (2022)
28. Yu, S., Jin, J., Xie, Y., Shen, J., Xuan, Q.: Ponzi scheme detection in ethereum transaction network. In: Dai, H.-N., Liu, X., Luo, D.X., Xiao, J., Chen, X. (eds.) BlockSys 2021. CCIS, vol. 1490, pp. 175–186. Springer, Singapore (2021). https://doi.org/10.1007/978-981-16-7993-3_14
29. Patel, V., Rajasegarar, S., Pan, L., Liu, J., Zhu, L.: EvAnGCN: evolving graph deep neural network based anomaly detection in blockchain. In: Chen, W., Yao, L., Cai, T., Pan, S., Shen, T., Li, X. (eds.) ADMA 2022 Part I. LNCS, vol. 13725, pp. 444–456. Springer, Cham (2022). https://doi.org/10.1007/978-3-031-22064-7_32
30. Yu, T., Chen, X., Xu, Z., Xu, J.: MP-GCN: a phishing nodes detection approach via graph convolution network for ethereum. Appl. Sci. **12**(14), 7294 (2022)
31. Jin, J., Zhou, J., Jin, C., Yu, S., Zheng, Z., Xuan, Q.: Dual-channel early warning framework for ethereum ponzi schemes. In: Meng, X., Xuan, Q., Yang, Y., Yue, Y., Zhang, Z.K. (eds.) BDSC 2022. CCIS, vol. 1640, pp. 260–274. Springer, Singapore (2022). https://doi.org/10.1007/978-981-19-7532-5_17
32. Patel, V., Pan, L., Rajasegarar, S.: Graph deep learning based anomaly detection in ethereum blockchain network. In: Kutyłowski, M., Zhang, J., Chen, C. (eds.) NSS 2020. LNCS, vol. 12570, pp. 132–148. Springer, Cham (2020). https://doi.org/10.1007/978-3-030-65745-1_8
33. Morishima, S.: Scalable anomaly detection in blockchain using graphics processing unit. Comput. Electr. Eng. **92**, 107087 (2021)
34. Li, S., Gou, G., Liu, C., Hou, C., Li, Z., Xiong, G.: TTAGN: temporal transaction aggregation graph network for ethereum phishing scams detection. In: Proceedings of the ACM Web Conference 2022, pp. 661–669 (2022)
35. Prokhorenkova, L., Gusev, G., Vorobev, A., Dorogush, A.V., Gulin, A.: CatBoost: unbiased boosting with categorical features. In: Advances in Neural Information Processing Systems, vol. 31 (2018)
36. Zhang, Y., Kang, S., Dai, W., Chen, S., Zhu, J.: Code will speak: Early detection of Ponzi smart contracts on Ethereum. In: 2021 IEEE International Conference on Services Computing (SCC), pp. 301–308. IEEE (2021)
37. Nerurkar, P., Busnel, Y., Ludinard, R., Shah, K., Bhirud, S., Patel, D.: Detecting illicit entities in bitcoin using supervised learning of ensemble decision trees. In: Proceedings of the 10th International Conference on Information Communication and Management, pp. 25–30 (2020)
38. Ostapowicz, M., Żbikowski, K.: Detecting fraudulent accounts on blockchain: a supervised approach. In: Cheng, R., Mamoulis, N., Sun, Y., Huang, X. (eds.) WISE 2020. LNCS, vol. 11881, pp. 18–31. Springer, Cham (2019). https://doi.org/10.1007/978-3-030-34223-4_2
39. Shayegan, M.J., Sabor, H.R., Uddin, M., Chen, C.L.: A collective anomaly detection technique to detect crypto wallet frauds on bitcoin network. Symmetry **14**(2), 328 (2022)
40. Sayadi, S., Rejeb, S.B., Choukair, Z.: Anomaly detection model over blockchain electronic transactions. In: 2019 15th International Wireless Communications & Mobile Computing Conference (IWCMC), pp. 895–900. IEEE (2019)
41. Khonji, M., Iraqi, Y., Jones, A.: Phishing detection: a literature survey. IEEE Commun. Surv. Tutorials **15**(4), 2091–2121 (2013)

42. Bartoletti, M., Carta, S., Cimoli, T., Saia, R.: Dissecting Ponzi schemes on Ethereum: identification, analysis, and impact. Futur. Gener. Comput. Syst. **102**, 259–277 (2020)
43. watcher.guru (2023). https://watcher.guru/
44. tokenview (2023). https://tokenview.io/
45. reddit (2023). https://old.reddit.com/r/CryptoCurrency/comments/101hnkr/eth
46. etherscan (2023). https://etherscan.io/
47. García, S., Ramírez-Gallego, S., Luengo, J., Benítez, J.M., Herrera, F.: Big data preprocessing: methods and prospects. Big Data Anal. **1**(1), 1–22 (2016)
48. Han, H., Wang, W.-Y., Mao, B.-H.: Borderline-SMOTE: a new over-sampling method in imbalanced data sets learning. In: Huang, D.-S., Zhang, X.-P., Huang, G.-B. (eds.) ICIC 2005. LNCS, vol. 3644, pp. 878–887. Springer, Heidelberg (2005). https://doi.org/10.1007/11538059_91
49. Khan, S.S., Madden, M.G.: One-class classification: taxonomy of study and review of techniques. Knowl. Eng. Rev. **29**(3), 345–374 (2014)
50. Yuan, Z., Yuan, Q., Wu, J.: Phishing detection on ethereum via learning representation of transaction subgraphs. In: Zheng, Z., Dai, H.-N., Fu, X., Chen, B. (eds.) BlockSys 2020. CCIS, vol. 1267, pp. 178–191. Springer, Singapore (2020). https://doi.org/10.1007/978-981-15-9213-3_14

A Systematic Literature Review on Smart Contract Vulnerability Detection by Symbolic Execution

Yanli Wang[1], Sifei Sheng[2], and Yanlin Wang[1]([✉])

[1] School of Software Engineering, Sun Yat-sen University, Zhuhai 519082, China
wangyli58@mail2.sysu.edu.cn, wangylin36@mail.sysu.edu.cn
[2] Knowledge-First Empowerment Academy, Houston TX77036, USA

Abstract. Symbolic execution emerges as a potent method for software testing, progressively tackling the unique complexities associated with smart contract testing. Leveraging path exploration and constraint-solving mechanisms, symbolic execution uncovers potential vulnerabilities in smart contracts, ones that other testing methodologies might overlook. An expanding suite of tools and frameworks, including Oyente, Mythril, and Osiris, facilitate the symbolic execution of smart contracts. This paper delves into the theoretical underpinnings of smart contracts and symbolic execution. Subsequently, we provide a comprehensive review of the prevailing smart contract vulnerability detection tools reliant on symbolic execution, assessing their performance and testing scope, among other aspects. Lastly, we deliberate on the prospective challenges and the trajectory of this field in the future.

Keywords: Symbolic Execution · Smart Contract · Vulnerability Detection · Blockchain · Literature Review

1 Introduction

Smart contracts [26,28] has emerged as an innovative technology that enables the automation of trust and the execution of transactions without intermediaries. However, the lack of proper testing and validation mechanisms in smart contracts has led to a significant number of vulnerabilities and security incidents. As a result, researchers have proposed several techniques to detect smart contract vulnerabilities, including static analysis, dynamic analysis, and symbolic execution. Symbolic execution is a powerful technique for detecting vulnerabilities in software by exploring all possible paths and inputs to a program. It involves creating a symbolic representation of the program's execution and systematically exploring all possible input values to uncover potential errors or security weaknesses.

In this literature review, we provide a comprehensive overview of the SOTA in smart contract vulnerability detection using symbolic execution. We explore

J. Chen et al. (Eds.): BlockSys 2023, CCIS 1896, pp. 226–241, 2024.
https://doi.org/10.1007/978-981-99-8101-4_16

the existing literature, identify the challenges, and discuss the limitations of the current approaches. Furthermore, we highlight the need for further research to address the identified challenges and limitations in the existing approaches.

Contributions. Our paper makes the following contributions: (1) We present a detailed overview of symbolic execution as applied to the detection of vulnerabilities in smart contracts. (2) We assess the performance of current tools in the field across multiple dimensions.

2 Background

2.1 Smart Contract Vulnerabilities

Smart contracts, which govern the states of blockchains, operate atop these distributed ledger systems. Ethereum, the most extensive proponent of smart contracts, employs the Ethereum Virtual Machine (EVM) for their execution. The EVM receives inputs from blockchain transactions, retrieves the contract code from the state, and subsequently executes the operations delineated in the contract code. This process may entail reading from or writing to the variables housed in the contract storage, among other actions.

The types of bugs uncovered in smart contracts differ markedly from those typically found in traditional programming contexts. This discrepancy is attributable, in part, to the fact that a smart contract's execution result is contingent upon the transactions, thereby creating potential vulnerabilities related to transaction-ordering dependencies. If malicious actors execute 'front-running' transactions, they could potentially expropriate funds. Additionally, the ability of a smart contract to invoke other contracts could give rise to vulnerabilities stemming from mishandled calling exceptions, enabling malevolent contracts to initiate attacks. This accentuates the necessity for rigorous caution.

2.2 Symbolic Execution

Symbolic execution is a technique for analyzing computer programs that systematically investigates multiple potential execution paths without necessitating specific input. Instead of utilizing fully defined input values, this method symbolically represents input values and employs a constraint solver to generate actual inputs.

Throughout the symbolic execution process, the code of the program undergoes symbolic implementation, generating a tree comprised of various execution paths. Each of these paths signifies a distinct possible combination of input values. By probing all conceivable execution paths, symbolic execution is capable of detecting flaws, encompassing runtime errors and security vulnerabilities.

Symbolic execution's applications extend across several facets of software engineering, including program verification, bug identification, and testing. Beyond this, it offers valuable insights into system behavior, for example, exposing security frailties in network protocols and facilitating the analysis of cryptographic protocols.

3   Research Methodology

Figure 1 shows the overview of our methodology, which adopts the approach proposed by Kitchenham et al. (Kitchenham and Charters, 2007) to conduct a systematic literature review. This approach comprises three fundamental steps: literature search, literature selection, and data analysis.

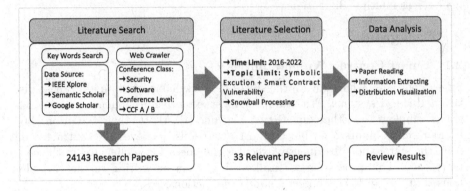

Fig. 1. Overview of research methodology design

3.1   Literature Search

To conduct a comprehensive search of relevant literature, we utilized several data sources, including IEEE Xplore, Semantic Scholar, and Google Scholar. To ensure the thoroughness of our search, we used the keywords "symbolic execution + smart contract" and "symbolic execution + vulnerability detection" in our search query. Additionally, we employed a web crawler [33] to scrape papers from top security and software-related conferences (CCF A/B) that were published between 2016 and 2022. To refine our search results, we retained literature with titles containing the keywords "smart contract", "symbolic execution", and "vulnerability detection". This process allowed us to obtain a comprehensive collection of relevant literature for our research.

3.2   Literature Selection

We set inclusion and exclusion criteria to ensure rigorous and comprehensive coverage of the relevant literature. Specifically, this review targets conference papers published between 2016 and 2022 that focus on the use of symbolic execution for smart contract vulnerability detection and have been published in peer-reviewed conference proceedings. By restricting the search to this particular subset of literature, we aim to provide a thorough and detailed examination of the current state-of-the-art in this domain.

To achieve the aforementioned objectives, it is necessary to establish clear and precise exclusion criteria. As such, we exclude articles that primarily address smart contract development, implementation, and testing but not vulnerability detection using symbolic execution. By doing so, we aim to ensure that our analysis focuses solely on papers that are most relevant to the specific topic of interest. Through this rigorous and selective approach, we can be confident in the completeness and accuracy of our findings.

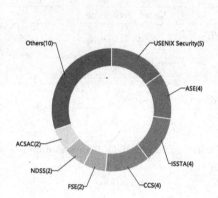

Fig. 2. The distribution of the conferences of paper selected

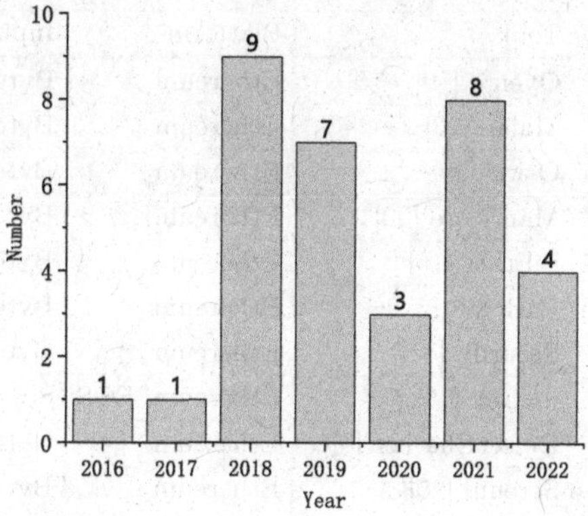

Fig. 3. The number of papers published between 2016 to 2022

The data extracted from papers consisted of the tool's name, paper title, publication year, conference name, etc. As illustrated in Fig. 2, this data was used to analyze the distribution of conferences where the selected papers were published. It is noteworthy that USENIX Security had the highest number of selected papers, totaling 5.

Furthermore, to gain insights into the temporal trends of the selected papers, we plotted the number of papers published between 2016 to 2022, as shown in Fig. 3. This analysis provides a comprehensive understanding of the research landscape over the years and is crucial for identifying emerging trends and research directions.

4   Overview of Existing Tools

Table 1 presents an overview of 22 tools that leverage symbolic execution for identifying vulnerabilities in smart contracts. Most tools focus on Ethereum. However, ExGen [15] focuses on EOS and EOSafe [11] is cross-platform. The input types accepted by the tools vary, with some accepting bytecode, source code, or an account address. Although some tools take source code as input, the first step in their processing is to compile the source code into bytecode.

Osiris [29] and Sereum [25] utilize taint analysis and tracking, respectively, while ExGen [15] and Slither [7] rely on the intermediate representation. Sailfish

[1], on the other hand, uses a storage dependency graph. SmarTest [27] and S-gram [18] utilize N-gram, a basic language model. ILF [10] and ContractFuzzer [14] use fuzzing as their primary technique. HoneyBadger [30] and SADPonzi [6] utilizes a heuristic-guided approach. MPro [35] leverages data dependency analysis, and Solar [8] utilizes a query language.

Table 1. Overview of tools using symbolic execution for smart contract vulnerability detection.

Tool	Platform	Input	Other Technique
Oyente [19]	Ethereum	Bytecode	–
Maian [23]	Ethereum	Bytecode	–
Osiris [29]	Ethereum	Bytecode	Taint Analysis
Manticore [20]	Ethereum	Bytecode	–
teEther [16]	Ethereum	Bytecode	–
Park [36]	Ethereum	Bytecode	–
Securify [31]	Ethereum	Bytecode	–
ExGen [15]	Ethereum, EOS	Source Code	Intermediate Representation
DefectChecker [4]	Ethereum	Bytecode	–
Sereum [25]	Ethereum	Bytecode	Taint Tracking
Nova/MTVD [12]	Ethereum	Bytecode	–
SmarTest [27]	Ethereum	Source Code	N-gram
ETHBMC [9]	Ethereum	Account Address	–
Solar [8]	Ethereum	Source Code	Query Language
Sailfish [1]	Ethereum	Source Code	Storage Dependency Graph
Slither [7]	Ethereum	Source Code	Intermediate Representation
ILF [10]	Ethereum	Source Code	Fuzzing
ContractFuzzer [14]	Ethereum	ABI	Fuzzing
HoneyBadger [30]	Ethereum	Bytecode	Heuristic-guided
MPro [35]	Ethereum	Source Code	Data Dependency Analysis
EOSafe [11]	EOS	Bytecode	–
SADPonzi [6]	Ethereum	Bytecode	Heuristic-guided
SolSEE [17]	Ethereum	Source Code	–
Annotary [32]	Ethereum	Source Code	–
S-gram [18]	Ethereum	Source Code	N-gram

5   Comparison of Existing Tools

5.1   Scope of Vulnerability Detection

Table 2 presents the vulnerability detection scope, based on currently available tools utilizing symbolic execution. We have chosen eight prevalent vulnerabilities for this analysis, encompassing Reentrancy (RE), Timestamp Dependence (TSD), Transaction-Ordering Dependence (TOD), and others. A total

Table 2. The scope of vulnerability detection based on symbolic execution vulnerability tools currently available. RE: Reentrancy; TSD: Timestamp Dependence; TOD: Transaction-Ordering Dependence; ME: Mishandled Exception; SC: Suicidal Contract; IB: Integer Bugs; CI: Call Injection; EL: Ether Leak

Tool	RE	TSD	TOD	ME	SC	IB	CI	EL
Oyente [19]	✓	✓	✓	✓	✓			
Maian [23]	✓			✓				✓
Osiris [29]	✓	✓	✓	✓		✓		
Mythril [22]	✓			✓	✓	✓		✓
teEther [16]					✓		✓	✓
Manticore [20]								✓
Park [36]	✓	✓	✓	✓	✓	✓		✓
Securify [31]	✓	✓	✓	✓			✓	✓
ExGen [15]	✓				✓	✓	✓	
DefectChecker [4]	✓	✓	✓	✓				
Sereum [25]	✓							
Nova/MTVD [12]					✓	✓		✓
SmarTest [27]					✓	✓		✓
ETHBMC [9]					✓			✓
Solar [8]	✓	✓						
Sailfish [1]	✓		✓					
Slither [7]	✓				✓		✓	✓
ILF [10]		✓		✓	✓			✓
ContractFuzzer [14]	✓	✓	✓	✓		✓		

of 19 tools have been incorporated into this table. Among these, ILF [10] and ContractFuzzer [14] are two prominent fuzzers.

Reentrancy (RE), also referred to as a recursive call attack, poses a significant risk during the invocation of external contracts that could potentially usurp control flow. This type of attack materializes when a malicious contract reinvokes the calling contract before the completion of the original function invocation, enabling multiple function invocations to intertwine in unexpected ways. Although various tools are equipped to detect reentrancy vulnerabilities, it persists as a critical issue in smart contract security. Oyente [19] uncovers Reentrancy by simulating the Ethereum Virtual Machine (EVM) code execution and scrutinizing the contract's Control Flow Graph (CFG). Tools derived from Oyente, such as Osiris [29], utilize a similar strategy to detect reentrancy bugs. Exgen [15] employs a technique known as Path-based Test Suite Generation to detect Reentrancy. Securify [31], on the other hand, identifies Reentrancy by establishing violation patterns that encapsulate sufficient conditions for this vulnerability, and then applies symbolic analysis to verify the existence of these patterns in the smart contract. Sailfish [1] detects reentrancy by mandating the existence of hazardous access, which allows it to account for cross-function reentrancy bugs and to exclusively model malicious reentrancy scenarios. Sereum [25] uncovers reentrancy attacks through run-time monitoring of EVM bytecode instructions. To achieve this, it augments an existing Ethereum client for the real-time oversight of contract execution. Solar [8] detects Reentrancy by synthesizing an attack program that manipulates the victim's public interface to meet the vulnerability query articulated by the security analyst. ContractFuzzer [14] uncovers Reentrancy vulnerabilities by utilizing AttackerAgent to attempt to siphon Ether from the smart contract via a Reentrant attack.

Timestamp Dependence (TSD) is a specific vulnerability inherent to systems based on blockchain. It manifests when the sequence of transactions is determined by timestamps, thereby enabling an attacker to manipulate these timestamps to their advantage. Oyente [19] identifies Timestamp Dependence by verifying if the timestamp is included in the path condition of an Ether flow.

Transaction Order Dependence (TOD) represents another vulnerability in blockchain-based systems, wherein the sequence of transactions can be rearranged by an attacker to their benefit. TOD vulnerabilities emerge due to the intrinsic parallelism in blockchain transaction processing. As different nodes within the blockchain network can process transactions in diverse orders, an attacker can exploit this variability by strategically reordering transactions. Oyente [19] identifies Transaction-Ordering Dependence by analyzing the contract's code to discern if it depends on the transaction order. Sailfish [1] detects Transaction-Ordering Dependence by determining whether the precondition of an Ether transfer, the Ether transfer amount, or the external call destination is data-flow dependent on some storage, and whether the statements corresponding to these three parameters form a hazardous pair. It supports all three TOD patterns recognized by Security: TOD Transfer, TOD Amount, and TOD Receiver.

Mishandled Exception (ME) emerges when the return value of a message call is not checked, leading to a continuation of execution even if the called contract throws an exception. Accidental failure of the call or deliberate forced failure by an attacker can trigger unanticipated behaviors in the subsequent program logic. Oyente [19] identifies mishandled exceptions by locating any external calls (implemented through SEND, CALL instructions) that are not followed by failure checks. These checks are conducted by ensuring the return value is non-zero.

Suicidal Contract (SC) arises when there are absent or insufficient access controls, thereby enabling malicious entities to self-destruct the contract. For instance, Maian [23] verifies whether a contract can be terminated after executing transactions provided by the symbolic analysis engine on the forked chain. Slither [7] identifies self-destruct functions in Ethereum smart contracts by analyzing the contract's code for any instances of self-destruct calls. Slither's intermediate representation, SlithIR, facilitates the application of common program analysis techniques, such as dataflow and taint tracking, which can aid in the detection of potential issues with self-destruct functions.

Integer bugs (IB) occur when an arithmetic operation exceeds the maximum or minimum limits of a type. For example, if a number is stored as a uint8 type, it signifies that the number is held as an 8-bit unsigned integer, ranging from 0 to $2^8 - 1$. During an arithmetic operation, an integer overflow may transpire. This situation arises when the operation's result tries to generate a numerical value exceeding the range that can be expressed with a specific number of bits. The resulting value may either surpass the maximum representable value or fall below the minimum representable value. Oyente [19] employs the UGT and ULT functions of the Z3 solver [21] to ascertain the occurrence of an integer overflow. In contrast, Osiris [29] adopts a dual methodology comprising both symbolic execution and taint analysis. By leveraging these two techniques, Osiris can effectively pinpoint potential integer bugs by exploring all possible execution paths and tracking the propagation of user-controlled inputs throughout the program.

Call Injection (CI) is a vulnerability that can surface in smart contracts when an attacker injects a malicious function call into the contract's code. This inserted function can then be executed by unsuspecting users or other smart contracts. teEther [16], as a representative tool, identifies vulnerabilities in smart contracts by conducting a comprehensive analysis of all unique Ethereum contracts. It utilizes a generic definition of vulnerable contracts to build a tool that can create an exploit for a contract using only its binary bytecode. teEther executes all the unique contracts, allocating up to 30 min for Control Flow Graph (CFG) reconstruction and an additional 30 min for identifying each exploit based on CALL, CALLCODE, DELEGATECALL, and SELFDESTRUCT.

Ether Leak (EL) arises due to insufficient or missing access controls, enabling malicious entities to withdraw some or all of the Ether from a contract account. This type of bug may occur when initialization functions are unintentionally exposed. For instance, if a function meant to be a constructor is erroneously named, its code may be included in the runtime bytecode and become callable by anyone, potentially leading to contract re-initialization. Maian [23] verifies whether a contract leaks Ether by sending transactions with inputs provided by the symbolic analysis engine to the contract. Manticore [20] detects Ether Leak by conducting dynamic symbolic execution on a program or smart contract.

Table 3 shows some vulnerability detection tools that were not mentioned in Table 2, mostly focused on addressing a specific type of problem.

HoneyBadger [30] is a tool utilized for identifying honeypot techniques in Ethereum smart contracts. It carries out symbolic analysis, cash flow analysis, and honeypot analysis on EVM bytecode, subsequently returning an in-depth report outlining the different honeypot techniques detected.

MPro [35] is a security analysis tool grounded in symbolic execution, developed to identify vulnerabilities in Ethereum smart contracts. MPro applies a novel optimization algorithm to minimize redundant symbolic execution and uses parallelization methods to enhance its performance. Additionally, MPro incorporates a new security analysis module explicitly designed for detecting reentrancy vulnerabilities.

EOSafe [11] is a security analysis tool specifically developed for EOSIO smart contracts. It comprises three modules: the Wasm Symbolic Execution Engine,

Table 3. Description of some symbolic execution-based vulnerability detection tools

Tool	Description
HoneyBadger [30]	A tool that employs symbolic execution and well-defined heuristics to expose honeypots.
Mpro [35]	A technique to analyze depth-n vulnerabilities in an efficient and scalable way.
EOSafe [11]	The first static analysis framework that can be used to automatically detect vulnerabilities in EOSIO smart contracts at the bytecode level.
SADPonzi [6]	A semantic-aware detection approach for identifying Ponzi schemes in Ethereum smart contracts.
SolSEE [17]	A source-level symbolic execution engine for Solidity smart contracts.
Annotary [32]	A concolic execution framework to analyze smart contracts for vulnerabilities, supported by annotations that developers write directly in the Solidity source code

the EOSIO Library Emulator, and the Vulnerability Scanner. To identify vulnerabilities in smart contracts, EOSafe uses a two-step process that initially finds suspicious functions, followed by vulnerability detection via symbolic execution and path constraints.

SADPonzi [6] is a tool that employs semantic awareness to detect Ponzi schemes in Ethereum smart contracts. It uses a heuristic-guided symbolic execution method that models the execution of operations related to investors, balancing accuracy and scalability. This approach has demonstrated superior accuracy and robustness compared to current machine learning-based techniques.

SolSEE [17] is a symbolic execution engine at the source level, specifically designed to analyze Solidity smart contracts. It offers advanced analysis flexibility and supports essential features of the Solidity language. SolSEE provides precise operational semantics and enables users to define a harness function to control the function call sequence during the verification process. It also detects and reports underflows and overflows of unsigned integers and verifies assertions' validity, enabling the specification of custom high-level properties of the analyzed smart contracts. SolSEE includes a web-based user interface and a visualizer to display analysis results.

Annotary [32] is a concolic execution tool assisting Solidity developers in writing secure and error-free smart contracts. In contrast to other tools that rely on predefined vulnerability patterns, Annotary offers a developer-centric approach. It allows developers to express their expectations using annotations directly in the Solidity code. Based on these annotations, Annotary then performs a concolic execution analysis of the compiled EVM bytecode and alerts the developer of potential violations.

5.2   Performance of Zero-Day Vulnerability Detection

Zero-day vulnerabilities refer to unknown software security flaws with no current fix. These are challenging to handle as hackers can exploit them before vendors have time to respond. Detecting zero-day vulnerabilities requires continuous software monitoring and advanced security technologies. Strategies to improve detection include using advanced static and dynamic analysis tools, machine learning algorithms for pattern detection, and formal verification methods. Despite these efforts, continuous research is needed due to software evolution and sophisticated attacks.

Maian [23] tool can find vulnerabilities directly from the bytecode of Ethereum smart contracts without requiring source code access. It has been used to analyze 970,898 contracts live on the public Ethereum blockchain and can find the infamous Parity bug that previous analyses failed to capture.

Exgen [15] has been evaluated against 162 EOS contracts for its capability to detect and exploit zero-day vulnerabilities. The results show that ExGen produces 50 exploits for 24 real-world contracts with zero-day vulnerabilities.

Sailfish [1] has discovered some unique vulnerabilities that were not detected by other tools. To demonstrate that Sailfish is capable of finding zero-day vulnerabilities, researchers manually selected 88 reentrancy-only contracts and 107 time-dependency-only contracts flagged only by Sailfish for analysis.

SmarTest [27] finds various zero-day bugs from smart contracts in the wild. The experiment conducted in November 2019 collected 2,743 smart contracts with an open-source license from Etherscan and ran SmarTest (trained on the CVE dataset) on the contracts. The two most significant bug patterns that SmarTest found from 7 contracts, excluding benign and uncertain cases, are reported in the section.

Sailfish [1] has discovered unique vulnerabilities that have not been detected by any other tool, including some examples of cross-function reentrancy, delegate-based reentrancy, CREAM finance reentrancy attack and transaction order dependency.

5.3   Performance of Exploitation

Exploits can be used to steal funds or manipulate contract logic. To address these risks, a number of smart contract vulnerability detection tools have been developed, many of which include an "exploitation" function that allows researchers and developers to simulate and identify potential exploits in a safe and controlled environment.

teEther [16] performs automatic exploit generation for smart contracts by executing on all the unique contracts and allowing up to 30 min for CFG reconstruction plus 30 min for finding each aCALL, CALLCODE, DELEGATECALL, and SELFDESTRUCT-based exploit. It generates exploits by identifying vulnerable contracts that allow an attacker to transfer Ether from the contract to an attacker-controlled address and then create a sequence of state-changing transactions followed by a critical transaction.

ETHBMC [9] uses a symbolic executor to generate concrete inputs that trigger the detected vulnerability. When a model is violated, ETHBMC can automatically generate a chain of transactions that demonstrates the detected vulnerability. This allows for easier analysis and understanding of the vulnerability. Additionally, ETHBMC can be used to generate exploits by finding inputs that cause the contract to behave in an unintended way, such as transferring funds to an attacker's account.

Solar [8] is an automated tool for synthesizing an attack program that exploits a known vulnerability in a smart contract. The input to Solar is a declarative specification of the potential vulnerability, and if the vulnerability is present in the contract, Solar generates an attack program that utilizes the contract's Application Binary Interface (ABI) and contains at least one concrete trace where the vulnerability is present. The tool has been successfully used to generate exploits for Gasless-send vulnerabilities in several benchmark contracts.

5.4 Performance in Other Aspects

Dynamic Symbolic Execution. Dynamic symbolic execution (DSE) is a technique that systematically explores all possible execution paths of a program by dynamically executing the program with symbolic values. In the context of smart contract vulnerability detection, DSE can generate test cases that exercise all possible execution paths of a smart contract and identify potential vulnerabilities. By applying DSE to smart contracts, we can ensure that all execution paths are thoroughly tested, including those that may be difficult to reach by manual testing. During our literature review, we observed that several scholars incorporated dynamic symbolic execution (DSE) into their vulnerability detection tools.

Manticore [20] is a dynamic symbolic execution tool that can explore a program's state space with a high degree of semantic awareness. During analysis, Manticore identifies a set of path predicates, which are constraints on the program's input, for the paths that it explores. These path predicates are then leveraged to generate program inputs that will cause the associated paths to execute. This process allows Manticore to effectively identify bugs and vulnerabilities in programs, making it a powerful tool for software security analysis.

Nova/MTVD [12] are implemented on top of a DSE framework for smart contracts, which utilizes dynamic symbolic execution to precisely label and differentiate symbolic variables. The framework employs a mature DSE technique for traditional programs but also includes modifications to address nonuniform data accesses in smart contracts.

Heuristic Algorithm. Heuristic algorithms are problem-solving methods that rely on rules of thumb or common sense to identify solutions. In the realm of smart contract vulnerability detection, heuristic algorithms can be valuable in navigating potential paths to pinpoint the location of vulnerabilities. In our literature review, we found that several scholars have integrated heuristic algorithms into their vulnerability detection tools.

SADPonzi [6] employs a heuristic-guided symbolic execution approach to extract semantic information for all possible paths within smart contracts. This technique facilitates the identification of transfer behaviors and distribution strategies employed in relation to investors. The heuristics used in the approach are established based on the definition of Ponzi schemes, which aid in directing the symbolic execution process and in detecting relevant strategies and behaviors.

HoneyBadger [30] uses heuristics to detect certain honeypot techniques, such as inheritance disorder. Nonetheless, certain details are solely accessible at the source code level rather than the bytecode level, which forces HoneyBadger to rely on other less accurate information to identify these methodologies. Using this approach may result in a decrease in the accuracy of detection and the introduction of some false positives. Therefore, while HoneyBadger utilizes heuristics to detect honeypot techniques, it also needs to combine other information for analysis to improve accuracy.

Language Model. A language model is a statistical model that captures the probability distribution of word sequences in a language. In the realm of smart contract vulnerability detection, a language model can be trained to grasp the syntax and semantics of smart contract code. Utilizing the language model on the smart contract code enables us to anticipate the possibility of a particular code sequence being susceptible to vulnerabilities. Our literature review shows that several scholars have integrated language models into their vulnerability detection tools.

S-gram [18] leverages an N-gram based Training Engine to develop a language model specialized for smart contracts. During the model construction stage, a Static Analyzer conducts a lightweight analysis of the smart contract corpus to generate semantic metadata, such as access dependency and transaction flow sensitivity, for each contract. Subsequently, the Tokenizer labels the semantic metadata and parses the contracts into a token sequence. S-gram then uses the N-gram based Training Engine to train the language model. In the security auditing phase, the model can be utilized to identify possible vulnerabilities.

SmarTest [27] uses a language model to improve its performance in detecting vulnerabilities. Specifically, SMARTEST leverages a pre-trained language model to generate input sequences that are more likely to trigger vulnerabilities. The language model is used to guide the symbolic execution process by generating input sequences that are semantically similar to those seen during training. This approach improves the efficiency and effectiveness of symbolic execution by reducing the search space and increasing the likelihood of finding vulnerabilities.

6 Challenges and Future Directions

6.1 Challenges

Execution Efficiency. The complex task of examining all possible paths of a smart contract through symbolic values poses significant challenges to execution efficiency, often limiting the accuracy and scalability of symbolic tools. Several researchers have suggested remedies such as parallel execution [36], path pruning [13], or bytecode analysis [13] to circumvent this hurdle.

Path Explosion. The exponential escalation of potential execution paths for a smart contract, owing to an increase in the number of branches and loops, leads to a phenomenon known as path explosion. This considerably extends the time and resources required for symbolic execution, thereby diminishing its coverage and precision [34]. Researchers have suggested numerous strategies to mitigate this issue, including heuristic learning, parallel execution [36], critical path coverage, and multi-objective optimization [34].

6.2 Future Directions

Deep Learning. Deep learning has proven successful in various domains for automated code analysis and holds promising potential for smart contract vulnerability detection. Future investigations could delve into the application of deep learning techniques for vulnerability detection, such as training a neural network to classify contracts as vulnerable or secure based on their bytecode or source code.

Interoperability. The execution of smart contracts across diverse blockchain platforms-each possessing its own programming languages, runtime environments, and security considerations-raises the challenge of interoperability. Detecting vulnerabilities becomes complex as the same vulnerability could manifest differently or have varying implications on distinct platforms. Future research could explore methods to detect vulnerabilities that are transferable across multiple smart contract platforms, or strategies for automatic translation of contracts between platforms for analysis.

7 Related Work

Symbolic execution is a powerful technique for automated software testing and analysis that has been extensively studied in recent years. In this context, Chen et al. (2013) [5] provide a comprehensive overview of dynamic symbolic execution, including its theoretical foundations, state-of-the-art solutions, and implementation challenges. Similarly, Pasareanu and Visser (2009) [24] survey the latest trends in symbolic execution, covering various approaches to path exploration and constraint solving. In addition to these general surveys, Cadar et al. [2] offer a preliminary assessment of symbolic execution for software testing, including its use in academia, research labs, and industry. Furthermore, Cadar and Sen [3] provide a comprehensive overview of modern symbolic execution techniques, including the key challenges they face, such as path exploration, constraint solving, and memory modeling. These papers provide a comprehensive background on symbolic execution for software testing, its applications, limitations, and technical challenges. As such, they can serve as a valuable resource for researchers investigating smart contract vulnerability detection using symbolic execution.

8   Conclusion

This review provides a comprehensive overview of prevailing symbolic execution tools, drawing comparisons between their respective performances in the realm of vulnerability detection. Since the inception of Oyente [19], the academic community has seen a surge of interest in the application of symbolic execution for software testing. Consequently, enhancing the efficiency of symbolic execution has emerged as a prominent research trajectory. Existing literature has illustrated attempts at boosting the exploration efficiency of symbolic execution through a myriad of strategies. These include the deployment of heuristic algorithms [6,30], dynamic symbolic execution techniques [12,20], and utilization of language models [18,27] for navigational guidance. In the current landscape, however, methods incorporating deep learning to guide symbolic execution path exploration remain sparse. This suggests a potential area for future research, with the prospect of deep learning methodologies as an emergent development trend in the field of symbolic execution.

Acknowledgments. This work is partially supported by fundings from the National Key R&D Program of China (2022YFB2702203).

References

1. Bose, P., Das, D., Chen, Y., Feng, Y., Kruegel, C., Vigna, G.: SAILFISH: vetting smart contract state-inconsistency bugs in seconds. In: S&P (2021)
2. Cadar, C., et al.: Symbolic execution for software testing in practice - preliminary assessment. In: ICSE (2011)
3. Cadar, C., Sen, K.: Symbolic execution for software testing: three decades later. Commun. ACM **56**, 82–90 (2013)
4. Chen, J., Xia, X., Lo, D., Grundy, J., Luo, X., Chen, T.: DEFECTCHECKER: automated smart contract defect detection by analyzing EVM bytecode. In: TSE (2022)
5. Chen, T., Zhang, X.S., Guo, S.Z., Li, H.Y., Wu, Y.: State of the art: dynamic symbolic execution for automated test generation. In: FGCS (2013)
6. Chen, W., et al.: SADPonzi: detecting and characterizing Ponzi schemes in Ethereum smart contracts. In: SIGMETRICS (2021)
7. Feist, J., Grieco, G., Groce, A.: Slither: a static analysis framework for smart contracts. In: ICSE (2019)
8. Feng, Y., Torlak, E., Bodik, R.: Summary-based symbolic evaluation for smart contracts. In: ASE (2020)
9. Frank, J., Aschermann, C., Holz, T.: ETHBMC: a bounded model checker for smart contracts. In: USENIX Security (2020)
10. He, J., Balunović, M., Ambroladze, N., Tsankov, P., Vechev, M.: Learning to fuzz from symbolic execution with application to smart contracts. In: CCS (2019)

11. He, N., et al.: Security analysis of EOSIO smart contracts. In: USENIX Security (2020)
12. Huang, J., Jiang, J., You, W., Liang, B.: Precise dynamic symbolic execution for nonuniform data access in smart contracts. In: TC (2022)
13. Jiang, B., Chen, Y., Wang, D., Ashraf, I., Chan, W.: WANA: symbolic execution of Wasm bytecode for extensible smart contract vulnerability detection. In: QRS (2021)
14. Jiang, B., Liu, Y., Chan, W.K.: ContractFuzzer: fuzzing smart contracts for vulnerability detection. In: ASE (2018)
15. Jin, L., Cao, Y., Chen, Y., Zhang, D., Campanoni, S.: EXGEN: cross-platform, automated exploit generation for smart contract vulnerabilities. In: TDSC (2022)
16. Krupp, J., Rossow, C.: TEETHER: gnawing at Ethereum to automatically exploit smart contracts. In: USENIX Security (2018)
17. Lin, S.W., Tolmach, P., Liu, Y., Li, Y.: SolSEE: a source-level symbolic execution engine for solidity. In: FSE (2022)
18. Liu, H., Liu, C., Zhao, W., Jiang, Y., Sun, J.: S-gram: towards semantic-aware security auditing for Ethereum smart contracts. In: ASE (2018)
19. Luu, L., Chu, D.H., Olickel, H., Saxena, P., Hobor, A.: Making smart contracts smarter. In: CCS (2016)
20. Mossberg, M., et al.: Manticore: a user-friendly symbolic execution framework for binaries and smart contracts. In: ASE (2019)
21. de Moura, L., Bjørner, N.: Z3: An efficient SMT solver (2008). https://github.com/Z3Prover/z3
22. Muelle, B., Honig, J., Swende, M.: Mythril: security analysis tool for EVM bytecode (2023)
23. Nikolić, I., Kolluri, A., Sergey, I., Saxena, P., Hobor, A.: Finding the greedy, prodigal, and suicidal contracts at scale. In: ACSAC (2018)
24. Păsăreanu, C.S., Visser, W.: A survey of new trends in symbolic execution for software testing and analysis. In: STTT (2009)
25. Rodler, M., Li, W., Karame, G.O., Davi, L.: Sereum: protecting existing smart contracts against re-entrancy attacks. In: NDSS (2019)
26. Sankar, L.S., Sindhu, M., Sethumadhavan, M.: Survey of consensus protocols on blockchain applications. In: International Conference on Advanced Computing and Communication Systems (ICACCS) (2017)
27. So, S., Hong, S., Oh, H.: SMARTEST: effectively hunting vulnerable transaction sequences in smart contracts through language model-guided symbolic execution. In: USENIX Security (2021)
28. Swan, M.: Blockchain: Blueprint for a New Economy. O'Reilly Media, Inc., Sebastopol (2015). https://dl.acm.org/doi/book/10.5555/3006358
29. Torres, C.F., Schütte, J., State, R.: Osiris: hunting for integer bugs in Ethereum smart contracts. In: ACSAC (2018)
30. Torres, C.F., Steichen, M.: The art of the scam: demystifying honeypots in Ethereum smart contracts. In: USENIX Security (2019)
31. Tsankov, P., Dan, A., Drachsler-Cohen, D., Gervais, A., Bünzli, F., Vechev, M.: Securify: practical security analysis of smart contracts. In: CCS (2018)
32. Weiss, K., Schütte, J.: Annotary: a concolic execution system for developing secure smart contracts. In: Sako, K., Schneider, S., Ryan, P.Y.A. (eds.) ESORICS 2019. LNCS, vol. 11735, pp. 747–766. Springer, Cham (2019). https://doi.org/10.1007/978-3-030-29959-0_36
33. yf1291: Crawl-conorjou (2021). https://github.com/yf1291/Crawl-ConOrJou

34. Zhang, L., Wang, J., Wang, W., Jin, Z., Su, Y., Chen, H.: Smart contract vulnerability detection combined with multi-objective detection. In: CN (2022)
35. Zhang, W., Banescu, S., Passos, L., Stewart, S., Ganesh, V.: MPro: combining static and symbolic analysis for scalable testing of smart contract. In: ISSRE (2019)
36. Zheng, P., Zheng, Z., Luo, X.: Park: accelerating smart contract vulnerability detection via parallel-fork symbolic execution. In: ISSTA (2022)

Sharding Technologies in Blockchain: Basics, State of the Art, and Challenges

Luyi Zhang[1], Yujue Wang[2], Yong Ding[1,3], Hai Liang[1(✉)], Changsong Yang[1], and Chunhai Li[4]

[1] Guangxi Key Laboratory of Cryptography and Information Security, School of Computer Science and Information Security, Guilin University of Electronic Technology, Guilin 541004, China
lianghai@guet.edu.cn
[2] Hangzhou Innovation Institute, Beihang University, Hangzhou 310052, China
[3] Cyberspace Security Research Center, Peng Cheng Laboratory, Shenzhen 518055, China
[4] School of Information and Communication, Guilin University of Electronic Technology, Guilin 541004, China

Abstract. Sharding is one of the key technologies of blockchain scalable characteristics widely used in cryptocurrencies, Internet of Things, supply chain management and other fields. It can achieve high performance scaling without reducing the decentralization of blockchain, thus solving the problems of insufficient scalability and low throughput of blockchain. In this paper, the characteristics of some classical sharding technologies are analyzed in terms of performance and implementation. The key mechanisms of sharding are summarized, including sharding formation, reshuffle, intra-shard consensus protocol, and cross-shard protocol. Also, the advantages and shortcomings of typical scalability schemes are summarized, including state channel, DAG, and side chain. We summarize the current challenges faced by sharding technology from intra-shard, and cross-shard, and provide an outlook on the development prospects and future research directions in this field.

Keywords: Blockchain · Sharding · Distributed Ledger · Scalability · Consensus

1 Introduction

Blockchain was oriented from the peer-to-peer electronic payment system in 2008 – Bitcoin [28], in which all nodes agree to transactions in a trustless decentralized model and realize a system different from the traditional trust model. With the characteristics of data transparency, integrity, and decentralization, although the blockchain has attracted widespread attention from academia and the business community, the problem of scalability hinders the wide application of blockchain [40].

J. Chen et al. (Eds.): BlockSys 2023, CCIS 1896, pp. 242–255, 2024.
https://doi.org/10.1007/978-981-99-8101-4_17

The scalability namely that the transaction throughput would increase with more participants joining in is not considered in a series of designs in Bitcoin. Specifically, Bitcoin can only process 7 transactions per second, and Ethereum takes 30 transactions per second, which is far from satisfying the needs of the existing large-scale payment system such as Visa whose transaction throughput can reach thousands of transactions per second. Moreover the approaches to optimizing ledger storage and improving storage efficiency [30] also restrict the application of blockchain in more fields. In this regard, many proposals have been introduced to improve the scalability of blockchain systems, such as sharding, state channel [14], side chain [4], and DAG [18].

Sharding was originally used for improving the scalability of the database by storing a few copies in different places [10,12,19]. Luu et al. [26] first introduced sharding into a blockchain, which is a relatively efficient approach to improve the scalability of the blockchain. The nodes participating in the network are divided into small blockchain networks called shards, which can be each regarded as a single blockchain and they can process transactions in parallel, significantly improving throughput. The difference between traditional blockchain and sharded blockchain is shown in Fig. 1.

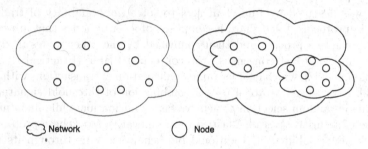

Fig. 1. The architecture of traditional and sharded blockchain (Left: traditional blockchain; Right: sharded blockchain)

Although sharding has effectively improved the scalability of the blockchain, it still has some deficiencies [11]. First, the entire sharding mechanism takes a lot to deal with tasks for sharding, e.g., requiring massive time and overheads during reshuffle for preventing nodes from committing malicious behaviors. Hence, it matters how to develop new sharding mechanisms to increase the effective time ratio of processing [1]. Second, as an extremely difficult part of sharding, sharding exacerbates the processing of cross-shard transactions because nodes have to communicate with one another for ledger transfer, which demands a certain method for realizing ledger status exchange among shards [33].

1.1 Our Contributions

The contributions of this paper are summarized as follows. First, some classic scalability technologies in blockchain are reviewed and analyzed. Second, the typical sharding technologies are reviewed, analyzed, and compared from different perspectives. Third, the challenges for enhancing existing sharding technologies are discussed.

1.2   Paper Organization

The remainder of this paper are organized as follows. Section 2 systematically introduces the typical technologies on scalability. Section 3 introduces sharding from different views. Section 4 introduces other scalability technologies in blockchain. The future challenge and conclusion are presented in Sects. 5 and 6 respectively.

2   Typical Sharding Technologies

Many representative technologies for improving the scalability of blockchain have been proposed including Elastico, OmniLedger, RapidChain, Sharper, Monoxide, and AHL, which are reviewed and analyzed in this section.

2.1   Elastico

Elastico was designed by Luu et al. [26] to solve the scalability of traditional blockchain protocols. Each shard is composed of a set of nodes that are selected through a random process and then confirmed by the other nodes in the network. It employs a fast consensus protocol, called PBFT (Practical Byzantine Fault Tolerance) [7], which enables rapid confirmation of transactions within each shard. This consensus protocol uses a combination of threshold signature and deterministic random selection to achieve fast confirmation while maintaining a high level of security. Overall, Elastico is an innovative blockchain protocol that addresses the scalability of traditional blockchain systems through its unique sharding approach and fast consensus protocol as well as includes several features that allow it to adapt to changes in the network, making it a promising solution for blockchain scalibity.

2.2   OmniLedger

OmniLedger proposed by Kokoris-Kogias et al. [23] divides the network into smaller sub-networks known as shards which enables the platform to achieve high transaction throughput. Moreover, the design of OmniLedger allows shards to dynamically adjust their size based on the workload and the number of active nodes in the network. To solve the scalability and security problems while remaining decentralized, OmniLedger engages the PBC (Parallelizing Block Commitments) mechanism that performs on par with centralized payment systems and handles cross-shard transactions atomically and provides a public randomness that is immune to bias for shard formation. Thus, OmniLedger offers a scalable solution to the traditional blockchain, whose sharding strategy and PBC, and fast consensus protocol make it a potential candidate for large-scale blockchain applications.

2.3   RapidChain

Though RapidChain [38] is based on sharding-based blockchain protocols like OmniLedger and Elastico, it succeeds in complete transaction processing sharding without the need for any trusted setup. RapidChain can be resilient to Byzantine faults up to 1/3 fraction of its participants and achieves complete sharding of the communication, computation, and storage overhead of processing transactions without assuming any trusted setup [38] and for efficient block propagation. Also, it introduces an optimal intra-shard consensus protocol that combines a variant of PBFT [7] with a gossip protocol. Thus, RapidChain provides a scalable solution via the mechanism of complete sharding, building on previous work in the field while introducing novel techniques for achieving efficient intra-shard consensus.

2.4   Sharper

SharPer is a permissioned blockchain that enables both intra-shard and cross-shard transactions by splitting nodes into shards and separating the ledger [3]. SharPer provides deterministic security in networks when more than half (if nodes are crash-only) or two-thirds (if nodes are Byzantine) of the nodes in each cluster (shard) are non-faulty and introduces two decentralized flattened consensus protocols to order cross-shard transactions without relying on centralized entities or trusted participants. Thus, SharPer has a promising feature that could make it an attractive solution for improving the scalability of the permissioned blockchain.

2.5   Monoxide

Monoxide is a scalable and permissionless blockchain system that divides workloads of communication, computation, storage, and memory for state representation into independent and parallel zones, and introduces Chu-ko-nu mining and eventual atomicity [36]. The eventual atomicity technique could provide consistency and resilience in asynchronous operating zones and allow for the efficient processing of cross-zone transactions. For the issue of poor throughput in conventional blockchain networks, Monoxide offers an asynchronous consensus zone blockchain network [36]. For the new network topology, efficient cross-shard transactions are suggested, and for the mining arithmetic dilution problem, the Chu-ko-nu mining method is proposed.

2.6   Nightshade

Along with segmenting the network into smaller node groups known as "shards", Nightshade [32] combines the chunks produced by each shard to make one large block, which provides a scalable and safe solution to execute transactions on a blockchain network while keeping the security and decentralization features crucial for blockchain.

2.7   Pyramid

Pyramid [20], the first layered sharding blockchain system where some shards may contain the complete records of several shards, allow the internal processing and validation of cross-shard transactions in these shards. A layered sharding consensus based on cooperation across shards is offered to ensure consistency among the relevant shards when committing cross-shard transactions.

3   Sharding from Different Perspectives

Blockchain is generally taken as a decentralized, pseudonym, and distributed database [24], and sharding is used to improve the reliability and reduce the storage of each node in a distributed database [22]. Additionally, the verification of transactions within each shard plays an important role in the blockchain. Hence, to achieve the sharding of blockchain, it is important to take into account both the data structure of the blockchain and the object of sharding. In this section, sharding will be discussed in different phases where blockchain works.

3.1   Shard Formation

Shard formation, which is typically the initial step in blockchain sharding, usually takes an approach that typically employs some random functions to provide unpredictability into account. To date, some classic solutions have been proposed. EpochRandomness is a random function used by Elastico [26]. Each node has to acquire a nonce that satisfies the following condition based on its IP and public key:

$$O = H(epochRandomness\|IP\|PK\|nonce) \leq 2^{\gamma-D}$$

where D is the workload size parameter of the predefined network node to solve a Proof of Work (PoW) problem [28], and γ is the output digit of the predefined H function. Each node calculates the O value, it indicates which shard the node belongs to, and will broadcast its location to other nodes.

In SharPer, nodes are assigned to clusters (shards) based on their geographical distribution, i.e., nodes that are in close proximity are assigned to the same cluster to reduce the latency of intra-cluster (shard) communication [3]. Instead of a trusted randomness beacon [12], OmniLedger adopted a distributed-randomness generation protocol RandHound [34] to provide unbiasability, unpredictability, third-party verifiability, and scalability [23]. Monoxide [36] uniformly partitions the space of user addresses into 2^k zones in a fixed and deterministic way and k denoted the sharding scale constant. In AHL [13], nodes derive their committee assignment by computing a random permutation π of $[1 : N]$ seeded by a random number. Also, AHL exploits TEE [27] to efficiently obtain the random number in a distributed and Byzantine environment, but it is still not completely secure in light of the fact that TEE relies on a single source of randomness.

3.2   Reshuffle

To prevent malicious nodes from colluding to cause sabotage, it is usually necessary to reorganize the nodes [29] after the organization of shards is completed, which is called reshuffle. There are typically two ways to reorganize shards, namely, the global one that takes longer than the initial shard organization, and the local one that involves transferring nodes across shards.

Global Reshuffle. Global shard reorganization redistributes nodes to shards like sharding formation when nodes are assigned to shards, thereby preventing nodes from colluding but requiring significant efforts [9]. Elastico [26] utilizes the randomness generation function to restructure the whole network nodes after each epoch, while the committee calculates a random number that will be disseminated to all nodes at the end of each epoch for the next round of sharding. Nodes across the network, upon receiving the random number, will determine their shard position through the random number. The reorganization of Elastico is effective in preventing node collusion [26], but it comes at a high cost, since the reorganization of nodes is global, resulting in significant temporal and spatial overhead. Moreover, the system is unable to function normally during the reorganization period, which has a significant impact.

Huang et al. propose MVCom [21] that optimizes the shard reorganization in Elastico [26] by designing a distributed algorithm that the most valuable part of the committee is selected for each round of several blockchain shards and the dynamic join-leave of the shard committee is supported. During the reorganization phase, Mvcom reduces the number of nodes that need to be reorganized, which greatly reduces the overhead. Thus this mechanism can strike a balance between the transaction throughput and transaction latency of the shard blockchain.

Local Reshuffle. Global shard reorganization can provide high system security, but it is time-intensive and resource-intensive and requires extensive communication. More efficient techniques of shard reorganization have been introduced, in which only a subset of nodes are redistributed [13], which prevents malicious nodes from colluding at lower costs of communication and time compared to Elastico [26].

RapidChain [38] puts forward the limited *cuckoo* rule [31] and divides other committees into two categories through reference committees. When a new node joins the blockchain, the reference committee would randomly add it to an active committee, and then randomly reassign a certain number of active nodes in the active committee to different negative committees which increases the number of active nodes in the passive committee while dealing with new nodes, indirectly increasing the activity of the entire system. RapidChain [38] demonstrates the concept of layering, although it is only a simple two-layer approach. Additionally, it utilizes the join-leave mechanism of nodes, combining with node reorganization to achieve dynamic changes of nodes within the shards. Moreover, there is a user-oriented shard reorganization, which is represented by SSChain [9]. A new node can pick the shard with the greatest income when it joins according to the gain function GPH (Gain Per Hash), and can also leave and rejoin when the income of the current shard is lower compared to alternative shards with high revenue. Unlike RapidChain [38], SSChain [9] delegates the task of shard reorganization to the users. Users select the shards they want to join based on a function that takes into account their income. However, this function-based allocation may lead to imbalance between shards.

3.3   Intra-shard Consensus

The consensus utilized for a transaction is referred to as intra-shard consensus if the participants of the transaction are from the same shard [25]. Most of the current sharding strategies employ PoW [28] or PBFT-based [7], two popular intra-shard consensus algorithms.

PoW-Based Consensus. Although PoW has been superseded by other consensus algorithms, it still draws attention as the result that its mathematically proved probabilistic security and simplicity [28]. As shown in Fig. 2, any consensus group can have a defensive capability of more than 51% thanks to Monoxide's Chu-ko-nu mining [36]. The hash of m blockheads that are going to release a block is calculated each time block is released, and these blockheads share a nonce. The current consensus group (shard) number b arranges the m block headers in sequence, constructs a Merkle tree, and then acquires

$$< MerkleRoot, b, m, nonce >$$

through hash when a block is produced. Later relevant information about the block will be broadcast to a specific consensus group ($b \leq i < b + m$) to ensure that other shards only produce one block. Therefore, even if a single consensus group experiences a delay, the block generated by other consensus groups remains unaffected.

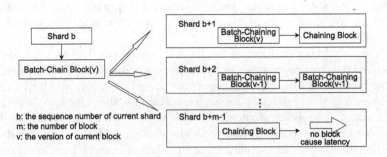

Fig. 2. Chu-ko-nu Mining of Monoxide

PBFT-Based Consensus. The intra-shard consensus based on PBFT is adopted by many sharding schemes such as Elastico [26] and Sharper [3]. Each shard member will append all the received identity solutions to the identity blockchain, creating a view with at least c shard members where c denotes the size of shards. When the shard formation is finished, the transactions are agreed upon using the PBFT protocol. As shown in Fig. 3, the PBFT protocol is divided into five stages, namely, *request*, *pre-prepare*, *prepare*, *commit*, and *reply*. A

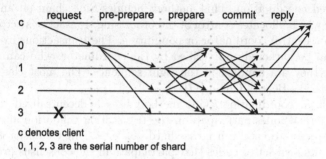

c denotes client
0, 1, 2, 3 are the serial number of shard

Fig. 3. PBFT Workflow

client sends a *request* message to the network to execute a transaction in *request* phase. Then in *pre-prepare* phase, the primary node receives the request message and assigns a sequence number to it. The primary then sends a *pre-prepare* message to all the other nodes in the shard, including the request message and the sequence number. Later, upon receiving the *pre-prepare* message, each node in the shard verifies the message and checks if it is not identical to the previous messages that have identical shard number and message serial number but different content. If the message is valid, the node sends a *prepare* message to all other nodes in the network including the *pre-prepare* message and its digital signature. When a node receives $2f + 1$ *prepare* messages, where f is the maximum number of Byzantine faults the system can tolerate, it sends a *commit* message to all the other nodes in the network, including the *pre-prepare* message, the *request* message, and its digital signature. When a node receives $2f + 1$ *commit* messages, it executes the *request* message and sends a *response* message to the client. In case the primary node becomes faulty or malicious, the network goes through a view change process to select a new primary node.

Even in the presence of Byzantine faults, PBFT ensures that all nodes in the network reach consensus on the same transaction order and state. However, because of its high communication and computational overhead, it is best suited for networks with fewer nodes. Additionally, PBFT ensures the finality of transactions, meaning that within a certain period of time, transactions will either be executed or rejected. However, it comes with centralization risks and overhead issues, and makes the system more complex.

3.4 Cross-Shard Consensus

In a sharded blockchain, establishing a consensus regarding transactions across many shards is known as cross-shard consensus [5], and cross-shard transactions are those that involve multiple shards or require coordination between them to maintain the consistency and integrity of the transaction. Cross-shard consensus can be categorized into two types based on the approach to obtaining consensus across several shards in a sharded blockchain:

- Centralized coordination: This method includes Side chain [4] and Relaycahin [37], which allocates control of the processing transactions across various shards to a central coordinator or committee. The transactions from various shards can be gathered and verified by the coordinator, who can also make sure that they are handled in the right sequence. The most classic case is Ethereum 2.0's Beacon Chain [17].
- Decentralized coordination: This method uses a decentralized mechanism where different nodes participate in the transaction validation and decision-making process to establish cross-shard consensus. In Chainspace [2], each shard has its own set of nodes that participate in the consensus process, and the nodes communicate with each other to achieve cross-shard consensus.

4   Other Scalability Technologies in Blockchain

Typically, blockchain scalability solutions consist of three layers. Layer 1 refers to the basic layer of a blockchain network such as block size and consensus [15,18, 35]. Layer 2 solutions are built on top of the base layer and use off-chain methods to increase scalability, such as state channel [14] and side chain [4]. Further, layer 3 solutions sit on top of Layer 2 solutions and provide additional functionality for blockchain, such as improving privacy with zero-knowledge proof [16], and other decentralized applications [6]. In a nutshell, these layers form a comprehensive approach to scaling blockchain technology while maintaining the decentralized and secure nature as much as possible.

4.1   State Channel

Aiming at resolving the problem of transaction confirmation latency, the state channel was proposed, which does not require submitting total transactions to the blockchain [14], but usually commits their start transaction and end transaction. Thus, many transactions would not be written into the blockchain in the consensus. For example, in a chess game, only the two steps of the game start and game end will participate in the consensus and be written into the blockchain but none of the steps between them need to be written into the blockchain. State channels are mostly used in scenarios requiring frequent transactions between accounts, but in other scenarios, they would not perform well and may be vulnerable to DoS attacks [39].

4.2   Directed Acyclic Graph

DAG [18] is inspired by the directed graph of blockchain transactions, which gives up the traditional blockchain structure and cancels the collection of transactions, instead adopting a graph structure composed of transactions that greatly reduces the granularity of the system and in which transactions no longer need to be verified together with other transactions meantime. Also, as a graph structure, DAG has more scalability ports than the traditional chain structure, which greatly improves transaction processing speed naturally. Users in the DAG network server as both miners and verification nodes, and they perform verification on transactions with each other. The high scalability and low transaction fees of DAG make it very suitable for scenarios with large transaction throughput. However, DAG is usually more vulnerable to centralization [18] and transaction inclusion collision attacks [8] while achieving high scalability.

4.3   Side Chain

The side chain allows building a new blockchain outside the main blockchain, which is called a side chain of the main chain. The side chain is independent and has its network and consensus algorithm as the main chain, improving the performance and enhancing the function of the main blockchain [4]. Naturally, between the main chain and side chain, there require special components to handle information exchange, e.g., the token transfer. When the main chain encounters too many transactions, some transactions can be transferred to the side chain for processing. Also, the main chain can assign the task to the side chain when it requires function extension that cannot be realized by the main chain itself routinely.

5   Summary and Challenges

5.1   Summary of Classic Schemes

With constant updating, iteration, and optimization of throughput, latency, and consensus protocol, sharding technology has significantly increased in robustness and scalability over the past few years. It can be seen from Table 1 that the sharding of permissionless blockchain is still the most prevalent one. Permissioned blockchain offers fewer use cases, but sharding in permissioned blockchain also makes some progress.

Although intra-shard consensus and cross-shard consensus are both for transaction verification, they have distinct characteristics in terms of implementation. The intra-shard consensus protocol is primarily based on PBFT-based protocols, whereas the cross-shard consensus protocol prioritizes system reliability and transaction atomicity. The PoW-based intra-shard consensus protocol is more secure than the PBFT-based intra-shard consensus protocol. However, the PBFT-based intra-shard consensus approach has the advantage of transaction finality and low energy consumption. Hence, some hybrid consensus sharding solutions combine both approaches by incorporating a PoW-based protocol to enhance the security of sharding in subsequent rounds of BFT protocols.

Table 1. Review of classic sharding technology

Attribute	Elastico [26]	OmniLedger [23]	RapidChain [38]	Monoxide [36]	SharPer [3]	AHL [13]
fault rate	$x^a/4$	$x/4$	$x/3$	$x/2$	$x/3^f$	$x/4$
TPS	16 blocks^b	$\approx 10k$ tx/s^c	≈ 7300 tx/s^d	≈ 11700tx/s^e	$\approx 14000tx/s^g$	$\approx 3000tx/s^h$
latency	110s	1s	8.7s	13 − 21s	3s	6 − 7s
sharding	epochRandomness	RandHound+VRF-based	Committee election	Committee election	Geographical distribution	TEE
intra-protocol	PBFT	ByzCoinX	Synchronous consensus	PoW	PBFT	2PC and 2PL
cross-protocol	–	Atomix	Routing	DHT+Relay	PBFT-like	–
reorganization	epochRandomness	RandHound+VRF-based	Bounded Cuck-oo rule	First k bit of address	–	–
identity	PoW	PoW	PoW	Hash	–	–
security	Probabilistic	Probabilistic	Probabilistic	Probabilistic	Deterministic	Probabilistic

^{a} Total number of nodes in the blockchain.
^{b} 100 nodes/shard and 16 shards in total.
^{c} 72 nodes/shards (malicious nodes account for 12.5%), a total of 25 shards.
^{d} 250 nodes/shard, 4000 nodes in total.
^{e} 36 nodes/shard, 2048 shards in total.
^{f} If nodes are Byzantine.
^{g} A network of 64 shards.
^{h} 33 nodes/shard and 30 shards in total.

5.2   Challenges

Intra-shard. Although the PBFT-based intra-shard consensus protocol consumes less energy than the PoW-based consensus protocol, it exhibits lower efficiency and over-confirmation of information in the process of information exchange. However, the PBFT-based consensus can be optimized by appropriately simplifying the reuse of information exchange and information verification to improve the efficiency of the protocol to a certain extent.

Cross-Shard. The proportion of cross-shard transactions is usually extremely elevated, which may have a greater impact on the throughput of the blockchain system. Although some cross-shard protocols can handle cross-shard transactions, the participation of clients is still required to ensure the effective progress of cross-shard transactions, which increases the pressure on clients. Moreover, it is also crucial for consensus to support light clients for achieving good state sharding – minimizing the ledger state stored by the client, and minimizing the number of operating steps required by the client in the cross-shard transaction verification process.

6   Conclusion

Sharding offers a promising solution to the scalability that has long plagued blockchain technology. Its ability to partition a network into smaller subsets (shards) allows for greater efficiency and faster processing of transactions, thus expanding the potential application cases of blockchain. Nevertheless, sharding also presents its own set of unique challenges and potential security risks, which must be addressed through thoughtful protocol design and implementation. Despite these challenges, the adoption of sharding is steadily growing in the blockchain community, and its successful implementation in various networks suggests a bright future for this technology. This paper summarized the performance and implementation aspects of certain classic sharding schemes. The key sharding scalability mechanisms are reviewed and analyzed, including sharding formation, reshuffle, intra-shard consensus protocol, and cross-shard consensus protocol. In addition, the benefits and drawbacks of existing scalability techniques, including state channel, DAG, and side chain are explained. In future work, it is necessary to make further improvements on the scalability, security, and versatility of blockchain technology.

Acknowledgments. This article is supported in part by the National Key R&D Program of China under project 2020YFB1006003, the Guangxi Natural Science Foundation of China under 2019GXNSFGA245004, the National Natural Science Foundation of China under projects 62162017 and 62172119, Zhejiang Provincial Natural Science Foundation of China under Grant No. LZ23F020012, the Guangdong Key R&D Program under project 2020B0101090002, and the Major Key Project of PCL under grant PCL2022A03.

References

1. Abraham, I., Malkhi, D., Nayak, K., Ren, L., Spiegelman, A.: Solidus: an incentive-compatible cryptocurrency based on permissionless byzantine consensus. CoRR abs/1612.02916 (2016). http://arxiv.org/abs/1612.02916
2. Al-Bassam, M., Sonnino, A., Bano, S., Hrycyszyn, D., Danezis, G.: Chainspace: a sharded smart contracts platform. In: 25th Annual Network and Distributed System Security Symposium, NDSS 2018, San Diego, California, USA, 18–21 February 2018. The Internet Society (2018)
3. Amiri, M.J., Agrawal, D., El Abbadi, A.: Sharper: sharding permissioned blockchains over network clusters. In: Proceedings of the 2021 International Conference on Management of Data, SIGMOD 2021, pp. 76–88. Association for Computing Machinery, New York (2021)
4. Back, A., et al.: Enabling blockchain innovations with pegged sidechains. White Paper (2014). https://blockstream.com/sidechains.pdf
5. Bandara, E., Liang, X., Foytik, P., Shetty, S., Ranasinghe, N., De Zoysa, K.: Rahasak-scalable blockchain architecture for enterprise applications. J. Syst. Architect. **116**, 102061 (2021)
6. Buterin, V.: A next-generation smart contract and decentralized application platform. White Paper (2014). https://github.com/ethereum/wiki/wiki/White-Paper
7. Castro, M., Liskov, B.: Practical byzantine fault tolerance. In: Proceedings of the Third Symposium on Operating Systems Design and Implementation, OSDI 1999, pp. 173–186. USENIX Association, USA (1999)
8. Chen, C., Chen, X., Fang, Z.: Tips: transaction inclusion protocol with signaling in DAG-based blockchain. IEEE J. Sel. Areas Commun. **40**(12), 3685–3701 (2022)
9. Chen, H., Wang, Y.: Sschain: a full sharding protocol for public blockchain without data migration overhead. Pervasive Mob. Comput. **59**, 101055 (2019). https://doi.org/10.1016/j.pmcj.2019.101055
10. Corbett, J.C., et al.: Spanner: Google's globally distributed database. ACM Trans. Comput. Syst. **31**(3), 1–22 (2013)

11. Croman, K., et al.: On scaling decentralized blockchains. In: Clark, J., Meiklejohn, S., Ryan, P.Y., Wallach, D., Brenner, M., Rohloff, K. (eds.) FC 2016. LNCS, vol. 9604, pp. 106–125. Springer (2016). https://doi.org/10.1007/978-3-662-53357-4_8

12. Danezis, G., Meiklejohn, S.: Centrally banked cryptocurrencies. In: 23rd Annual Network and Distributed System Security Symposium, NDSS 2016, San Diego, California, USA, 21–24 February 2016. The Internet Society (2016)

13. Dang, H., Dinh, T.T.A., Loghin, D., Chang, E.C., Lin, Q., Ooi, B.C.: Towards scaling blockchain systems via sharding. In: Proceedings of the 2019 International Conference on Management of Data, SIGMOD 2019, pp. 123–140. Association for Computing Machinery, New York (2019)

14. Dziembowski, S., Faust, S., Hostáková, K.: General state channel networks. In: Proceedings of the 2018 ACM SIGSAC Conference on Computer and Communications Security, CCS 2018, pp. 949–966. Association for Computing Machinery, New York (2018)

15. Elrond, A.: Highly scalable public blockchain via adaptive state sharding and secure proof of stake (2019). https://whitepaper.io/document/510/elrond-whitepaper

16. Espel, T., Katz, L., Robin, G.: Proposal for protocol on a quorum blockchain with zero knowledge. IACR Cryptol. ePrint Arch., 1093 (2017). http://eprint.iacr.org/2017/1093

17. Foundation, E.: The beacon chain. https://benjaminion.xyz/eth2-annotated-spec/phase0/beacon-chain/

18. Gao, Z., et al.: State-of-the-art survey of consensus mechanisms on DAG-based distributed ledger. J. Softw. 31(4), 1124–1142 (2019)

19. Glendenning, L., Beschastnikh, I., Krishnamurthy, A., Anderson, T.: Scalable consistency in scatter. In: Proceedings of the Twenty-Third ACM Symposium on Operating Systems Principles, SOSP 2011, pp. 15–28. Association for Computing Machinery, New York (2011)

20. Hong, Z., Guo, S., Li, P., Chen, W.: Pyramid: A layered sharding blockchain system. In: 40th IEEE Conference on Computer Communications, INFOCOM 2021, Vancouver, BC, Canada, 10–13 May 2021, pp. 1–10. IEEE (2021)

21. Huang, H., Huang, Z., Peng, X., Zheng, Z., Guo, S.: MVCom: scheduling most valuable committees for the large-scale sharded blockchain. In: 2021 IEEE 41st International Conference on Distributed Computing Systems (ICDCS), pp. 629–639 (2021)

22. Jia, D., Xin, J., Wang, Z., Wang, G.: Optimized data storage method for sharding-based blockchain. IEEE Access 9, 67890–67900 (2021)

23. Kokoris-Kogias, E., Jovanovic, P., Gasser, L., Gailly, N., Syta, E., Ford, B.: Omniledger: a secure, scale-out, decentralized ledger via sharding. In: 2018 IEEE Symposium on Security and Privacy (SP), pp. 583–598 (2018)

24. Li, C., Xu, Y., Tang, J., Liu, W.: Quantum blockchain: a decentralized, encrypted and distributed database based on quantum mechanics. J. Quantum Comput. 1(2), 49–63 (2019)

25. Liu, Y., Liu, J., Wu, Q., Yu, H., Hei, Y., Zhou, Z.: SSHC: a secure and scalable hybrid consensus protocol for sharding blockchains with a formal security framework. IEEE Trans. Dependable Secure Comput. 19(3), 2070–2088 (2022)

26. Luu, L., Narayanan, V., Zheng, C., Baweja, K., Gilbert, S., Saxena, P.: A secure sharding protocol for open blockchains. In: Proceedings of the 2016 ACM SIGSAC Conference on Computer and Communications Security, CCS 2016, pp. 17–30. Association for Computing Machinery, New York (2016)

27. McKeen, F., et al.: Innovative instructions and software model for isolated execution. In: Proceedings of the 2nd International Workshop on Hardware and Architectural Support for Security and Privacy, HASP 2013, p. 1. Association for Computing Machinery, New York (2013)

28. Nakamoto, S.: Bitcoin: A peer-to-peer electronic cash system. White Paper (2008). https://bitcoin.org/bitcoin.pdf

29. Peng, Z., Wu, H., Xiao, B., Guo, S.: VQL: providing query efficiency and data authenticity in blockchain systems. In: 2019 IEEE 35th International Conference on Data Engineering Workshops (ICDEW), pp. 1–6 (2019)

30. Qi, X., Zhang, Z., Jin, C., Zhou, A.: BFT-store: storage partition for permissioned blockchain via erasure coding. In: 2020 IEEE 36th International Conference on Data Engineering (ICDE), pp. 1926–1929 (2020)

31. Sen, S., Freedman, M.J.: Commensal cuckoo: secure group partitioning for large-scale services. SIGOPS Oper. Syst. Rev. **46**(1), 33–39 (2012)

32. Skidanov, A., Polosukhin, I.: Nightshade: Near protocol sharding design. White Paper (2019). https://nearprotocol.com/downloads/Nightshade.pdf

33. Sonnino, A., Bano, S., Al-Bassam, M., Danezis, G.: Replay attacks and defenses against cross-shard consensus in sharded distributed ledgers. In: 2020 IEEE European Symposium on Security and Privacy (EuroS&P), pp. 294–308 (2020)

34. Syta, E., et al.: Scalable bias-resistant distributed randomness. In: 2017 IEEE Symposium on Security and Privacy (SP), pp. 444–460 (2017)

35. Team, H.: The blockchain using randomness to reinforce proof of stake. https://harmony.one/whitepaper.pdf

36. Wang, J., Wang, H.: Monoxide: scale out blockchain with asynchronous consensus zones. In: Proceedings of the 16th USENIX Conference on Networked Systems Design and Implementation, NSDI 2019, pp. 95–112. USENIX Association, USA (2019)

37. Wood, G.: Polkadot: vision for a heterogeneous multi-chain framework. White paper (2016). https://polkadot.network/whitepaper/

38. Zamani, M., Movahedi, M., Raykova, M.: Rapidchain: scaling blockchain via full sharding. In: Proceedings of the 2018 ACM SIGSAC Conference on Computer and Communications Security, CCS 2018, pp. 931–948. Association for Computing Machinery, New York (2018)

39. Zhang, P., Zhou, M.: Security and trust in blockchains: architecture, key technologies, and open issues. IEEE Trans. Comput. Soc. Syst. **7**(3), 790–801 (2020)

40. Zheng, Z., Xie, S., Dai, H., Chen, X., Wang, H.: An overview of blockchain technology: architecture, consensus, and future trends. In: 2017 IEEE International Congress on Big Data (BigData Congress), pp. 557–564 (2017)

Federated Learning for Blockchain

A Blockchain-Enabled Decentralized Federated Learning System with Transparent and Open Incentive and Audit Contracts

Zeju Cai[1], Jianguo Chen[1(✉)], Zulong Diao[2,3], and Xiang Hua[1]

[1] School of Software Engineering, Sun Yat-Sen University, Zhuhai 519000, China
chenjg33@mail.sysu.edu.cn
[2] Institute of Computing Technology, Chinese Academy of Sciences, Beijing 100864, China
[3] Purple Mountain Laboratories, Nanjing 210000, China

Abstract. Federated learning is an innovative and secure artificial intelligence model that ensures distributed privacy protection. However, FL faces serious challenges such as potential single point failures, lack of transparency in audits, and insufficient incentives for participants. In this paper, to address the above challenges, we propose a Blockchain-enabled Decentralized Federated Learning (BC-DFL) system with transparent and open incentive and audit mechanisms. We design a two-stage model training contract that enables a transparent and decentralized FL process. In the first stage, local models are collected, and after reaching the predetermined conditions, the winning nodes of blockchain mining perform model aggregation in the second stage. In addition, to reduce the block size, we leverage the Inter-Planetary File System to convert local models into hashes and record them on the blockchain. Moreover, to incentivize desirable behavior and deter malicious actions, we further propose a rewarding formula and corresponding incentive contract. Our smart contracts incorporate a mutual evaluation mechanism for nodes, which enables fair rewards for benign nodes while punishing those with nefarious intent. The experimental results reveal that the proposed system achieves a high anti-single point of failure value and high incentive goal while maintaining similar accuracy to the original FL system. The source code is available on GitHub.

Keywords: Blockchain · Decentralized federated learning · Privacy · Security issue · Smart contract · Incentive mechanism

1 Introduction

As one of the most promising avenues for privacy-preserving computing, Federated Learning (FL) has garnered considerable interest in recent years. FL is a distributed Artificial Intelligence (AI) technology that enables distributed training of machine learning and deep learning models [13]. The goal of FL is to

J. Chen et al. (Eds.): BlockSys 2023, CCIS 1896, pp. 259–269, 2024.
https://doi.org/10.1007/978-981-99-8101-4_18

achieve collaborative modelling and improve the efficacy of AI models while maintaining data privacy and complying with legal requirements [9,15]. Initially proposed by Google in 2016 to address the challenge of updating the local AI models for Android users, FL involves each participant training a local model based on local data [5]. The local models are then sent to the central server to aggregate and create a global model. FL's numerous advantages have attracted widespread attention from both the academic and industrial communities [18].

Despite the potential benefits, traditional FL suffers from several serious challenges such as potential single point failures, lack of transparency in audits, and insufficient incentives for participants [1,11,17]. While the technique successfully prevents the leakage of original data, the central aggregation server remains vulnerable to single point of failure. This can easily become a performance bottleneck and security risk for federated learning [11]. In addition, most FL systems lack transparent incentive mechanisms, and data owners incur network and communication overhead when assisting with FL training. Moreover, current FL systems also lack a transparent and open audit mechanism that would enable system backtracking and identification of malicious nodes in the event of system failures [1]. Therefore, it is critical to address the challenges of how to compensate these data owners and reward high-quality data providers [17].

The integration of blockchain technology provides a potential solution to the issues faced by traditional FL [21]. Blockchain is essentially a distributed ledger that runs on a decentralized system and is jointly maintained by each participating node [3]. The data on the blockchain is transparent and immutable, making it resistant to tampering and fraud [8,16]. The decentralized and trustless nature of blockchain also eliminates the need for a trusted third-party entity, allowing for reliable data recording in a distrusted environment [10,12]. The use of smart contracts on the blockchain can further automate the execution of federated learning algorithms and create a transparent and open operational framework [2,4,14]. By integrating FL with blockchain, a feature-rich, ecologically complete, credible, and secure system can be built.

In this paper, we propose a novel Blockchain-enabled Decentralized Federated Learning (BC-DFL) system that aims to address the challenges faced by traditional FL, while providing enhanced transparency and security. Our proposed system offers a promising solution to the challenges faced by traditional federated learning and provides a secure and privacy-preserving mechanism for distributed machine learning.

The contributions of this paper are summarized as follows:

- We incorporate blockchain and smart contract techniques into FL and propose a blockchain-enabled decentralized federated learning system with transparent and open incentive and audit mechanisms. The BC-DFL framework mitigates single point of failure and records the intermediate gradient of each node on the blockchain to enable transparent and open program operation and data auditing.
- We utilize InterPlanetary File System (IPFS) to convert the local models into hashes before saving them to the blockchain. This method greatly reduces the

volume of the blockchain and block size during communication, resulting in faster blockchain performance.
- We further design an innovative incentive mechanism that rewards nodes contributing significantly to training, compensates participating nodes and penalizes malicious nodes. The calculation basis of this mechanism is disclosed through the blockchain's smart contract.

2   Related Work

In the realm of traditional FL, the central server has been identified as a potential single point of failure and a bottleneck to system performance. Therefore, replacing it has long been a focus of research in this field [7,19]. In [7], Hu *et al.* leveraged the gossip protocol to implement the upload and download process of traditional federated learning gradients, effectively supplanting the role of the central server. Similarly, in [19], Qu *et al.* proposed a decentralized FL framework that relies on exchanging models with one-hop neighbors in the network. However, these decentralized solutions require relatively complex system design and lack the ability to conduct open and transparent audits of data during model training.

From the perspective of incentive mechanism, FL nodes need to pay a certain amount of computing, network, and storage resources to participate in the FL training process. Therefore, learning task publishers need to use incentive mechanisms to compensate for those nodes that contribute more to model training [20,22]. At the same time, the incentive mechanism can also punish nodes that attempt to disrupt the learning process. In [22], Yu *et al.* dynamically divides a given budget in a context-aware manner among data owners in a federation by jointly maximizing the collective utility while minimizing the inequality among the data owners. In [20], Tu *et al.* apply game theory to better motivate federated learning trainers to participate in training. However, most of the calculations for incentives in these schemes are placed on the central server, and there is a lack of an open and transparent way to disclose the calculation basis for incentives.

3   Proposed Blockchain-Enabled Decentralized Federated Learning System

In this section, we propose a blockchain-enabled decentralized federated learning (BC-DFL) system, which enhances the transparency and security of the FL system and solves the single point of failure problem in traditional FL systems. Firstly, we will introduce the overall architecture in Subsect. 3.1, and then provide a detailed description of the smart contracts in Subsect. 3.2.

3.1   Overall Architecture

Our proposed BC-DFL system consists of a single type of working node, where all nodes are clients with the same status and permissions. These working nodes handle local model training and blockchain maintenance. The overall architecture of the proposed BC-DFL framework is shown in Fig. 1.

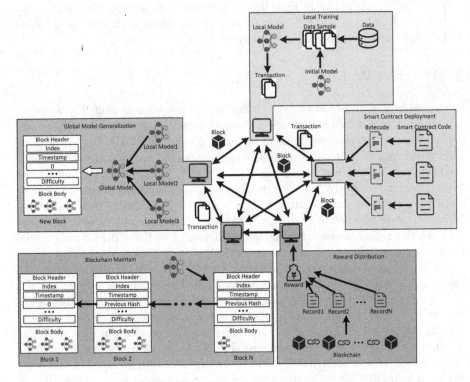

Fig. 1. The overall architecture of the proposed BC-DFL system.

As shown in Fig. 1, our BC-DFL framework uses the decentralized nature of blockchain to eliminate the potential defect of the single point of failure in traditional FL systems.

In our approach, we leverage smart contracts to replace the traditional role of parameter servers in FL. Smart contracts are used for tasks such as model validation, model aggregation, node rewards, and penalties for malicious nodes. These contracts provide transparent and open mechanisms for rewards. Additionally, because blockchain is a distributed ledger, it can be used to store various information during the training process, including hash values of local and global models on the client side, the accuracy of cross-validation models, and other relevant information. By utilizing the immutability of blockchain, we create a reliable source of audit data.

Based on the above ideas, Firstly, We design a node registration contract that facilitates the selection of appropriate nodes for participation in the FL training process. Subsequently, we design a two-stage model training contract that enables a transparent and decentralized FL process. To incentivize desirable behaviour and deter malicious actions, we further propose a rewarding formula and corresponding incentive contract. Our systems incorporate a mutual evaluation mechanism for nodes, which enables fair rewards for benign nodes while punishing those with nefarious intent. The system functions through the following subfunctions:

Smart Contract Deployment: Prior to the start of the model learning task, the Machine Learning (ML)/Deep Learning (DL) task publisher writes the smart contract programs required for model training. He/she compiles the contract programs into bytecode and deploys them into the blockchain system. The smart contracts must include functions such as node registration, model training methods, training end conditions, and node reward basis records. Any blockchain node can check the content of each smart contract. If the node believes that the contract is acceptable, it can join the training through the registration function of the smart contract.

Local Training: The local ML/DL model on each working node in the BC-DFL system is trained according to the ML/DL task requirements. Before training begins, each working node receives the hash of the latest global model from the blockchain system. The hash value will be used to download the corresponding global model from the Inter-Planetary File System (IPFS) system. Local training is conducted by each client, which samples from its own data set. After training, the model is uploaded to IPFS system, and the hash value of the model is stored on the blockchain.

Global Model Aggregation: When the number of local models or the waiting time for local models reaches a certain threshold, the smart contract for model aggregation is triggered. The global model is obtained by a weighted update of the local model, and the obtained global model is also uploaded to the IPFS system. At the same time, the hash value of the model is stored in the blockchain.

Reward Distribution: During the FL training process, the reward basis of nodes will be transparently recorded on the blockchain through smart contracts. After the training is over, the central server executes rewards and punishments according to the recorded reward basis.

3.2   Designed Smart Contracts for BC-DFL

In this section, we design three smart contracts for the proposed BC-DFL system to facilitate node registration, model training, and reward distribution. Then, we deploy the following types of smart contracts in the BC-DFL system.

(1) **Node Registration Contract.**

   This contract serves to assist nodes that wish to participate in the training to join the system. It also conducts a review of the registered nodes, including identity and data review, to ensure that the nodes meet the necessary training requirements.

(2) **Model Training Contract.**

This contract specifies the number of local models required for global model aggregation, as well as the upper limit of the waiting time. Once the number of local models reaches the requirement or the waiting time exceeds the threshold, the model training contract is called to aggregate the global model. The new global model is generated by performing a weighted update of the local models of all nodes:

$$W_t^G = \sum_{i=1}^{N} \alpha_i W_t^i, \tag{1}$$

where W_t^G represents the global model in the t-th round of training, W_t^i represents the local model of node i in the t-th round of training, and α_i represents the aggregation weight of node i. After the new global model is generated, each client can obtain the hash value of the latest model by calling the Model Training Contract.

(3) **Reward Allocation Contract.**

This contract measures the contribution of each node by recording their participation in each global update, the quality of the local model they provide, and their honesty in verifying other people's models. The quality of the model is assessed using the local test set of each node in the system, and the final local model quality evaluation is obtained by taking the average of the best and worst 20% of the test results of all nodes. To prevent some nodes from maliciously reducing the accuracy of other nodes, we penalize nodes that provide test results that are significantly different from the average. The reward value R_i for node i is computed as follows:

$$R_i = \sum_{t=1}^{T} [\phi_1(i,t)\beta_1 \triangle(Acc_t^i, Acc_t^G) + \beta_2\phi_1(i,t)] - \sum_{t=1}^{T} \sum_{k=1}^{\phi_2(i,t)} \beta_3 e^{|Test_t^i - Test_t^G|}, \tag{2}$$

where T represents the total number of training rounds, $\phi_1(i,t)$ indicates whether node i participated in the training in the t-th iteration (1 if yes, 0 otherwise), and $\phi_2(i,t)$ represents the number of times that node i provided inaccurate model accuracy in round t. $\beta_i (i \in [1,6])$ are weighting parameters and $\triangle(Acc_t^i, Acc_t^G)$ is defined as follows:

$$\triangle(Acc_t^i, Acc_t^G) = \begin{cases} e^{\beta_4(Acc_t^i - Acc_t^G)}, & Acc_t^i - Acc_t^G \geq \sigma_1 \\ \beta_5(Acc_t^i - Acc_t^G), & 0 \leq Acc_t^i - Acc_t^G < \sigma_1 \\ 0, & -\sigma_1 \leq Acc_t^i - Acc_t^G < 0 \\ -e^{\beta_6(Acc_t^G - Acc_t^i)}, & Acc_t^i - Acc_t^G < -\sigma_1 \end{cases} \tag{3}$$

where σ_1 and σ_2 are threshold parameters. The significance of the formula design is that for very good or very poor local models, the rewards or penalties are given in an exponential form. This reward distribution contract enables the fair and transparent distribution of rewards to participating nodes based on their contributions to the training.

The purpose of $beta_i, (i \in [1,6])$ is to adapt the reward formula to different training tasks. For instance, depending on the degree of heterogeneity of the dataset, even if a node trains and submits its local model honestly, the accuracy of its local model may still be low because the distribution of the node's local dataset may be different from that of other nodes. In such cases, setting β_6 too large and σ_1 too small may harm the interests of honest nodes and discourage their training enthusiasm. Furthermore, if the task issuer believes that rewarding the local model for high training accuracy is unnecessary (as it may lead to a local optimum), then β_4 can be reduced while increasing the value of σ_1.

4 Experiments

In this section, we present experimental results to evaluate the effectiveness of our proposed BC-DFL system using the MNIST dataset.

4.1 Experiment Setup

We use an Intel Core i5-12400F processor to perform our experiments in a Windows 11 operating system environment. The PyTorch version employed was 1.13.1+cpu, while the programming language used was Python 3.7.12. Distributed file storage was facilitated by IPFS version 0.17.0. For our FL framework, we leverage the fedml [6], while the underlying blockchain was based on Ethereum. Most of the existing papers on blockchain-enabled federated learning have not disclosed the code. To promote reproducibility and transparency, we have publicly shared our code on GitHub, available at https://github.com/Vateer/BC-DFL.

4.2 Experimental Results

Accuracy Comparison. Figure 2 shows the average testing accuracy of our proposed system and traditional FL system is consistent within the allowable error range, without the presence of a poison attack. Notably, the proposed framework applies blockchain technology to facilitate decentralized aggregation, while retaining the same gradient and aggregation methods as traditional FL.

Anti Single Point of Failure Experiment. Figure 3 demonstrates the robustness of our proposed BC-DFL system against a single point of failure. To evaluate the system's ability to handle node downtime, we initiated a blockchain with four nodes and gradually decreased the number of nodes, simulating the occurrence of node failure. As shown in the figure, the FL process can continue even when some nodes in the blockchain are down, as long as there are still surviving nodes. This experiment validates the resilience of our proposed system against disruptions caused by node failures.

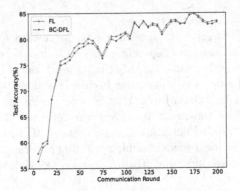

Fig. 2. Accuracy evolution between BC and BC-DFL.

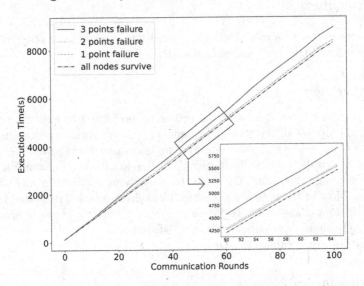

Fig. 3. Anti single point of failure experiment.

Incentive Mechanism Experiment. Our proposed reward mechanism's effectiveness is displayed in Fig. 4. We established FL settings utilizing a data poisoning attack with varying proportions of malicious nodes (10%, 20%, 30%, 40%). Overall, there are 500 clients present in this environment, and 10 clients are randomly selected per communication round to participate in the training process. In this experiment, we set $\beta_i = [1, 1, 1, 0.1, 1, 0.1](i \in [1, 6])$. The final average reward value for both benign nodes and malicious nodes is computed. Due to the limited number of clients partaking in the training, the final average reward value will diminish the rewards or penalties obtained by these clients. Importantly, it should be mentioned that we may be unable to identify malicious clients in some scenarios due to the data set being non-independent and identically distributed. Even a benign client may produce a model with a low

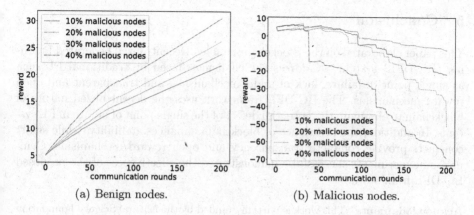

(a) Benign nodes.   (b) Malicious nodes.

Fig. 4. Reward comparison under different malicious node percentages.

accuracy rate, hence passing as a potential malicious client. Nonetheless, our proposed algorithm can generally correctly identify and punish malicious nodes while also rewarding benign nodes.

At the same time, we sought to determine an appropriate β_6 value to effectively deter poison attacks by malicious nodes in the network. Specifically, we evaluated various β_6 values in the context of a 10% malicious node scenario, and the associated findings are presented in the accompanying figure. Notably, as we increased beta, we observed that the reward value of malicious Nodes also increased. We believe that to punish malicious nodes, the value of β_6 should be higher than 0.15 (Fig. 5).

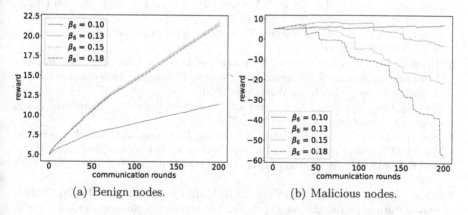

(a) Benign nodes.   (b) Malicious nodes.

Fig. 5. Reward comparison under different value of β_6 in Eq. (3).

5   Conclusion

This paper elaborated on the Blockchain-enabled Decentralized Federated Learning (BC-DFL) system to address the challenges faced by traditional FL such as single point of failure, lack of audit mechanisms, and transparent and open reward mechanisms. The BC-DFL framework uses the decentralized nature of blockchain to eliminate the potential defect of the single point of failure in FL systems. In addition, the invariance of blockchain enhances audibility, while smart contracts provide complete transparency and open reward mechanisms. Comparison experiments successfully demonstrated the effectiveness of the proposed BC-DFL framework.

Acknowledgments. This work is partially funded by the Natural Science Foundation of Guang Dong Province under Grant 2023A1515011179.

References

1. Awan, S., Li, F., Luo, B., Liu, M.: Poster: a reliable and accountable privacy-preserving federated learning framework using the blockchain. In: Proceedings of the 2019 ACM SIGSAC Conference on Computer and Communications Security, pp. 2561–2563 (2019)
2. Chen, Y., et al.: DIM-DS: dynamic incentive model for data sharing in federated learning based on smart contracts and evolutionary game theory. IEEE Internet Things J. **9**(23), 24572–24584 (2022). https://doi.org/10.1109/JIOT.2022.3191671
3. Dai, H.N., Zheng, Z., Zhang, Y.: Blockchain for internet of things: a survey. IEEE Internet Things J. **6**(5), 8076–8094 (2019)
4. Gao, L., Li, L., Chen, Y., Xu, C., Xu, M.: FGFL: a blockchain-based fair incentive governor for federated learning. J. Parallel Distrib. Comput. **163**, 283–299 (2022). https://doi.org/10.1016/j.jpdc.2022.01.019
5. Hard, A., et al.: Federated learning for mobile keyboard prediction. arXiv preprint arXiv:1811.03604 (2018)
6. He, C., et al.: FedML: a research library and benchmark for federated machine learning. In: Advances in Neural Information Processing Systems, Best Paper Award at Federate Learning Workshop (2020)
7. Hu, C., Jiang, J., Wang, Z.: Decentralized federated learning: a segmented gossip approach. arXiv preprint arXiv:1908.07782 (2019)
8. Jia, B., Zhang, X., Liu, J., Zhang, Y., Huang, K., Liang, Y.: Blockchain-enabled federated learning data protection aggregation scheme with differential privacy and homomorphic encryption in IIoT. IEEE Trans. Industr. Inf. **18**(6), 4049–4058 (2021)
9. Konečnỳ, J., McMahan, H.B., Yu, F.X., Richtárik, P., Suresh, A.T., Bacon, D.: Federated learning: strategies for improving communication efficiency. arXiv preprint arXiv:1610.05492 (2016)
10. Kouhizadeh, M., Sarkis, J.: Blockchain practices, potentials, and perspectives in greening supply chains. Sustainability **10**(10), 3652 (2018)
11. Li, J., et al.: Blockchain assisted decentralized federated learning (BLADE-FL): performance analysis and resource allocation. IEEE Trans. Parallel Distrib. Syst. **33**(10), 2401–2415 (2021)

12. Li, X., Jiang, P., Chen, T., Luo, X., Wen, Q.: A survey on the security of blockchain systems. Futur. Gener. Comput. Syst. **107**, 841–853 (2020)
13. Liu, Y., Peng, J., Kang, J., Iliyasu, A.M., Niyato, D., Abd El-Latif, A.A.: A secure federated learning framework for 5G networks. IEEE Wirel. Commun. **27**(4), 24–31 (2020)
14. Ma, C., et al.: When federated learning meets blockchain: a new distributed learning paradigm. IEEE Comput. Intell. Mag. **17**(3), 26–33 (2022). https://doi.org/10.1109/MCI.2022.3180932
15. McMahan, B., Moore, E., Ramage, D., Hampson, S., y Arcas, B.A.: Communication-efficient learning of deep networks from decentralized data. In: Artificial Intelligence and Statistics, pp. 1273–1282. PMLR (2017)
16. Monrat, A.A., Schelén, O., Andersson, K.: A survey of blockchain from the perspectives of applications, challenges, and opportunities. IEEE Access **7**, 117134–117151 (2019)
17. Qu, Y., et al.: Decentralized privacy using blockchain-enabled federated learning in fog computing. IEEE Internet Things J. **7**(6), 5171–5183 (2020)
18. Qu, Y., Uddin, M.P., Gan, C., Xiang, Y., Gao, L., Yearwood, J.: Blockchain-enabled federated learning: a survey. ACM Comput. Surv. **55**(4), 1–35 (2022)
19. Qu, Y., et al.: Decentralized federated learning for UAV networks: architecture, challenges, and opportunities. IEEE Netw. **35**(6), 156–162 (2021)
20. Tu, X., Zhu, K., Luong, N.C., Niyato, D., Zhang, Y., Li, J.: Incentive mechanisms for federated learning: from economic and game theoretic perspective. IEEE Trans. Cogn. Commun. Netw. **8**, 1566–1593 (2022)
21. Xu, C., Qu, Y., Eklund, P.W., Xiang, Y., Gao, L.: BAFL: an efficient blockchain-based asynchronous federated learning framework. In: 2021 IEEE Symposium on Computers and Communications (ISCC), pp. 1–6. IEEE (2021)
22. Yu, H., et al.: A fairness-aware incentive scheme for federated learning. In: Proceedings of the AAAI/ACM Conference on AI, Ethics, and Society, pp. 393–399 (2020)

Blockchain-Based Federated Learning for IoT Sharing: Incentive Scheme with Reputation Mechanism

Ting Cai[1], Xiaoli Li[2], Wuhui Chen[3], Zimei Wei[1], and Zhiwei Ye[1(✉)]

[1] School of Computer Science and Engineering, Hubei University of Technology,
Wuhan 430068, China
{caiting,hgcsyzw}@hbut.edu.cn
[2] School of Computer Science and Engineering, Hubei University of Arts
and Science, Xiangyang 441053, China
[3] School of Computer Science and Engineering, Sun Yat-sen University,
Guangzhou 510006, China

Abstract. Huge amounts of data produced by millions of IoT devices are expected to be shared and leveraged as the cornerstone of real-world IoT applications, such as industrial IoT, smart grid, and intelligent transportation system. However, there still exist bottlenecks when implementing IoT sharing, such as the privacy leakage of user data, IoT data quality, and incentives for sharing these data. In this paper, we propose an online incentive framework for model sharing based on blockchain and federated learning to improve the privacy protection of IoT data. To ensure the quality of submitted data, a reputation mechanism is further designed to punish the users who do not complete the model-sharing task. Based on these settings, the model sharing problem based on federated learning is formulated as an online incentive mechanism, then we use deep reinforcement learning to obtain optimal sets of sharing users with the goal of maximizing long-term social welfare. Numerical results indicate the effectiveness of the proposed framework and incentive mechanism in IoT sharing.

Keywords: IoT sharing · Blockchain · Federated learning · Incentive mechanism · Deep reinforcement learning

1 Introduction

Thanks to various kinds of sensors and embedded smart devices, the Internet of Things (IoT) can generate and collect data in real time, which has a profound impact on our daily life. A 2019 survey of International Data Corporation found that there was an incredible total amount of about 18.3 trillion gigabytes of data generated globally through IoT devices [1]. As the number of connected devices increases, by 2025, there will be 55.7 billion connected devices worldwide, 75% of which will be connected to the IoT [2]. Undoubtedly, this trend will boost the rapid growth of the total amount of data in the IoT.

© The Author(s), under exclusive license to Springer Nature Singapore Pte Ltd. 2024
J. Chen et al. (Eds.): BlockSys 2023, CCIS 1896, pp. 270–284, 2024.
https://doi.org/10.1007/978-981-99-8101-4_19

Massive IoT data is the backbone for the progressive realization of various applications, like smart city and smart grid [3]. However, IoT users are mostly unwilling to share or forward data. Here list two main reasons.

- No incentives. Sharing data requires consuming energy, computing resources and bandwidth, which seems to be not cost-effective to users.
- Privacy risk. It exists the potential risk of privacy leakages, like information as the position of an individual, and enterprise business data.

There are some proposals for solving the above challenges. A basic idea is to design proper incentive mechanisms. Most studies focus on incentives through auction algorithms and game theory [3,12,15]. Although they apply to sharing, there still exist some issues as follows: first, traditional central servers have been widely adopted in the majority of architectures of IoT sharing, which will suffer a single point of failure and low scalability; second, the leakage of privacy has not been fully considered for users, for example, the malicious may obtain sensitive data by invading a central server. Therefore, data security and privacy protection should be taken into account in incentive mechanisms.

We try to introduce blockchain to build a decentralized IoT-sharing architecture with security and trustworthiness. Given the high leakage risk of sharing data, we employ federated learning (FL) to allow users only to share their local training model, but not the raw data. We integrate an incentive mechanism into the decentralized FL model-sharing framework. Compare to other solutions, we implement online incentive IoT sharing with enhanced privacy and data quality.

1.1 Related Works

Many scholars propose incentive mechanisms based on auction algorithms or Stackelberg game to maximize social welfare or minimize social cost. Xu et al. [3] use the Stackelberg game to design an incentive mechanism, which guarantees efficient user recruitment and maximize the utilities of all participants. Gao et al. [4] design an auction-based incentive mechanism for VM resource allocation in order to maximize the total social welfare. However, attacking their centralized servers could break the sharing process or even cause privacy issues.

Blockchain is brought to yield decentralization, security, and trustworthiness for sharing [5]. Yuan et al. [6] build decentralized trusted blockchain-based data sharing with congestion control in the IoV. Pu et al. [7] leverage edge servers to build up the blockchain and implement a sharing scheme with recovery and revocability in the IoT. However these studies select joined users without considering the data quality, it is probably to receive a large amount of low-quality data. Furthermore, lacking the assessment criterion for data quality will decrease the enthusiasm of users who submit data with high quality.

Besides, federated learning is introduced into data sharing to share only trained models instead of the user's original data [8]. And Jing et al. [9] propose a blockchain-based satellite MEC framework using federated learning to improve recognition accuracy and data privacy. But none of the studies consider how to motivate IoT users to participate in model sharing.

1.2 Contributions

To solve the above limitations, we propose an online model-sharing incentive system that combines blockchain and federated learning. It could be implemented in IoT sharing to prevent the privacy leakage of user data, ensure data quality, and arise incentives. Our major contributions are presented as below:

- We design a general framework for IoT model sharing based on blockchain and federated learning techniques.
- We further incorporate a reputation scheme to guarantee the high quality of local training models.
- We formulate the model-sharing process as an online incentive mechanism, and use the Proximal Policy Optimization algorithm to find the optimal solution.

2 Blockchain and Federated Learning Framework for IoT Model Sharing Incentives

2.1 Framework Roles

The involved main roles in our proposed framework include Consortium Blockchain, Model Sharing Platform, IoT Users and Edge Nodes, as shown in Fig. 1.

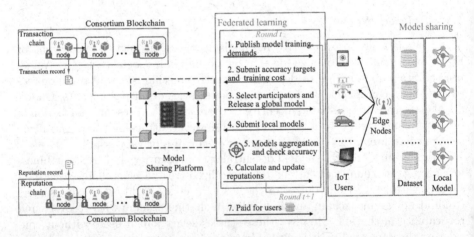

Fig. 1. The online incentive framework based on blockchain and federated learning for IoT model sharing.

Consortium Blockchain. Thanks to the features of decentralization, immutable and traceable, we adopt the consortium blockchain to guarantee user trust and data security. Specifically, we build up two blockchains, one is for recording transaction information between users and the platform, and the other is used as a reputation recorded chain.

Model Sharing Platform. The platform is to publish the FL content and requirements of model-sharing tasks, including data types, training devices, machine learning models, etc., and is responsible for aggregating received models from each IoT user to generate the global model.

IoT Users. The IoT users who participated in the model sharing will train the model with local data, then submit a local well-trained model to the model-sharing platform for aggregation.

Edge Nodes. The edge nodes are responsible for maintaining the communication between model-sharing platform and IoT users, verifying the legitimacy of user submitted transactions, packaging transactions to generate new blocks, and making a consensus on the block.

2.2   Online Incentive Workflows for Model Sharing

Our framework conducts multiple rounds of global iterations, i.e., the processes of model sharing. Each round t is described as follows.

1) Step 1: Publish the model training demands: The model-sharing platform publishes demands on model training, including specific data types, training devices, learning methods, etc.

2) Step 2: Submit model accuracy and training cost: The IoT Users submit the target of model accuracy and training costs to the platform.

3) Step 3: Select participants and release a global model: The platform first directly rejects the engagement of IoT users whose reputation are below a certain value. Then, it chooses participants according to the DRL algorithm, and delivers the global model and hyperparameters to them.

4) Step 4: Submit the local model: The selected participants train model locally using their smart devices and data, then submit them to the platform.

5) Step 5: Aggregate models and check model accuracy: The platform uses the FedAvg algorithm [10] to aggregate user's submitted models, and checks whether they have reached the claimed accuracy target. If yes, the user can be paid and the reputation value increases. Otherwise, there is no pay and the reputation value decreases.

6) Step 6: Calculate and update reputation: Calculate the reputation for each IoT user and record them in the reputation chain. If it reaches convergence or the maximum number of iterations, we move to Step 7. Otherwise, we start a new round of model sharing from Step 1.

7) Step 7: Pay users with rewards: The platform pays users reward accordingly, only to the participants who reach the claimed accuracy.

In each round, the platform gets the reputation value of IoT users from the reputation chain, while the users whose reputation value is below a standard level can be directly eliminated. After receiving the trained models, the platform checks whether a submitted model achieves its claimed accuracy. The unachieved users are deemed not to have completed the current model-sharing task, thus giving no pay, and lowering some reputation values as a penalty.

3   Problem Formulation

In this section, we formulate how to calculate the costs of local training, utilities of IoT users, reputation value, utilities of the model-sharing platform, and the utility function of incentives. The main notations are summarized in Table 1.

Table 1. List of Notation Definitions

Notation	Definition
u_i^t	Utility of i-th user in t-th round
p_i^t	i^{th} user's rewards obtained from the platform in t-th round
E_i^t	Training costs submitted by i-th user in t-th round
u_p^t	Utility of the platform in t-th model-sharing round
$R(\cdot)$	The value function of model-sharing platform
u_{sw}^{total}	Social welfare for $total$ times sharing, i.e., a long-term social welfare
u_{sc}^{total}	Social costs for $total$ times sharing, i.e., a long-term social cost
W^t	Set of selected users participating in model sharing through an online incentive algorithm in t-th model-sharing round
ϵ_i^t	The accuracy of ith user's local model in t-th round
$E_{t,i}^{cmp}$	The power consumed by i-th user on each local iteration in t-th round
$T_{t,i}^{cmp}$	Time costs by i-th user on each local iteration in t-th round
$E_{t,i}^{com}$	The power consumed by i-th user for uploading models to the platform in t-th model-sharing round
$T_{t,i}^{com}$	i^{th} user's transmission time for uploading models to the platform in t-th model-sharing round
$E_{t,i}$	Energy consumption of each local updates for i-th user in t-th round
$T_{t,i}$	Time consumption of each local updates for i-th user in t-th round
M_i^t	The quality of ith user's local model in t-th round
C_i^t	Reputation value for i-th user in t-th round

3.1   Cost and Utility of Sharing Users

For each round, N users participate, where each user $i \in N$ takes local data samples d_i for local training. Such sample data can be either texts or pictures. To facilitate training, IoT users need to use their own smart devices to preprocess their collected data to labeled data. Notably, we assume the data collected by the same user has the same size.

For user i, the required CPU cycles of the computing unit of the data sample is denoted as c_i during round t. The required CPU cycles to perform a local machine training process is $c_i d_i$. We denote f_i as the frequency of CPU cycles, and the power consumed by user i during each local training iteration can be defined as follows:

$$E_{t,i}^{cmp} = \sum_{1}^{c_i d_i} \zeta_i f_i^2 = \zeta_i c_i d_i f_i^2, \tag{1}$$

where ζ_i is the effective capacitances for user i's smart devices.

In addition, the time cost of user i for each local iteration can be calculated by the following:

$$T_{t,i}^{cmp} = \frac{c_i d_i}{f_i}. \tag{2}$$

For each round, multiple IoT users use local data to train models and upload well-trained models to the platform for aggregation. The total number of iterations is affected by users' data quality, which even ultimately affects the accuracy of the final model [11]. Thus, we denote the model accuracy of user i's local training in round t by ϵ_i^t. Since the accuracy of the final global model is a constant value, the number of liberations for updating locally once in round t can be defined as $iter_i^t = \log(1/\epsilon_i^t)$ [12,13]. We neglect the download transfer time between users and the platform, so the transmission time only considers the training time and the upload time. We assume the position of IoT users remains unchanged, from joining in until the end of sharing. Therefore, the transmission rate for user i in round t is as follows:

$$r_i^t = B_i^t \ln\left(1 + \frac{h_i^t \rho_i^t}{N_0^{t,i}}\right), \tag{3}$$

where B_i^t is channel bandwidth, $N_0^{t,i}$ is channel noise, ρ_i^t is transmission power, and h_i^t is the channel gain of point-to-point connections in round t. Here, hyperparameters of the training model like neural network, activation functions, etc., are set by the platform. We assume a constant σ to be the size of data uploaded by users to the platform, i.e., a model parameter. In round t, the transmission time for user i's local updated model is written as

$$T_{t,i}^{com} = \frac{\sigma}{r_i^t}. \tag{4}$$

Accordingly, the energy consumption of uploading user i's local model in round t is given by

$$E_{t,i}^{com} = T_{t,i}^{com} \rho_i^t. \tag{5}$$

Based on Eq. (2) and Eq. (4), the total time for user i's local updates during round t can be calculated by

$$T_{t,i} = iter_i^t \times T_{t,i}^{cmp} + T_{t,i}^{com} = \log\left(\frac{1}{\epsilon_i^t}\right)\frac{c_i d_i}{f_i} + \frac{\sigma}{B_i^t \ln\left(1 + \frac{h_i^t \rho_i^t}{N_0^{t,i}}\right)}. \tag{6}$$

Based on Eq. (1) and Eq. (5), the total energy consumption for user i's local updates during round t can be represented as

$$E_{t,i} = iter_i^t \times E_{t,i}^{cmp} + E_{t,i}^{com} = \log\left(\frac{1}{\epsilon_i^t}\right)\zeta_i c_i d_i f_i^2 + \frac{\sigma \rho_i^t}{B_i^t \ln\left(1 + \frac{h_i^t \rho_i^t}{N_0^{t,i}}\right)}. \tag{7}$$

In round t, we denote user paid obtaining from the platform by p_i^t, and define the set of selected users participating in model sharing as W^t. Thus, the utility of user i is

$$u_i^t = \begin{cases} p_i^t - E_{t,i}, & i \in W^t; \\ 0, & i \notin W^t. \end{cases} \qquad (8)$$

Notably, only the selected IoT users reaching claimed accuracy targets can be paid by the platform. If not selected to participate in model sharing, the user's utility is 0.

3.2 Reputation Mechanism

We define C_i^t as user i's reputation value in round t. The term x is the total number of user i's participation in model sharing, and y indicates the number of failed tasks for user i. The terms ω_f and ω_s are two adjustment factors related to reputation value, which guarantee the decreased value C_i^{t-1} of user reputations after a failed task can be bigger than the increased value C_i^{t+1} of user reputations after a successful task, i.e., $C_i^{t-1} > C_i^{t+1}$. Note that those whose reputations decrease to a certain threshold value will be judged as trust-breaking users, who are longer allowed to participate in the model sharing.

After each round, the platform will recalculate the value of user reputations and submit them to the reputation chain. Here, $flag$ is defined as a flag variable, where $flag = 0$ means a task is failed; and $flag = 1$ indicates a task is successful. Then, user i's reputation value can be expressed as follows:

$$\begin{cases} C_i^{t,pre}, & x < 5, flag = 0; \\ \max\left(C_i^{t,pre} * \left(1 - \frac{x-y}{x} * \omega_f\right), 0\right), & x \geq 5, flag = 0; \\ \min\left(C_i^{t,pre} * \left(1 + \frac{x-y}{x} * \omega_s\right), 1\right), & flag = 1, \end{cases} \qquad (9)$$

where $C_i^{t,pre}$ is user i's reputation value before i joins in round t. When the total number of user-conducted tasks is less than 5, the value of user reputation remains unchanged even if the task is failed. Only a failed task conducted by the user whose number of tasks outweighs 5, the value of user's reputation will be decreased. The adjustment factors ω_f and ω_s are used to determine the extent to the value of reputation increases and decreases.

3.3 Utility of Platform

In this section, we define the utilities of the platform as two parts, one part relates to the quality of submitted models, and the other part considers the time satisfaction for users' local training. First, we define the quality of data for user i in model-sharing round t as

$$q_i^t = \frac{\varphi_i^t}{\log\left(\frac{1}{\epsilon_i^t}\right)}, \qquad (10)$$

where φ_i^t is a coefficient related to the number of iterations for local model training. Obviously, a bigger q_i^t will reach a higher model accuracy with fewer iterations.

Apart from hyperparameters, the platform will release a maximum waiting time T_{max}^t for each iteration in round t. Once a user fails in submitting the model within the time T_{max}^t, the platform will mark it as a failed task and give no pay. According to Eq. (10), we give the formula of model quality assessment as follows:

$$M_i^t = \frac{\varphi_i^t}{\log\left(\frac{1}{\epsilon_i^t}\right)} \log\left(\frac{T_{max}^t - T_{t,i}}{T_{max}^t} + 1\right),$$ (11)

where $\log\left(\frac{T_{max}^t - T_{t,i}}{T_{max}^t} + 1\right)$ represents the time satisfactory for users' local training. And the shorter time is, the higher of platform's satisfaction. Then, the utility of the platform can be expressed as

$$u_p^{total} = R\left(\sum_{t=1}^{total}\sum_{i\in W^t} M_i^t\right) - \sum_{t=1}^{total}\sum_{i\in W^t} p_i^t,$$ (12)

where $total$ is the total number of global iterations required by a whole federated learning process, i.e., total rounds of the model sharing. The term $R(\cdot)$ represents the value function of the platform, which is determined by both model quality and time satisfaction. And there is $R(0) = 0, R'(\cdot) > 0, R''(\cdot) < 0$, i.e., the diminishing marginal utility [15].

3.4   Optimization Goal of Incentive Sharing

Since there are multiple rounds of model sharing between users and the platform, we focus on how to achieve greater long-term social welfare. In our framework, each round of global iterations is taken as one model-sharing process. When the current global model has converged or reached the upper limit of iteration numbers, the platform will end that model sharing. Then, we define the social welfare for an entire federated learning process as

$$u_{sw}^{total} = u_p^{total} + \sum_{t=1}^{total}\sum_{i\in W^t} u_i^t = R\left(\sum_{t=1}^{total}\sum_{i\in W^t} M_i^t\right) - \sum_{t=1}^{total}\sum_{i\in W^t} E_{t,i}.$$ (13)

The social cost of model sharing incentives is

$$u_{sc}^{total} = \sum_{t=1}^{total}\sum_{i\in W} E_{t,i}.$$ (14)

To ensure the paid to users can outperform user costs, we define the paid to user i in round t as the following:

$$p_i^t = \max\left(u_{sw}^{total}(W_i) - u_{sw}^{total}(W_{-i}) + b_i^t, E_{t,i}\right),$$ (15)

where $u_{sw,-i}^{total}$ is the social welfare of an entire federated learning process for all users apart from user i. Note that only the selected user participants who perform tasks successfully can get paid; otherwise, the set of paid is 0.

4   DRL-Based Algorithm Design

As already discussed before, we aim at maximizing long-term social welfare for model sharing. User selections in each round of model sharing are only related to the previous rounds but not to the subsequent rounds, which resort to the Markov decision process (MDP). Therefore, we formulate the model sharing for each round as an MDP, then use the Proximal Policy Optimization (PPO) algorithm to find the optimal user selection policy for model sharing. Next, we identify state space, action space, and reward function as follows.

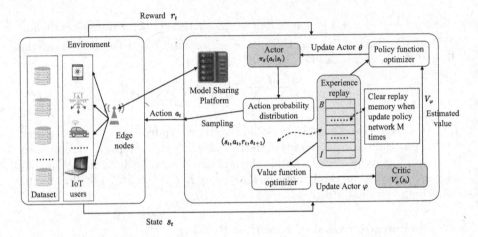

Fig. 2. The architecture of PPO-based online incentive algorithm.

4.1   State Space

In each round, the agent will take the state observed from the environment, including the user's model quality and training cost. Therefore, we define the state space as follows:

$$s_t = \left(M_1^t, E_{t,1}, M_2^t, E_{t,2}, ..., M_{sum}^{t-1}, E_{sum}^{t-1} \right), \tag{16}$$

where M_i^t is the model quality for user i at epoch t, $E_{t,i}$ is the training cost of user i's submitted model at epoch t. The last two terms defined in s_t are used as the memory variables, especially for recording the information of previous rounds in model sharing. Here, M_{sum}^{t-1} represents the total quality of models of selected participants for $t - 1$ episodes, and E_{sum}^{t-1} indicates the total cost of selected participants for $t - 1$ episodes during model sharing.

4.2   Action Space

The proposed incentive sharing framework aims to maximize long-term social welfare. The DRL agent will select which users to participate in model sharing according to the current state s_t, i.e., model quality and training costs. Thus, the action space for epoch t can be given as

$$a_t = \left(z_1^t, z_2^t, ..., z_i^t, ... \right),$$ (17)

where z_i^t determines whether to add user i to the model sharing at epoch t. Here, $z_i^t \leq 0$ indicates user i is rejected to join; while $z_i^t > 0$ means user i is allowed to participate in model sharing.

Algorithm 1: PPO-based Online Incentive Sharing Algorithm

---

1 **Initialize:** parameters of the policy network θ, the value network φ, discount factor γ, loss coefficient c, and the current state s_0;
2 **for** $episode = 0, 1, 2, ..., E$ **do**
3   **for** $epoch\ k \in 0, 1, ..., K$ **do**
4   Input the state s_k to the policy network π_θ and obtain the action a_k;
5   Calculate the reward r_k for agent k according to Eq. (18);
6   Interact with the environment to obtain the next state s_{k+1};
7   Store (s_k, a_k, r_k, s_{k+1}) into the replay memory;
8   Set the parameter of policy network $\hat{\theta}$ to θ;
9   **if** $(k+1)\, \% B = 0$ **then**
10   **for** $e = 0, 1, 2, ..., M$ **do**
11   Sample from the replay memory and calculate L_k^A, L_k^{VF} according to Eq. (20) and Eq. (21);
12   Update θ and φ as in Eq. (19);
13   **end**
14   Empty the replay memory;
15   **end**
16   **end**
17 **end**
18 Set the maximum number of global iterations for federated learning, i.e., $total$;
19 **for** $k = 0, 1, 2, ..., total$ **do**
20   Observe the environment, like users' model quality and training cost, to obtain the current state s_k;
21   Input the state s_k to the policy network π_θ and obtain the action a_k;
22   Choose users paticipating in model sharing from the user set N according to the action a_k;
23   Paticipanted users download the latest global model ω_k from the platform and use local data to update;
24   Each IoT user uploads its locally updated model ω_k^i to the model sharing platform;
25   The platform uses the FedAvg algorithm to aggregate the upload local models and generate the new global model ω_{k+1};
26 **end**

4.3   Reward Function

The reward function is defined to maximize social welfare. We assume that one episode contains *total* epochs, i.e., a whole model-sharing process based on federated learning has *total* rounds, each round of which requires selecting users that maximize long-term social welfare. Thus, we have

$$
r_t = \begin{cases} 0, \ t < total; \\ R\left(\sum_{j=1}^{total}\sum_{i \in W^j} M_i^j\right) - \sum_{j=1}^{total}\sum_{i \in W^j} E_i^j, t = total. \end{cases} \tag{18}
$$

Note that the reward is set to 0 till the last epoch. That is, only when the federated learning task is ended, the environment will feedback on the social welfare to the agent as a reward.

4.4   Workflow of PPO

The workflow of PPO illustrates in Fig. 2. Through interactions between the environment and the PPO agent, the selection of the optimal users are performed adaptively. Specifically, the policy network and value function in our proposed algorithm are updated as follows:

$$
\theta^{e+1} = \underset{\theta}{argmax}\, \mathbf{E}_k\left[L_k^A\left(\theta^e\right) - cL_k^{VF}\left(\theta^e\right)\right], \tag{19}
$$

$$
L_k^A\left(\theta^e\right) = \min\left[r_k^e\left(\theta^e\right)A\left(s_k, a_k\right), g\left(\epsilon, A\left(s_k, a_k\right)\right)\right], \tag{20}
$$

$$
L_k^{VF}\left(\theta^e\right) = \left(V\left(s_k\right) - V_{targ}^k\right)^2, \tag{21}
$$

where V_{targ}^k is discounted rewards from epoch k to the end of an episode. Finally, we formally present the proposed PPO-based online incentive algorithm in Algorithm 1.

5   Numerical Results

We implement transaction chain and reputation chain by using Fisco Bcos and python-SDK. To test our proposed model-sharing framework based on federated learning, we take MNIST [14] as the training dataset and use PyTorch to develop the DRL algorithm, and FedAvg [10] is adopted to simulate multiple rounds of model sharing. For federated learning, we set up 50 participated users, 10 local iterations for each user, and 10 global iterations for model sharing. For the simulation setting of our PPO-based incentive mechanism, we consider discount factor $\gamma = 0.995$, clip function $\epsilon = 0.2$, and the global iterations are set to $epoch = 20$, $episode = 500$ in each complete federate learning process. The main parameters are listed in Table 2.

We compare our incentive algorithm with other incentive baselines: i) **offline optimal auction** [15], in which all collected information during the complete multiple rounds of model sharing must be input to the algorithm at one time; ii)

online greedy auction is modified from our previous work, i.e., offline optimal auction algorithm [15], which only takes in the user information of the current round and focuses on maximizing social welfare for the current round; and iii) **random selection**, the IoT users in which are randomly selected to participate in the model sharing.

Figure 3 shows the convergence performance of our proposed PPO-based online incentive algorithm. We observe that our algorithm can achieve a drastically-increased long-term social welfare during the early stage of training and then quickly reaches convergence.

Table 2. Parameter Setting in the Simulation

Parameter	Setting
The range of users' model accuracy	$[0.2, 0.92]$
CPU cycles for model-sharing users	$c_i = 5$
Size of dataset unit	$d_i = 10$
CPU frequency	$f_i = 1$
Number of effective capacitors	$\zeta = 2, \varphi^t = 0.5$
The time of data transmission	$T_{t,i}^{com} = 10$
Consumed power for data transmission	$E_{t,i}^{com} = 20$
The maximum training time that platform can tolerate	$T_{\max}^t = 150^{[56,62]}$

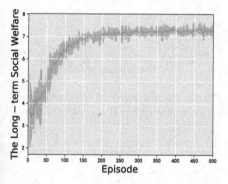 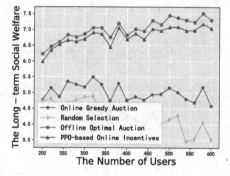

Fig. 3. Evaluation of convergence performance.

Fig. 4. The long-term social welfare under different numbers of users.

Figure 4 shows the long-term social welfare of the proposed PPO-based online incentives under different numbers of users. From Fig. 4, we observe that our algorithm is significantly better than online greedy auction, the performance of which is closely near to offline optimal auction. Random selection has the worst performance. Although the performance of online greedy auction is better than random selection, it is far worse than offline optimal auction. Thus, we can conclude that directly changing offline optimal auction to an online manner can not receive better long-term social welfare. Most importantly, our algorithm shows good performance in dynamic online model-sharing scenarios.

Figure 5 shows the long-term social cost under different numbers of users. We can observe that, the social costs of online greedy auction and random selection are increasing with the increasing of user amount. However, the social costs of offline optimal auction and our PPO-based online incentives have remained low rates in growth. The reason is that online greedy auction only focuses on maximizing social welfare for the current round, which inevitably causes a continuous increase as the number of users increases. By contrast, our algorithm focuses on long-term social welfare so as not to blindly add more engaged participants when the user increases.

Figure 6 tests the number of selected participants under different numbers of users. Similar to Fig. 5, the growth rates of the offline optimal auction and our PPO-based online incentives keep at a relatively low level. From Fig. 6 and Fig. 5, we can conclude that our algorithm aims to maximize long-term social welfare, rather than focusing solely on the current utilities.

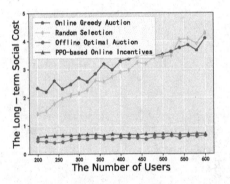 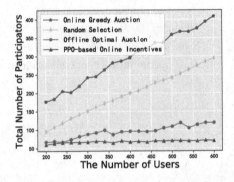

Fig. 5. The long-term social cost under different numbers of users.

Fig. 6. Total number of selected participants under different numbers of users.

6   Conclusion

In this paper, we studied data privacy protection, data quality guarantees, and incentive mechanism design for IoT sharing. We proposed a privacy-preserving framework with federated learning for data training. Blockchain technology is utilized to design a decentralized federated learning architecture with transaction chain and reputation chain for secure model training and guaranteed data quality. Furthermore, to incentive IoT users to participate in data sharing, we formulate multiple rounds of model-sharing processes to an online incentive mechanism with the goal of maximizing long-term social welfare. Numerical results show the effectiveness of our proposed framework and incentive mechanism for IoT sharing.

Acknowledgements. The work described in this paper was supported by the National Natural Science Foundation of China (62302154, 62306108), the Doctoral Scientific Research Foundation of Hubei University of Technology (XJ2022006701), and the Key Research and Development Program of Hubei Province (2023BEB024).

References

1. De Prieëlle, F., De Reuver, M., Rezaei, J.: The role of ecosystem data governance in adoption of data platforms by internet-of-things data providers: case of Dutch horticulture industry. IEEE Trans. Eng. Manage. **69**(4), 940–950 (2020)
2. Chen, W., Qiu, X., Cai, T., Dai, H.N., Zheng, Z., Zhang, Y.: Deep reinforcement learning for internet of things: a comprehensive survey. IEEE Commun. Surv. Tutor. **23**(3), 1659–1692 (2021)
3. Xu, Y., Xiao, M., Wu, J., Zhang, S., Gao, G.: Incentive mechanism for spatial crowdsourcing with unknown social-aware workers: a three-stage Stackelberg game approach. IEEE Trans. Mob. Comput. (2022). https://doi.org/10.1109/TMC.2022.3157687
4. Gao, G., Xiao, M., Wu, J., Huang, H., Wang, S., Chen, G.: Auction-based VM allocation for deadline-sensitive tasks in distributed edge cloud. IEEE Trans. Serv. Comput. **14**(6), 1727–1741 (2021)
5. Liu, Y., Hao, X., Ren, W., Xiong, R., Zhu, T., Choo, K.K.R., Min, G.: A blockchain-based decentralized, fair and authenticated information sharing scheme in zero trust internet-of-things. IEEE Trans. Comput. **27**(2), 501–512 (2023)
6. Yuan, M., et al.: TRUCON: blockchain-based trusted data sharing with congestion control in internet of vehicles. IEEE Trans. Intell. Transp. Syst. **24**(3), 3489–3500 (2023)
7. Pu, Y., Hu, C., Deng, S., Alrawais, A.: R^2PEDS: a recoverable and revocable privacy-preserving edge data sharing scheme. IEEE Internet Things J. **7**(9), 8077–8089 (2020)
8. Lu, Y., Huang, X., Dai, Y., Maharjan, S., Zhang, Y.: Blockchain and federated learning for privacy-preserved data sharing in industrial IoT. IEEE Trans. Industr. Inf. **16**(6), 4177–4186 (2019)
9. Jing, Y., Wang, J., Jiang, C., Zhan, Y.: Satellite MEC with federated learning: architectures, technologies and challenges. IEEE Netw. **36**(5), 106–112 (2022)
10. Brendan McMahan, H., Moore, E., Ramage, D., Hampson, S., Arcas, B.A.Y.: Communication-efficient learning of deep networks from decentralized data. In: Proceedings of Machine Learning Research: Proceedings of the 20th International Conference on Artificial Intelligence and Statistics, Fort Lauderdale, FL, USA, pp. 1273–1282. PMLR, AISTATS (2017)
11. Tran, N.H., Bao, W., Zomaya, A., Nguyen, M.N., Hong, C.S.: Federated learning over wireless networks: optimization model design and analysis. In: IEEE INFO-COM 2019-IEEE Conference on Computer Communications, pp. 1387–1395. IEEE (2019)
12. Tu, X., Zhu, K., Luong, N.C., Niyato, D., Zhang, Y., Li, J.: Incentive mechanisms for federated learning: from economic and game theoretic perspective. IEEE Trans. Cogn. Commun. Netw. **8**(3), 1566–1593 (2022)
13. Luo, B., Li, X., Wang, S., Huang, J., Tassiulas, L.: Cost-effective federated learning design. In: IEEE INFOCOM 2021-IEEE Conference on Computer Communications, pp. 1–10. IEEE (2021)

14. Wang, M., Deng, W.: Oracle-MNIST: a realistic image dataset for benchmarking machine learning algorithms. arXiv preprint arXiv:2205.09442 (2022)
15. Chen, W., Chen, Y., Chen, X., Zheng, Z.: Toward secure data sharing for the IoV: a quality-driven incentive mechanism with on-chain and off-chain guarantees. IEEE Internet Things J. **7**(3), 1625–1640 (2019)

An Optimized Scheme of Federated Learning Based on Differential Privacy

Yang Li[1,2]([⊠]), Jin Xu[1,2], Jianming Zhu[1,2], and Xiuli Wang[1,2]

[1] School of Information, Central University of Finance and Economics, Beijing 100081, China
liyang@cufe.edu.cn
[2] Engineering Research Center of State Financial Security, Ministry of Education, Central University of Finance and Economics, Beijing 102206, China

Abstract. With the arrival of the Web3 era, data has seen an explosive growth. The use of differential privacy mechanisms in federated learning has been proposed to protect user privacy and avoid security threats from data sharing. The core idea of this approach is that multiple clients train their local data, add noise to their client parameters, and then transmit them to a central server for parameter aggregation. However, there are still defects that need to be addressed. First, it is difficult to resist attacks from malicious clients, which means that user privacy is not fully protected. Second, it is challenging to add an appropriate amount of noise to achieve high model accuracy. Therefore, this paper proposes a bidirectional adaptive noise addition federated learning scheme, which adds adaptive noise satisfying the differential privacy mechanism to both the central server and clients to improve model accuracy. Considering the heterogeneity of client hardware, this paper samples gradients and samples separately to reduce communication costs and uses RMSprop to accelerate model training on both clients and central servers. Experimental results show that the proposed scheme enhances user privacy protection while maintaining high efficiency.

Keywords: gradient and clients sampling · differential privacy · federated learning

1 Introduction

Usually, the performance of the machine learning model depends on the amount of data and the quality of the data. In the traditional training method, all the data needs to be collected together before the model training. However, some data may involve user privacy. But, some users believe that collecting personal data may threaten personal privacy and refuses to provide relevant data, so it will result in forming data islands among users data sharing [1]. Therefore, how to use data more efficiently while protecting privacy has received widespread attention from industry and academia.

To solve above problems, federated learning is an effective approach to choose to perverse users' privacy. The main idea is central server send initial model to all clients for training. In each round of communication, clients' model parameters are upload to central server, which select a suitable algorithm to calculate client's parameters, after several rounds of exchanging parameters, the final model is obtained.

J. Chen et al. (Eds.): BlockSys 2023, CCIS 1896, pp. 285–295, 2024.
https://doi.org/10.1007/978-981-99-8101-4_20

2 Related Work

Since the training of machine learning models requires a large amount of user data, in 2016, Google proposed a distributed machine learning system, federated learning [2], which can train models without collecting all data. It is widely used in many fields, such as healthcare, finance and industry [3–5]. The users of federated learning use local data to train the model, and then upload the clients' gradient to the server to update the global model. So federated learning can solve the problem of data silos and ensure data security. However, federated learning still has some problems, such as gradient security, communication overhead, and data distribution [6].

Liu [7] added the historical experience to the traditional SGD method to reduce communication overhead, the updated method is momentum gradient descent (MGD). Experiments show that, the training speed of the model can be significantly accelerated to achieve better accuracy. The sparse federated learning scheme adopted in paper [8] could reduce communication overhead, computational overhead and achieve better model accuracy, but the data protection ability of the scheme is reduced. In [12], the author modified the optimizer and clipped the data appropriately to achieve a faster convergence speed in order to maintain high accuracy of the model. However, the author doesn't study the impact of the number of clients.

As mentioned above, the application of differential privacy in federated learning can better protect the clients and server from adversary attacks. Based on the above problems, this paper improves the traditional differential privacy federated learning to a novel federated learning approach with bidirectional adaptive differential privacy. By setting a global Gaussian noise, clients and server exchange data with bidirectional adaptive noise. In order to improve the convergence speed, this paper also uses gradient sampling and adaptive learning rate.

This paper proposes a bidirectional adaptive differential privacy federated learning scheme based on traditional differential privacy federated learning. By setting the total Gaussian noise, the client uses the RMSprop optimizer and adaptively adds Gaussian noise according to the gradient variation of the optimizer. The server uses the same optimizer to stabilize the aggregation results of the model. The noise value obtained by subtracting the total Gaussian noise from the maximum noise added by the client is added to the server to achieve global differential privacy protection. In addition, training is performed through client sampling, gradient sampling, and sample sampling to improve the convergence speed of the model. Finally, the effectiveness of the proposed scheme is verified by comparing with the existing one-way noise adding algorithm and one-way adaptive noise adding algorithm.

3 Preliminaries

Federal learning based on differential privacy mechanism is a scheme to achieve good privacy protection effect in the process of parameter transmission by adding noise satisfying differential privacy to the parameters of client or central server. The differential privacy mechanism guarantees the privacy security of the database. Assuming that there is only one data difference between two databases, using differential privacy to perturb the original data can make it difficult to distinguish the two databases [13]. The differential privacy formula [14] is as follows:

Definition 1: Given a query function $q = D \rightarrow R^d$, where D is the input dataset and R^d is d-dimensional real vector returned for the query function. For any two adjacent data sets D_1, D_2 that differ by only one data record, the global sensitivity of the query function q is as follows:

$$\Delta q = \max_{D_1, D_2} q(D_1) - q(D_2) \tag{1}$$

Definition 2: A randomized algorithm M with domain $\mathbb{N}^{|x|}$ is (ε, δ)- differential privacy if for all $S \subseteq Range(M)$ and for all $x, y \in \mathbb{N}^{|x|}$ such that $x - y_1 \leq 1$:

$$\Pr[M(x) \in S] \leq \exp(\varepsilon) \Pr[M(y) \in S] + \delta \tag{2}$$

where the probability space is over the coin flips of the algorithm M. If $\delta = 0$, then the random algorithm is ε-differential privacy, and $\varepsilon \in (0, 1)$.

Lemma 1: Given a data set $D = \{D_1, \cdots, D_n\}$, each data set in D is disjoint, and $A = \{A_1, \cdots, A_n\}$ is a set of algorithms that satisfy-differential privacy, then the algorithm $A_i(D_i) = \{A_1(D_1), \cdots, A_n(D_n)\}$ will satisfy $\max(\varepsilon \in_{i \in [1,...n]})$-differential privacy.

By adding differential privacy noise to the gradient of federated learning, user information is protected from adversary attacks. Laplace noise and Gaussian noise are commonly used in noise adding methods. The formula is as follows:

$$M(d) \triangleq f(d) + N\left(0, C^2 \sigma^2\right) \tag{3}$$

where $N\left(0, C^2 \sigma^2\right)$ is the Gaussian distribution or the Laplacian distribution, the mean is 0, the variance is $C^2 \sigma^2$, C is gradient norm bound, and σ is the noise level.

4   Method Design

4.1 Our Approach FedBADP

In this section, we propose a novel federated learning with bidirectional adaptive differential privacy, which uses local noise and central noise to enhance privacy preserving. At the same time, in order to reduce the communication overhead and improve the accuracy of the model, we use partial data to train model and upload parameter to the server. Besides, we use the RMSprop optimizer to optimize the model in client, and also uses the RMSprop optimizer in the central server to stabilize the model parameters under the influence of DP (Fig. 1).

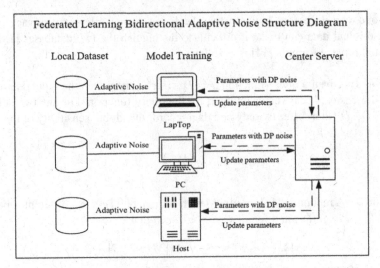

Fig. 1. Federated Learning Bidirectional Adaptive Noise Structure Diagram.

Most of the existing studies believe that the local client is honest, and only add noise to the client to resist the dishonest central server. However, Geyer [15] considered that the malicious clients had a risk of disclosing user data, and proposed a scheme of adding noise in central server to prevent malicious clients from recovering useful information. Therefore, in order to prevent dishonest central server and clients from destroying user data privacy, noise should be added to both clients and central server to enhance user privacy preserving.

The federated learning scheme proposed by Mcmahan [4] requires all clients to participate in model training. It need higher hardware and communication capabilities for clients. Besides, the model training time will become longer. In this scheme, by sampling the client, a certain proportion of users are randomly selected to participate in the model training. According to the experiment in reference [15], clients could choose the appropriate sampling ratio to achieve a better training accuracy. Therefore, this paper adds noise to the randomly selected clients by setting different sampling rates.

The local devices have to meet strict requirements if all the data of clients participate in the model training, and it is difficult to complete the training in a short time with these large amount of data. In this paper, the training samples are randomly sampled with sampling rate $q = L/N$, where N is the total number of local samples and L is the number of samples participating in the training. Through data sampling, the calculation overhead of the client can be reduced and it can reach a better model accuracy.

In traditional federated learning, the central server sends the model to the clients. The client uses its own data to train model, and the updated parameters are sent to the central server for parameter aggregation without any desensitization. As stated in [13], attackers can still recover useful information from gradients. In order to prevent the inference attack of the central server, the clients add artificial noise to the updated gradient and perturb the data to enhance the user's data security. The method used in this paper is to clip the gradient of the sample, the clients to add Gaussian mechanism (ε, δ)-differential privacy.

The traditional SGD has a slow convergence speed and is easy to fall into the local optimal solution. Therefore, it is necessary to rely on experience to select an appropriate learning rate to achieve the global optimal solution. In this paper, we proposed that using RMSprop optimizer in both the clients and server, and by exponential weighted average method to eliminate the fluctuation problem in the process of gradient descent, which can solve the above problems as much as possible. The main idea is that maintain the magnitude of the derivative in a dimension and the result of the exponential weighted average at the same order of magnitude. So this approach can reduce the fluctuation problem of loss function.

Since the original noise scheme cannot change with the gradients, there will be more redundant noise or insufficient noise, which may lead to privacy leakage. Therefore, we propose an adaptive noise scheme, which sets a max privacy budget. The local clients and the central server adopt adaptive noise-adding method to perturb the parameters of each dimension. If the parameter variation is larger, the more noise is added, and the opposite is the same. The adaptive noise formulas are as follows:

$$\sigma_{l_i} = \frac{g_t}{\sqrt{E[g^2]_t + \tau}}\sigma \tag{4}$$

$$\sigma_A^2 = \sigma_L^2 + \sigma_C^2 \tag{5}$$

where σ is the max noise according to the initial privacy budget ε, σ_{l_i} is the adaptive noise added by the i dimensional parameters of the local client, and the privacy budget ε_i can be calculated from the noise σ_{l_i}. In order to prevent the noise from reducing model accuracy, it is difficult to protect the user data if the added noise is deficiency. So we set a ε_i range, the adaptive noise will meet the noise requirements in different scenes as much as possible. σ_L^2 is the noise added by the local client, σ_C^2 is the noise added by the central server, so σ_A^2 is the total noise.

Adaptive noise is added according to the change of the current gradient. When the gradient changes greatly, the gradients' variation will be relatively large, and the adaptive noise still can reach the protection ability. However, if the variation parameters is small, the adaptive noise will be added less, and difficult to protect the data. Therefore, we set a minimum value of the adaptive noise in our algorithm.

$$\sigma = \max(\sigma_{low}, \sigma) \tag{6}$$

where σ is the adaptive added noise, and σ_{low} is the lowest value of the adaptive noise. Before adding the noise, the algorithm will choose the larger one as the adaptive noise.

After clipping the gradient, the clients add Gaussian noise to the parameters of each dimension, and the C_L needs to choose an appropriate value to ensure that both the user privacy preserving and a better model accuracy can be achieved quickly. Therefore, the way to add noise is to select the norm median of each dimension parameter as C_L. The formulas for adding noise to the central server is:

$$\overline{\overline{w_t^i}} = \overline{w_t^i} + N\left(0, C_L^2 \sigma_{l_i}^2\right) \tag{7}$$

$$C_L = median(\|w_1\|_2, \cdots, \|w_i\|_2) \tag{8}$$

where C_L takes the median of the norm of all dimensional parameters' l_2, $N\left(0, C_L^2 \sigma_{l_i}^2\right)$ is the Gaussian distribution, the mean of which is 0 and the variance is $C_L^2 \sigma_{l_i}^2$. $\overline{w_t^i}$ is the parameter clipped by each dimension in the current communication round of a client, and $\overline{\overline{w_t^i}}$ is the parameter after adding noise.

Usually, majority current schemes are adding noise to the clipped parameters to adjust the adaptive noise. In our algorithm, the noise is added to the clipped gradient before sending to the central server, and after the RMSprop optimizer stabilizes the parameters, the noise is added to central server again. By this way, this model can resist attacks from malicious clients. In this process, we don't limit client's gradient range, it is not necessary to clip the gradient at the central server.

After the central server receives the parameters from all clients, it needs to weight each client's parameters for model aggregation. We set the weight is n/m, where n is the local data of the client, and m is the data of all clients in a communication round. The central server aggregates parameters according to the weights of the clients, and the updated parameters add Gaussian noise to protect each client's data security. Therefore, the parameters of the final aggregation are composed of two different parts of the noise, and broadcasted to all clients for the next round of model training. The central server parameter aggregation formula is as follows:

$$w_t = \sum_{i=1}^{N} \frac{n}{m} w_t^i + N\left(0, C_C^2 \sigma_C^2\right) \tag{9}$$

where w_t^i is the parameter uploaded by the client, and we sum all clients' w_t^i by weight n/m. N is the number of clients participating in the model training for the current communication round. C_C is the noise sensitivity, and σ_C is the noise added by the central server. In order to calculate the total amount of noise added, the noise is adaptively added by the client, and the remaining noise is added to the central server's parameters.

Table 1. Algorithm of Bidirectional Adaptive Differential Privacy Federated Learning

---

Algorithm 1 Bidirectional Adaptive DP-Federated Learning

Input: sample $\{x_1, x_2, \cdots, x_N\}$, learning rate η, batch size, privacy budget ϵ, client sampling c

Output: parameter w_t, noise σ

1: Initialize: randomly set w_t

2: Client:

3: For each round of iterations do:

4:    Random sampling of c models participating from all clients

5:    Central server broadcasts initial model parameters to c servers

6:    Each client c Using differential privacy federated learning training model:

7:        Every client using sample rate q

8:        Train the model to get the model gradient

9:        Taking Gradient Median to Update Parameters w_t

10:        Calculate C_L

11:        For i in all dimensions:

12:            $\overline{w_t^i} = w_t^i / \max(1, \frac{\|w_t^i\|_2}{c})$

13:            $\overline{\overline{w_t^i}} = \overline{w_t^i} + N(0, C_L^2 \sigma_{l_i}^2)$

14:        End For

15:        $\sigma_L^2 = \sum_{i=1,\cdots k} \sigma_{l_i}^2$

16:    End For

17: Central server:

18:    Receive all client uploaded parameters w_l

19:    $w_t = \sum_{i=1}^N \frac{n}{m} w_t^i$

20:    $w_{t+1} = w_t + N(0, C_C^2 \sigma_C^2)$

---

5 Simulation Results and Discussion

5.1 Simulation Design

The network layer is constructed as the convolutional layer of 16 units, the maximum pooling layer of 2×2, the convolutional layer of 32 units and the maximum pooling layer of 2×2. After each convolutional layer, we use the Relu activation, and then the result of the maximum pooling layer is flattened to $7 \times 7 \times 32$. The prediction result is linearly output through the fully connected network. Each convolution layer uses the convolution kernel of 5×5 with a stride of 1 and a padding of 2, to prevent the image from becoming too small to fit the training dataset, which may cause a worse training result. Besides, we use RMSprop optimizer on both client and server to improve the model accuracy.

5.2 Relationship Between Adaptive Noise and Model Accuracy

In Fig. 2, this paper chooses different adaptive noise for comparation. We randomly sample 50% from 100 clients and set the minimum noise value in clients and server. Besides, the data sampling rate in the client is 20%, learning rate is 0.001, and batch size is 64 as the experimental parameters.

As shown in Fig. 2(a), as the accuracy fluctuates greatly before the 30th rounds, the added noise has little effect on the accuracy. When the communication round reaches 40th, the model tends to converge, and the accuracy without limit is the highest, reaching 96.4%. The model with a minimum noise of 9 has the highest accuracy up to 92.96%.

Due to the complexity of the Fashion-MNIST dataset, as shown in Fig. 2(b), the accuracy fluctuates significantly in the early stage. After several rounds of information exchange, the model tends to converge. The highest accuracy without limiting the noise size is 82.93%, and the highest accuracy of the model with a minimum noise of 9 is 76.78%.

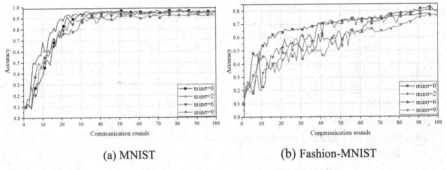

(a) MNIST   (b) Fashion-MNIST

Fig. 2. Relationship between Adaptive Noise and Model Accuracy.

5.3 Relationship Between Sample Sampling Rate and Model Accuracy

Figure 3 shows the analysis of local sample sampling rate using MNIST and Fashion-MNIST datasets, and the other parameters are the same as in Fig. 2. In the experiment, we set different sampling rate to observe the influence of the convergence speed and model accuracy. When the sampling rate is 20%, the data contains more information, so the accuracy is higher than $q = 10\%$ in early rounds, but the training time will increase greatly, and the final accuracy is almost the same as $q = 10\%$. The experimental results show that even if the number of samples increases, the effective information in the samples will not increase.

Our algorithm uses local date's 10%, and randomly selects half of 100 clients to participate in training. Finally, our model accuracy is 0.91% higher than CRD [11]. On the premise of consistent result, the number of training samples used in the model is reduced to 10%, and the proportion of clients is reduced 10% also, but the result is almost the same. Therefore, the sampling rate 10% is used in future experiments to reduce the computational load of local clients.

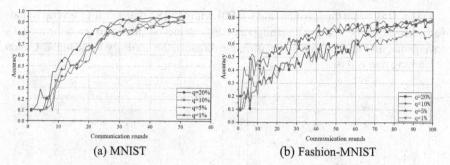

(a) MNIST   (b) Fashion-MNIST

Fig. 3. Relationship between Sample Sampling Rate and Model Accuracy.

5.4 The Relationship Between the Total Number of Clients, Sampling Rate and Model Accuracy

Figure 4 is trained with different sampling rates of client. The experimental result show that when the total number of local clients is less, the higher the sampling rates is, the fewer times the model aggregations can achieve high accuracy. The number of clients in the experiment is 100 and 500, and the client sampling rates are 22%, 50% and 100% respectively.

In Fig. 4(a), when 100 clients participating simulation without sampling, 40 rounds of aggregation can achieve convergence, and the accuracy is up to 96.29%. When the number of clients increases and the sample rate decreases, it is necessary to communicate with the central server more times to achieve the highest accuracy. The Fashion-MNIST dataset experiment in Fig. 5(b) also proves the above conclusion.

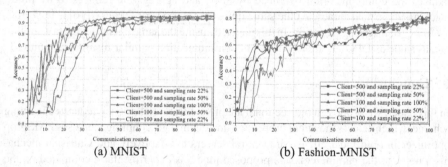

(a) MNIST   (b) Fashion-MNIST

Fig. 4. The relationship between the total number of clients, sampling rate and model accuracy.

5.5 Relationship Between Learning Rate and Model Accuracy

In Fig. 5, by comparing the initial learning rate of the RMSprop optimizer, the influence of the learning rate on accuracy and convergence speed is verified. Choosing the appropriate learning rate can not only protect privacy, but also reduce unnecessary communication overhead.

In Fig. 5(a), when the learning rate is 0.001 with MNIST dataset, after several rounds of adaptive adjustment, a fixed learning rate can be achieved quickly to reach the model's convergence. In Fig. 4(b), due to the different datasets, the accuracy is the highest when the learning rate is 0.01.

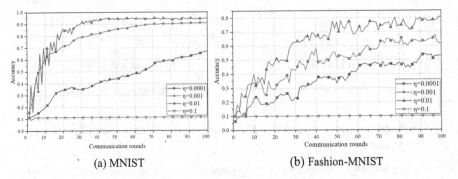

(a) MNIST   (b) Fashion-MNIST

Fig. 5. Relationship between Learning Rate and Model Accuracy.

When the learning rate is 0.1, due to the higher learning rate, the adaptive noise added in the 100 rounds model aggregation also increases. Simultaneously, the data availability is reduced, and the accuracy is lower. If the learning rate set too small, the adaptive noise cannot meet the requirements of protecting user privacy, the model converges slowly also, and the accuracy is difficult to achieve the ideal value.

Through the comparison of different algorithms in Table 1, compared with the 700 aggregations and the model accuracy 97% in DP-SGD [14], but the model in our paper reduces the communication overhead by 88%, and aggregation reduces to 81 times, reaching 96.85% accuracy. At the same time, the accuracy of DPOPT [16] is 96% after 100 times of model aggregation. In this paper, by using the same clients and data sampling rate as same as DPOPT, after 60 times of communication, similar results are achieved.

6   Conclusion

In this paper, we propose a bidirectional adaptive differential privacy federated learning scheme, which selects the client proportion and client data sampling, and uses RMSprop optimizer in both local clients and central servers to adaptively add Gaussian mechanism noise to the parameters. The proposed model is experimentally compared on the MNIST and Fashion-MNIST Non-IID datasets in terms of noise magnitude, model accuracy, communication rounds, and sampling rate. Experimental results show that the proposed FedBADP scheme outperforms other algorithms and can significantly reduce communication costs through sampling.

Acknowledgments. This research is funded by the 2022 Central University of Finance and Economics Education and Teaching Reform Fund (No. 2022ZXJG35), Emerging Interdisciplinary Project of CUFE, the National Natural Science Foundation of China (No. 61906220) and Ministry of Education of Humanities and Social Science project (No. 19YJCZH178).

References

1. Artificial Intelligence Project Team of Webank. Federated Learning White Paper V2.0. https://aisp-1251170195.cos.ap-hongkong.myqcloud.com/wp-content/uploads/pdf. Accessed 13 Feb 2023
2. Mcmahan, H.B.F., Moore, E,.S., Ramage D, T.: Communication-efficient learning of deep networks from decentralized data. In: Artificial Intelligence and Statistics. PMLR, pp. 1273–1282 (2017)
3. Tu, X.F., Zhu K.S., Luong N.C.T.: Incentive mechanisms for federated learning: from economic and game theoretic perspective. CoRR abs, 2111.11850 (2021)
4. Chen, J.F., Sun, C.S., Zhou, X.T.: Local privacy protection for power data prediction model based on federated learning and homomorphic encryption. Inf. Secur. Res. 9(03), 228–234(2023)
5. Su, Y.F., Liu, W.S.: Secure protection method for federated learning model based on secure shuffling and differential privacy. Inf. Secur. Res. 8(03), 270–276 (2022)
6. Li, T.F., Sahu, A.K.S., Talwalkar, A.T.: Federated learning: challenges, methods, and future directions. IEEE Sig. Process. Mag. 37, 50–60 (2020)
7. Liu, W.F., Chen, L.S., Chen Y.T.: Accelerating federated learning via momentum gradient descent. IEEE Trans. Parallel Distrib. Syst. 31(8), 1754–66 (2020)
8. Liu, X.F., Li, Y.S., Wang, Q,T.: Sparse personalized federated learning via maximizing correlation. arXiv preprint, arXiv.2107.05330 (2021)
9. Melis, L.F., Song C.S., Cristofaro, E.D.T.: Inference attacks against collaborative learning. CoRR abs, 1805.04049 (2018)
10. Abadi, M.F., Chu, A.S.: Deep learning with differential privacy. In: Proceedings of the 2016 ACM SIGSAC Conference on Computer and Communications Security, pp. 308–318 (2016)
11. Wei, K.F., Li, J.S., Ding, M.T.: User-level privacy-preserving federated learning: analysis and performance optimization. IEEE Trans. Mob. Comput. 21(9), 3388–3401 (2022)
12. Wu, X.F., Zhang, Y.S., Shi, M.T.: An adaptive federated learning scheme with differential privacy preserving. Future Gener. Comput. Syst. 127, 362–72 (2022)
13. Roth, A.F., Dwork, C.S.: The algorithmic foundations of differential privacy. 1st edn. Found. Trends Theor. Comput. Sci. 9(3–4), 211–407 (2013)
14. Li, N.F., Lyu, M.S., Su, D.T.: Differential privacy: from theory to practice. Synth. Lect. Inf. Secur. Priv. Trust 8(4), 1–138 (2016)
15. Geyer, R.C.F., Klein, T.S., Nabi, M.T.: Differentially private federated learning: a client level perspective. arXiv preprint, arXiv.1712.07557 (2017)
16. Xiang, L.F., Yang, J.S., Li, B.T.: Differentially-private deep learning from an optimization perspective. In: Proceedings of the IEEE Conference on Computer Communications, pp. 559–567 (2019)

Author Index

Printed in the United States
by Baker & Taylor Publisher Services

Printed in the United States
by Baker & Taylor Publisher Services